9 44

INTRODUCTIONS TO FILM STUDIES

THE FRENCH NEW WAVE

A NEW LOOK

NAOMI GREENE

WALLFLOWER

LONDON and NEW YORK

A Wallflower Press Book
Published by
Columbia University Press
Publishers Since 1893
New York • Chichester, West Sussex

Wallflower Press® is a registered trademark of Columbia University Press.

A complete CIP record is available from the Library of Congress

ISBN 978-1-905674-12-1 (pbk. : alk. paper)
ISBN 978-0-231-85066-7 (e-book)

Columbia University Press books are printed on permanent and acid-free paper.
This book is printed on paper with recycled content.

Printed in the United States of America

p 10 9 8 7 6 5 4 3 2

Cover image: Catherine Deneuve and François Truffant (1970), the Kobal Collection
Book and cover design by Rob Bowden Design

CONTENTS

ACKNOWLEDGEMENTS

I would like to say thank you to the following people:

To Michael Witt for generously sharing his insights into Godard.
To Marie Ariane Thompson and Charles Wolfe who took time out
from very busy schedules to help me with images in this book.
To Chas Thompson for his generous expertise in preparing the
manuscript.
To Jacqueline Downs at Wallflower Press for her unflagging support.

1   DEFINING TRAITS OF THE NEW WAVE

The French New Wave – *la nouvelle vague* – is usually viewed from one or more overlapping perspectives. To begin with, it is seen as a vital period in the history of French cinema. As if from nowhere, films now regarded as classics – *Les Quatre cents coups* (*The 400 Blows*, 1959), *Hiroshima mon amour* (1959) and *À bout de souffle* (*Breathless*, 1960) – burst upon the scene in the late 1950s and early 1960s. As highly personal films made on extremely low budgets, they changed – at least for a time – the ways in which French films were made, produced and perceived. The importance of the New Wave is such that French critics often place the phenomenon at the epicentre of a broad continuum, frequently expressed in the form of a family tree of filmmakers, of French film. In this admittedly very special family tree, Jean Renoir, director of pre-war classics such as *La Grande illusion* (*Grand Illusion*, 1937) and *La Règle du jeu* (*Rules of the Game*, 1939), becomes the 'good uncle' or 'godfather' of New Wave directors; directors such as ethnographic filmmaker Jean Rouch and poet Jean Cocteau are seen as its 'uncles' (see Frodon 1995: 31; Bergala 1998: 37, 40).

Looking at this continuum from the perspective of what happened after the New Wave, critics stress its impact on later generations of directors. For example, in a book devoted to post-New Wave cinema, Jill Forbes notes that French filmmakers of the 1970s and 1980s (for example, Maurice Pialat, Bertrand Tavernier, Jean Eustache) felt the 'constant necessity' to position themselves 'positively or negatively in relation to the *nouvelle vague*' (Forbes 1992: 3). Calling the New Wave the 'best-known French film movement of the post-war period', Ginette Vincendeau proceeds to observe that it constitutes a 'critical standard against which French cinema has been judged ever since' (Vincendeau 2000: 111). Even Susan Hayward, who seems more sceptical of the centrality of the New Wave than other critics, acknowledges that it 'forced a reconsideration of production practices' and a 'democratisation' of the camera which, by the 1970s, allowed 'formerly marginalised voices and people into filmmaking (e.g. Women, Blacks and Beurs)' (Hayward 2005: 235).

A critical era in French cinematic history, the New Wave has also had an enormous impact on the international scene. Along with films by Italian directors like Michelangelo Antonioni and Federico Fellini, or those by Swedish filmmaker Ingmar Bergman, French New Wave films constitute one of the defining moments in the wave of self-reflexive cinematic modernism that emerged in the 1950s and 1960s. They were, as Jean-Luc Godard put it, 'both cinema and, at the same time, the explanation of cinema' (Godard 1968: 99). Even more broadly, the New Wave has frequently been taken as the virtual embodiment of an innovative, low-budget, cinema of youthful directors. Indeed, in the eyes of Ginette Vincendeau, the very term 'designates a "freer" approach to film, outside traditional production and stylistic norms (professionalism, studios, literary sources, large budgets, stars), an approach which privileges spontaneity and the individual expression of the auteur-director' (1996: 109).

It is largely this last aspect of the New Wave that, in the course the 1960s and 1970s, influenced filmmakers from all over the world. In his introduction to *Second Wave* (1970), a book devoted to eight young directors from different countries, Ian Cameron notes that if the New Wave did not inspire all the directors studied in the book, it 'created the pre-conditions for their acceptance' (Cameron 1970: 64). Challenging the American model of commercial cinema, the New Wave encouraged directors to see themselves as part of a worldwide confraternity of kindred spirits. Never before, perhaps, has a movement that began in one country had such global resonance. Indeed, Antoine de Baecque is doubtlessly correct when he suggests that the 'real success' of the New Wave was 'international'. What he calls the 'aesthetic and economic model' of *la nouvelle vague* was felt in countries as diverse as Italy, Poland, England, Hungary, Czechoslovakia, Japan, Brazil and the United States. Taking us back to the notion of a family continuum, de Baecque expands it to include directors such as Bernardo Bertolucci, Jerzy Skolimowski, Nagisa Oshima, Karel Reisz, Alain Tanner and Martin

Scorsese. All of these filmmakers, he insists, should be regarded as 'legitimate' or 'illegitimate' sons of the New Wave (de Baecque 1998: 150).

To explore the nature and evolution of the New Wave, as well as the contours of what de Baecque deems its 'aesthetic and economic model', this study begins with a brief historical overview of the New Wave and a discussion of what are usually considered its defining traits. Then, using a lens that is at once social and economic, cultural and historical, it traces the nature and arc of this phenomenon. Thus, Chapter 2 analyses the ways in which the intense filmic culture of postwar France set the stage for the cinematic explosion of the late 1950s. Chapter 3 explores experimental and independent films of the 1950s while Chapter 4 is devoted to the films of 1958–60 that virtually embodied *la nouvelle vague*. The book concludes with a discussion of New Wave films of the early 1960s and with a brief look at the legacy/legacies of the movement.

Up until now, at least, there has been relatively little disagreement about the importance of the New Wave, but critics are not always in accord when it comes to its precise contours or its internal coherence. For example, while most commentators feel that the New Wave faded after the early 1960s, Susan Hayward posits two distinct moments in its evolution—what she calls a 'first' New Wave (1958–1962) and a 'second', more political, New Wave (1966–1968) (Hayward 2005: 205). Nor do critics always agree about which directors can effectively be labelled 'new wave'. Some commentators, like James Monaco, author of one of the first books in English about the *nouvelle vague*, tend to confine the term to the directors at the nucleus of the phenomenon. Often referred to as the Young Turks, this group – notably Jean-Luc Godard, François Truffaut, Eric Rohmer, Jacques Rivette and Claude Chabrol – worked together as young critics on the influential film journal *Les cahiers du cinéma* before launching their careers as directors. At the other end of the critical spectrum, Alan Williams uses the term very broadly to designate what he calls 'a brief period of upheaval and innovation in the late 1950s and early 1960s' (1992: 328). But most critics take what is probably a more compelling position somewhere between these two extremes. For example, in a broad and yet precise definition of the New Wave, Michael Witt and Michael Temple suggest that its ranks consisted of three major groups of filmmakers: (1) the Young Turks of *Cahiers*; (2) the older group of so-called Left Bank (or *rive gauche*) filmmakers (notably Agnès Varda, Alain Resnais and Chris Marker) who not only lived on the Left Bank of Paris but were also on the left politically; (3) a number of 'satellite' figures – principally, Jacques Demy, Louis Malle, Jean-Daniel Pollet and Jacques Rozier – who shared some or all of what Witt and Temple call the 'aspirations of the New Wave' (2004: 183). Echoing this classification, Antoine de Baecque adds two more groups to the list of directors affiliated with the New Wave: on the one hand, those allied with the documentary or *cinéma vérité* (Jean Rouch, Pierre Schendoerffer); on the other, those coming from commercial cinema (Roger Vadim, Louis Malle, Claude Sautet) (1998: 100).

Ironically, perhaps, the directors closest to the heart of the New Wave – that is, the so-called Young Turks – have consistently taken a sceptical view of categories and definitions such as these. For example, at a 1960 roundtable devoted to the question of the New Wave, the participants – among them Truffaut, Godard and Rohmer – could only agree on the following formula: 'The New Wave is merely diversity' (cited in Frodon 1995: 23). In their view, the New Wave was, above all, a question of shared friendships and affinities that included a common revolt – what Truffaut called a series of 'refusals' – against the films and filmmaking practices of the preceding generation.

New Wave directors were alike, insisted Truffaut, only insofar as they made films about things close to their hearts. As early as 1959, in fact, Truffaut maintained that the slogan 'New Wave' had been forged essentially by reviewers and journalists. 'Outside France', he said, 'people seemed to believe there was an association of young French directors who got together regularly and had a plan, a common aesthetic … in fact there was never anything like that and it was all a fiction, made up from those outside' (1988: 39–40). Echoing Truffaut's insistence that New Wave directors lacked a 'common aesthetic', Claude Chabrol observed that, unlike the Surrealists, New Wave directors 'did not form a group … We did not carry out a revolution. All that we did was enable some young directors to get started – each with his own style – at an era when French cinema was ossified' (quoted in Braucourt 1971: 128). As for Godard, in his 1998 series of films devoted to the history of cinema, *Histoire(s) du cinéma*, he sadly suggests that the hopes he shared with his friends at the time of the New Wave had never been realised. Referring to Truffaut's film, *Les Quatre cents coups* (an expression suggesting a period of youthful delinquency), Godard observes: 'Our only error was to believe that it was just a beginning

... that the four hundred blows would continue / when really they were growing weak.'

Most, if not all, critics seem to share the feeling of the Young Turks that they never constituted a 'school'.[1] And most would agree, too, that the range of New Wave films was tremendously diverse. At the same time, though, most would argue that the New Wave represents far more than a moment of shared friendships and affinities. At the most basic level – and here there is virtually no disagreement – the New Wave was, clearly, a vast, unprecedented, changing of the generational guard. Suddenly, one generation of directors eclipsed their predecessors. As they did so, they brought with them new performers (Jean-Paul Belmondo, Jean-Pierre Léaud, Jean-Claude Brialy, Jeanne Moreau, Bernadette Lafont, Anna Karina), new scriptwriters (Jean Gruault, Paul Gégauff) and new cinematographers (Henri Decaë, Raoul Coutard). 'I don't think it had ever happened before or after in the history of cinema', observed director Louis Malle, 'that a group of directors in their mid-twenties suddenly broke through and took over' (1993: 31). Admittedly, not all New Wave directors were as young as Godard and Truffaut who launched their first features while still in their twenties. And some – notably the Left Bank directors – had made distinguished documentaries well before 1958 or 1959. But the fact remains that virtually all came to widespread public attention and prominence in the heady years that stretched from 1958 to 1962.

To describe the extent of the changes that took place during this moment of upheaval, commentators frequently have recourse to telling statistics. For example, Michel Marie points out that while 20 per cent of French films were shot by only nine directors in the period that stretched from 1945 to 1957, at least 160 new filmmakers made their first features between January 1959 and the end of 1962 (1997: 15). (The December 1962 issue of *Les cahiers du cinéma* enumerates the names of 162 directors who made their first feature film between 1958 and 1962.) Looking at these astonishing statistics from a somewhat different angle, Jean-Michel Frodon notes that while an average of 16 first films were made each year from 1950 through 1958, that figure more than doubled – to 33 – between 1958 and 1962 (1995: 20). Struck by the virtual explosion of first films made in these years, Jacques Siclier went so far as to declare that 'nothing like this has ever been recorded before in the French cinema' (1961b: 116).

Emerging at a remarkable rate in the late 1950s, young directors also challenged established modes of making and producing films. Such modes were particularly rigid in postwar France where the world of cinema remained a carefully guarded fortress still governed by institutions and rules established during the Occupation. Two principal organisations controlled the world of film: the COIC (Comité de l'organisation des industries du cinéma) or, as it became known after the war, the CNC (Centre national de la cinématographie) and a professional school, the IDHEC (Institut des hautes études cinématographiques). The CNC was placed in charge of an important economic mechanism of state support of film by which a portion of each film ticket sold would be reinvested in future French film production.) In this carefully controlled climate, anyone who wanted to make a film had to obtain an official document much like a union card. The most conventional way of obtaining such a card was through a long apprenticeship served with established directors. After the war, another path to becoming a director was put into place: one could learn the craft, as it were, by making short films – which were mainly documentaries – that were customarily shown before the feature.

This second path was essentially that followed by the Left Bank directors or 'first generation' of the New Wave: that is, Alain Resnais, Chris Marker, and (although she was younger than Resnais and Marker) Agnès Varda. As Chapter 3 will make clear, although many of these documentaries were commissioned works, they were also deeply personal and highly experimental films that clearly rank among the most interesting films of the 1950s. In contrast, the Young Turks essentially rejected both methods of becoming a director. Inspired by a youthful passion for cinema, they did not have the patience for a long apprenticeship – especially one with directors they may not have admired. Summing up their attitude, a brash Chabrol deemed such an apprenticeship totally useless. 'Everything you need to know in order to direct', declared the young critic, 'can be learned in four hours' (quoted in Siclier 1961a: 15). While it is true that (with the exception of Chabrol), the Young Turks did make short films, it was really their work as film critics – an issue explored in Chapter 2 – that prepared them to become directors in their own right.

The path chosen by the Young Turks was clearly a highly unorthodox one in the rigid climate of the 1950s. But it did hark back to an earlier period in France – that is, the 1920s – that also witnessed an intertwined flowering of French film and film criticism and theory. At that time, avant-garde directors such as Louis Delluc and Germaine Dulac – as well as Jean Cocteau and the Surrealists – made films even as they theorised and wrote about the medium itself. Reviving this long-lost tradition, the young critics of *Les cahiers du cinéma* were quite explicit about what they saw as the inseparability of writing about films and making them. 'By acting as a critic', said Chabrol, 'one winds up discovering a method, an aesthetic. In the end ... a personal aesthetic' (1962: 3). Along similar lines, that same year Godard insisted that there could be no better preparation for making films than writing and thinking about them. 'All of us at *Cahiers*', he declared in the course of an important interview, 'saw ourselves as future directors. Going to *ciné-clubs* and the Cinémathèque was already a way of thinking cinema and thinking about cinema. Writing was already making cinema because, between writing and filmmaking, there is only a quantitative, not a qualitative, difference ... As a critic I already considered myself a filmmaker' (1968: 284–5).

When the *Cahiers* critics actually began to make their first films – to pass from writing to directing – the path they took was also an unconventional one. Emulating independent filmmakers like Jean-Pierre Melville, they used personal funds to auto-produce their first films on a shoestring. At the same time – and this, certainly, has fuelled the aura of legend that surrounds the New Wave – they gave one another moral and financial support even as they collaborated on each others' films. In this respect, a 1956 short by Jacques Rivette, *Le coup du berger*, is exemplary. Often called the 'first film' of the New Wave, *Le coup du berger* was produced by Chabrol (an inheritance bequeathed to his wife allowed him to form his own production company) with the help of one of the far-sighted producers, Pierre Braunberger, who was to play an important role in the New Wave.[2] Pointing to the collaborative nature of early New Wave films, Rivette and Chabrol were given credit for the scenario of the film while Godard and Truffaut acted in it. Observing that Rivette encouraged them all to make films, Truffaut noted that *Le coup du berger* 'was exemplary as much for the way it was made as for its production style and ambitions. It was produced by Chabrol, shot in Chabrol's apartment in only two weeks by Rivette on a borrowed camera with just enough money to cover the film stock, and featured friends such as Jean-Claude Brialy and Doniol-Valcroze as actors' (1988: 42).

Before long the collaborative energies and friendships at work in *Le coup du berger* would result in striking debuts. The triumph of Chabrol's second feature, *Les cousins* (*The Cousins*, 1959) allowed him to produce Eric Rohmer's *Le signe du lion* (*The Sign of Leo*, 1959) and to help finance the production of Rivette's *Paris nous appartient* (*Paris Belongs to Us*, 1960). Moreover, along with Truffaut, Chabrol helped persuade producer Georges de Beauregard to finance Godard's first feature. Since Godard was still unknown, Beauregard asked Truffaut and Chabrol – who had already made a name for themselves – to be included in the credits for the film. Thus, Truffaut received credit for the scenario of *À bout de souffle* (in fact, he had submitted an idea for the film) while Chabrol was given the fictitious post of 'artistic advisor'.

As one young director after another made his (or, in the case of Varda, her) debut, it became strikingly clear that it was not only the methods of production that distinguished early New Wave features from those of the preceding generation. For these films were in sharp contrast with those of their elders – particularly with the prestigious films that belonged to the so-called Tradition of Quality. Mainly associated with ageing directors who had begun working well before the war (Marcel Carné, Claude Autant-Lara, Christian-Jacque, Marc Allégret), or who made their first films during the Occupation (Yves Allégret, André Cayette, Henri-Georges Clouzot), the highly-regarded films of the Tradition of Quality were usually marked by lavish sets and costumes and by the presence of glamorous stars (Michelle Morgan, Gérard Philippe) given to highly theatrical performances. Based on carefully crafted scripts, they usually fell into well-worn categories or genres: literary adaptations (often based on classic French novels of the nineteenth century by authors like Stendhal and Zola); thrillers or *film noirs* that harked back to the poetic realist tradition of the 1930s; and psychological melodramas that often bore tendentiously on contemporary social issues.

Well before they made their own filmmaking debuts, the Young Turks had made known their antipathy for the Tradition of Quality and all that it represented. Beginning in 1954, in the pages of *Les cahiers du cinéma*, they had launched what would become a sustained attack on the films of their elders. Scornfully deeming the Tradition of Quality an old-fashioned cinema or what they called *le cinéma du papa*, they decried it for a variety of reasons: its dependence on literary scripts, its theatrical artificiality and its divorce from contemporary reality. It was, they charged, a cinema made by skilled craftsmen – not by inspired artists who were responsible for every aspect of the film and who put their very souls into their work. In its stead, they demanded films that would be as personal, as individual, as novels. Indeed, they insisted that directors were as much the 'authors' of their films as were any novelists. 'The only films I like', declared an intransigent Godard, 'are those that resemble their authors' (1968: 190). At the same time, they also espoused a cinema that – fleeing the spectre of filmed theatre – would exploit all the resources of cinematic language.

Not surprisingly, in virtually all these respects, early New Wave features offered the sharpest of contrasts with those of the Tradition of Quality. In so doing, they also established what might be seen as an 'aesthetic' of their own. Pointing to the all-important role of the director/author, they juxtaposed sound and image in new ways and foregrounded the role of editing and camerawork. Clearly, many of the choices embraced by New Wave directors were dictated by economic necessity as much as ideological conviction. For example, unable to film in the costly studios used for pro-ductions of the Tradition of Quality, New Wave directors shot their films in the streets of Paris with natural light and ambient sound. Similarly unable to afford established stars, they used young unknowns whose naturalistic acting and gift for improvisation contrasted greatly with the theatrical dec-lamations of an older generation of performers. At the same time, though, these choices implied a changed relationship to reality. For example, as Truffaut observed in 1959, the fact that they had to make do with one take (rather than the more costly two or three) meant that their films lacked 'the usual icy perfection of French films' even as they 'touched the public by their spontaneity' (1988: 45). In this manner, he felt, they 'captured more of the truth, the truth of the streets, the truth of performance and the actor … In any case one reaches a profound truth by a superficial one and sophisticated cinema had lost even superficial truth' (ibid.).

Truffaut's insistence on the notion of truth(s) – both superficial and profound – opens onto a critical dimension of the New Wave. For the phenomenon was not only about new modes of production or changed filmmaking techniques (location shooting, natural lighting, a mobile and often intrusive camera) or, even, a new conception of the director's role as a complete *auteur*. At its core lay an overarching need to draw close – as the Italian neo-realists they greatly admired had done – to reality itself.

It was, precisely, the absence of reality or 'truth' that, in the eyes of the Young Turks, was so sorely lacking in the Tradition of Quality. 'The shared trait that united all those at *Cahiers*', notes Jean Douchet, 'was based on a postulate: it is necessary for a film to tell the truth about the world' (1999: 193). Obviously, this 'truth' assumed a different cast for each director. For Godard, who wanted to 'to strip reality of its appearances', it had an ontological dimension; for Rivette, who was obsessed with the artifice of theatre, it implied a meditation on the relationship between 'truth' and 'lies'. For older directors Alain Resnais and Chris Marker, the search for 'truth' often bore on the realities of history and memory; for the Young Turks it involved, instead, the realities of everyday life: the nature of rela-tionships, the desires and aspirations of French youth, the pace of life in Paris. But if the directors of the New Wave were attuned to different 'truths', they agreed on a fundamental point: that is, the search for 'truth' meant breaking down the barriers that had long divided documentary and fiction. Suggesting that all great films revealed the inseparability of documentary and fiction, Godard went so far as to declare that, in part, the New Wave could be defined by its creation of 'a new relationship between fiction and reality' (1968: 315).

Impelled by the need to seize reality, New Wave films emerged at a time of momentous political, social and cultural change. From a political viewpoint, this period was shadowed by the bitter and divisive struggle to retain a colonial foothold in Algeria. Recalled to power to avert a pos-sible civil war, Charles de Gaulle – the man who had saved the 'honour' of France in the dark days of World War II – was forced to preside over the end of empire. (After losing Indochina in 1954, France had to grant Algeria its independence in 1962.) In the course of this traumatic period, post-war hopes for social change were fading – leaving a kind of moral, if not nihilistic, vacuum in their wake. From an economic standpoint, too, the period was one of enormous change. The 1950s and early 1960s marked the midpoint of *les trentes glorieuses* – the 'thirty glorious years' of the postwar economic boom. Along with growing prosperity, this period was marked by dramatic demographic, institutional and social transforma-tions. A wave of consumerism and newfound affluence advanced hand-in-hand with a weakening of traditional mores and longstanding social structures. Rural areas and villages declined; huge anonymous housing projects on the outskirts of cities replaced familiar neighbourhoods; television decisively entered French homes even as mass culture – often coming from across the Atlantic – gave an allure to everything that seemed 'new'.

Amidst these economic, social and cultural changes, a new generation – its ranks swelled by a postwar baby boom – was coming of age. This was, of course, the generation of the Young Turks themselves. And, as commentator Antoine de Baecque points out, this fundamental 'convergence' – that is between the generation of young people that emerged at this time and the 'wave' of young directors who began their careers in the late 1950s – was fundamental to what he calls the 'mythology' of the New Wave. In a work whose very title suggests this critical convergence, *La Nouvelle Vague: Portrait d'une jeunesse*, de Baecque asserts that at this time 'something unique happened … a generation of French people … was almost contemporaneous with a cinematic idea and praxis that was called "New Wave". This correspondence alone … transformed a particular moment in the history of cinema into a mythology of modern times' (de Baecque 1998: 17). Coming from the ranks of the new generation, the young filmmakers of the late 1950s caught the bewildering alienation, the search for money and love, experienced by young people as they confronted a world in which traditional moral codes and political aspirations no longer held sway. Mirroring the chaotic world that surrounded this emerging generation, filmmakers 'stylised', in the words of de Baecque, 'the immediacy of its history' (1998: 16).

Significantly, the very term 'new wave' was first applied not to the young filmmakers of the late 1950s but, rather, to the generation of young French people who would be portrayed in their films. It was a term that sprang from a growing fascination with the attitudes and beliefs of the nation's youth – a fascination that was reflected in, and promoted by, the media. Starting in 1955 with a special issue of the journal *La Nef*, the media – magazines, reviews and books – began to probe into the lives of the generation that would lead France into the future. Everything about this new generation – its cultural tastes, sexual life, religious beliefs and social behaviour – was subject to investigation and debate. One such investigative probe – carried out by the journal *L'Express* – would lead to the term 'new wave'. (Founded in 1954 and modelled after American news magazines, *L'Express* sought to position itself on the cutting-edge of changes in French life.) In August of 1957, *L'Express* began a vast poll of young people:

the questions asked ranged from 'Are you happy?' to 'Do you feel lucky or unlucky to be living in the present?' Each week it published the most representative and interesting responses. 'We have prepared a vast questionnaire', *L'Express* told its readers, 'for young people from all locales, all social classes, designed to reveal for the first time, in depth, just what our new French generation – *la nouvelle vague* – is like. Their ideals, their beliefs, their education, their desires ... what are they?' (quoted in Neupert 2002: 14). Along with a commentary by journalist Françoise Giroud, the results of the poll were published in *L'Express* on 3 October 1957 under the title *'La Nouvelle vague arrive!'* By the following June, the term had gained such currency that *L'Express* began referring to itself as *le journal de la nouvelle vague*.

In light of this prevailing sense of a dramatic generational shift, it is not surprising that the term *nouvelle vague* was soon applied to film. At first, as Jean-Michel Frodon notes, the term was used sociologically – that is, to designate films that 'revealed new mores, depicted with ... a refreshing frankness' (1995: 21). Before long, however, it assumed a different sense when Pierre Billard, writing in a relatively specialised film journal, *Cinéma*, applied it to the emerging generation (those born after 1918) of young French directors. But it was the Cannes Film Festival of 1959 that, finally, launched the idea of a cinematic *nouvelle vague* – an idea that would soon spread around the world. For the festival witnessed the decisive triumph of three films by young directors: Alain Resnais' *Hiroshima mon amour*, François Truffaut's *Les Quatre cents coups* and Marcel Camus' *Orfeu negro* (*Black Orpheus*). (*Les Quatre cents coups* won Truffaut the prize for best director while Resnais' film garnered the International Critics' Prize.) In the wake of the festival, when *L'Express* used the term *nouvelle vague*, it no longer designated the emerging generation of French youth but, instead, new films by young directors. Consolidating the idea of a cinematic *nouvelle vague*, the festival also brought the phenomenon to international attention. For months after the festival what had transpired at Cannes was discussed in newspapers and journals around the world even as the films themselves were distributed abroad. As the New Wave became known outside France so, too, did the writings of the *Cahiers* critics and the positions they embraced.

If directors like Godard and Truffaut shared the same age – and many of the moral and sentimental dilemmas – of the young people who flocked to their films, they resembled them in another critical respect. Suggesting still another 'convergence', this resemblance also leads to one of the most striking impulses of the New Wave. That is, the young directors of the late 1950s belonged to, embodied, a generation that adored films. Throughout the 1950s, young people went to the cinema in great numbers: for example, those between 15 and 24 constituted 43 per cent of the spectators in Parisian movie houses. Moreover, for this generation of ardent filmgoers, cinema was much more than a mere escape: in the bleak landscape of postwar France – a world marked by the memory of the Occupation and its many moral hypocrisies – films represented what de Baecque describes as a kind of 'shared mythological world, a way of assimilating the imaginary of lost paradises and of reaching the utopian dimension of life' (1998: 71). Not surprisingly American films – often in lush colours and with larger-than-life, romantic characters – were particularly attractive to a generation raised in the greyness and deprivations of the Occupation and its aftermath. Significantly, while earlier generations of sensitive young people wanted to write novels, those of the so-called generation of 1960 wanted, above all, to make films. 'The cinema', observed Jacques Siclier, 'has become the preferred means of expression for ... the 1960 generation' (1961b: 117–18).

The intense love of cinema, or *cinéphilie*, experienced by this generation of young people was at the very heart of the New Wave. If, as Godard had it, one pole of the New Wave was defined by a 'new relationship between fiction and reality', its other pole could be characterised, in his words, as the 'nostalgia for a cinema that no longer exists' (1968: 315). Deeply imbued with this nostalgia, the Young Turks, in particular, injected their intense *cinéphilie*, their extensive historical and critical awareness, into their films. Filled with allusions to other films, with homages to beloved directors, with shots and techniques that kept audiences aware that they were watching a film, their films embodied the self-reflexivity that is often placed at the core of cinematic modernism. Indeed, in the eyes of many commentators, it is above all this self-reflexivity – this alliance of what Godard called 'art and the theory of art' – that gives the New Wave its decidedly modern dimension. For example, Fabrice Revault d'Allones argues that even when pre-*nouvelle vague* films – like, say, those of Jean Cocteau – broke with dominant modes of French cinema, they were not 'modern' in the sense of those made by the *Cahiers* group. 'Modern cinema', declares d'Allones unequivocally, 'is represented by those at *Cahiers* and by people close to them like Rozier (or, later, Varda)' (1988: 78). Looking at this aspect of the New Wave from a still broader perspective, French critic Serge Daney argues that New Wave *cinéphilisme* fuelled the high modernist sense that the language of film – as well as its public – transcended national barriers (Daney 1998: 65). Underscoring this sense of universality, in one of his most striking epigrams, Godard observed that he and his friends had added an additional country to the map of the world: a country whose name was Cinema.

School(s) for cinema: Ciné-clubs and the French Cinémathèque

As we have just suggested, the idea of 'cinema' embodied in the New Wave represents the culminating point of a period of intense *cinéphilie* that – together with a long meditation on film – began in the immediate postwar years. Never before had filmmakers been so aware of their place and role in the continuum of film history. 'We are the first filmmakers', declared Godard, 'who know that Griffith exists. Even Carné, Delluc, and René Clair did not have any real critical or historical training when they made their first films' (Godard 1968: 286).

The historical awareness Godard is evoking was fuelled by two institutions that took shape in the immediate postwar period: the French Cinémathèque and two principal extended networks of film clubs, or *ciné-clubs*.[1] Freed from wartime restrictions prohibiting public meetings, these film clubs embodied and reflected the climate of cultural ferment, marked by hopes of social and political renewal, which took hold as the nation emerged from the claustrophobic years of the Occupation. Offering a window into worlds long hidden from French eyes, *ciné-clubs* helped fuel the growing sense that cinema was not merely a popular form of entertainment but, as Eric Rohmer put it, 'the classical art of the twentieth century'. Underscoring the role played by these clubs in terms of the New Wave, French film historian and critic René Prédal goes so far as to suggest that 'without the *ciné-club* movement, there would doubtlessly not have been a *nouvelle vague*, because it was the clubs which created the sense of waiting, the aspirations ... that the films of 1958–1960 would fulfill' (1991: 61).

While the *ciné-club* movement began after the war, the roots of the Cinémathèque actually go back to 1935. At that time, two friends – future director Georges Franju and Henri Langlois, the latter an obsessive lover and collector of films who would become the heart and soul of the Cinémathèque – established a kind of *ciné-club*, the Cercle du cinéma, which showed films from Langlois' ever-growing personal collection. Towards the end of the war, in December 1944, Langlois – who had taken every measure to hide his films from the Germans during the Occupation – resurrected the Cercle du cinéma. Four years later, in October 1948, installed in a nineteenth-century building on the Avenue de Messine, the Cercle was transformed into the Cinémathèque. Also known as Le Musée du cinéma, it did, in fact, function as a museum – one of the first such institutions dedicated to the collection, preservation and exhibition of films.

Both the Cinémathèque and the *ciné-clubs* did far more than merely show films. That is, both felt it their mission to teach viewers how to comprehend and analyse the unique nature of cinematic language. Thus, for example, to free viewers from literary models, Langlois might programme films together that, on the surface, were very different – for example, a drama with a comedy or a western with a historical epic – but which had, perhaps, some formal affinities. Or, he might show foreign films without subtitles, or silent films without music, so that the utmost attention had to be paid to plastic values and visual images – in other words, to the form of the film. Emphasising the pedagogical role played by the Cinémathèque, Jean Douchet suggests that it constituted the nation's 'true film school' – one which used consummate works of the past to inspire and train the filmmakers of tomorrow. Comparing the Cinémathèque to no less an institution than the Louvre, Douchet observes that 'Henri Langlois launched a generation of filmmakers who discovered the cinema of the past at the French Cinémathèque, just as Matisse and Picasso reinvented twentieth century painting by imitating Ingres, Delacroix, and Manet in the Louvre. The New Wave was creative because it imitated Rossellini, Dreyer, Bresson, Lang, Hitchcock, and Renoir' (1999: 9). Perhaps no one has paid more eloquent tribute to Langlois' role in shaping the Young Turks – who were, in fact, referred to as the 'children of the Cinémathèque' – than Godard.

In *Histoire(s) du cinéma*, the director says simply: 'one night we were at Langlois' place / and then there was light.'

Imbued with a pedagogical mission, both the Cinémathèque and the *ciné-clubs* showed a wide diversity of films that often could not be seen anywhere else: silent classics; avant-garde and/or scandalous films like Kenneth Anger's *Fireworks* (1947) or Jean Genet's *Un chant d'amour* (*A Song of Love*, 1950); prewar French films that had long been prohibited such as Jean Vigo's anarchistic short *Zéro de conduit* (*Zero for Conduct*, 1933). American films (which had been banned during the war) and contemporary Italian neo-realist dramas had a particularly dramatic impact. In addition to showing films, moreover, the *ciné-clubs* also engaged in a variety of film-related activities. They sponsored journals where young film devotees could articulate their own ideas; so, too, did they organise debates, film forums and even festivals. For example, in July 1949, one of the leading *ciné-clubs*, *Objectif 49* – headed mainly by critics André Bazin and Alexandre Astruc with poet-filmmaker Jean Cocteau as honorary president – organised an important film festival in Biarritz. Dubbed 'Le festival du film maudit', it was designed as the 'anti-Cannes' festival in that it highlighted important films that, for one reason or another, were not shown at France's leading film festival or at regular movie houses. Even more importantly, perhaps, it was at Biarritz that the future Young Turks – who had travelled from Paris to the South of France – first became aware of themselves as a new generation of film enthusiasts and critics.

As the festival of Biarritz made very clear, all these activities offered a forum, a place, where young enthusiasts could meet, discuss ideas and forge friendships. In fact, many of the friendships that would play an important role in shaping the New Wave were first cemented at these venues. For example, Alain Resnais and Chris Marker – who would become collaborators as well as life-long friends – first came to know one another at film showings organised by André Bazin. And the Young Turks first met at the Latin Quarter *ciné-club* which was run by Eric Rohmer. In fact, although Rohmer was older than the other Young Turks, he is always associated with them precisely because of their shared experience of the *ciné-club* movement. The breeding ground of the Young Turks, this important club also sponsored a short-lived journal, *La Gazette du cinéma*, where the Young Turks honed the critical skills they would eventually bring to *Les cahiers du cinéma*.

At the centre of all these activities was a man destined to become known as the 'godfather' of the New Wave as well as one of the most influential theorists and critics in the history of French film: André Bazin. In fact, Phil Powrie and Keith Reader are not wrong when they suggest that Bazin's critical work is 'arguably still the most important by a single author in the history of French writing about film' (Powrie/Reader 2002: 58). Trained as a teacher – a stammer prevented him from carrying out this calling – Bazin was deeply influenced by existentialism and by the currents of radical or social Catholicism (that emphasised both a personal or intuitive relation with the divine as well as the need for social ideals) that emerged in the postwar climate. At the same time, of course, Bazin was a great lover of cinema. And it was through cinema that he was able to meld and to express these various impulses: that is, his original pedagogical vocation, his deep spirituality and his belief in the need for social commitment. Not only did he approach film from a deeply moral perspective but, by bringing filmic culture to the people, he sought to carry out a vocation at once educational, spiritual and social. In his eyes, as Antoine de Baecque observes, 'cinema was the keystone in the new education designed for [a] people emerging from the misfortunes of war' (2003: 35).

Bazin's conviction that cinema could play a critical pedagogical role prompted him to work tirelessly in the *ciné-club* movement. Even before the end of the war he had founded a *ciné-club* where he showed films that the Vichy government had banned for political reasons. After the war, he presented films virtually every day – not only in *ciné-clubs* but also in schools and factories. In addition to these activities, Bazin was also prolific as a critic, journalist and theoretician of film. He contributed to the Catholic journal *Esprit* as well as to two important (albeit short-lived) film journals that sprung up after the war: *La revue du cinéma* (the precursor of *Les cahiers du cinéma*) and (until Cold War polarities hardened ideological positions) to the Communist weekly *L'ecran français*. Above all, perhaps, as co-founder and editor of *Les cahiers du cinéma*, he exerted a profound influence on the young men who would constitute the nucleus of the New Wave. Far more intransigent than the gentle and ecumenical Bazin – Truffaut referred to him as 'the saint with a corduroy cap' – the Young Turks would ultimately differ from their mentor on many issues. But they would never cease to ask the question, vital to Bazin, which became the title of his collected essays: 'What is Cinema?'

Critical landmarks

André Bazin: What is Cinema?

It is generally agreed that Bazin's first important essay, 'Ontology of the Photographic Image', represents the starting point of the meditation on film that stretched from the immediate postwar era to the pages of *Les cahiers du cinéma* and, ultimately, to the films of the New Wave. Invariably assigned a prominent place in chronologies of the New Wave, this 1945 essay revolves around an issue at the philosophical heart of the movement: the relationship of cinema to reality. In examining this fundamental issue, Bazin draws, significantly, not on earlier film theorists – in fact, his essay is often seen as the beginning of a new era in film theory – but, rather, on two important thinkers of the postwar period: that is, Jean-Paul Sartre and André Malraux. Like Sartre, Bazin is concerned with the very nature of phenomenal reality or, more precisely, with the ways in which art captures and expresses that reality; like Malraux, Bazin posits the notion of 'stages' in the history of art even as he shares Malraux's romantic view of art itself as a defence against the erosions of time and the finality of death. Towards the beginning of his essay, in fact, he cites a remark by Malraux that will be at the heart of his subsequent argument. 'Cinema', he says, 'is nothing other than the most developed aspect of the principle of plastic realism that [first] appeared in the Renaissance' (1958: 12).

In Bazin's view, this crucial principle – that cinema represents a new stage in artistic 'realism' – is valid for one essential reason. That is, whereas a plastic art like painting is essentially 'subjective' in that the 'reality' reproduced in a painting is inevitably filtered through the artist's mind and hand, cinema and photography – because they rely on mechanical means to reproduce reality – are 'objective'. Underscoring the notion of 'mechanical reproduction', he argues that, with photography 'nothing intervenes between the initial object and its representation except for another object. For the first time an image of the world is formed automatically, without the creative intervention of man' (1958: 15). Taking this notion a step further, he argues that this very 'objectivity' of photography – the 'absence' of human intervention – gives it a 'power of credibility' not found in painting (ibid.). 'Photography', he insists, 'is the beneficiary of a transfer of reality from the thing to its representation' (1958: 16). Capturing the object in a given moment of time and space, photography also frees it from 'temporal contingencies' even as it rescues it from its 'own corruption' (ibid.).

It is precisely in respect to time that cinema takes a giant leap forward compared to photography, says Bazin. The advent of cinema, which photographs things in motion, meant that 'for the first time, like a mummy of change, the image of things is also that of their duration' (ibid.). After making the case that cinema is not only closer to reality or more 'credible' than any of the arts that preceded it, Bazin takes still another theoretical leap. In doing so, he reveals his spiritual concerns even as he strikes what is clearly a metaphysical note. For, now, he suggests that the object is actually transformed by virtue of being photographed. The camera is able, as it were, to make reality reveal itself – or to allow us to perceive it – in a new way. By freeing the object reproduced from our 'piled up preconceptions', by cleansing it of the 'spiritual grime' with which our eyes have covered it, the camera lens presents it to us in its 'virginal' state. Dubbing photography (and, by implication, cinema) 'the most important event in the history of the plastic arts', he declares that 'it allows us to admire in the reproduction the original that our eyes would not have known how to love' (1958: 19).

Not surprisingly, Bazin's deeply held belief about the nature and mission of cinema – that is, his insistence that it respects and reveals reality – colours his attitude towards various filmmakers as well as towards different modalities of cinematic language. In terms of cinematic language, he consistently extols the virtue of depth of focus or composition in depth as opposed to montage in the belief that the former is 'closer' to reality. Whereas, he argues, montage – be it intellectual (Sergei Eisenstein), temporal/spatial (D. W. Griffith) or psychological (classic American film) – fragments reality, depth of field allows us to experience the continuity and ambiguity of reality much as we do in real life even as it leaves us relatively free to interpret what we are seeing. Taking his argument one step further, he leaves the terrain of psychology for that of metaphysics. For, at this point, he affirms his belief that depth of field allows us to experience not only the 'ambiguity' of reality but, also, what he calls its fundamental 'mystery'. As an example of this, he turns to *La Règle du jeu*. In this pre-war classic, asserts Bazin, Renoir discovered 'the secret of a film narrative capable of expressing everything without fragmenting the world, of revealing the hidden meaning of beings and things without destroying [their] natural unity' (1958: 146).

As his remarks about Renoir make clear, Bazin interwove theory and criticism in an intensely personal manner. Nowhere is this more apparent than in a series of important essays he devoted to Italian neo-realism, the film movement that is often seen as the precursor of the New Wave. Foreshadowing the critical stance that would characterise the Young Turks, these essays are permeated by an implicit – and, sometimes, an explicit – comparison between, on the one hand, French films of the Tradition of Quality and, on the other, neo-realist classics by directors such as Roberto Rossellini and Vittorio de Sica. (Unlike the Young Turks – who loved Rossellini but not de Sica – Bazin greatly admired both directors.) In Bazin's view, not only are many films of the Tradition of Quality marked by what he sees as an obsessive concern with 'stylistics and literary elegance', but, also, they seem to take place in a kind of historical and social vacuum – in what he called a 'neutral social and historical context' – totally divorced from the contemporary world. In contrast, neo-realist films – from Rossellini's *Roma, città aperta* (*Rome, Open City*, 1945) and *Paisà* (*Paisan*, 1947) to de Sica's *Ladri di biciclette* (*The Bicycle Thieves*, 1948) and *Umberto D* (1952) – look squarely, painfully, at the cruel realities of the war and at the social and economic problems of postwar Italy.

Above and beyond their concern with the social context, continues Bazin, neo-realist films differ from the literary and often artificial works in the Tradition of Quality in still another important respect. Permeated by a 'love of reality for its own sake', they never subject reality to preconceived codes and meaning; despite the left-wing thrust of their films, people and places never become 'symbols' or 'signs' (Bazin 1962: 15, 16). For example, although a film such as *Ladri di biciclette* clearly conveys a social message – it implicitly denounces a world in which the poor must resort to stealing from one another – it never 'reduces events and beings to a political or economic Manicheaism' (1962: 49). Respecting what Bazin calls the 'phenomenological integrity' of the world, the film portrays events in all their 'factual weight, singularity and ambiguity' (1962: 50). Furthermore, in its respect for what Bazin calls the 'ontological ambiguity or reality', the film assumes a moral and spiritual dimension that, for Bazin, lies at the heart of cinema's most profound vocation. In refusing to betray the 'essence' of things – in allowing them to 'exist freely for themselves' – de Sica enables

Ladri di biciclette (1948): in Bazin's view, a neo-realist film that refuses to 'play tricks' with reality

us to 'perceive the true language of reality, the irrefutable word that only love can express' (1962: 80, 81).

Thus introduced and championed in France by Bazin, Italian neo-realism would have a profound effect on the Young Turks. As young critics, their admiration for neo-realism exacerbated the disdain they felt for the Tradition of Quality. For them, Rossellini was, perhaps, *the* towering director of the postwar period. 'Rossellini', declared Godard, 'is the only one with a correct [*juste*] and total vision of things. He films them in the only possible way' (1968: 297). Once they began making films it became clear how much they owed to what might be seen as the neo-realist aesthetic: that is, an aesthetic marked by shooting on location and the use of natural light, by the absence of stars and by the rejection of a carefully crafted narrative in favour of a loose storyline marked by the ellipses and ambiguities that characterised 'real' life. It is true that they often sought to capture 'reality' in ways quite different from those exemplified in neo-realist films and/or espoused by Bazin. But they clearly shared Bazin's conviction that cinema had a moral (if not spiritual) vocation to embrace the 'real'. Like their mentor, they too believed – as Bazin argues so powerfully throughout

his essays on neo-realism – that aesthetic choices imply a given relationship with reality, a particular way of perceiving, and representing, the
world. Indeed, long before Godard who in a well-known aphorism likened
a travelling shot to 'an affair of morality', Bazin encouraged his disciples to
see how deeply every aesthetic or stylistic decision betrays a worldview at
once phenomenological, moral and spiritual.

Alexandre Astruc: La caméra-stylo

In 1946, in a review of Orson Welles' *The Magnificent Ambersons* published
in *L'écran français* on 19 November, Bazin explicitly raised the notion of a
'cinema of authors'. 'Orson Welles', wrote Bazin, 'is undoubtedly one of
the five or six filmmakers in the world worthy of the title of author – one of
the five or six who carry within themselves a vision of the world' (Tacchella
1990: 244). Two years after Bazin wrote those words, Alexandre Astruc
expanded on this critical notion in an essay entitled 'The Birth of a New
Avant-Garde: La Caméra-Stylo'. A man of many talents, Astruc was a novelist and filmmaker as well as an essayist and critic. A founding member of
the important film club *Objectif 49*, he also assisted at the birth of *Les cahiers du cinéma*. Still, it seems safe to say that, of all his activities, he is best
remembered for this essay in which he compared the camera to a pen.

Often likened to a 'manifesto' of the New Wave, Astruc's essay was
published in *L'écran français* on 30 March 1948. Here, Astruc issues a
ringing call for a 'cinema of authors' even as he explores one of the issues
central to the New Wave: the specific nature of film language. Like Bazin,
Astruc rejects the notion – embraced by certain theorists of the silent era
– that this language is essentially a purely visual one characterised largely
by the use of montage. Although he does not share Bazin's aversion to
montage on moral or phenomenological grounds, he is careful to point out
that it does not constitute the specific language, or what he calls the idea,
of a film. 'It will soon be possible', he asserts, 'to write ideas directly on film
without even having to resort to those heavy associations of images that
were the delight of the silent cinema … To suggest the passing of time, there
is no need to show falling leaves and then apple trees in blossom' (1968:
19). But nor, he says, can a film be equated with its script. Challenging
the important role accorded to a well-crafted script in the Tradition of
Quality, he goes on to affirm his belief that 'cinema will gradually break
free from … the immediate and concrete demands of the narrative, to be-

come a means of writing just as flexible and subtle as written language' (1968: 18).

As this remark suggests, Astruc is concerned not only with the language of film but also with its status as an art, and with what he views as the all important role of the director. Convinced that cinema has to take its rightful place in a pantheon of the arts, he compares it to literature, the form of expression that, in France, has perhaps generated more respect than any other. Insisting that 'the profundity and meaning' of films can rival that found in the novels of William Faulkner and Malraux, or in the essays of Sartre and Albert Camus, he argues that the 'cinema of today is capable of expressing any kind of reality' (Astruc 1968: 20, 21). He continues – and it is here that he comes to the central role played by the director – that just as a novelist is the 'author' of his books, the director is the 'author', or *auteur*, of his films. While the novelist 'writes' with a pen, the film director 'writes' with the camera. It is for this reason that he labels what he views as the coming age of cinema as that of the *caméra-stylo* (or camera-pen). Further underscoring this essential idea, he declares that directing a film 'is no longer a means of illustrating or presenting a scene, but a true act of writing' (1968: 22). And with these words, Astruc laid the foundation for one of the most important notions associated with *Les cahiers du cinéma* and, later, with the New Wave: that of cinematic *auteurism*. Scriptwriters did not cease to exist; but there was no longer any question that the 'author' of a film was none other than its director.

Eric Rohmer: mise-en-scène

Astruc's discussion of *la caméra-stylo* was followed, a few months later, by still another essay devoted to the specific nature of filmic language. Written by future director Eric Rohmer – who was still writing under his birth name, Maurice Schérer – this essay (which appeared in *La revue du cinéma*) was entitled 'Cinema: the art of space'. In a sense, Rohmer's essay seems to answer Bazin's fundamental question about the nature of cinema, for Rohmer defines cinema as 'the art of space'. Rejecting (like Astruc and Bazin) earlier definitions of cinema that revolved around the use of montage or editing, Rohmer argues that the time has come to examine the unique ways in which cinema uses space: 'the expressive value of the relationship of [spatial] dimensions or the movement of lines within the area of the screen', he writes, 'can be the object of rigorous attention' (1989: 33). A meticulous investigation into the nature of cinematic space, Rohmer's essay – like that of Astruc – also challenges the highly literary films of the Tradition of Quality. But he does so for a slightly different reason. He argues that because of their insistence on literary values and 'words', such films have 'discouraged the viewer from seeing' (Rohmer 1989: 45). Now, he says, instead of listening to words, or 'understanding' the narrative thrust of actions, we need to perceive how spatial relations and movements can convey thought and emotion.

Densely analytical and philosophical, Rohmer's essay did not have the resonance of Astruc's resounding call for a cinema of *auteurs*. But it is of interest for several reasons. Pointing to Rohmer's future role as the so-called 'theoretician' of the Young Turks (as well as the editor of *Les cahiers du cinéma* in 1957, shortly before Bazin's death in 1958), it also revealed the intertwined nexus of theory and practice at work in the directors of the New Wave. To begin with, its insistence on cinematic 'space' announced the centrality of space – or, more precisely, of different places – in Rohmer's own films. From a still broader viewpoint, the essay foreshadowed one of the central notions – *mise-en-scène* – proposed by the Young Turks in their attempt to elucidate the specific nature of filmic language. As articulated by the young critics of *Les cahiers du cinéma*, the term seemed to denote the ways in which a given work used elements specific to film: the placement and movement of the camera, the organisation of beings and things within each frame, the movement within each frame and from shot to shot. Deemed the 'very essence' of a film by Bazin, *mise-en-scène* was defined by *Les cahiers du cinéma* critic Fereydoun Hoveyda as 'nothing other than the technique that each *auteur* invents in order to express himself and establish the specificity of his work' (Hoveyda 1986: 142). Of the various definitions of *mise-en-scène* proposed over the years, it is, perhaps, Jacques Rivette's that most clearly echoes the ideas put forward by Rohmer in his 1948 essay. Rivette defines *mise-en-scène* as 'a precise complex of people and decors, a network of relations, a moving architecture of relationships somehow suspended in space' (Rivette 1954: 44).

Once Rohmer and his friends began writing for *Les cahiers du cinéma*, they would discuss directors in terms of their use of *mise-en-scène*. Adumbrating this approach, in his seminal essay Rohmer examines the different ways in which great cinematic *auteurs* have manipulated space to convey how we experience the world. Speaking, for example, of the comedies of René Clair, Rohmer makes the point that, in his films (as in those of the great comics of the silent screen) the slightest intentions of the characters 'are immediately translated into spatial language' (Rohmer 1989: 38). Likening what he views as the 'geometrical action' of Buster Keaton to the 'inhuman world' of Kafka, Rohmer also uses quasi geometrical terms to describe a famous battle scene in Sergei Eisenstein's *Alexander Nevsky* (1938). Here, the clash between Slavic and Teutonic knights is seen as the 'pure collision and rebounding of two masses in space' (1989: 41). In the context of his analysis of German expressionism, Rohmer pays particular homage to F. W. Murnau. Focusing on Murnau's version of the Dracula myth, *Nosferatu* (1922), Rohmer suggests that Murnau's film 'is totally constructed around visual themes which correspond to concepts that have psychological or metaphysical resonances (suction, absorption, ascendancy, crushing) within us' (1989: 42).

Les cahiers du cinéma

The issues raised in the essays just discussed – Bazin's concern with the nature of 'realism' and his fervent admiration of neo-realism, Astruc's call for a cinema of *auteurs*, Rohmer's definition of cinema as the 'art of space' – run throughout the pages of the journal which became an integral part of the phenomenon of the New Wave: *Les cahiers du cinéma*. Nourished by the postwar climate of *cinéphilie*, *Les cahiers du cinéma*, which was founded in 1951, was the successor to another film journal, *La revue du cinéma*, which ran from 1920–31 and then again from 1946–49. (The first issue of *Les cahiers du cinéma* was dedicated to the editor of *La revue du cinéma*, Jean-George Auriol, who had recently died in a car accident.) Not only did *Les cahiers du cinéma* pursue many of the lines of enquiry that had marked *La revue du cinéma* but, also, it was headed by men – André Bazin, Jacques Doniol-Valcroze, Pierre Kast and Eric Rohmer – associated with Auriol's review. Before long, this generation of theorists and critics was joined by the younger *cinéphiles* – Jean-Luc Godard, François Truffaut, Claude Chabrol and Jacques Rivette. Propelled both by a passion for cinema as well as an instinct for rebellion, the Young Turks – who were also referred to (minus Chabrol) as the Gang of Four (Godard, Truffaut, Rivette and Rohmer)– took extreme positions that were often deeply (and perhaps deliberately) polemical. If their writings on film turned *Les cahiers du cinéma* into what was arguably the most exciting film journal of the postwar period, they also suggested the shape(s) their own cinema would take.

The tone – at once polemical and passionate – that would characterise the writings of the Young Turks was ushered in by Truffaut's violent attack on the Tradition of Quality, 'A Certain Tendency of French Cinema', an essay published in the January 1954 issue of *Les cahiers du cinéma*. Unlike Bazin's measured and nuanced critique of the Tradition of Quality, Truffaut's essay was both virulent and highly personal in nature. The young critic (he was barely 22) spared neither France's leading directors (Claude Autant-Lara, Jean Delannoy, Yves Allégret, René Clément) nor its most respected scriptwriters. In fact, much of his attack was directed against Jean Aurenche and Pierre Bost – venerated scriptwriters known for their adaptations of literary classics. In Truffaut's eyes, Aurenche and Bost embodied a cinema of scriptwriters concerned with literary elegance, rather than a cinema of directors/*auteurs* able to exploit all the resources specific to cinematic language. Declaring that there is no 'possible peaceful co-existence' (Truffaut 1987: 204) between, on the one hand, films dominated by scriptwriters and, on the other, those created by true *auteurs* such as Jean Renoir and Robert Bresson, the young critic scornfully characterised directors like Yves Allegret and Jean Delannoy as mere 'caricatures' of an *auteur* like Bresson. As for Aurenche and Bost, Truffaut dismissed them, saying that:

> an adaptation [is] of value only when written by a *man of the cinema*. Aurenche and Bost are essentially literary men and I reproach them for being scornful of the cinema by underestimating it ... When they hand in their scenarios, the film is done; the *metteur-en-scène*, in their eyes, is the gentleman who adds the pictures to it ... and, alas, it's true. (1987: 199, 203)

In addition to its reliance on literary scripts, the Tradition of Quality evoked Truffaut's ire for another reason. In his opinion, its worldview was as 'false' – based, he charged, on 'formulas, word games, maxims' – as it was 'negative' (Truffaut 1987: 204). Marked by what Truffaut considered a secular left-wing and anti-clerical bias, it portrayed human beings, he said, as 'abject' and 'grotesque' (ibid.). Once again, Aurenche and Bost

– who were decidedly on the left – were particular targets of his wrath. Discussing Aurenche's proposed 1951 adaptation of *The Diary of a Country Priest*, a work by Catholic novelist Georges Bernanos, Truffaut argued that Aurenche had actually betrayed the spiritual dimension of the novel in favour of his own left-wing views. Clearly designed to challenge what Truffaut saw as the reigning left-wing orthodoxy in intellectual circles – in fact, Truffaut's essay prompted fellow critic and man of the left, Pierre Kast, to charge that the review was being taken over by the 'priestly faction' – the political passions raised by Truffaut's essay foreshadowed the polemics that would soon swirl around the Young Turks. Denounced as right-wing 'anarchists' and 'hussars', they were bitterly attacked, in particular, in the pages of the left-wing film journal, *Positif*.[2]

Looking back at 'A Certain Tendency of French Cinema', Antoine de Baecque assigns it a vital place in the chronology of the New Wave: this brief essay by an unknown young critic signalled nothing less than 'the death decree of a certain French cinema, *la Qualité française*, and, with the same stroke of the pen, the birth certificate of another, the New Wave' (2003: 135). Certainly, Truffaut's essay left no doubt about the advent of a new generation – one that shared neither the artistic tastes nor the moral values of its parents. In the wake of Truffaut's essay, moreover, it was, increasingly, the intransigent Young Turks who set the tone for *Les cahiers du cinéma*. (Their final triumph would come towards the beginning of 1957 when Rohmer became editor-in-chief of the journal.) And, following Truffaut's lead, they left no doubt about the absolute nature of the dividing line between those directors who qualified as true *auteurs* and those who were merely artisans at best and 'caricatures' at worst. 'From then on', writes editor and critic of *Les cahiers du cinéma*, Jacques Doniol-Valcroze, of this turning point, 'it was known that we were for Renoir, Rossellini, Hitchcock, Bresson … and against X, Y and Z. From then on there was a doctrine, the *politique des auteurs*, even if it lacked flexibility' (Doniol-Valcroze 1959: 68).

One of the best-known concepts associated with the Young Turks of *Les cahiers du cinéma*, the *politique des auteurs* was a controversial extension of the *auteur* theory first posited by Astruc. In practice, as Doniol-Valcroze suggests, it essentially meant that the Young Turks divided film directors into two camps: on the one hand, the majority whom they ignored or dismissed; on the other, the happy few who (like Hitchcock, Rossellini or Welles) were eagerly sought after and eulogised as *auteurs*. Their faith in the happy few was absolute: in their eyes, an *auteur* could never fail since all that he did was automatically part of an important *oeuvre*. Indeed, Truffaut made this point in characteristically polemical fashion when, paraphrasing an epigram by French playwright Jean Giraudoux, he declared that 'there are no works, there are only authors' (Truffaut 1955: 47).

The emphasis that the Young Turks placed on the all-important role of the director meant that they tended to ignore the myriad other factors involved in making films: the constraints of genre, the role played by Hollywood studios in the case of certain American films, the influence of the surrounding social and political context. For example, dismissing the Japanese context of Kenji Mizoguchi's films, Rivette declared that, in fact, the director's films speak the 'universal language' of *mise-en-scène* (Rivette 1958: 28). 'If', he continued, 'music is a universal language so is *mise-en-scène*. That's what we need to learn, and not Japanese, to understand Mizoguchi's language' (ibid.). Embracing a deeply romantic conception of the artist, the young critics extolled what they saw as the sheer 'poetry' of cinema. As a rapturous Rohmer wrote of the American director Nicholas Ray: '*Cahiers* readers know that we deem Nicholas Ray to be one of the greatest – Rivette would say the greatest, and I would willingly endorse that – of the new generation of Americans filmmakers ... [he] is one of the few to possess his own style, his own vision of the world, his own poetry; he is an auteur, a great auteur' (Rohmer 1985: 111).

Not unexpectedly, the dogmatism and extremism of the Young Turks gave rise to heated debates and polemics. In the polarising climate of the Cold War, their passionate defence of chosen American *auteurs* was particularly controversial. Critics on the left took their infatuation with American cinema – as well as their refusal to accord any weight to the economic and political context – as one more proof that they were very much on the right. (Speaking of their praise of American director Samuel Fuller, Communist critic and film historian Georges Sadoul – doubtlessly appalled by the rabid anti-Communism of some of Fuller's films made at the time of the Cold War – wrote, in an unpublished letter to Doniol-Valcroze, that 'the only reason to defend such films is a question of pure and simple anti-red propaganda' (quoted in de Baecque 2003: 178)). But objections were not confined to politics. Not only did the highly commercial American cinema the Young Turks often embraced seem antithetical to the notion of an all-important *auteur* but, in the eyes of many, it was difficult to think that a director of B movies like Nicholas Ray was an *auteur* able to rival established masters like Carl Dreyer or Murnau. 'The closer *Cahiers* critics moved to what had been traditionally conceived as the "conveyor belt" end of the cinema spectrum', writes Jim Hillier in his introduction to an anthology of *Les cahiers du cinéma*, 'the more their "serious" discussion of filmmakers seemed outrageously inappropriate' (1986: 7).

The controversies that swirled around the *politique des auteurs* eventually prompted Bazin to write an important 1957 essay, 'On *la politique des auteurs*', in which he questioned some of the more extreme positions espoused by his younger colleagues. Insisting that every film be judged on its own merit, Bazin also suggested that the biographical approach informing the *politique des auteurs* – which focused, above all, on the personality of the director – was only one possible critical approach among many. At the same time, he also maintained that all artists are inevitably touched by the world – at once social, historical and technical – surrounding them. 'What is genius anyway', he asked, 'if not a certain combination of unquestionably personal talents, a gift from the fairies, and a moment of history?' (1968: 144). In terms of Hollywood films, Bazin's conviction that film is at once a 'popular and an industrial' art led him to stress the role played by the studio system itself – what he called the 'vitality, and, in a sense, the excellence of a tradition' (1968: 143–4). Using the example of *Citizen Kane* (1941) to make this point, he declared that if the film was a creation of *auteur* Orson Welles, it was also 'an RKO product' that owed 'a tremendous debt to superb technicians such as cameraman Gregg Toland' (1968: 148).

Bazin was not wrong: clearly the *politique des auteurs* led to extremist positions that, especially in the light of today's concern with the weight of social/cultural institutions and of popular culture, appear impossible to justify. But, at the same time, it also had a profound and widespread impact on perceptions of, and attitudes towards, films and filmmakers. It was the critics of *Les cahiers du cinéma* who first made people aware, for example, that a director like Hitchcock was not only a master entertainer but also a great artist; so, too, was it the Young Turks who made it possible to speak, say, of *Meet Me in St Louis* (1944) not only as an MGM musical or a film starring Judy Garland but also as an important work directed by Vincente Minnelli. Just as importantly – at least in terms of the present study – the *politique des auteurs* takes us to the core of some of the complex links between theory and practice that characterised the New Wave. On the one hand, the attraction the Young Turks felt for certain *auteurs* helped shape their concept of, and desire for, a new kind of cinema; on the other, in describing the work of beloved *auteurs* – from Rossellini to Howard Hawks and Hitchcock, or from Welles to Ray – they might well have been speaking of the contours that their own films were soon to assume. As a young critic, Truffaut – writing under the pseudonym of Robert Lachenay – once declared unequivocally: 'I think it is important that a director should be able to recognise himself in the portrait that we draw of him and his films' (Truffaut 1985: 108). Taking this remark one step further, one might say that a kind of self-portrait of the young critics emerges from the meditation on films and filmmakers they set forth in the pages of *Les cahiers du cinéma* throughout the 1950s.

Seen from this perspective, their remarks on Rossellini are of particular interest. For if Godard considered the maker of *Roma, città aperta* as the only director with a 'correct' view of things, Rivette drew a portrait of Rossellini that pointed to what would become at least three defining impulses of the New Wave: he praised Rossellini for his refusal to make films that fall into conventional categories (documentary, fiction, travelogue), for his grasp of contemporary reality, and for the highly personal nature of his films. Speaking, for example, of the heterogeneous nature of Rossellini's 1953 film, *Viaggio in Italia (Journey to Italy)*, Rivette noted that it is a film that 'comprises almost everything … metaphysical essay, confession, log-book, intimate journal' (Rivette 1985: 108). In this same essay, Rivette took care to underscore what he saw as the intensely modern dimension of Rossellini's films. Observing that they refused the relatively safe parameters of a traditional narrative, he went on to say that they captured not only contemporary anxieties but also the fragmented, arbitrary and open-ended nature of life in the present. Insisting that Rossellini's 'hurried' low-budget films 'contain the only real portrait of our times', Rivette told his readers that they could not fail to realise that, in these films, the 'arbitrary groups, [the] absolutely theoretical collections of people eaten away by lassitude and boredom … [reflect] the irrefutable, accusing image of our heteroclite, dissident, discordant societies' (Rivette 1985: 195).

Lastly, if Rivette saw Rossellini as the 'most modern of filmmakers', he also considered him among the most 'personal' of directors. It is true, of course, that in the eyes of the Young Turks every *auteur* was characterised by a personal vision of the world, a way of making films that was uniquely his (or, more rarely, her) own. Each possessed, as Rohmer wrote of Nicholas Ray, 'his own style, his own vision of the world, his own poetry' (Rohmer 1985: 111). But, above and beyond this 'poetry', Rossellini's films – or at least some of them – were personal in yet another respect: they clearly referred to aspects of his own life. For example, by casting actress Ingrid Bergman – who was Rossellini's lover and then his wife – in certain roles in *Siamo donne* (*Of Life and Love*, 1953) and *Viaggio in Italia*, Rossellini seemed to refer explicitly to his own sentimental dramas and dilemmas. Noting that in these works Rossellini carried 'freedom of expression' to its utmost level by speaking of himself, Jacques Rivette went on to observe that, here, Rossellini 'is no longer filming just his ideas, as in *Stromboli* (1950) or *Europa 51* (1952), but the most everyday details of his life' (Rivette 1985: 196).

The personal dimension that the Young Turks so prized in Rossellini's work might well be seen as *the* defining impulse of *la nouvelle vague*. In revealing his own life on screen, in marking films with his own sensibility or 'poetry', Rossellini was able to close the gap – so despised by the Young Turks – between cinema and life. It was precisely this gap that, once they became directors, the Young Turks of *Les cahiers du cinéma* would challenge in one film after another. Not all of their works were as explicitly autobiographical as, say, Truffaut's *Les Quatre cents coups* or Godard's *Une femme est une femme* (*A Woman is a Woman*, 1961). But, all bear witness to the quest for a personal stylistics and to the desire for a changed relationship with 'reality'. Nor were these impulses limited to the Young Turks. Quite the contrary: a desire to bring cinema closer to 'life' can be seen in filmmakers as disparate as Alain Resnais and Jean Rouch, as different from one another as Chris Marker and Jean-Pierre Melville. Well before the critics of *Les cahiers du cinéma* turned from criticism to filmmaking, in fact, directors such as these – who were mainly older than the Young Turks – were making highly personal films marked, albeit in different ways, by a new relationship with 'reality'. Experimenting with new ways of making and producing films, these directors prepared the way for the cinematic explosion of the late 1950s even as they, too, played a vital role in the New Wave.

3   PRELUDE: FILM EXPERIMENTS OF THE 1950s

As I have just suggested, at the same time that the Young Turks were pursuing a certain idea of cinema in the pages of *Les cahiers du cinéma*, a number of iconoclastic directors were making it clear that change was in the air. Many, if not all, of these changes came from the margins: from independent filmmakers like Jean-Pierre Melville and Jean Rouch as well as from the so-called 'first generation' of the New Wave. Highly personal short films by Chris Marker, Agnès Varda and, especially, Alain Resnais took cinema into unexplored terrain so decisively that, by 1957, a special issue of *Les cahiers du cinéma* deemed them part of a 'coherent movement, a genre' that revealed the talents of young filmmakers. Around the same time, more commercial directors like Roger Vadim and Louis Malle began to explore contemporary reality even as they captured the mores of an emerging generation of young people. Challenging the fortress-like world of French cinema in a variety of ways, virtually all these films – as the Young Turks were quick to sense and to point out – suggested the presence of something 'new' on the horizon.

Jean-Pierre Melville

Born in 1917, Jean-Pierre Melville has been variously described as the 'undisputed father' (Simsolo 2000) and as the 'inventor' (Siclier 1961a: 56) of the New Wave. Whether or not Melville can be said to have 'invented' the New Wave, of all the French *auteurs* admired by the Young Turks, in all probability none offered a sensibility as close to theirs as Melville. For one thing, throughout much of his career, his films resembled New Wave features in that (to use a phrase he applied to the New Wave) they were 'artisanal' in nature – in other words they 'were shot on location, without stars, without a standard crew, with a very fast film stock and with no distributor, without authorisation or servitude to anyone' (Neupert 2002: 71). For another, the fiercely independent Melville – who once declared that a director had to be 'free, courageous and intransigent' (Melville 1971: 9) – was the very model of a director/producer who had complete control of his own films. In Chabrol's words, he was 'a living example of what it was possible to be outside of conventions … We certainly would not have dreamed of making the films that we did without Melville' (1996: 74).

A 'living example' of an independent filmmaker, Melville shared both the ardent *cinéphilie* of the Young Turks as well as their pronounced taste for American culture and film. In an insightful study of the director, Ginette Vincendeau points out that, after World War Two, Melville moved in the same cultural and intellectual milieu – marked by a love of American literature and jazz as well as a propensity to haunt left-bank night spots featuring sultry *chanteuses* – that would later 'produce the New Wave' (Vincendeau 2003: 9). Melville even changed his given name, Jean-Pierre Grumbach, to that of Melville out of admiration for the author of *Moby Dick* – an artist who, by his own admission, 'meant more to [him] than any other' (1971: 18). His love for Hollywood films in particular – Chabrol was only half joking when he deemed Melville the 'last filmmaker to make American B melodramas' (1996: 75) – prompted him to wear dark glasses, a trench coat and a characteristic Stetson hat as if he were a character in a western or gangster film. More importantly, perhaps, like the Young Turks, he learned about cinema not by attending film school or serving as someone's assistant but by sheer dint of watching films. Telling one interviewer that he made his first film with a hand-cranked camera at the tender age of six, he went on to say it was by watching films that he learned to make them. 'To create films', he said, 'you must be madly in love with cinema … You also need a huge cinematic baggage. In 1947 [the year of his first feature] I was unbeatable … I knew everything, even the credit titles by heart. I have always learned cinema, I have never ceased to learn [it]' (1971: 20).

Melville's independence came into very sharp focus at the beginning of his career. Denied work in a studio because of the Byzantine regulations governing French cinema, he responded by establishing his own production company – Melville Productions – and began to make films on a tiny budget. His first feature, *Le silence de la mer* (1947/48), was an adaptation of a celebrated novel of wartime resistance by Vercors published clandes- tinely in 1943 and distributed through Resistance channels. In adapting this novel to the screen, Melville faced a variety of hurdles. In addition to a tiny budget – the film cost less than twenty per cent of an average feature – Melville lacked the necessary film credentials, the required number of technicians, as well as permission to film the book.[1] Still, despite what he described as moments of deep discouragement he forged ahead and shot the film in twenty days. In so doing, he said, he opposed what he saw as the 'dictatorial' nature of the 'syndicalist structure of the French industry' (Melville 1971: 34) as well as filmic conventions of the day. Prefiguring New Wave features in its use of location shooting and unknown performers, *Le silence de la mer* also made important stylistic innovations. The most strik- ing of these was, undoubtedly, Melville's decision to have the protagonists of the film remain silent and to convey their thoughts by a voice-over which speaks the words of Vercors' text.

If *Le silence de la mer* revealed Melville's intransigence and daring, his fourth film, *Bob le flambeur* (*Bob the Gambler*, 1955), staked out the ter- ritory – that of thrillers and gangster films – that, with few exceptions, he would inhabit for the rest of his career. A tale about an ageing and lonely gambler who lives by his own code and dreams of one last heist, Melville's melancholy thriller harks back both to French poetic realist films of the late 1930s and to American thrillers and gangster films of the 1930s and 1940s. But even as *Bob le flambeur* evokes these cinematic traditions, it also changes them in ways that seem to announce the transformation of genre that would take place in early New Wave features. To begin with – and this would become increasingly clear in Melville's subsequent thrillers – the film stylises the elements of genre: that is, the characters are stripped of individuality so that they somehow become icons or pure cinematic forms (the bar-girl, the thief, the chief of police). In the course of this process, as commentators have frequently noted, Melville's cinema reinvents '*film noir* by the exacerbation of its codes' even as it becomes 'a meditation on the disappearance of genres' (Jousse & Toubiana 1996: 63). And, at the same time, Melville also transforms the thriller genre by long digressions that somehow work against, or interrupt, its characteristic narrative flow. For example, *Bob le flambeur* begins with a celebrated lengthy sequence devoted not to the protagonist of the film nor to its plot but rather to the Parisian *quartier*, Montmartre, where Bob gambles and lives. (Melville himself had lived in Montmartre and knew the *quartier* and its inhabitants well.) Critic Jean-François Rauger might well be describing this sequence when he suggests that what he calls the 'distended' narrative of *Bob le flambeur* is one in which the 'rules of genre are turned upside down by a sauntering progression which is the opposite of the functionalism that governs the principle of crime thrillers' (1996: 72).

If the opening sequence of *Bob le flambeur* 'distends' the narrative, it also announces the important role that Paris would assume in early New Wave features. Moreover, master cameraman Henri Decaë, who had first worked with Melville on *Le silence de la mer* and who would soon become one of the two major cinematographers of the New Wave, was largely responsible for the portrait of Paris that emerges from *Bob le flambeur*. Praising Decaë's work, in 1958 Eric Rohmer declared that he was 'the glory of the new school of cameramen, the destroyer of the thousand taboos that prevented his elders from accepting the imperatives of modern filmmaking' (quoted in Douchet 1999: 110). Usually credited with applying classical studio aesthetics – those bearing, for example, on the way faces are lit or the contrasting values of shadow and light – to shooting on location, it was while working with Melville that Decaë perfected the use of the highly sensitive film stock (which made it possible to shoot in very low light) that he would later use to advantage in New Wave films. Recalling his work on *Bob le flambeur*, Decaë also linked his experiments on that film to his later work with New Wave directors. In order to film Paris at night, he observed, 'we used very fast film [which] allowed for a wide opening with very little light. We shot at night on Place Pigalle without any floodlights. It was as a result of this work that I was hired by all the New Wave people: Chabrol, Truffaut, Malle' (quoted in Bergala 1998: 40). One of Melville's most faithful collaborators, Decaë was nothing less than a living link between the flamboyant director and the young men of *la nouvelle vague*.

Jean Rouch

Born the same year as Melville, in 1917, Jean Rouch has been described as both a 'precursor' and a 'fellow traveller' of the New Wave. He was a 'precursor' certainly, insofar as his early films had a profound impact on those who would form the nucleus of the New Wave: marked by a Bazinian desire to embrace the real, they challenged existing genres and categories including the dividing line between fiction and documentary. He was also a 'fellow traveller' because he played an important role in the actual phenomenon of the New Wave. In particular, his 1960 film, *Chronique d'un été (Chronicle of a Summer)*, pioneered so-called *cinéma vérité* techniques – especially the use of hand-held camera and synchronous sound – that would influence and dovetail with impulses at work in directors such as Godard and Marker. 'Although few people know it', declared Jacques Rivette in 1968, 'Rouch has been the motor behind French cinema for the last ten years. In a certain way, Rouch is more important than Godard in terms of the evolution of French cinema. Godard follows a path that works only for him … while Rouch's films can serve as examples' (1999: 308).

Like the Young Turks themselves, Rouch was an ardent *cinéphile*. Even before the war, in 1937, he began attending the Cinémathèque where, in his words, he was 'nourished' by the great classics of film. (Many years later, from 1987 to 1993, he served a term as director of the Cinémathèque.) It was at the Cinémathèque that, in the late 1940s, he first meet youthful *cinéphiles* who would become the notorious band of *Les cahiers du cinéma*. But he actually came to make films by a circuitous route. Initially trained as a civil engineer, Rouch found he had both a passion and a calling for ethnography when he was sent to Africa during World War Two to build bridges and roads. Before long, he became aware that, for him, ethnography was inseparable from cinema. He told one interviewer that as early as 1941, while he was watching a dance of spirit possession, he realised that the scene he was witnessing 'can't be described, or written, or sketched, or photographed. It has to be filmed' (Rouch 1996a: 10).

Rouch's conviction that cinema constituted a vital ethnographic tool eventually led him to become a co-founder of the ethnographic film section at the national French museum of anthropology/ethnology, *le Musée de l'Homme*. But long before that he made another major discovery that would have enormous repercussions for both ethnography and film. He saw that film allowed him to engage in an important 'dialogue' with his subjects. When his subjects saw themselves on screen, 'they suddenly understood the "look" that I directed towards them and they immediately began to criticise me. It is the first time that I had a true dialogue with the people that I studied' (quoted in Prédal 1996: 38). His concern with this 'dialogue' – his desire to achieve nothing less than what he described as the 'irreplaceable quality of real contact between those who film and those who are filmed' (Rouch 1996b: 43) – eventually led him to embrace an approach characterised by what he called 'shared anthropology'. This meant that the indigenous people whose lives he observed and documented would no longer be passive subjects but would actively participate in the ethnographic project devoted to them. In this way, Rouch noted, knowledge would no longer be the privilege of Western observers – 'a stolen secret, devoured in the Western temples of knowledge' – but, rather, the 'result of an endless quest where ethnographers and those whom they study meet on a path' (Rouch 2003: 101).

If Rouch's desire to interact with his subjects distanced him from traditional ethnographers, it also had profound implications for film. His quest to come ever closer to his subjects implied, in his mind, that he had to capture not only the external life of his African participants but, also, their inner feelings, their unexpressed desires, their deepest fantasies – what he called their 'imaginary world'(Rouch 2003: 185). And, in order to capture their 'imaginary world', he somehow not only to abolish the distance that separated Western observers from their subjects but also – and it is this impulse that reverberates throughout the New Wave – the barriers that separated documentary from fiction. Directly challenging these barriers, he declared that 'fiction is the only way to penetrate reality' (ibid.). Elaborating on this critical notion, he remarked that, for him, 'as an ethnographer and filmmaker, there is almost no boundary between documentary film and films of fiction. The cinema, the art of the double, is already the transition from the real world to the imaginary world, and ethnography, the science of the thought systems of others, is a permanent crossing point from one conceptual universe to another' (ibid.).

What Rouch calls the 'transition from the real world to the imaginary world' is at the core of his first major feature, *Moi, un noir* (1958).[2] Here, as in subsequent films, Rouch made striking stylistic and technical innovations in order to capture the 'conceptual universe' of his subjects. On one level, the film resembles a conventional documentary insofar as it charts the difficult lives of impoverished young Nigerians who have migrated to Treichville, a suburb of Abidjan, capital of present-day Ghana, in search of work and a livelihood. It does not spare us the all-too-obvious miseries of their existence: we see that work is difficult to find, temporary, back-breaking. But, on another level, the film is anything but conventional. For Rouch is concerned not only with the external existence of his subjects but with their 'imaginary world' and their 'fantasies'. To explore this inner world, Rouch had his subjects participate in the making of the film: that is, he showed them a rough cut and asked them to improvise an accompanying narration. He then added their narration to the film so that, on the finished soundtrack, his African subjects not only comment on their actions and feelings but also act out their fantasies. Taking us ever deeper into the realm of theatre and the imaginary, they see themselves as iconic celebrities of popular culture. For example, the main protagonist, who calls himself Robinson, sees himself both as the actor Edward G. Robinson and, at one point, as the famous boxer Sugar Ray Robinson. At the intersection of theatre and reality, or of documentary and fiction, Robinson's imaginary universe is at once totally unreal and yet the most concrete and eloquent sign of his desperate existence.

Behind Robinson's imaginary universe, moreover, lie even more complex and intertwined layers of documentary and fiction. While Robinson seems to be an impoverished worker who dreams of being a celebrity, in truth, the young man we see on screen, Oumarou Ganda, was a young student who later became a filmmaker in his own right. So, the 'imaginary' existence he describes is, in effect, a kind of theatrical construct which captures the 'truth' of a life which is not really his own. Commenting on the complex layers of 'truth' and 'fiction' in the film, Jean-André Fieschi writes that 'what Rouch is the first to film here is no longer behaviour or dream or subjective discourse but the indissoluble mix which binds one to the other. The filmmaker's desire is the desire to abandon himself to the desire of his characters' (1973: 260). Similarly struck by what Fieschi calls an 'indissoluble mix', Jean-Luc Godard – who, interestingly, had studied anthropology – felt that *Moi, un noir* was as daring for its time as *Roma, città aperta* had been for an earlier era. Discussing the mix of documentary and fiction that, in his view, characterised *Moi, un noir* as it does all great films, Godard went on to say that Rouch searches for truth not 'because it is scandalous but because it is amusing, tragic, gracious, crazy, whatever. The important thing is that it is truth' (1968: 219). Not surprisingly, as Michel Marie points out, Godard's admiration for Rouch would later inspire him to incorporate themes and techniques first witnessed in *Moi, un noir* – in particular, those bearing on Rouch's unconventional approach to dialogue and language – into his own first feature, *À bout de souffle* (Marie 2000: 167–168).

Rouch's quest to capture the 'truth' of his subjects did not end with *Moi, un noir*. Two years later, in still another path-breaking documentary, *Chronique d'un été*, he pioneered the use of *cinéma vérité* techniques that would soon be enthusiastically embraced by New Wave directors. Here, using a new lightweight camera with portable recording equipment, he recorded, *for the first time in France*, in synchronous sound. (To manipulate his camera Rouch had the help of Canadian cameraman Michel Brault and Raoul Coutard, the man who would soon be Godard's cinematographer.) Subjects no longer had to record their comments while watching a rough cut of the images as they had for *Moi, un noir*; instead, they could speak directly to the director, to each another and to the viewer. Finally, Rouch had achieved the 'dialogue' he had desired for so long. 'At last', he said, 'we had a technique ... we knew how to proceed. It was the *"caméra-stylo"* that you sharpen and write with whenever you want, as much as you can, and wherever you want' (2003: 167).

A critical moment in terms of Rouch's own filmmaking, the use of *cinéma vérité* techniques in *Chronique d'un été* also ushered in a new moment in French cinema. The director hardly exaggerated when he observed that, after *Chronique d'un été*, 'everyone wanted to walk with the camera' (Rouch 2003: 225). Not surprisingly, no one wanted it more than the young directors of the New Wave. Eager to draw ever closer to 'reality', they quickly embraced techniques associated with *cinéma vérité*: that is, the use of a hand-held camera and synchronous sound, shooting on location in natural light, the presence of direct unscripted interviewers and non-professional actors. Underscoring the sense of freedom ushered in by the use of light cameras and live recording, Nestor Almendros, who would later serve as chief cameraman for Rohmer and Truffaut, observed that 'ever since we've been able to work without being tied down with heavy equipment for live recording, people have started talking, they have come alive on screen as never before. Our freedom is also their freedom, and by improving our ability to listen, we sharpen our ability to look' (quoted in Douchet 1999: 223). Film historian René Prédal makes the point that, for a period of time, it was virtually impossible to separate the aesthetic of *cinéma vérité* from that of the New Wave itself. 'Officially inaugurated in France with *Chronique d'un été*', writes Prédal, 'the history of *cinéma vérité* was grafted upon that of *la nouvelle vague* that, for a time, it accompanied and, most of all, nourished' (1991: 184).

The first French example of *cinéma vérité*, *Chronique d'un été* – which was made in collaboration with sociologist Edgar Morin – was also the first film in which Rouch's interviewees were not Africans but people he referred to as members of his own tribe – that is, Parisians. Turning his lens to his compatriots, Rouch also interrogates the 'truth' of his own film. For, after the bulk of the interviews are completed, his subjects are shown, on camera, watching the sequences shot thus far. They are then asked to comment upon their reactions to what they have just seen. Has making the film changed their lives? What do they think about their own performances? Were they and the others truthful or acting for the camera? Not surprisingly, responses differ. For one, a certain participant appears to be 'acting'; for another, she is, instead, intensely 'real'. Sometimes, someone who is acting appears the most 'real'. After the subjects have expressed their views, other 'truths' are revealed when the directors are similarly interviewed and asked for *their* reactions. Adding layer after layer of self-reflexivity to the film, these spiralling scenes of self-analysis point not only to the inseparability of 'appearance' and 'reality' but, also, to the presence of multiple 'truths'. Asked to comment on the film's search for 'truth', Rouch indulged in a French love of paradox even as he suggested that the only 'truth' was that of cinema itself: camera and editing choices and techniques created the sense of 'truth' that emerged from *cinéma vérité*. 'With the *ciné*-eye and the *ciné*-ear we recorded in sound and image a *ciné-vérité*, Vertov's *kinopravda*. This does not mean the cinema of truth, but the truth of cinema (Rouch 203: 167).

Voices from the Left Bank

No less than Rouch, albeit in different ways, the so-called 'first generation' of the New Wave or Left Bank filmmakers – Alain Resnais, Chris Marker and Agnès Varda – challenged the conventions of documentary even as they also engaged in a relentless pursuit of 'truth'.[3] For them, too, fiction and documentary were complementary realms that, approached in new ways, would lead not only to new forms of film but, also, to new perceptions of reality itself. Referring to the divide between early filmmakers Auguste and Louis Lumière and Georges Méliès, Agnès Varda might well have been speaking for all three directors when she insisted on the intertwined nature of documentary (the Lumières) and imagination (Méliès): 'I really try for a Lumière/Méliès cinema ... Using the superb cinematographic matter [consisting of] the faces of people really enmeshed in their situation ... And using, as well, this imagery from the dream-cinema, all the baggage and iconography ... of our mental world' (quoted in Flitterman-Lewis 1990: 242).

While Rouch clearly occupies his own niche in the history of French cinema, Left Bank directors are generally considered part of the resurgence of documentary that marked the postwar period. To some extent, this resurgence was due to the climate of the times: the recent trauma of the War and Occupation encouraged, in the words of René Prédal, 'the documentary spirit to bear witness to the situation of the nation' (1991: 109). But institutional factors were also at work. A system put into place under the Occupation – and which remained in effect until 1955 – required cinemas to show a short film along with the feature. Since it was easier to obtain institutional support for making documentaries than for fictional shorts, a great many documentaries – about four hundred – were produced between 1939 and 1944.[4]

Just as importantly, as suggested earlier, documentaries also represented one of the few ways of approaching the fortress-like world of French cinema. In making documentaries, young directors enjoyed a freedom, a liberty of expression, not to be found elsewhere. Instead of serving an unfulfilling apprenticeship to the important directors of the day, aspiring filmmakers were able to make films that were often intensely personal, as quintessentially the work of *auteurs*, as were the later films of the Young Turks. Few critics would disagree with René Prédal who, after comparing the personal tone and new subject matter of such documentaries to the stale repetitions of the Tradition of Quality, observes that 'the documentaries of the 1950s are personal, committed, intelligent and passionate' (1991: 110).

Like the Young Turks, Left Bank directors never saw themselves as an artistic 'school' or cinematic 'group'. 'I'm friendly with Marker and Resnais', observed Varda in 1960, 'but we don't form a group. We share a certain way of thinking, a certain complicity ... I often have the impression that I have the same kind of plastic vocabulary as Resnais, and the same desire to have fun as Marker – a certain way of seeing and speaking about funny things' (1960: 5). The friendship and 'complicity' they shared led, especially at the beginning, to collaborative efforts. As early as 1950, Marker and Resnais collaborated to make a striking documentary about African art, *Les statues meurent aussi* (*Statues also Die*, 1950/1953); the credits for Marker's first solo film, *Dimanche à Pékin* (*Sunday in Peking*, 1956), include Varda as 'Chinese consultant'. For her first film, *La pointe courte* (1954), Varda asked Resnais to serve as editor. Resnais' eventual participation in this project – he had initially demurred on the grounds that her experiments were 'too close' to his – produced consequences that extended far beyond the film itself. Not only did Resnais stimulate Varda's interest in cinema, he introduced her to the Young Turks of *Les cahiers du cinéma*. This in turn led to a kind of crossover collaboration when Varda cast Godard in a film-within-a-film in *Cléo de 5 à 7* (*Cléo from 5 to 7*, 1961). Recalling her first meeting with the Young Turks, Varda underscored their passion and intensity as well as her sense of being the sole female in a world of men. 'I was there', she remarked, 'as if by accident, feeling very small and ignorant – the only girl among the boys of *Cahiers*' (1994: 13).

But along with these ties of friendship and collaboration, Left Bank directors also shared fundamental impulses that frequently distinguished them sharply from the Young Turks. A generation removed from the young *cinéphiles* of *Les cahiers du cinéma*, Resnais and Marker had experienced the war and its aftermath far more directly than their younger colleagues. (In fact, Marker served as a parachutist with the American army.) Deeply marked by the traumas of the recent past, they went on to make films that bore witness to the terrible weight of history. Resnais, in particular, would confront some of the worst nightmares of the twentieth century: the indiscriminate bombing of civilian populations (*Guernica*, 1950), the atrocities of the concentration camps (*Nuit et brouillard* (*Night and Fog*, 1955)), the horrors of the atomic bomb (*Hiroshima mon amour*). Moreover, this historical awareness frequently had a global dimension not seen in the works of the Young Turks. While the latter (at least initially) rarely left Paris, Resnais and Marker shot their first films in, respectively, Japan and China. As critic Claire Clouzot notes, while the inspiration of the Young Turks was 'autobiographical and neo-romantic, the Left Bank directors and their scriptwriters sought inspiration in the repercussions of the cataclysm of the war, in the atomic threat and in the absurdity of the world' (1972: 56).

Along with this intense historical awareness went a deep political consciousness. Here, too, the contrast with the Young Turks is noteworthy. At least at the beginning of their careers, the critics of *Les cahiers du cinéma* – this was especially true of Truffaut – were often described as right-wing 'dandies' or 'hussars.[5] In contrast, Left Bank directors took their place among the nation's committed left-wing artists and intellectuals. According to Claire Clouzot, they took stands 'in favour of peace and revolution (whether in Cuba, China or Spain) and against the wars in Algeria and Vietnam, [against] all forms of racism and fascism, [against] colonialism [and] repression' (Clouzot 1972: 54). But in addition to speaking out and taking stands, they also made films impregnated with their political beliefs. For example, Varda's films consistently bear witness to a concern with those on the bottom rung of the social ladder; those of Chris Marker explore the nature of revolutionary struggle and the possibility of a better, more just, society.

The political divide between the Left Bank directors and the Young Turks takes on a very sharp edge when it comes to the historical event that dominated France in the late 1950s: the Algerian War. With the problematic exception of Godard's *Le petit soldat* (*The Little Soldier*, 1962), which was quickly banned, the films of the Young Turks contain no overt trace of the conflict that was so bitterly denounced by those on the left. In contrast, despite the rules of censorship then in force, Left Bank directors referred to the struggle – and to the larger issue of French colonialism – in one film after another. *Les statues meurent aussi* implicitly denounces the ravages of French colonialism while Marker's *Le joli mai* – a 1963 *cinéma vérité* film (made in collaboration with Pierre Lhomme) that resembles Rouch's *Chronique d'un été* – investigates the legacy of colonialism and racism within France itself. (Banned for ten years, *Les statues meurent aussi* was released – in a mutilated version – only after the Algerian War came to an end.) In *Muriel* (1963), Resnais deals with one of the most disturbing and controversial aspects of the Algerian War: the use of torture on the part of the French military. And Varda's first major feature, *Cléo de 5 à 7*, is punctuated by references to the war in Algeria and to anti-war protests in Paris.

In addition to their political and historical awareness, Left Bank directors were also far more immersed in, and inspired by, the other arts of painting, theatre and literature than were their younger colleagues. Resnais was deeply attracted both to the visual arts – early documentaries dealt with painters such as Van Gogh, Gauguin and Picasso – and to the world of theatre. An aspiring stage actor before he took up the study of film editing, he once expressed his life-long love of theatre (and of theatrical language) saying: 'I've always been obsessed by the idea that it should be possible to create a soundtrack as beautiful, as magical, as the language of Shakespeare' (quoted in Benayoun 1980: 31). Like Resnais, Varda was also drawn to theatre, literature and the visual arts. After studying art history (from 1951 to 1961) at the École du Louvre, she served as the official photographer for productions at the Théâtre National Populaire. Perhaps the most intensely literary of the three directors, Chris Marker wrote fiction and essays – like his friend André Bazin, he also contributed to the Catholic humanist journal *Esprit* – before making films.

Not only were all three directors drawn to literature but all had distinct affinities with the so-called 'new novelists' – Alain Robbe-Grillet, Marguerite Duras and Nathalie Sarraute – of the 1950s. In this context, it is significant that Resnais – who throughout his career would choose distinguished men and women of letters to write scripts for his films – collaborated with both Duras (*Hiroshima mon amour*) and Robbe-Grillet (*L'anneé dernière à Marienbad* (*Last Year at Marienbad*, 1961)). In addition to such collaborations, the films of the Left Bank directors are marked by many of the themes that characterise the 'new novel' – the weight of memory and the past, the behaviour of people caught in the meshes of desire and obsession, the correspondences between inner and outer landscapes. So, too, do they frequently use a highly literary language – one whose theatrical cadences and poetic repetitions offered the sharpest of contrasts with the improvised dialogue and contemporary speech patterns generally seen in the films of the Young Turks.

In terms of politics and sensibilities then, the directors of the Left Bank and the Young Turks of *Les cahiers du cinéma* were undeniably very far apart. But at the same time they shared a fundamental trait, what Noël Simsolo (2000) has called a 'certain idea of cinema'. For both groups viewed cinema as an intensely personal calling, not a *métier* to be embraced like any other. Impelled by a desire to seize the real – be it in the inner life of individuals or the realities of history – they too challenged existing conventions even as they experimented with new forms. In so doing, implicitly or explicitly, they posed the phenomenological and existential questions – What is the nature of the image? What is its relationship to reality? How best can film uncover the 'truth' of reality? – at the philosophical heart of the New Wave.

Alain Resnais

Underscoring the important role played by Alain Resnais in relation to the New Wave, Antoine de Baecque observes that his short documentaries of the 1950s laid the groundwork for the 'flowering' of first features that came at the end of the decade (1998: 65). Seen from this perspective, it is significant, surely, that no one was more enthusiastic about Resnais' shorts than Godard. Writing in the pages of *Les cahiers du cinéma*, the young critic went so far as to declare that 'if film shorts did not exist Alain Resnais would surely have invented them' (Godard 1968: 193). It was undoubtedly the deeply experimental nature of Resnais' cinema – the sense that, as Godard had it, Resnais rethought all the 'possibilities of cinematographic technique' even as he 'started over from zero' (ibid.) – that won such praise from Godard. Comparing Resnais' mastery of editing to that of the great Soviet director Sergei Eisenstein, Godard unequivocally declared that for both directors editing 'means organising cinematographically, that is, anticipating dramatically, composing musically and – in still other, more beautiful, words – *mettre en scène*' (1968: 194).

Godard was not wrong: the most striking aspect of Resnais' cinema is probably his highly personal use of editing or montage. But what Godard does not say here – and, indeed, what would hardly have been clear at the time – was how profoundly Resnais' quest for a new cinematographic language, his 'starting over from zero', was influenced by a historical imperative. That is, in the immediate postwar period, the memory of recent horrors – Auschwitz as well as Hiroshima – seemed to demand new modes of thought and expression. Never before, perhaps, had traditional perceptions and forms seemed so inadequate and hollow, so unable to capture the 'real'. In this climate, as critic Serge Daney has observed, Resnais was more than a filmmaker – he was a 'seismograph'. Resnais, says Daney,

> was burdened with the terrible task of capturing the founding event of modernity: that, in the cinema as elsewhere, one had to deal with one more character: *the human race*. Now this character had just been denied (the concentration camps), atomised (the bomb), and diminished (torture). Traditional cinema was incapable of capturing this. It was necessary to find a form. Thus Resnais. (1986: 164)

The 'form' that Resnais chose was one that, collapsing inner and outer landscapes, subjectivity and objectivity, sought to capture the slightest nuances of feeling and desire – what he called the very 'mechanism' of thought. Indeed, in the eyes of French philosopher Gilles Deleuze, Resnais invented something totally new in the history of cinema – what Deleuze calls a 'cinema of thought' (1985: 271). In part, Resnais' approach was so radical because he refused to acknowledge that inner realities were less important, or even less 'real', than those of the external world. Deeply influenced by Surrealism – the artistic movement that championed the role of the imagination together with that of the irrational and the unconscious – Resnais once declared that 'filming what goes on in one's head is not subjectivity but another reality' (quoted in Bounoure 1962: 84). At the same time – and here too Resnais took a radical stance – he insisted that thought itself was not necessarily linked to particular characters or individuals. Indeed, in 1961 he observed: 'I'm more interested in feelings than in characters. I think that we can create a cinema without psychologically defined characters, one where the play of feelings would circulate just as, in a contemporary painting, the play of forms manages to be stronger than the action' (quoted in Pingaud 1961: 87–8).

The subjects of Resnais' early shorts could hardly be more varied: they range from films about art and artists to a documentary about the French national library; from a meditation on the Spanish Civil War to one of the most important films ever made about the Holocaust. But whatever the subject of these films, they attempt to seize and represent the ways in which emotions and desires, dreams and memories, shape the ways in which we see the world. In all these films, camerawork and editing, music and visual rhythms, work together to capture what Deleuze calls 'thought' or what another French philosopher, Youssef Ishaghpour, refers to as 'psychic functioning' (1982: 182). Resnais does not reject the 'objective' world: for example, *Guernica* – which consists largely of images drawn from Picasso's famous painting of the same title – begins with an 'objective' photograph of the Spanish town of Guernica laid to waste by fascist bombs. But this photographic evidence of a terrible historical event is no more important than the way the bombing of Guernica has been remembered, and rendered, by Picasso's images and by the words and commentary of poet Paul Eluard. Moreover, in all these films – and here too the subject matters little – the 'psychic functioning' explored by Resnais is bathed in the climate of melancholy and mourning that, in films like *Guernica* or *Nuit et brouillard*, is so clearly the result of historical trauma.

Both the melancholic nature of Resnais' cinema and his desire to capture the recesses of 'psychic functioning' were apparent in his first important short, *Van Gogh* (1948). In this work, Resnais does not give us an 'objective' documentary about the Dutch painter. Rather, he attempts to capture Van Gogh's anguished mind purely through the landscapes and portraits the painter executed towards the end of his life. Reflecting on this film, Resnais remarked that he wanted to see if, by virtue of montage, things painted by Van Gogh – trees, houses and people – could be made to 'play the role of real objects in a *récit* and if, in this case, it was possible to substitute for the spectator, almost without his knowing, the inner world of an artist for the real world that is revealed by photography' (quoted in Prédal 1968: 21). To make us experience this 'inner world', Resnais edits images drawn from Van Gogh's paintings into a montage sequence that becomes increasingly frenzied as the film progresses. Propelled from image to image, we are drawn into the obsessed and off-centre world of the painter; within this visionary world, we have the impression that we are on a journey to the innermost regions of thought where the 'madness' of the painter, who committed suicide after painting these images, lies hidden. In this imaginary world, writes a poetic Gilles Deleuze, 'the layers of inner life and those of the exterior world, speed up, grow longer, cut into each other with increasing speeds until the screen goes black at the end' (1985: 272).

In the case of both *Van Gogh* and *Guernica*, the 'psychic functioning' evoked by Resnais can be ascribed to specific individuals; so, too, can the melancholy of the film be explained in terms of definable reasons (individual madness, historical trauma). But in other shorts, as suggested earlier, Resnais' approach is even more radical: that is, he divorces the 'psychic mechanism' at work from any concrete psychological anchor; at the same time, he refuses to give us a discernible cause or reason to explain the anguish that is so clearly visible. This is the case, for example, of *Toute la mémoire du monde*, a 1956 documentary about the French national library that was commissioned by a governmental agency concerned with cultural affairs. At first glance, the subject of this film would hardly seem to lend itself to Resnais' obsession with the melancholy of individuals (*Van Gogh*) or the memory of historical horror (*Guernica*). And, yet, even as Resnais gives us all the 'objective' facts about the library (its history, content, mode of operation), he also imbues it with all the anguish and melancholy seen in those earlier films. Transformed by camerawork (especially by seemingly interminable tracking shots as well as high-angle shots), by lighting and rhythm, the library becomes as unreal as any imaginary structure in a film of science fiction. Robert Benayoun describes the library as a 'cathedral, a fortress, an astrodome, an undersea and spatial station' (1980: 55); to Gilles Deleuze, it suggests nothing other than a 'gigantic memory' where 'men themselves are no longer anything but mental functions or neuronic messengers' (1985: 159).

Above all, perhaps – and this takes us to the acute historical aware-ness at the core of Resnais' cinema – whether or not this was intentional on Resnais' part, it seems to me that the claustrophobic library of *Toute la mémoire du monde*, with its dark halls and seemingly-endless corridors, evokes the haunting spectre of the empty concentration camp seen in *Nuit et brouillard*. In the library, it is books, rather than people, that are inventoried, stamped, locked away. Again and again, critics have likened the library to places not unlike the camps: that is, to a prison or, even, a tomb. Underscoring the presence of 'heavy gates and grills', of 'keys turn-ing in locks', Noel Burch emphasizes the sense of imprisonment that clings to this monument of memory. 'Finally', he writes, 'having got past all the barriers separating the "prisoners" from the outside world, we reach the "cell-blocks": the stacks, with their long dark aisles filled by the echoing footsteps of invisible guards' (1959: 59). Along similar lines, Peter Harcourt notes that, as seen by Resnais, the collections in the library become 'huge prisons that confine one's past, huge tombs in which man's past records can be buried'. The 'depository of the past', he continues, 'is seen as a great prison in which one can wander endlessly along extended corridors' (Harcourt 1973: 50). As such reactions suggest, in this film the library virtu-ally incarnates the 'play of feelings' that gives Resnais' cinema its distinc-tive cast.

Chris Marker

For Chris Marker, as for Resnais, the realities of the 'imagination' are as 'real' and important as those of the outer world. He, too, is obsessed with memory and the reach of the past. But, in addition to these concerns, another issue permeates Marker's cinema: for, like his friend André Bazin, he is concerned with the relationship between the image and what it represents or (as Bazin would have it) between cinema and reality. But if Marker resembles Bazin in this respect, the conclusions he reaches could hardly be more different from those embraced by the great critic. While Bazin argued that cinema can embrace, and reveal, reality, Marker's films underscore the chasm that lies between images and what they represent. Like Godard – who would later sum up this issue in a well-known aphorism proclaimed in his film *Vent d'est* (*Wind from the East*, 1969): 'It's not a just [correct] image, it's just an image' – Marker seems determined to prevent us from 'believing' in what we see. His films continually suggest that images themselves – filtered through modes of feeling and imagination, conditioned by earlier images as well as preconceptions – cry out for interpretation. Undermining and challenging the transparency of the image, they ask us to reflect on the ways we (re)construct memories, tell stories, use and interpret images. 'It is in this attempt to understand and interpret the world and its images', writes Jean-Luc Alpigiano, 'that Marker's cinema differs from the conceptions of Bazin who feels that it should be sufficient to show it' (1998: 26).

This fundamental difference between Marker and Bazin is related to still another fault line between these two thinkers. While Bazin favours long-takes in the belief that they bring us closer to phenomenal reality, Marker tends to use the intellectual montage associated with the directors of early Soviet cinema. In this kind of montage, ideas spring not from the images themselves but, rather, from their juxtaposition. Moreover, while directors of silent features had to limit themselves to the juxtaposition of visual images, Marker can – and does – extend this principle to the juxtaposition of sound and image. Thus, as Bazin observed in an illuminating essay on Marker's films, images frequently refer not only to preceding images but, rather, to what has just been said (2003: 44). If the long takes (as well as the concordance of sound and image) favoured by Bazin somehow invite us to sink into the world, Marker's highly cerebral approach to montage, as well as his tendency to divorce sound and image, demand, rather, that we interpret what is shown – that we extract 'meaning' from the collision not only of images but, also, from that of sound and images.

Moreover – and here we come to what may be the most unconventional and deeply personal impulse at work in Marker's cinema – the counterpoint between image and sound is one that frequently privileges sound. Commenting upon this distinctive characteristic of Marker's cinema, Bazin points out that while commentary usually 'completes [the] organisation of sense' provided by the (visual) montage, the reverse often occurs in Marker's cinema. 'I would say', Bazin observes of Marker's films, 'that the primary material is intelligence, that its immediate means of expression is language, and that the image only intervenes in the third position, in reference to this verbal intelligence' (ibid.). The central role played by what Bazin calls 'intelligence' is one of the principal reasons, surely, that Marker's films have often been likened to personal essays. Not only do his films undermine conventional distinctions between documentary and fiction but, also, they interweave poetry and sociology, memory and history, past and present, in the most personal ways imaginable. To borrow Rivette's description of Rossellini's *Viaggio in Italia*, Marker's films 'comprise almost everything … metaphysical essay, confession, log-book, intimate journal' (Rivette 1985: 199).

From the very first, Marker's films revealed the intensely personal and heteroclite nature of his cinema. Throughout his documentaries of the 1950s, reflections on history and politics are accompanied by a meditation on the meaning of cultural images or signs. For example, in *Dimanche à Pékin* – which was shot in the Chinese capital five years after Mao's triumphant victory in 1949 – Marker seeks to find, and record, the 'new' China of Communist dreams. But, from the beginning, it is apparent that what he sees is conditioned by feelings, imagination, memory. Mixing past and present, the real and the unreal, the opening commentary tells us that 'nothing is more beautiful than Paris if not the memory of Paris. And nothing is more beautiful than Peking if not the memory of Peking. As for me, here in Paris, I remember Peking and I count my treasures. Without knowing it, I've been dreaming of Peking for thirty years.'

As Marker wanders the streets of the Chinese capital, he anxiously interrogates what lies behind the images that fill the screen. What do the images of modern Peking, asks the voice-over, reveal of China's fabled past? Of the future dreamed of, envisaged, by Mao's revolutionaries? How are the images recorded by his camera related to the images of the mythological China that have haunted the Western imagination for so long? Are there any signs, any vestiges, of the legendary China – the land of Genghis Khan and Jules Verne – dreamed of in the West? Raising one question after another, the commentary repeatedly warns us that images are not what they seem. Stone animals guard Ming tombs where no one is buried; imposing arches lead nowhere. Seeking the China of the past, Marker discovers only traces: men performing ancient martial arts, shadow boxers, upturned roofs. In search of the China of the future, Marker films children at work and play; interacting with them at school, he apologises – ironically? – for interrupting the 'march of history'. To conclude this most personal of cinematic essays, he reminds us of the need to understand China 'with whom we shall have to share history'.

In his next film, *Lettre de Sibérie* (*Letter from Siberia*, 1958), Marker turns from the Chinese capital to the outermost regions of the Soviet Union. Confronted with the heavy hand of Soviet propaganda, his characteristic irony is exacerbated – 'ducks', he informs us solemnly, 'are by nature given to collectives' – even as the need for interpretation, for wariness in the face of the slogans that obscure and distort the real, is felt more intensely. In fact, in an oft-cited sequence, Marker reveals how easily the same images can be interpreted in radically different ways. In three successive sequences we see the same shots of a town in Siberia. But each time we hear a different commentary which, in effect, changes the way we view and interpret the images. In the first sequence, as if hearing the voice of Soviet propaganda, we are told that the town is a modern one populated by 'happy Soviet workers' intent on making it 'a good place to live'. This is followed by a sequence reflecting Western views of the town as gloomy, where unhappy workers are treated like 'slaves'. Finally, we are given a 'neutral' or objective commentary which tells us that we are seeing a town where modern houses are gradually replacing decrepit areas and where the workers are striving to make much needed improvements. But Marker's scepticism, his hermeneutical investigation, is relentless. For even this 'objective' view, he finally declares, is not correct since it freezes realities that are constantly evolving. Objectivity, he insists, 'does not distort the reality of Siberia but it stops it, judges it, and therefore distorts it just the same. What counts is [Siberia's] *élan* and its diversity.' This leads the director to a seemingly paradoxical conclusion: perhaps, he says, it is not actual documentary shots that will allow us to understand Siberia but, rather, 'imaginary newsreels'. And, indeed, at this point, he begins to create 'unreal' newsreels that may well reveal more about Siberia than actual documentary footage.

Agnès Varda

The complex relationship between the world of the imagination and that of 'reality' also haunts the cinema of Agnès Varda. In fact her first film, a feature entitled *La pointe courte*, is permeated by what Alison Smith describes as 'the tension between recording and creating reality, between the objective and the subjective, documentary and imaginative invention' (1998: 4). An innovative film in every respect, *La pointe courte* – which was shot on location in the southern French town of Sète – makes it very clear why Varda has been described as the 'mother' or 'godmother' of the New Wave.[6] To begin with, at least four years before the Young Turks made their first films on a shoestring, the 24-year-old Varda created her own production company to make this feature-length work. Without training or experience (other than that as a photographer), without the necessary authorisations, and with very little money she stuck to her project. When the funds provided by an inheritance from her father and a loan from her mother (who mortgaged her house) proved insufficient, she asked her collaborators (including editor Alain Resnais and composer Georges Delerue) and actors (Sylvia Monfort and Philippe Noiret) to form a kind of cooperative whereby they would be paid if and when the film made money. (It took 13 years before everyone was fully paid.) When the film was finally completed, the inexperienced director did not know how to have her work distributed. Luckily, André Bazin – to whom Varda would dedicate a later short – came to the rescue by writing a favourable article on the film and by helping Varda to set up an important private screening.

Once the film was shown (in a small art-house cinema on the Left Bank), there could be no doubt that Varda's stylistic daring equalled her bravery – what Melville might have called her 'intransigence' – in producing the film. For, like virtually all of Varda's subsequent films, *La pointe courte* defied established categories. Neither a documentary nor a work of fiction, it was, instead, a kind of highly personal amalgam of the two. The film – inspired, Varda has said, by the juxtaposition of two narratives in Faulkner's novel, *The Wild Palms* (1939) – intercuts documentary sequences with those depicting a kind of fictional narrative. In the docu-

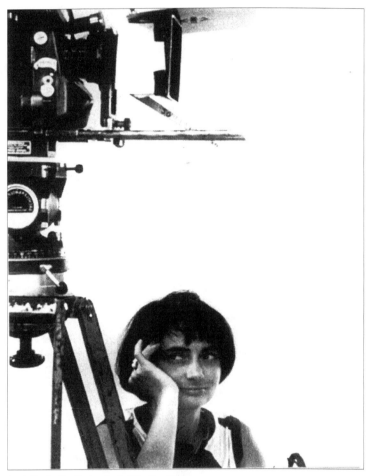

Agnès Varda: the 'Godmother' of the New Wave

mentary sequences – which seemed so 'real' that they give rise to comparisons with Italian neo-realism – Varda portrayed the lives of fishermen and their families in La pointe, a section of Sète, that she knew well from her childhood in this city. Here, there are no actors or scripted dramas but only the details and dramas of everyday life: clothes hanging on the line, boats returning to port, the machinations of the fishermen who want to outwit a visiting health inspector, the death of a child, the difficult romance of two young people. The fictional narrative, instead, features actors who portray the marital difficulties of a young couple newly arrived in La pointe courte. In contrast to the naturalistic dialogue of the fisher folk seen in the documentary sequences, the husband and wife, as if reading a text, speak in a highly literary and artificial manner.

Although commentators have speculated on the precise nature of the relationship between the two parts of the film, Varda herself observed that she deliberately left this relationship open or ambiguous so that spectators could 'create oppositions and superimpositions' (1994: 227). At the same time, the ambiguities of the film clearly reflected her preference for what she saw as the complexities of literature as opposed to the simplicities and artificial constraints of most films. Musing that most films did not deal with the 'problems of existence', in the course of an important 1960 interview she went on to confess that she had the feeling that cinema 'did not speak of things that were alive and important [and] that it was not free, especially in regard to form, and that irritated me. I wanted to make a film as you would a novel' (1960: 8). But, above and beyond her taste for formal innovation and for real problems – for 'things that were alive and important' – the two parts of the film also corresponded to what she described as her acute sense of the 'two sides' of everything. Even while making the film, she said, she 'felt the two sides of everything, the side of men and the side of women, black and white, wood and iron, the world of reality stemming from observing people and the mental world where the mind wanders and invents structures and forms' (1994: 39).

What Varda describes as the 'two sides' of everything – the 'observable' side of reality and the 'mental world where the mind wanders' – are very much in evidence in the three shorts that followed La pointe courte. Described by Godard as 'diamonds that shine in a thousand facets', two of these – O Saisons, ô Châteaux (1957) and Du côté de la côte (1958) – were commissioned documentaries dealing with regions of France. L'Opéra-Mouffe (1958) was, instead, an avant-garde work made for a festival of experimental films in Brussels. Despite these different points of departure, all three, significantly, were about concrete, observable, 'places' or, more precisely, about what Varda saw as the important relationship between people and places. 'I believe', she once remarked, 'that people are made not only of the places where they were raised but of those they love. I believe that surroundings live within us' (1960: 14). But at the same time, all three are also permeated by the 'wandering life of the mind'. For example, in *Du côté de la côte*, a documentary about the French Riviera, the places and people observed become a springboard for imagined dramas, for reflections on the beauty and the fragility of life, for an investigation of the surreal and grotesque elements that lie below the surface of daily existence.

Of the three films, it is, not unexpectedly, *L'Opéra-Mouffe* – dubbed a 'subjective documentary' by Varda – that most seamlessly blends the internal and the external, the world of observable reality and that of the mind. Like Resnais' shorts, *L'Opéra-Mouffe* portrays the outer world as it is seen and transformed by the press of subjective feelings and desires. But, Varda's film differs from Resnais' in that, here, the gaze directed towards the outer world is clearly that of a woman. (Indeed, Sandy Flitterman-Lewis considers this film a 'landmark in feminist cinema' because of its emphasis on female subjectivity (1990: 264)). Infused with what Varda called a 'woman's cinematic vocabulary', the film portrays a bustling market street (rue Mouffetard) in the Latin Quarter of Paris as seen through the hypersensitive eyes of a pregnant woman.[7] Accompanied by the vibrant music of Georges Delerue, the film – which is otherwise silent – becomes a kind of visual and musical record of the woman's thoughts, sensations and impressions as she watches the busy world of the street. Reflecting her hopes and fears, the street appears welcoming, threatening, sinister. Lyrical shots of lovers at the beginning give way, towards the end, to shots of people who are old, perhaps homeless, crippled. Subjective fears are relayed through the most concrete of images: a shot of a pregnant belly is followed by one of a melon being brutally sliced open to release its seeds; grotesque carnival masks hint at fears of deformity and death.

One of Varda's most personal films, *L'Opéra-Mouffe* was not only shot by the director herself but, also, sprang directly from a profoundly subjective experience, for she herself was pregnant with her first child when she made it.[8] (In fact, the pregnant belly seen in the opening shot is her own.) While Varda took care to emphasise that the rather fearful and anguished woman's vision reflected in the film was not totally her own, she did acknowledge that it was imbued with the heightened sensitivity – marked by a return to 'instincts' and the presence of 'new sensations' – that accompanied her pregnancy. Looking back at this aspect of *L'Opéra-*

Et Dieu créa la femme (1956): an image of changing moralities

Mouffe in 1994, she emphasised, once again, her desire to create a work able to document not only the realities of the outside world but also the truths of the imagination. 'I was happy', she said, 'to have transmitted the particular emotion of my pregnancy ... I was modern enough to do breathing exercises but as primitive as it can be when it came to vibrating with new sensations. And [I was happy] to have found a cinematic expression for them, between the truth of a Cartier-Bresson and the dream images of so-called art cinema' (1994: 115).

Changing Mores

Roger Vadim

Reflecting on the New Wave, film historian René Prédal suggests that it had two kinds of precursors or, in his words, 'godfathers': 'illegitimate' (those who took an independent path to filmmaking) and 'legitimate' (those who worked within the system). Of the 'legitimate godfathers', Roger Vadim was, probably, the most important. Vadim's first film, *Et Dieu créa la femme* (*And God Created Woman*, 1956), a family drama in lush Technicolor reminiscent of certain Hollywood melodramas of the 1950s, clearly did not challenge the conventions of narrative cinema. But it *did* portray the rapidly changing generational, social, cultural and, especially, sexual landscape of postwar France. In so doing, it achieved a success – a *succès de scandale* in France, Vadim's film was a great commercial draw in the United States – which would have profound implications for the New Wave. Writing in 1961, Jacques Siclier called Vadim the 'most famous precursor of the New Wave' (1961a: 69). Echoing this judgement, nearly fifty years later film historian David Cook observed that 'more than any other single figure in French cinema, [Vadim] opened the doors of the industry to his generation and provided the economic justification for the New Wave' (2004: 441).

Et Dieu créa la femme owed its success and notoriety, above all, to the electric presence of its female star, a very young Brigitte Bardot who, at the time, was married to Vadim. Although Bardot had appeared in earlier films, it was Vadim's that transformed her from an aspiring starlet into the very symbol of a new kind of sexuality, a contemporary female icon for an emerging generation of viewers. As Ginette Vincendeau observes, the sense of 'newness' that clung to Bardot was fuelled by several factors: the actress's youth, her sexual frankness, her embrace of spontaneity (marked by the patterns of everyday speech, casual clothes, and so forth) and even her training (unlike the classically-trained stage actresses of an earlier generation, Bardot began her career as a dancer and a model). But Vincendeau goes on to make the important point that, despite this 'newness', the fact that Bardot was still seen (and filmed) as an object of male desire meant that 'her appeal depended on "old" values: on traditional myths of femininity and on the display of her body, though a body repackaged for the times: nude, more "natural", on location, in colour and Cinemascope' (2000: 84).

In the film, Bardot plays a young woman, Juliette, who lives in the seaside town of St Tropez and whose defiant eroticism, and disdain for bourgeois hypocrisies, is both scandalous and – to a series of different men – infinitely desirable. In recent years, it is true, some feminists have complained that, in the end, Bardot is 'tamed' by her husband. After discovering that his wife has slept with his brother, Juliette's husband (played by a very young Jean-Louis Trintignant) slaps her – a rebuke that his young wife seems to find fitting and, perhaps, exciting. But what dominates this film, what lingers in the memory, is not this rather conventional ending:

rather, it is the sheer eroticism of Bardot's presence – the way in which she revels in her body. Exerting her charms upon her suitors in this film, Bardot became one of the world's most potent sex symbols; the only French star whose glamour rivalled that of Marilyn Monroe, she was a 'sex kitten' to be desired by men, copied by women. Most critics would probably not put it as crudely as Pierre Billard who wrote that 'Roger Vadim owed his reputation as a modern director to Bardot's breasts' (1995: 625). But even the most sober commentators have recourse to extravagant metaphors in order to stress the force of Bardot's appeal. With Bardot, writes Jean Douchet, 'a wild, liberated, animal presence burst across the screen. It undermined and revolutionised social customs, not just in France but around the world' (1999: 143). Observing that Bardot's erotic force 'swept away all moral and social conventions', René Prédal makes the crucial point that it was largely due to Bardot – and to the success of *Et Dieu créa la femme* – that for a time the New Wave itself became 'synonymous with youth, free love and joyous sexuality' (1991: 117).

Significantly, no one was more enthusiastic about the film, or about the new kind of sexuality that Bardot represented, than the Young Turks. In their eyes, Vadim's sexual frankness – and Bardot's incandescent appeal – meant that sexuality and the 'body' appeared as they really were in modern life. Declaring that Bardot was 'magnificent', Truffaut praised *Et Dieu créa la femme* as 'a typical film of our generation' (1975: 328). Truffaut's enthusiasm was matched by that of Godard. In his review of Vadim's second film, *Sait-on jamais?*, Godard hailed the director for 'breathing the air of today' and deemed him the 'best of the young French directors working [at that point]' (1968: 82). A few years later, Godard paid Vadim what was, perhaps, a still greater compliment. Not only did he himself cast Bardot in his 1963 film, *Le mépris (Contempt)* but, also, he shot her in ways that deliberately recalled her celebrated appearance in *Et Dieu créa la femme*. In so doing, he managed at once to pay homage to her body and to make the viewer reflect on the ways in which cinema uses, and misuses, sexuality.

Louis Malle

Although Vadim continued making films, as a director he is remembered, above all, for *Et Dieu créa la femme*. The case is very different when it comes to Louis Malle. After making his debut in the late 1950s, Malle proceeded to enjoy a long and distinguished career that included many memorable

L'ascenseur à l'échafaud (1957): a 'new amorality' in the air

films. In relation to the New Wave, too, Malle played a very different – and far more complex – role than Vadim. While *Et Dieu créa la femme* may have paved the way for young directors, the work itself was a conventional melodrama which had neither the look nor the feel of a New Wave film. In contrast, in certain respects, the first film by Louis Malle, *L'ascenseur à l'échafaud* (*Lift to the Scaffold*, 1957) had a great deal in common with early films by the Young Turks.[9] Commentators are split, in fact, on whether or not Malle should be seen as a part of the New Wave. At one extreme, Alan Williams argues that 'Malle was at the very heart of the *nouvelle vague*' (1992: 340); at the other, Jacques Siclier declares that Malle was funda-mentally a 'brilliant stylist' rather than a true *auteur* in the manner of his New Wave contemporaries (1961a: 64). Midway between the two, René Prédal voices what is, perhaps, the more general consensus: that Malle was essentially an 'independent *auteur*' whose first films coincided with those of the New Wave (1989: 16).

Wherever one places Malle in relation to the New Wave, there is little doubt, as suggested earlier, that *L'ascenseur à l'échafaud*, like early films by Godard and Truffaut, represented a changing of the guard. From a formal point of view, Malle's film clearly pointed ahead to techniques associated with the New Wave: shot on location in the streets of Paris by cinematographer Henri Decaë, it featured a fairly loose narrative structure along with a jazz score – improvised by legendary trumpeter Miles Davis – that was defiantly modern. At the same time, it was also firmly rooted in contemporary reality. In marked contrast to the romantic and familiar view of Paris as a charming place of neighbourhood cafés and welcoming bistros, the city seen here is already the relatively anonymous capital that was taking shape in the postwar years. 'Traditionally', observed Malle, 'it was always the René Clair Paris that French films presented, and I took care to show one of the first modern buildings in Paris. I invented a motel ... I showed a Paris not of the future, but at least a modern city, a world already somewhat dehumanised' (1993: 16). Most importantly, perhaps, like *Et Dieu créa la femme*, Malle's film made it clear that social attitudes had changed – that a 'new amorality' was in the air. Focused on two lovers (played by Jeanne Moreau and Maurice Ronet) who hatch a doomed plot to kill the woman's husband, the film underscored, in particular, the woman's passion and sensuality – as well as her total indifference to any morality. And if Brigitte Bardot embodied a new kind of sensuality, so, too – albeit in a very different key – did Jeanne Moreau. A classically-trained actress, the beautiful Moreau would soon be seen as the embodiment of the so-called eternal feminine. Strong yet passionate, ready to give everything for love – and to demand everything of it – she conveyed what Vincendeau deems an 'existential' sexuality which was at once sensuous, serious and cerebral (2000: 12).

The contours of Moreau's persona came into even sharper focus in Malle's next film, *Les amants* (*The Lovers*, 1958). (Apparently the actress, who had a hand in shaping the script, infused the character with aspects of her own personality.) Here, the irresolvable conflict between the 'authenticity' of passion and the claims of society is even sharper, less freighted with ambiguity, than in *L'ascenseur à l'échafaud*. In this film, Moreau plays a kind of latter-day Emma Bovary: like Flaubert's heroine in the titular novel, she is a beautiful young wife and mother slowly suffocating from the aridness of provincial bourgeois life. Finally, a romantic *coup de foudre* frees her from her lifeless and shallow existence: after a night of passion spent with a bohemian architect she has just met – a night depicted in what was considered shocking detail – she decides to abandon everything. Leaving behind her child as well as her husband, in the early morning she sets off with the architect – heading towards a future that is both frightening and liberating.

Significantly, *Les amants* evoked great enthusiasm on the part of the Young Turks. It was Jacques Doniol-Valcroze who declared that *Les amants* 'is a very important film. It marks the rise of a new generation within a French cinema that, since the war, has resembled a closed shop for fifty years' (Doniol-Valcroze: 110). In the eyes of Truffaut, Malle's second film was superior to both *Et Dieu créa la femme* and *L'ascenseur à l'échafaud* – better, even, than his friend Chabrol's first film, *Le beau Serge* (*Handsome Serge*, 1958). Deeming *Les amants* 'a fascinating film', he went so far as to compare Malle's work to Renoir's. Paying Malle a great compliment, the young critic wrote that *Les amants* 'progresses with the spontaneity of Renoir's old films: that is, it gives you the feeling of discovering things along with the filmmaker rather than coming after him' (1975: 331). (In light of this comparison it is interesting that, in this film, Malle pays homage to Renoir by casting an actor from *La Règle du jeu*, Gaston Modot.) And while Godard's *Le mépris* evoked and played off *Et Dieu créa la femme*, Truffaut's third film – *Jules et Jim* (1961) – echoes aspects of *Les amants*. Shot by Henri Decaë, and accompanied by the kind of novelistic voice-over featured in *Les amants*, *Jules et Jim* stars Jeanne Moreau once again playing a liberated, passionate woman who refuses to make any concessions to social norms. Looking at Moreau's performance in this film, one can well understand why Vincendeau considers her the New Wave star par excellence (2000: 130).[10] Often considered Truffaut's masterpiece – and, certainly, one of the classics of French cinema – *Jules et Jim* suggests not only the continuities that link Malle to the Young Turks but, also, just how far the New Wave had come in a few short years.

4   EUPHORIA

'In 1959', remarked Truffaut famously, 'we were living a dream – everything was happening in ways that would have been inconceivable two years earlier' (1988: 56). What Truffaut calls a 'dream' was made possible by the release of six striking features by young directors: *Le beau Serge* and *Les cousins* by Claude Chabrol, *Les Quatre cents coups* by François Truffaut, *Hiroshima mon amour* by Alain Resnais, *Orfeu negro* by Marcel Camus and *À bout de souffle* by Jean-Luc Godard. Coming close on the heels of one another – *Les Quatre cents coups*, *Hiroshima mon amour* and *Orfeu negro* were all seen at the Cannes festival of 1959 – they firmly established the notion of a cinematic New Wave in the minds of both the press and the public. Reflecting on this phenomenon, Truffaut remarked that if only one of the films released in 1958–59 had appeared, 'little would have been said'. But, he continued, the release of all 'really had an effect and we had innumerable telephone calls asking us to get together and be photographed as a group' (1962: 48). As each film offered yet more proof that a new generation of filmmakers had arrived, it also brought its particular 'touch', in the words of Antoine de Baecque, to the 'collective portrait of the New Wave' that emerged so decisively at this exciting time (1998: 88).

Le beau Serge and *Les cousins*

Even before the revelation of the New Wave at the Cannes festival of 1959, Chabrol had managed to launch his career with two features: *Le beau Serge* (shown out of competition at the Cannes festival of 1958) and *Les cousins*. Often seen as companion pieces, the two films were, indeed, conceived around the same time. Chabrol began with *Le beau Serge* – an extremely low-budget feature written, produced and directed by Chabrol himself – because it was less expensive to produce. The foreign distribution rights the director received for this film, together with a sum from the CNC, allowed him to proceed with *Les cousins*. Thus, as fellow *Les cahiers du cinéma* critic and (later) filmmaker Jacques Doniol-Valcroze remarked at the time, Chabrol – who had never gone to film school, never served as anyone's assistant and never even made a short – broke into filmmaking by sheer 'audacity' (quoted in Douchet 1999: 128).

In certain respects, *Le beau Serge* is probably the most old-fashioned of the New Wave features released in the course of this period. A psychological melodrama about two childhood friends who choose very different paths in life, the film explores the murkier zones of human behaviour in ways that evoke a long tradition of French *moralistes* dating back to Blaise Pascal and Jean de La Fontaine. Along with a *moraliste*'s eye for the hidden corners of thought and action, the film also suggests the religious character – marked by a concern with guilt and redemption – that would shadow Chabrol's films. (Along with Eric Rohmer, Chabrol is usually seen as part of the 'Catholic' wing of the Young Turks.) But if, in these respects, the film seemed rooted in the past, it also revealed impulses that clearly signalled a New Wave sensibility. To begin with, it starred young, unknown performers – Gérard Blain, Bernadette Lafont and Jean-Claude Brialy – who, before long, would become familiar faces in New Wave films. Moreover, shot on location (by Henri Decaë) in the village of Sardent, it captured the texture and feel of a very specific place in a quasi-documentary fashion. As would be the case in almost all New Wave features, it was a place rooted in the director's own experience: Chabrol had spent the Occupation years in Sardent living with his grandmother and, at one point, had actually shown films in a barn he dubbed 'Cinéma de Sardentais'. Underscoring the resonance that the village held for him, in one interview Chabrol remarked that the idea for his first feature stemmed from a desire to shoot a film 'in wintertime Sardent. For me, the region represented childhood and winter' (1962: 3).

Inspired by a period in Chabrol's own past, the film evokes the sense of village life both through its casting – in addition to young unknowns, Chabrol used non-professionals drawn from Sardent – and through its attention to the rhythms and details of everyday life. The camera lingers on the coming and going of Sardent's inhabitants – from the children who play on the village square to the locals who gather in the café or bistro to exchange information and to gossip. Revealing the importance that he attached to these scenes, Chabrol expressed regret that he was forced to cut similar ones because of time constraints. (The film was reduced from its original length of two and a half hours to the requisite 93 minutes.) Referring to Marcel Pagnol, a director of the 1930s known for his portrayal of village life in the South of France, Chabrol observed that the original film had 'a whole Pagnol side. You saw the baker making his bread, the gossips in the stores, the schoolchildren running along the streams. That's where I made my cuts. Now, what seems to me the best [aspect of the film] is precisely the life of the village' (1976: 141). But even with these cuts, Chabrol's evocation of the environment – his use of real places and people, his attention to everyday detail, his sensitivity to changes in light and season – was so striking that the film quickly gave rise to comparisons with neo-realism. When *Le beau Serge* first appeared, Robin Wood and Michael Walker observed, 'it looked like an attempt at developing a French neo-realist school, with Chabrol shooting entirely on location, using the real inhabitants of a real village, showing a consistent concern to represent the surface details of the environment and the people's lives with the greatest possible fidelity' (1970: 11).

In addition to its 'fidelity' to the lives and surroundings of its characters, *Le beau Serge* announced itself as a New Wave film in another important respect. It revealed the influence of *cinéphilie* – the respect for old masters – shared by the Young Turks. In particular, like many of Chabrol's subsequent films, it evoked the work of one of the filmmakers most admired by the Young Turks: Alfred Hitchcock. In fact, it is largely because of the Young Turks – whose feelings for Hitchcock (and Hawks) were so intense that they were sometimes dubbed 'Hitchcocko-Hawksiens' by their older colleagues – that Hitchcock, previously regarded principally as a popular entertainer, began to receive the recognition so readily accorded him today. Significantly, the Young Turks discussed Hitchcock not only in the pages of *Les cahiers du cinéma* but also in two notable studies of his films. In 1957 Rohmer and Chabrol collaborated on a work later translated into English as *Hitchcock: The First Forty-Four Films* (Rohmer & Chabrol 1979); in 1966 Truffaut published an extended series of important interviews with the filmmaker called, simply, *Hitchcock* (Truffaut 1967). Nearly half a century later, Godard expressed his admiration for the maker of *North by Northwest* (a film released while the Young Turks were writing for *Les cahiers du cinéma*): in his 1998 series of films about the history of film, *Histoire(s) du cinéma*, Godard deems Hitchcock nothing less than the 'greatest creator of forms of the twentieth century'.

Still, whilst all the Young Turks felt deeply about Hitchcock's films, they obviously held a special resonance for Chabrol. On the most superficial level Chabrol, like Hitchcock, liked to make a fleeting appearance in his own films. (In *Le beau Serge*, he is glimpsed on the village square in the midst of a conversation with assistant director Philippe de Broca.) On a much deeper level, Chabrol also used the thriller genre to explore shifting zones of guilt and complicity. Analysing these in their study of Hitchcock, Rohmer and Chabrol underscore the director's use of a fundamental narrative/psychological stratagem that they label a process of 'exchange', by which the attributes or qualities of one character (for example, guilt or suspicion) are gradually transferred to another. In the wake of this study, critics have discerned a similar stratagem of 'exchange' in Chabrol's own films.[1] For example, in *Le beau Serge*, the character initially seen as 'good' and 'moral' gradually reveals hidden or repressed layers of egoism and insecurity, of fear and jealousy. As these layers come into focus, the spectator is forced to re-evaluate earlier impressions and assumptions. 'What interests me', confessed Chabrol, 'is to tease the audience along, to set it chasing off in one direction, and then to turn things inside out' (Chabrol 1970/71: 6). Imbued with suspense, the process of turning 'things inside out' also points to the gap – at the heart of Chabrol's films as well, perhaps, as those of Hitchcock – between appearance and reality.

If Chabrol's shares Hitchcock's taste for disquieting and suspenseful 'exchanges', he resembles the master of suspense in still another way: that is, he continually uses *mise-en-scène* and camera movements to heighten our sense of shifting realities and perceptions. Often, we glimpse psychological mechanisms and motives not through what the characters say or do but, rather, through the ways they are filmed. Speaking of this aspect of his work, Chabrol once observed that the 'subject' of his films did not reside in their plots – although he grudgingly admitted that plots were necessary – but, rather, in their 'characters and form' (quoted in Braucourt 1971: 122). While this aspect of Chabrol's films would become more assured with the passage of time, *Le beau Serge* already suggests his unconventional and highly expressive use of the camera. Half-pans or tracking shots gradually transform a subjective shot (that is, one in which we see something from a character's point of view) into an objective one; or else objective shots may become subjective so that, as Joel Magny observes, 'the one looking becomes the one looked at, and vice versa' (1987: 40). Reflecting the sense of shifting perceptions – or what the director called the 'play of masks' (Wood & Walker 1979: 15) – that characterise Chabrol's films, such shots also point to the tremendous importance the Young Turks ascribed to the resources peculiar to the language of film.

In various respects, then, *Le beau Serge* suggested the shape of things to come. The film's personal dimension, its documentary-like evocation of a particular time and place, its cinematic echoes as well as its unconventional use of cinematographic language – all these would soon be seen as defining impulses of the New Wave. Still, it was Chabrol's second film, *Les cousins*, which clearly announced the arrival of a 'new wave' of young directors. In part, this was a result of timing: by the time *Les cousins* was released, the media had begun to speak of the emergence of a new generation, a *nouvelle vague*, of young French men and women. But it is also true that Chabrol's film gave a compelling portrait of the very generation of young people whose beliefs and attitudes were being anxiously interrogated in the media. Moreover, the film seemed to confirm the growing sense that the new generation was one of disillusioned, if not nihilistic, hedonists who lacked the ideals and moral compass of their parents. Both reflecting and dovetailing with the media's fascination with youth, *Les cousins* became not only the fifth most popular film of 1959 but also the very emblem of the New Wave. 'Thanks to its story, style and financial success', writes Richard Neupert, '*Les cousins* quickly became ... a poster child for the New Wave' (2002: 143).

Written by Chabrol and Paul Géguaff – a friend from Chabrol's days as a young *cinéphile* who would become one of his most faithful collaborators – *Les cousins* is set in still another milieu that Chabrol knew well from personal experience. It takes place largely in the Latin Quarter of Paris where he had spent time as a law student. Just as *Le beau Serge* had given audiences a sense of provincial life, *Les cousins* explores not only the different locales of the city but also the different emotions – the feelings of liberation as well as of alienation and loneliness – associated with life in the capital. Pointing to the centrality of Paris in New Wave features, *Les cousins* contains an iconic city scene which, as Jean Douchet remarks, would become a 'mythic device' in one film of the New Wave after another. Here, we are whirled through the streets of Paris in a convertible as a seemingly exultant camera swoops from the streets to the spires of the cathedral and the tops of the trees. For Chabrol, notes Douchet, as for the other Young Turks, 'the street reflected the aspirations of the young people who made it theirs. It embodied the dominant fantasy of riding around in a sporty convertible (there is no New Wave film, good or bad, without this mythic device)' (1999: 123).

Although *Le beau Serge* and *Les cousins* unfold in very different surroundings, the stories they tell – more precisely, the moral fables they embody – are similar. Like *Le beau Serge*, *Les cousins* portrays two young men who offer a study in contrasts. (Reflecting Chabrol's tendency to work repeatedly with the same performers, the film stars the two young actors – Gérard Blain and Jean-Claude Brialy – also seen in *Le beau Serge*.) This time, they are cousins rather than friends. As the film opens, Charles (Blain), a young man from the provinces, has just arrived in Paris. While there, he will prepare for his law exams and stay with his cousin, François (Brialy). A good student and dutiful son who writes long letters to his mother, Charles is also earnest and naïve: when his cousin introduces him to a young woman, Florence (Juliette Mayniel), he falls instantly in love and is crushed when she begins an affair with François. In sharp contrast to Charles, François is a sophisticated Parisian dandy who is as casual about women as he is cavalier about his studies. Whereas Charles blurts out whatever he thinks or feels, François is given to artifice and theatre. He displays an attraction to what Chabrol called the 'seductions' and 'dangers' of Nazism/Fascism. Given to neo-fascist rituals and mythologies, he solemnly recites Goethe, listens to Wagner and even dresses up as a Nazi officer.[2] Hedonistic and amoral as well as theatrical, he indulges himself in all the attractions – nightclubs, parties and fast cars – that Paris can offer.

Finally, in a twist of fate, it is the playboy François who passes his exam and not the plodding Charles. Crushed and desolate, Charles wanders along the banks of the Seine and appears to think momentarily of suicide. But, instead, he returns home and – as if all the frustrations he has experienced have suddenly exploded – he places one bullet in an empty gun and aims it at his sleeping cousin. Like everything else he has done, however, the attempt fails. But now François awakens. Horsing around, he aims the gun – which he believes empty – and fires it at Charles. Unlike Charles, *he* is successful: to his shock and dismay, he has killed his cousin. As if, finally, real life has broken in on the theatrical illusions with which he has surrounded himself, he wanders, aimlessly, around the room. To the swelling sounds of Wagner's music, the camera moves in for a final close-up of the radio as it broadcasts the *Liebestod*.

In *Les cousins*, as in *Le beau Serge* and virtually all of Chabrol's subsequent films, initial impressions prove deceptive even as moral systems give way under the pressures of emotions and desire. As the film progresses, the seemingly virtuous Charles, who had all our sympathy at the beginning, undergoes a kind of metamorphosis or 'exchange'. Midway through the film, we begin to sense that his earnestness masks a deep sense of insecurity and that he clings obsessively to his studies to escape the pressures of real life. Unable to deal with his rejection at the hands of Florence, he is also unable to confront or acknowledge his real nature or his deepest feelings. 'I'm always struck by the fact', observed Chabrol, 'that people are rarely ready to recognise themselves as they are. I'm horrified by their lack of lucidity' (quoted in Braucourt 1971: 123). Like the 'virtuous' character in *Le beau Serge*, Charles becomes increasingly masochistic even as he commits what Chabrol views as a 'sin': he cuts himself off from those around him. Displaying his mastery of *mise-en-scène* and camera shots, Chabrol repeatedly underscores Charles' deliberate rejection of others – and its accompanying solitude – through visual means. Within his cousin's apartment, for example, Charles remains in a kind of solitary cubicle or cell while others party around him; leaving the university with a band of friends, Charles is framed – and isolated – by the camera. The most telling sequence, perhaps, occurs after he has failed his exam. Here, he sees Florence through the plate-glass window of a restaurant. No less than the walls of his cubicle, the glass isolates him as if imprisoning him within the inner walls of his rigidity, his insecurity and his despair.

If *Les cousins* prompts us to question initial assumptions, it also casts doubt on traditional morality. In this respect, the film reflected the temper of a new generation that was emerging in a world marked by social dislocations and cultural change. The old strictures to which Charles clings so obsessively – the admonition that hard work will lead to success or that true love will conquer all – are proved hollow. But, neither does Chabrol endorse the 'new' morality or, rather, the 'amorality', which marked many young people at this time. In the end, François' hedonistic approach to life is no more appealing, or fruitful, than Charles' old-fashioned morality. In fact, in a revealing remark, Chabrol observed that he preferred the 'old' morality to the 'new'. 'I come back to traditional morality', he said, 'which understands these old imbecilic givens of good and evil and which is in formal contradiction with the present evolution of mores. The new morality ... is even stupider than [the old]' (quoted in Braucourt 1971: 126).

What Chabrol deemed the 'stupidity' of the new morality is made very clear early in the film, in a nightclub sequence which features young people eager, perhaps desperate, to lose themselves in what Chabrol called the 'stupefying' and 'alienating' factors – such as promiscuous sex and alcohol – of modern life. 'Each of my films set in Paris', said the director, 'involves a sequence set in a nightclub – and each time it's more terrifying' (quoted in Braucourt 1971: 138). Even more 'terrifying' than the nightclub sequences, perhaps, are those that portray wild parties – complete with orgiastic sex and hysterical outbursts, with alcohol and drugs – that take place at François' apartment. Accompanied by expressionist touches (flickering candles, foreboding shadows) that recall Chabrol's love for German director Fritz Lang – 'I had a passion for Lang before Hitchcock ... without Lang, Hitchcock would not have existed' (Chabrol 1970/71: 4) – these scenes leave no doubt about the seductions as well as the dangers of the 'new' morality.

Les Quatre cents coups

Released in March 1959, *Les cousins* appeared shortly before the event that would seal the triumph of the New Wave: the revelation of Truffaut's *Les Quatre cents coups* and of Resnais' *Hiroshima mon amour* at the Cannes festival of 1959. But even before the festival opened, there were indications that change was in the air. For none of the nation's most venerated directors – men such as Marcel Carné, René Clement, René Clair and Claude Autant-Lara – were among the filmmakers whose works were selected to represent France at Cannes. Instead, the three chosen films were first (or, in the case of Marcel Camus, second) features by young direc-

Les Quatre cents coups (1959): Truffaut portrays the 'most everyday details' of his life

tors: Camus' *Orfeu negro*, Resnais' *Hiroshima mon amour* and Truffaut's *Les Quatre cents coups*. Upon learning that his friend's film would represent France, Godard had good reason to exult. In his view, this selection signalled a fundamental change in French cinema. 'For the first time', he wrote, 'a youthful film has been officially designated by those in charge to show to the whole world the true face of French cinema ... The face of French cinema has changed' (1968: 247).

Before the festival began, André Malraux, then Minister of Culture, had asked to see the chosen films for himself. It was his view that the 'film of François Truffaut is good, that of Marcel Camus less good, that of Resnais very good' (quoted in de Baecque 1998: 81). Malraux was certainly correct: Truffaut's film *was* good. Still, no one could have expected the tremendous welcome that it was accorded. Only the year before, Truffaut had found himself a *persona non grata* at Cannes because, in his role as a critic for *Arts*, he had insulted an important official and called the festival a 'failure dominated by machinations, compromises and missteps'. The following year he returned in triumph with a film that was a sensation. Photographs reveal the 14-year-old lead of the film, Jean-Pierre Léaud, being carried aloft by the President of the Jury, Jean Cocteau, a venerated figure who long supported the Young Turks. Newspapers and magazines were quick to celebrate the phenomenon. A headline in *France-Soir* proclaimed: 'A 28-year-old director: François Truffaut, A 14-year-old star: Jean-Pierre Léaud. A triumph at Cannes: *Les Quatre cents coups*' (quoted in de Baecque 1998: 84). Devoting four pages to the enormous excitement caused by the film, the widely-read magazine *Paris-Match* dubbed Cannes 'the festival of prodigal sons' (ibid.). *Elle* rapturously declared that the festival witnessed nothing less than 'the renaissance of French cinema' (ibid.). As the success of what was now seen as the New Wave resonated around the world – the foreign sales alone of *Les Quatre cents coups* amounted to ten times the budget of the film and went on to win the New York critics award for best film of the year– more conventional films began to seem old-fashioned. Noting that Truffaut's feature marked a watershed date in postwar French cinema, the critics from *Les cahiers du cinéma* covering the festival observed that it forced even traditional producers 'to ask themselves nervous questions even as they attempted to produce similar films' (Various authors 1959: 42).

If *Les Quatre cents coups* marked a date in the history of postwar French cinema it was also, of course, a personal triumph for the young critic and for the kind of cinema he had championed throughout the 1950s. In a discussion of the 1957 Cannes festival, Truffaut had described the film of the 'future' in the following terms. 'Tomorrow's film', he declared, 'will not be made by bureaucrats behind the camera but by artists for whom shooting a film constitutes a formidable and exalting adventure. Tomorrow's film will resemble the person who makes it … Tomorrow's film will be an act of love' (1987: 224). Once *Les Quatre cents coups* – which was made on a very limited budget with the help of Truffaut's father-in-law – appeared, no one could doubt that his film was just such an 'exalting adventure' and an extremely personal 'act of love'.[3] Nor could any one doubt that the film 'resembled' its maker. Of course, when Truffaut and the other Young Turks insisted that every real film constituted a 'portrait' of its maker, they referred, above all, to the uniquely personal way in which each film saw and represented the world – a vision embodied in its *mise-en-scène*. But, in the case of *Les Quatre cents coups*, it was not only its *mise-en-scène* that stamped it indelibly as a film by Truffaut as it 'resembled' its young director in a more obvious way: it would be difficult to imagine a more profoundly autobiographical work. In this respect alone, the film corresponded to

Truffaut's 1957 blueprint of the film of 'tomorrow' even as it offered the sharpest of contrasts with the more impersonal and lavish productions of the Tradition of Quality.

In *Les Quatre cents coups* Truffaut traces the portrait of Antoine Doinel, a 13-year-old Parisian. Despite his best efforts, Antoine is surrounded by problems at home and school. In the classroom, he is faced with an authoritarian instructor who mocks him and is blind to his poetic nature; at home, in the cramped apartment he shares with his parents, his shrewish mother denies him the affection he so obviously craves. She is married to a man – it is later revealed that he is not Antoine's real father – who is well meaning but ineffectual and bumbling. Antoine finds refuge from his constricting life through escapades with his best friend René. But, eventually, in a series of mishaps, one of these adventures leads him to steal a typewriter. Unable to sell the stolen machine, he tries to return it only to be apprehended by a security guard. His frustrated parents, who feel they can no longer cope with him, send him to a home for juvenile delinquents. He escapes and runs away until he finds himself at the edge of the sea. The film ends with a freeze frame of his haunted face. His future remains unknown.

To create his portrait of Antoine, Truffaut drew heavily on aspects of his personality as well as incidents of his life. Indeed, the resemblance between Antoine and Truffaut is so marked that the fictional character – who would figure in three more films by Truffaut – has often been described as Truffaut's 'alter ego'. It is doubtlessly true, as Truffaut pointed out repeatedly, that the young actor who played the role, Jean-Perre Léaud, changed Truffaut's original conception of Antoine by infusing it with aspects of his own personality. 'I saw Antoine', said Truffaut, 'as more fragile, wilder, less aggressive; Jean-Pierre gave him health, aggressiveness, courage' (1988: 91). It is also true that Truffaut – perhaps to spare his parents pain and embarrassment at the way they were portrayed – insisted that the film was not autobiographical. But there is no mistaking the fact that detail after detail of Truffaut's adolescence – from the *quartier* where he lived to his troubled relationship with his mother, from his love of Balzac to his friendship with René (whose real name was Robert Lachenay) – is reflected in the film. Like Antoine, Truffaut never knew his father: indeed, one critic suggests that an English phrase repeated by Antoine and his comrades in class – 'where is the father?' – is imbued with autobiographical echoes

(Auzel 1990: 40). Even Antoine's stay in a home for juvenile delinquents is based on a real incident. While Antoine lands in trouble for stealing a typewriter, Truffaut was sent to a similar institution for having misappropriated funds in connection with a *ciné-club* he tried to establish when he was barely 16. It was at this critical juncture, in fact, that Truffaut's life took a very different turn from that which apparently awaits the fleeing Antoine. Unlike Antoine, Truffaut did not escape from the institution where he was confined. Rather, André Bazin – whom he had first met in connection with his abortive film club – assured his release by assuming parental responsibility for him. In so doing, Bazin became the most important of Truffaut's so-called 'spiritual' fathers – an august group that included Roberto Rossellini, Jean Renoir and Henri Langlois. In a sad twist of fate, Bazin – to whom Truffaut dedicated his first feature – died just at the time when his young protégé began filming *Les Quatre cents coups*.

Truffaut's friendship with Bazin points to still another deeply autobiographical dimension of the film – one that takes us to the heart of the New Wave: Antoine, who plays truant to go to the local cinema, shares the fascination with cinema that marked Truffaut's childhood and adolescence. Looking back at the role that cinema played in his adolescence, Truffaut observed that it was much more than a passion or even a simple refuge. 'I hardly have the impression that I'm exaggerating', he remarked, 'when I say that cinema saved my life. I used to describe it as a "drug" before that word became so fashionable' (1988: 19). Throughout the film, in fact, cinematic echoes – pointing to some of the director's favourite films and directors – bear witness to the ardent love of film that may well have 'saved' Truffaut's life. For example, a scene where pupils slip away one by one in the course of an excursion recalls a similar scene in Jean Vigo's classic film about schoolboys, *Zéro de conduite*; the bizarre furnishings of a spare room in René's apartment suggest a similar room in Melville and Cocteau's *Les enfants terribles* (*The Strange Ones*, 1950); a scene where Jeanne Moreau and Jean-Claude Brialy make a cameo appearance looking for a lost dog plays off the opening of Jean Renoir's 1932 classic, *Boudu sauvé des eaux* (*Boudu Saved From Drowning*).

Above and beyond the evident *cinéphilie* of *Les Quatre cents coups*, Truffaut makes clear his love for cinema by the very way he films. Describing the films he loved, he once observed that 'I was in favour of what was ridiculous, audacious, daring ... Lyricism, always, always lyricism' (ibid.).

Challenging existing conventions, Truffaut manipulates all the resources of cinematic language even as he gives ample proof of his taste for 'lyricism' and 'audacity'. The film constantly conveys emotions and heightens dramatic intensity through visual motifs, *mise-en-scène* and camerawork. For example, the fundamental contrast between freedom and imprisonment that pervades the film is expressed both through contrasting visual spaces – the cramped apartment and the confined rooms of the school versus the freedom of the city and the outdoors – and through camerawork. 'At home or school', writes Anne Gillain, 'the narration is dominated by static shots and close-ups, while outside, long and mobile shots prevail. These alternations give the film its powerful rhythm of tension and release' (2000: 144). As Gillain suggests, as if exulting in the freedom of the streets, in outdoor sequences Truffaut's mobile and often intrusive camera seems to swoop and fly; indoors, as if it shared the unease and claustrophobia felt by Antoine, it barely moves. Thus, in a celebrated sequence in which a psychologist at the home for juvenile delinquents interviews Antoine, the camera does not leave the boy's face. This means that the scene – which traditionally would have been filmed in shot/reverse-shot – becomes a compelling, almost *cinéma vérité*, interview broken only by dissolves.[4] In contrast with the static nature of this sequence, when Antoine escapes from the institution, the camera follows him with a long and extremely mobile tracking shot only to end with a fixed frame when Antoine's flight is finally halted by the sea.

If Truffaut's innovative use of filmic language struck a decidedly new chord, so too did the seemingly spontaneous nature of his film. Location shooting, digressions, improvisational techniques – all these worked together to create a sense of lived reality rarely seen in French films since the 1930s. 'I would not be capable', observed Truffaut, 'of preparing a film with an exact shooting script, prepared in advance, shot by shot … My imagination interacts with reality … I believe in improvisation' (1988: 96). Thus, instead of writing dialogue for the young schoolboys who figure in *Les Quatre cents coups*, he encouraged them to use their own words. So too did he leave Antoine free to invent own responses in the critical interview scene with the psychologist. 'I wanted his vocabulary', said Truffaut of his young hero, 'his hesitations, his total spontaneity' (1988: 92).

The sense of spontaneity, of lived reality, created by these improvisational techniques is enhanced further by Truffaut's focus on the most ordinary details – what the director called the 'little everyday incidents' – of life. Rejecting the plot complications and melodramatic confrontations that he had hated in the Tradition of Quality, Truffaut lingers on seemingly insignificant or extraneous details and actions that, ultimately, contribute not to the film's narrative but, rather, to its dense emotional texture. A good example of this comes towards the beginning of *Les Quatre cents coups*: in a long sequence that evokes the climate of fear and apprehension that reigns in the schoolroom, we witness the growing sense of frustration and desperation of a young pupil as he attempts to write a composition free of forbidden ink smudges. Still another long sequence conveys the rhythms of Antoine's daily life: here, he goes about the most ordinary chores as he sets the table, cleans the stove and brings the rubbish downstairs. Creating an almost documentary feel – 'I wanted a film', said Truffaut, 'which would resemble a documentary without being one' (1988: 105) – the sequence adds to the texture of the film rather than to any narrative flow. Rejecting the artificial constraints of most narratives, Truffaut also avoids, of course, conventional closure. Concluding his film in the most open-ended and ambiguous manner, he leaves it to the audience to wonder about the shape of Antoine's future.

Hiroshima mon amour

One could hardly find a better illustration of the tremendous diversity of New Wave films than by comparing the two that Minister of Culture André Malraux deemed 'good' and 'very good'. For in almost every way, *Les Quatre cents coups* and *Hiroshima mon amour* offer a study in contrasts. Marked by an improvisational tone, Truffaut's first feature is a semi-autobiographical work that deals with the 'little incidents' constituting the fabric of an adolescent's life. *Hiroshima mon amour*, instead, is a meticulously structured and highly theatrical work that opens on the larger stage of history: it deals not only with the so-called *années noires* of the Occupation but also with the horrors unleashed when the atom bomb was dropped on Hiroshima. Whereas the heart-felt humanism of *Les Quatre cents coups* arouses the viewer's empathy – Truffaut himself saw his work as more 'instinctive than intellectual' – the complex narrative of *Hiroshima mon amour* distances the viewer even as it demands his/her intellectual participation.

To these obvious differences, moreover, must be added still another. More overarching, perhaps, it bears upon the very nature of innovation that marked New Wave features. While *Les Quatre cents coups* clearly blew a breath of fresh air into what had become the staleness of French cinema, at the same time it also harked back to earlier films such as *Zéro de conduite* and *Boudu sauvé des eaux*. Its portrait of children, in particular, prompted comparisons with directors such as Vigo and Rossellini. In the case of *Hiroshima mon amour*, however, no similar antecedents came to mind.

It is true, as suggested earlier, that Godard compared Resnais' mastery of editing to that of Eisenstein. Still, in a round-table discussion of *Hiroshima mon amour* by *Les cahiers du cinéma*, Godard also made the explicit point that *Hiroshima mon amour* called to mind not earlier films but, rather, modernist works in the other arts. In its relentless psychological probing and intricate narrative structure, it evoked novels by William Faulkner and James Joyce, or paintings by Georges Braque and Picasso, or, even, musical compositions by Stravinsky. Underscoring the radically new nature of the film, Godard declared that *Hiroshima mon amour* 'has absolutely no cinematic points of reference. You can say of *Hiroshima* that it is like Faulkner + Stravinsky, but you cannot say that it is like this filmmaker + that filmmaker … one has the impression of seeing a film that would have been impossible to predict in light of what one knew about cinema' (quoted in de Baecque & Tesson 1999: 37).

The film that no one could have 'predicted' had a fairly conventional start. Resnais, who was known for his film about the concentration camps, *Nuit et brouillard*, was asked to make a documentary about the atom bomb and the cause of world peace. At first, afraid that he could only repeat what he had already done in *Nuit et brouillard*, Resnais was reluctant to accept the project. But then, largely because of two factors that clearly would give the film a new dimension, he changed his mind. On the one hand, Japanese producers suggested a co-production that would take place both in Japan and in France and that would have protagonists drawn from the two countries. On the other, perhaps more importantly, the highly respected novelist Marguerite Duras agreed to do the script. The result was a film that – merging one of Duras' favourite themes (the melancholy passion of a woman) with Resnais' concern with history and memory – became a landmark in French cinema.

The melancholy lovers of Alain Resnais' *Hiroshima mon amour* (1959)

Set in Hiroshima, the film depicts a passionate affair between a Japanese man – described by Duras in a deliberately ambiguous way as an 'engineer or an architect' (Duras 1961: 8) – and a young French actress who has come to this particular city to make a film in the cause of world peace. The strong desire and love the woman feels for the Japanese man calls forth long-hidden memories of an earlier love affair. For the first time in her life, she tells someone about that earlier passion. Her memories are conveyed not only though what she says but, above all, by flashback sequences. Set in her hometown of Nevers in France, these sequences – which are brief and mysterious at the beginning of the film – gradually intrude upon and eclipse the scenes that unfold in the present. The tale they tell is one of love and transgression, of grief and death. We eventually learn that during the war, the young woman was desperately in love with a German soldier who was killed before her eyes. In the course of the purges that followed Liberation, she was punished for this guilty love by having her head shaved. Her distraught parents, seeing their daughter mad with grief and despair, locked her in the basement of her house where, in her anguish, she clawed the walls until her fingers bled. Finally, one night, under cover of darkness, she fled to Paris where she began life anew. There she married, began a career and had two children. But she never related the events of her past to anyone – not even to her husband. Now, after revealing her long-buried history to her Japanese lover, she feels that she has betrayed the memory of the German soldier. Even the most profound love, she realises, can be related and, by that very token, forgotten. In a kind of daze brought on by the anguish of remembering, as well as the threat of forgetting, she spends the night wandering the streets of modern-day Hiroshima. Everywhere she goes she is followed by the Japanese man who implores her to stay there with him.

If, as Godard had it, *Hiroshima mon amour* had no visible precedents, it was at least partly because of its intricate mixture of private drama and historical trauma. Underscoring the unconventional and polemical nature of this mixture, Truffaut declared that it was nothing short of 'astonishing'. In *Hiroshima mon amour*, he wrote, 'there was everything that you are not supposed to do: mix adultery and the atomic bomb, a very general problem and a very special one, a social problem and a political one and, within the political one, the mixture of a great problem – the bomb – with the smaller one of the scandals of the purges. It is really an astonishing mixture' (1988: 52). Implicit in the film's very title – which pairs the city of Hiroshima, a symbol of suffering and death, with words that speak of love – this mixture is at the heart of the film's celebrated opening sequence. Here, passion and death, history and memory, come together as we see shots of what appear to be intertwined bodies that glisten with drops that suggest, at once, the ardour of lovemaking as well as the ashes provoked by a nuclear explosion. In Duras' words: 'In the beginning of the film we don't see this chance couple. Neither her nor him. Instead we see mutilated bodies – the heads, the hips – moving – in the throes of love or death – and covered successively with the ashes, the dew, of atomic death – and the sweat of love fulfilled' (1961: 8).

Penetrated by the ashes of 'atomic death ... and the sweat of love fulfilled', the opening sequence of *Hiroshima mon amour* also suggests the very personal and dramatically unconventional mixture of documentary (the traces of ash deposited by the atomic bomb) and fiction (the passionate love affair between the Japanese man and the French woman) at the core of the film. In part, of course, this mixture was the result of the collaboration between Duras, known for her novels, and Resnais, known for his documentaries. But it also suggests Resnais' unconventional approach to documentary. Again and again, as suggested earlier, Resnais had introduced 'subjective' elements into his early documentaries in an attempt to capture the very 'mechanism' of thought and memory. Returning to this vital issue in *Hiroshima mon amour*, Resnais turns his film into a kind of meditation on the nature of representation, the very meaning of the 'document', and the ways in which history is 'documented'. Here, the spectre of conventional documentary or what critic Marie-Claire Ropars-Wuilleumier calls the 'documentary illusion' is explicitly evoked – and rejected – within the film itself (1990: 179). The film the young French actress has come to make in Hiroshima is, presumably, the kind of conventional documentary – one that uses the city as a background to document and recreate the terrible aftermath of the bomb – that Resnais had never wanted to make.

But what kind of film can be made about Hiroshima? How can events that resist or defy understanding and representation be documented and represented? Resnais had already posed this question explicitly in his 1955 work about the concentration camps, *Nuit et brouillard*. In that film, Resnais' camera travels through an empty camp as the commentary – written by novelist and camp survivor, Jean Cayrol – insistently reminds us of both the need and the impossibility of remembering and/or representing an experience that cannot be understood or imagined by those who were not there. As the camera tracks through the dormitories of the now-empty camp, the text insists that 'no description, no picture' can restore the 'true dimension' of the camps. It asks:

> What remains of the reality of these camps, despised by those who made them, incomprehensible to those who suffered here...? No description, no picture can restore their true dimension: endless, uninterrupted fear ... Of this brick dormitory, of these threatened sleepers, we can only show you the shell, the shadow.

In *Hiroshima mon amour*, Resnais returns to this question. But now – taking us to the mixture of documentary and fiction that pervades the film – he places it within a fictional context. The opening dialogue between the lovers – in the course of which the Japanese man repeatedly asks the woman what she has 'seen' in Hiroshima – is, in effect, a discussion about the very impossibility of seeing, or speaking of, Hiroshima. In Duras' words their 'initial exchange is allegorical. In short, an operatic exchange. Impossible to talk about Hiroshima. All one can do is talk about the impossibility of talking about Hiroshima' (1961: 9). In this 'operatic exchange' Resnais intercuts what might be called 'the shell, the shadow' of horror – archival traces of the devastation wrought by the bomb (museum exhibits, photographs) – into the dialogue between the lovers. At the same time, the dialogue underscores the fact that the horrors we witness are mere 'traces' of the past. As we see the interlaced bodies of the lovers, we hear words that will be repeated again and again. The man calmly intones: 'You saw nothing at Hiroshima.' And the woman responds: 'I saw everything. Everything.' Each time as she describes what she 'saw', the camera, with inexorable tracking shots that seem to take us to the recesses of memory, shows this to the viewer: photographs and exhibits, reconstructions of deformed survivors, pieces of burnt flesh and of pulverised metal – all 'traces' and 'documents' of the inconceivable. 'I know everything', the woman finally insists. The Japanese man calmly responds: 'Nothing. You know nothing.'

If this sequence underscores the limits of representation – the fact that no one who was not there can understand the reality of Hiroshima – it also embodies the radical nature of Resnais' cinema. For even as he shows us the 'traces' of horror, he reminds us that they are merely the 'shadow' of what occurred. Evoking events that could hardly be more 'real', he takes care to banish any illusion of realism. As if to underscore Resnais' adamant refusal to 'recreate' a world that defies knowledge and understanding, everything about the film seems designed to keep us at a distance, to remind us that what we are seeing is not 'real'. Just as the incantatory and repetitive language of the lovers has little in common with the cadences of normal speech, they themselves bear little resemblance to the psychologically developed characters of most films. Known only as 'he' and 'she' throughout the film, they are, rather, the very embodiment of historical experience and suffering. Indeed, at the end of the film the lovers call each other by the names of the places that symbolise suffering at once collective and individual. He, of course, is 'Hiroshima'; she, 'Nevers'. Just as in *Guernica* we remember the Spanish civil war through Picasso's painting, we 'remember' Hiroshima through the woman's enormous pain. Refusing to disassociate individual suffering from historical trauma, Resnais' film, as Youssef Ishaghpour observes, makes it clear that history is the 'form of existence' of his characters and that 'their existence is historical' (1982: 190).

À bout de souffle

Two films, suggests Antoine de Baecque, constitute what he calls the 'aesthetic manifesto' of the New Wave: *Hiroshima mon amour* and Godard's first feature, *À bout de souffle*. Although de Baecque does not expand on this idea, it is not difficult to see why he should single out these two films in particular. Not only did both directors reject traditional cinema – one built on the illusion of reality – far more explicitly and decisively than their cohorts, they also virtually enlarged both the language and the horizons of cinema. Challenging what films might speak about they captured realities that previously were rarely (if ever) seen on screen. In one important respect, of course, the films of Resnais and Godard are in sharp contrast. While it is generally agreed that *Hiroshima mon amour* had no cinematic precedents, *À bout de souffle* consistently and deliberately harks back to earlier films, in particular to French *film noir* and American thrillers. Permeated by what Godard called the 'nostalgia for a cinema that no longer exists' (Godard 1968: 315), *À bout de souffle* is, in fact, dedicated to Monogram Studios – maker of the American B melodramas that Godard loved as a young critic.

The film's protagonist – a petty conman and thief named Michel Poiccard (played by Jean-Paul Belmondo in the role that would make him a star) – might well be seen as a latter-day version of the doomed outsiders embodied by Jean Gabin and Humphrey Bogart in films of the 1930s and 1940s. As the film opens, Michel is on his way from the South of France to Paris in a stolen car when he shoots and kills a policeman who pulls him over to the side of the road. Now, suddenly, he is a fugitive. When he reaches Paris, Michel attempts to persuade Patricia (Jean Seberg), a young American ex-patriot with whom he has had a brief fling, to escape to Italy with him. She is reluctant, unable to commit herself to him. Finally, almost as if to resolve the deep ambivalence she feels, she betrays him to the police. When he learns what she has done he initially refuses to flee. He is too weary, perhaps, or too despondent. But he does attempt to warn a comrade about the imminent arrival of the police. In so doing, he runs into the street where the approaching officers shoot him in the back. Before dying, he tells Patricia – who has witnessed the scene – that she is really *dégueulasse* (horrible or disgusting). The film ends with a close-up of her uncomprehending face as she asks the meaning of *déguelasse*.

Around the same time he made *À bout de souffle*, that is, in 1959, Godard voiced an idea fundamental not only to his first feature but to his entire cinema. Underscoring what he saw as the intertwined nature of documentary and fiction, Godard declared unequivocally that 'all great fictional films lean towards documentary just as all great documentaries lean toward fiction' (1968: 225). Returning to this same idea a few years later, in the course of a 1962 interview, he made it clear that by documentary he also meant 'life' or 'reality' while the notion of fiction, for him, encompassed that of 'cinema', 'theatre', 'spectacle', and the 'imaginary'. 'By virtue of being a realist', he said, 'one discovers the theatre … behind the theatre there is life; and behind life, the theatre. I began with the imaginary and I discovered the real; but, behind the real, once again there is the imaginary' (1968: 298). A bit further on in the course of this same interview, he applied the dialectic between the 'imaginary' and the 'real' to his own films. 'If I analyse myself today', he observed, 'I see that basically I have always wanted to do a research film [*film de recherche*] in the form of a spectacle. The documentary part concerns someone in a particular situation. The spectacle part comes when this person is made into a gangster or a secret agent' (1968: 299).

The combination of what Godard describes as research or documentary and spectacle takes us to the core of *À bout de souffle*. The 'spectacle' side of the film resides, clearly, in its plot: an existentialist thriller about a conman on the run – and one who is betrayed by the woman he loves – *À bout de souffle* situates itself in a well-defined tradition of *film noir*. Indeed, it repeatedly and explicitly evokes aspects of such American productions: not only does Michel make gestures like those of Humphrey Bogart but, as in many gangster films, we learn of Michel's impending doom through changing newspaper headlines. At the same time *À bout de souffle* has a striking 'documentary' side. If its narrative is clearly the stuff of 'fiction' or 'theatre', its portrayal of people and places suggests, instead, Godard's ardent desire to capture what he called the realities of 'modern' life. 'If I have a dream,' he remarked only half facetiously in 1967, 'it would be to become the director of French news one day. All my films have constituted reports on the situation of the country, news documents

À bout de souffle (1960): on the streets of Paris

– treated, perhaps, in a special manner but in relationship to modern reality' (1968: 392).

As in the case of many New Wave films, in *À bout de souffle* Godard's exploration of 'modern reality' begins with place or location. Like *Les cousins* and *Les Quatre cents coups*, *À bout de souffle* captures Paris in a way not seen since the films of Renoir in the 1930s. Shot on location in the city's streets, the film conveys the noise and confusion, the crowds and rhythms, of the French capital. For example, in a famous scene in which the camera follows Michel and Patricia as they walk up and down the fashionable boulevard of the Champs-Elysées, ambient noise cuts into and eclipses their dialogue even as cars and pedestrians seem to jostle for our attention. Speaking of the vital role played by location shooting in this film, Godard suggested that people 'live differently in different decors'. Before *À bout de souffle*, he said, 'no film showed the nature [of the Champs-Elysées]. My characters see it sixty times a day … I wanted to show them in it' (1968: 296).

The sense of raw reality that clings to the city extends, moreover, to the ways in which the characters speak and behave. Underscoring Godard's 'revolutionary' use of language, Michel Marie goes so far as to suggest that the hero of *À bout de souffle* 'was the first film character to violate the refined sound conventions of 1959 French cinema by using popular slang and the most trivial spoken French' (Marie 2000: 166). And while the roles played by Patricia and Michel may be the stuff of fiction – woman as betrayer, doomed gangster fighting for his life as the police close in on him – they themselves are very real individuals. Unlike the stylised, one-dimensional gangsters of many thrillers, Michel is a complex man who enjoys sophisticated puns, corrects people's grammar and loves Mozart's clarinet concerto. As for Patricia, she is surely the first gangster's moll, as it were, who is about to attend the Sorbonne and who worries about the shape of her future career. Moreover, their relationship reflects a very particular social and historical moment – one marked by changing sexual roles and by the collapse of the old morality. While Patricia's betrayal of Michel may suggest a certain timeworn misogyny, her conflicted feelings about Michel, as well as her desire to achieve something on her own, clearly foreshadow the coming explosion of the movement for women's liberation.

Godard's evident interest in the existential and social climate that surrounds his characters opens upon still another distinctive – and defining – aspect of the film. He frequently analyses personal and social issues in long digressive sequences that fragment, or remove us from, the narrative flow. Imbued with the play of ideas, and marked by a plethora of quotes or citations, these digressions help transform his films into what he himself dubbed cinematic 'essays'. As he continued making films, the 'essayist' dimension of his cinema grew stronger and stronger even as it frequently eclipsed the narrative. But even *À bout de souffle* – where the narrative flow is stronger than in subsequent works – contains long digressive discussions. For example, in a well-known sequence that takes place in Patricia's hotel room, the lovers engage in an extended conversation – replete with allusions to works by Faulkner, Shakespeare and Picasso – about the problems and issues they are facing. They wonder about the different ways in which men and women think and behave, and speculate about the gap between a long romantic tradition of idealised love and the modern tug-of-war between the two sexes. Later on, Godard returns to these questions in still another long sequence. Here, paying homage to Jean-Pierre Melville, he casts the director of *Bob le flambeur* as a famous writer who, as an expert on 'love', is eagerly interviewed by a host of reporters, including Patricia. The questions they throw at him reflect the issues that run throughout the film. How are American and French women different? Is there a difference between sex and love? Patricia herself poses one of the most telling – and personal – of questions: what, she asks, is the role of women in modern society? Like most men – or, at least, like Michel – he refuses to take her very serious question seriously because, he says, she is too attractive.

A cinematic 'essay' that documents and explores the troubled social and sexual landscape of contemporary France, *À bout de souffle* is also – perhaps above all – a film about cinema itself. This brings us back, of course, to the intertwined layers of 'fiction' and 'reality' at the core of the film. For if Godard dreamed of being the 'director of the French news' one day, he also had another dream: that of 'remaking' cinema. 'What I wanted', he remarked of *À bout de souffle*, 'was to start with a conventional story and to remake – but differently – all of cinema made thus far. I also wanted to create the impression that I had just found or experienced cinematographic techniques [*procédés*] for the first time' (1968: 288). In *À bout de souffle*, the process of 'remaking' cinema begins, in a sense, with acts of destruction. For the film leaves no doubt about Godard's desire to do away with a certain kind of cinema – one built on the illusion of reality – along with the rules that hold it in place. To this end, the director deliberately, defiantly, breaks with preceding conventions even as he insistently calls attention to the very process of making a film. For example: he has characters address the audience directly, shoots into the light so that their faces are obscured, makes use of jump-cuts, disregards narrative coherence, ignores continuity shots and renders dialogue inaudible through the use of ambient noise. 'Right from the beginning', writes Michel Marie of the sequence in which Michel is seen driving to Paris, '[the film] ruthlessly violates the moribund codes of spatial and graphic continuity editing which were so scrupulously observed by professional editors in 1959' (Marie 2000: 163).

Speaking of these transgressions and others, in a well-known essay on Godard, Susan Sontag deems the director nothing less than a 'deliberate destroyer' of cinema – one who ranks with great figures of modernism in the other arts. While Godard may not be the first such 'destroyer', observes Sontag, he is 'certainly the most persistent and prolific and timely. His approach to established rules of film technique like the unobtrusive cut, consistency of point of view, and clear storyline is comparable to Schoenberg's repudiation of … tonal language … or to the challenge of the Cubists' (1969: 150). Similarly underscoring Godard's role as a 'destroyer', in an essay entitled 'The Cinema of Poetry', Pier Paolo Pasolini also compares the director to one of the great figures of modernist painting, Georges Braque. Noting that Godard deliberately and consistently subjects reality to a process of 'brutal' fragmentation, Pasolini suggests that beneath all of Godard's films runs another 'film made for the pure pleasure of restoring a reality fragmented by technique and reconstructed by a brutal, mechanical and disharmonious Braque' (1972: 187).

As Pasolini appears to suggest, like other great figures of modernism, if Godard 'destroys' traditional art it is because he wants to create something 'new' – to 'remake' cinema. In his case, he wants to capture not only the social realities so sorely lacking in the Tradition of Quality but, in some sense, underlying ontological reality. Impelled by a desire to somehow take cinema beyond the normal limits, he wants to use the camera, in the words of Michael Witt, 'as a scientific "scope" through which to penetrate the surface of reality' (1994: 36). Expressing this fundamental desire as early as 1952, Godard voiced what would be a life-long aim: 'artistic creation', he said, 'is not painting ones soul in things but painting the soul of things' (1968: 37). Echoing this same desire, in *À bout de souffle*, Michel tells Patricia that he would like to know what is 'behind' her face. If this desire to capture the 'soul' of things, to see what lies hidden 'behind' appearances, leads Godard to reject the mere 'illusion' of reality, it also prompts him, as critic Alain Bergala has pointed out, to use techniques associated with documentary (location shooting, improvised or seemingly improvised sequences, synchronous sound, the use of 'real' people) and to allow his camera to linger on faces and objects as if to make them reveal their innermost being.

Bergala's observations on Godard are drawn from an important essay in which he discusses some of the defining traits of high cinematic modernism. In his view, modernism – a period exemplified by the New Wave in general and by Godard in particular – was characterised, above all, by a search for 'truth', by a passionate investigation of the relationship between cinema and 'life'. 'The important thing', writes Bergala, 'was less to respect reality (modernism was not a kind of neo-realism) than to make it disgorge, cinematographically, its fragment of truth' (1983: 5). It is here, in its passionate search for 'truth' or for what Bergala also calls the 'true inscription of reality', that Godard's cinema most clearly evokes the ghost of Bazin. It is evident that, in certain respects, his films could hardly be more different from those championed by the great critic. If he uses long-held shots, he also favours rapid and intrusive editing that seems to destroy what was fundamental to Bazin: a sense of the essential wholeness or continuity of reality. Yet, seen from another perspective, Godard and Bazin share one fundamental belief: both view cinema as an instrument of 'truth' able to penetrate the veil of appearances. Indeed, calling Godard a 'Bazinian fundamentalist' Michael Temple observes that for every constructivist or anti-Bazinian slogan uttered by Godard – for example, 'it's not a just image, it's just an image' – one can find an opposing statement such as 'photography is the truth and cinema is the truth twenty-four times per second' (see Temple 1994: 84). Godard's belief in the essential 'truth' of cinema may have wavered over the years; still, there is no question that this issue lies at the heart of his cinema and at the philosophical core of the New Wave.

5   AFTERSHOCKS

The euphoria of 1959–60, the sense, as Truffaut had it, that the young directors were living a 'dream', did not last long. Scarcely a year after the media
hailed the triumph of the New Wave, newspapers and journals began to
attack *la nouvelle vague* and even to proclaim its death. Punning on the
word *vague* (which means 'vague' as well as 'wave'), screenwriter Michel
Audiard declared unequivocally that 'the New Wave is dead. And we see
that, in the end, it was more 'vague' than new' (quoted in de Baecque 1998:
136). Confronted with this sharp turn of the critical pendulum, commentators proposed a variety of explanations. While Truffaut sensed a desire for
'revenge' on the part of the Old Guard, Pierre Kast suggested that the New
Wave was being blamed for the general decline in movie ticket sales taking
place in these years. Clearly, the increasingly polarised climate of the Cold
War helped fuel political attacks from both the right and the left. While
right-wing critics and viewers despised what they saw as the 'amorality' of
New Wave films, those on the left were upset by the fact that these films
seemed to lack political commitment as well as a social 'message'.[1]
    Above and beyond these factors, was the simple fact that – in con-
trast with the astounding success of *Les cousins* or *Les Quatre cents coups*
– subsequent films by the Young Turks were critical and box-office failures.
While critical opinion has undergone a dramatic shift in regard to films such
as Chabrol's *Les bonnes femmes* (*The Good Girls*, 1960), Truffaut's *Tirez sur
le pianiste* (*Shoot the Piano Player*, 1960) and Godard's *Une femme est une
femme*, when these films were first released they disappointed critics and
audiences alike. Nor did the tepid reception of Eric Rohmer's first feature

(made in 1959, *Le signe du lion* was released in 1962) or that of Jacques Rivette (*Paris nous appartient* released in 1960) change the sense that the New Wave was a thing of the past. Indeed, writing in 1961, Jacques Siclier lamented the fact that, in two short years, 'the situation of the French cinema has been radically transformed' (Siclier 1961b: 116).

Still, looking back, it is clear that – although fashion-minded critics were quick to pronounce the 'death' of the New Wave – the early 1960s witnessed a number of films permeated by New Wave impulses. Indeed, while the 'end' of the phenomenon is by no means clear-cut, most commentators suggest that the New Wave lasted until 1962 or 1963. For example, the editors of *The French Cinema Book* feel *la nouvelle vague* went from 1958 to 1962 (Witt & Temple 2004: 183). So, too, does Antoine de Baecque take 1962 as the year when the phenomenon began to recede. After that date, he writes, 'only Godard – with films like *Le mépris*, *Pierrot le fou*, *Week-end* and *La Chinoise* – managed to prolong, and radicalise, the spirit of the New Wave in France' (De Baecque 1998: 149).

In the remaining pages of this study I would like to take a brief look at a number of films, spanning the years 1959 to 1962, which bear witness to the continuing repercussions of the New Wave. For example, shot on location in different areas of Paris, the films by Varda, Rohmer and Rivette turn the city into a virtual protagonist even as they suggest the important role it played in the New Wave imagination. At the same time, albeit in different ways, they blend documentary and fiction in an unconventional and highly personal fashion. In so doing, they point to what Godard might have called the inextricable links between the 'imaginary' and the 'real'. Still another important dimension of the New Wave is exemplified in Godard's *Une femme est une femme* and Truffaut's *Tirez sur le pianiste*. For in their second features, both directors – buoyed, perhaps, by the success of their first films – ventured onto still riskier terrain. This means that not only are both films visibly impregnated with what Godard called the 'nostalgia for a cinema that no longer exists' (1968: 315), but, also, that both play with, and transform, genre in dramatically new ways.

Parisian peregrinations: Varda, Rohmer, Rivette

Considered one of the most important films of the early 1960s, Agnès Varda's *Cléo de 5 à 7* has also been hailed by feminist critics as a landmark film about a woman's self-awakening. As the film opens, its protagonist, a beautiful young Parisian singer named Cléo, is anxiously awaiting the results of an important medical test. She consults a fortune-teller only to have the Tarot cards confirm her worst fears: she will soon die from cancer. Shaken and near hysteria, the young woman returns home where she has a brief visit with her elderly lover followed by a fruitless session with her songwriters. In the course of these encounters, Cléo reveals not only her terrible anxiety but also her preoccupation – underscored by the presence of mirrors and other reflecting surfaces – with her beauty and her 'image'. Concerned, above all, with the way she 'looks' to others, she reassures herself about her illness by telling herself 'as long as I'm beautiful I'm alive'. Midway through the film, however, the existential crisis she is facing appears to prompt a change in her. Casting off the blonde wig and seductive clothes she has worn thus far, she dons a simple black dress before venturing out, once again, into the city. Even as her appearance changes, she starts to connect with her real being and with the world around her. 'She begins', explained Varda, 'to see things and people in a simpler fashion' (1994: 48). Graced with this new 'simplicity' and openness, she allows herself to become friendly with a young soldier, on leave from the war in Algeria, whom she meets in a park. Immediately drawn to one another, they go to the hospital to learn the results of Cléo's medical exam. The doctor reassures her – we do not know if he is telling the truth or not – that she will be fine after a few months of treatment. The film ends as Cléo turns to her newfound friend and tells him: 'I am almost happy.'

Cléo de 5 à 7 was apparently sparked by producer George Beauregard's suggestion that Varda – known for her shorts about particular places – make an inexpensive one in black and white about Paris. With this as a starting point, Varda proceeded to make a film that, like her documentaries of the 1950s, reveals the unique blend of documentary and fiction that typifies virtually all her work: at once an 'objective' portrait of the city, it is also permeated by the intensely subjective, fear-ridden view of its protagonist. Speaking of the intricate mixture of documentary and fiction that characterises *Cléo de 5 à 7*, Varda remarked that from the start she conceived of this film as a subjective work – one that transformed what she saw as the 'diffuse fear' of the city (the fear of 'being lost and misunderstood') into Cléo's fear of a possible diagnosis of cancer. And, indeed, throughout the film we are made aware of the intensity of subjective vision: the ways in

Jean-Luc Godard (left) and Anna Karina (right) costumed for the film-within-a-film seen by Cléo in Agnès Varda's *Cléo de 5 à 7* (1961)

which Cléo's anxieties condition how she sees the city. As seen through her anguished eyes, Paris is a place of pitfalls and dangers. Wherever she goes she sees portents of danger and death: images of broken mirrors and funeral homes insistently greet her. As if reflecting the young woman's sense that her very body is under assault, one of the most striking scenes portrays bodily functions in a grotesque, quasi surreal, light. Here, Cléo watches enthralled as a street entertainer swallows a wiggling live frog; as soon as the frog's legs disappear down his throat, he regurgitates and, without missing a beat, begins his act anew for the entranced spectators.

The emphasis on subjective vision that pervades the film is explicitly underscored, moreover, in a short film-within-a-film that Cléo watches in the company of a friend. Made to resemble an early slapstick comedy, the film's star is no one other than Varda's good friend, Jean-Luc Godard. Imbued with the sense of friendship and collaboration that characterised early New Wave features, the film-within-a-film also suggests how profoundly subjective vision conditions the way we see the world. For here Godard plays a young swain who finally comes to the realisation that his worldview – more precisely, whether the world is 'happy' or 'sad' – depends on whether or not he is wearing his sunglasses!

If the short film is an unconventional reminder of the pervasiveness of subjective vision, Varda uses similarly unconventional means to evoke the other pole of her film: its objective or documentary cast. To begin with, each segment is prefaced by titles that not only indicate its length – for example, 16:31–16:37 – but, also, serve to emphasise the fact that the duration of the film (two hours) corresponds to 'real' time. Noting that the time and duration of the film were 'real', Varda observed that so too were the 'itineraries and the distances' that mark Cléo's journey (first on foot, then by cab and bus) through the city. Furthermore, the documentary impulse that governs Varda's approach to time and place also extends to the ways in which the director captures the city's inhabitants. As in a documentary, the camera lingers on people's faces: shots of old women gossiping in a corner, or those of a couple quarrelling in a cafe, suggest the multitude of very real urban dramas that lie outside Cléo's intensely subjective field of vision.

A complex portrait – at once subjective and objective – of Paris and its people, *Cléo de 5 à 7* assumes a documentary cast in still another respect. The film also captures the atmosphere of a very particular historical and social moment. Both the presence of the soldier, as well as a radio broadcast overheard in a taxi, are explicit reminders of the continuing war in Algeria and of its repercussions in France. From a still broader perspective, the film as a whole – which portrays, after all, a period of anxious waiting – bears witness to the sense of unease and paralysis that gripped the country before the actual end of the war. Indeed, as the Communist critic, Georges Sadoul, wrote at the time: 'The reality of Cléo is first and foremost the profound reality of our time, of the year 1961, when the [war] seemed eternal … Ninety minutes in the life of a Parisian can contain the anguish and preoccupations of a nation' (quoted in Varda 1994: 235).

No less than Agnès Varda, Eric Rohmer also sought to capture the realities of a particular time and place. Underscoring his desire to capture what he called the 'truth' and 'objectivity' of space and time, in the course of a 1965 interview, Rohmer took care to point out that the strength of that desire – his attraction to 'reality' itself – helped distinguish him from directors such as Godard and Resnais. While they were concerned with the ways in which things were filmed, he was principally interested in what he called the 'autonomous existence' of what is filmed, or *la chose filmée*. Taking this essentially Bazinian preoccupation with the 'autonomous existence' of reality one step further, he went on to say that he would like to make a film 'where the camera is absolutely invisible' (1999: 242). But, he acknowledged, filming reality was a difficult, if not impossible, task. 'I have the feeling', he observed, 'that reality will always be more beautiful than my film. At the same time, only cinema can give us the vision of this reality such as it is' (ibid.).

In *Le signe du lion*, 'reality such as it is', or the 'truth' of space and time, bear on Paris itself. In fact, Rohmer once remarked that his first feature was nothing other than a *grande promenade* or long walk through the French capital. It is true that this *grande promenade* is actually taken by the film's protagonist: a hapless violinist who, through a strange set of circumstances, finds himself penniless and homeless on the streets of Paris in the dog days of summer when all his friends are away. Still, as commentators have frequently noted, the real protagonist of the film is hardly the violinist but Paris itself – a summertime city of broiling streets and deserted avenues made unbearable by the August sun. Noting the central role played by the capital in Rohmer's film, critic Claude Beylie describes it as a kind of documentary 'reportage' on 'the hard and implacable city, full of a million hostile faces, that is plunged into a stupor by the sun, an omnipresent monster with tentacles' (1999: 105).

As suggested earlier, *Le signe du lion* did not find favour with audiences. Its failure at the box office meant, in fact, that Rohmer was forced to turn his second film, *La boulangère de Monceau* (*The Girl at the Monceau Bakery*, 1962), which was originally conceived as a feature, into a 16mm short.[2] Despite its brevity, however, far more than *Le signe du lion*, *La boulangère de Monceau* indicated the play of documentary and fiction that marks almost all of Rohmer's films. It combines Rohmer's interest in place with his taste for what he called 'moral' tales (and, later, proverbs). As the film opens, it is, once again place – Paris – that is paramount. In a voice-over commentary that accompanies most of the film, the protagonist describes the small neighbourhood where the action will unfold. (The actual voice we hear is that of future director Bertrand Tavernier.) As if he were giving us a peculiar kind of geography lesson, he explains the layout of the adjacent streets, the relative density of the *quartier*, and so on. Indeed, his explanation is so detailed that critic Michel Marie has likened it to a 'maniacal presentation of the urban topography where the narrator will wander' (2003: 84). The rest of the film suggests, moreover, that

Rohmer shares his character's obsession with 'urban topography', for not only does the camera follow the protagonist as he repeatedly walks up and down the same streets but it also frequently lets its gaze linger on street signs as if to remind us exactly where we are.

As the film progresses, it soon becomes clear that the place portrayed – the protagonist's neighbourhood – constitutes the setting for what Rohmer calls a 'moral' tale. In fact, *La boulangère de Monceau* is the first of six films that the director grouped together under the rubrique of *Contes Moraux (Moral Tales)*. In this film, as in many of his subsequent works – including his first truly successful film, *Ma nuit chez Maud (My Night at Maud's*, 1969) – the 'moral' emerges from a kind of quirky triangle in which a man hesitates between two women. Soon after the film begins, we learn that its protagonist is smitten with Sylvie, a young woman he has seen in the neighbourhood and whom he finally meets at the local bakery. They agree to have coffee together the next time they meet; but, after this encouraging start, Sylvie seems to vanish from the area. In frustration, the protagonist decides to seduce another young woman, Jacqueline, who works at another local bakery. But before he can take Jacqueline to dinner he meets Sylvie again. A sprained ankle, she explains, had forced her to stay home. Ignoring his date with Jacqueline, he sets out with Sylvie. In the last scene, Sylvie and the protagonist are seen entering the bakery: we are told that they 'married about six months later'.

As in most of Rohmer's moral tales, the narrative of *La boulangère de Monceau* is slight. Speaking of a later film, he might well have been describing not only *La boulangère de Monceau* but his entire *oeuvre* when he remarked that 'the narrative is at the service of the place, it's there to underscore the place. That's what I call the search for truth; that's the truth that interests me' (1999: 243). But if the narrative is there 'at the service of place', it also reveals what might be seen as still another kind of 'truth'. For Rohmer is interested not only in the 'truth' of place but also in the 'truths' that lie hidden in the human heart. A latter-day *moraliste*, the director is concerned, above all, with the ethical behaviour of his characters. 'What interests me', he observed, 'is showing human beings and that man is a moral being. My characters are not purely aesthetic beings. They have a moral reality that interests me in the same way as their physical reality' (ibid.).

As in almost all his films, in *La boulangère de Monceau* this 'moral reality' emerges from the discrepancy between, on the one hand, what his characters say and, on the other, what they do – in other words, from the ways in which they rationalise and justify actions that are clearly less than admirable not only in our eyes but also in theirs. For example, the protagonist of the film justifies his decision to seduce a woman he does not love: he must 'punish' her, he tells himself, for her presumption in thinking *he* would be interested in someone so commonplace. Later, he dismisses his date with Jacqueline on the grounds that it would be a 'vice' to go out with her once he has seen Sylvie again. Here, as always in Rohmer's films, it is largely left to the spectator to tease out the motives of the characters, to see the ways in which we justify raw or primitive emotions – fear, desire, a narcissistic concern with self-image – by casuistic reasoning.

In *La boulangère de Monceau*, Rohmer gives us the impression that Paris, or at least that corner of it where the action unfolds, can be known and described. In contrast, the Paris seen in Jacques Rivette's first feature, *Paris nous appartient,* is not only unknowable but, instead, a sinister and confusing maze.³ Of all the films of the Young Turks, it is surely *Paris nous appartient* that offers the most stylised – and, perhaps, the most intensely subjective – portrait of the French capital. The title may tell us that 'Paris nous appartient'; but the film itself illustrates that just the reverse is true. The recognisable and often charming Paris seen in, say, *Les Quatre cents coups* is transformed by Rivette into an ominous city – not unlike the New York or Los Angeles portrayed in *film noir* thrillers – of desolate grey dawns, unfamiliar streets, miserable courtyards and back alleys. Bathed in expressionist shadows, this tone is set from the very first: in a sequence punctuated by discordant notes and strange noises, the camera speeds relentlessly through an unfamiliar and desolate landscape marked by houses, trees and railroad lines. Only the fleeting glimpse of a sign in a railroad station tells us that this strange world we are entering is, in fact, none other than Paris.

The disorientation and apprehension created by this opening sequence persists throughout the film. Set in 1957, the film concerns a vast plot of a fascist conspiracy that may or may not be true. The main characters – who are gradually drawn into the mystery – are artists, students and bohemians who live on the Left Bank: their ranks include Anne, a young student of literature, and her brother, Pierre; Gérard, an aspiring theatre director; and Philip Kaufman, an American novelist who has fled the United States because of McCarthyite witch hunts. It is, in fact, Philip who first warns of this conspiracy by insisting that the suicide of a Spanish refugee was really a murder. He tells Anne that Gérard (who she seems to be falling in love with) will be the next victim. In an attempt to investigate this shadowy conspiracy, Anne follows one lead after another only to meet with endless denials and mysterious clues that go nowhere. After many twists and turns of the plot, Gérard does, in fact, die. But, we soon learn, his death was a real suicide. And this revelation is followed by still another: it turns out that the conspiracy never existed – it was a figment of Philip's deeply paranoid imagination. As all goes up in smoke, Pierre dies in the confusion, and finally Anne sits by a lake outside Paris. The film comes to an end with images of birds that skim the surface of the water before – like the plot? – they disappear into the sky.

In its convoluted and literary plot, as well as its expressionist portrait of a sinister Paris, Rivette's film clearly stands apart from other New Wave features. But, in other respects, it has much in common with other films by the Young Turks. To begin with, reminding us of Rivette's past as an ardent *cinéphile*, it too is replete with the cinematic echoes seen in, say, *À bout de souffle* and *Les Quatre cents coups*. One sequence, in fact, pays explicit homage to the master of German expressionism, Fritz Lang: towards the end of the film the assembled characters view a segment of Lang's 1926 film, *Metropolis*. Apart from this explicit homage, the expressionist shadows that pervade the film – as well as the sinister conspiracy itself – suggest the frightening world that surrounds Lang's mastermind of evil, Dr Mabuse. In addition to these allusions to Lang, the film also evokes, as Italian critic Adriano Aprà has observed, two other sets of cinematic 'codes' or echoes. In Aprà's view, the film places neo-realist characters (drawn from everyday life) into a world marked by the iconography (clues, conspiracies, mysterious deaths) of detective thrillers (1974: 100).

Penetrated by the intense *cinéphilie* of the Young Turks, the film also testifies to what is, perhaps, an even more fundamental New Wave trait. It is explicitly concerned with the nature of 'truth' or, more precisely, what Godard saw as the interplay of 'reality' and 'illusion' (understood as theatre, spectacle and fiction) at the heart of all great films. Indeed, the issue of 'illusion' is, in a sense, the very subject of the film: for, after all, the conspiracy itself – the 'event' that drives the narrative – is ultimately proven to be nothing more than a fiction dreamed up by a paranoid mind. 'I tried', said Rivette, 'to tell the story of an idea, with the aid of the detective story

Paris nous appartient (1960): the play of reality and illusion

form; that is to say that instead of *unveiling* primary intentions at the end of the story, the dénouement can't do anything but abolish them: "Nothing took place but the place"' (quoted in Monaco 1976: 315). A film about an 'illusion', *Paris nous appartient* also foregrounds what is often seen as the art of illusion *par excellence*: that is, theatre. Announcing the presence of theatre that will run throughout Rivette's cinema, *Paris nous appartient* incorporates lengthy rehearsal sequences of the play Gérard is directing – Shakespeare's *Pericles, Prince of Tyre* – into the film itself.

But Rivette's film is not merely about 'illusions', for it also demonstrates the ways in which 'illusion' and 'reality' – or what Godard might have called the 'imaginary' and the 'real' – are inevitably intertwined. The conspiracy is false; still, its consequences could hardly be more real. At least in part because of Anne's investigation, both Gérard and her brother met their deaths. At the same time, as Aprà points out, the unreal conspiracy also serves to bind characters to one another. 'It is almost as if the film tells us about the characters' attempts to give form to their own phantasms and to promote them in a social aim [that offers] an escape from their own isola-tion' (1974: 100). Echoing the play of illusion and reality that surrounds the conspiracy, Rivette also underscores the 'truths' that inhere to theatre and spectacle. For example, Gérard courts Anne with lines taken from a play by Molière – lines that are at once totally theatrical and totally true.

A film about 'illusion' and 'reality', *Paris nous appartient* is ultimately – and this too takes us to a fundamental New Wave impulse – a self-reflective work about cinema itself. For no less than theatre, cinema is also built on 'lies' that are, simultaneously, both true and false. In this sense, it is not hard to see how the theatrical sequences in Rivette's films are not only about theatre but, also – perhaps above all – about cinema itself. Indeed, at one point in *Paris nous appartient* Rivette seems to conflate the two arts: Gérard's observations about the 'incoherence' of *Pericles* can be taken, surely, not only as a comment on life itself but, also, on the 'incoherence' of Rivette's film. Discussing the all-important presence of theatre within his films, Rivette placed himself in a long line of filmmakers whose ranks included not only much-admired older directors (for example, George Cukor, Jean Rouch, Jean Cocteau and Kenji Mizoguchi) but, also, his friend and cohort Godard. Categorically declaring that 'all films are about theatre', he went on to say that it was hardly surprising 'if, among the films we like, there are so many that foreground this issue ... Because the subject [of theatre] involves truth and lies and there is no other [subject] in cinema: it is necessarily an interrogation about truth using means which necessarily lie ... Taking this as the subject of a film is mere honesty: therefore, it must be done' (1999: 295).

The 'shattering' of genre: Truffaut and Godard

Like *Paris nous appartient*, both Truffaut's second film, *Tirez sur le pianiste* and Godard's third, *Une femme est une femme* are marked by an extreme self-reflexivity. But the form it takes is very different from that seen in *Paris nous appartient*, for both films deliberately evoke specific cinematic genres even as they transform them in radically new ways. While *Tirez sur le pianiste* is a highly calculated and uneasy mix of several genres, *Une femme est une femme* is largely a pastiche of American musical comedies of the 1950s. Imbued with the intense *cinéphilie* of both directors, the extremely self-reflective nature of these films appealed, as Truffaut had it, to those 'fanatic' about cinema rather than the larger public.

Truffaut's films are usually placed in one of the following categories: the largely autobiographical films of the so-called Antoine Doinel cycle

François Truffaut on the set of *Tirez sur le pianiste* (1960)

(which follow the young protagonist of *Les Quatre cents coups* as he matures into adulthood, marriage and fatherhood); literary adaptations (often set in the past) such as *Jules et Jim*; contemporary love stories ranging from *La peau douce* (*The Soft Skin*, 1964) to *La femme d'à côte* (*The Woman Next Door*, 1981); films explicitly about cinema and/or theatre like *La nuit américaine* (*Day for Night*, 1975) and *Le dernier métro* (*The Last Metro*, 1980); and detective films or thrillers including *Tirez sur le pianiste* or his homage to Hitchcock, *La mariée était en noir* (*The Bride Wore Black*, 1968). At the same time, through, it must be said that any attempt to categorise Truffaut's films inevitably falls short because virtually every one contains at least some elements of the others. In this last respect, *Tirez sur le pianiste* is surely exemplary, for Truffaut's second film is at once a psychological melodrama about an artist, a passionate romance, a story about children, a detective thriller and, ultimately, a tragedy. It may be precisely this blend of elements that prompts critics Antoine de Baecque and Serge Toubiana to suggest that *Tirez sur le pianiste* is, in fact, Truffaut's 'true New Wave film' (Toubiana & de Baecque 2000: 157).

As the film opens, its protagonist, Charlie Kohler – played by singing star Charles Aznavour – is playing a honky-tonk piano in a working-class Parisian bistro. Subsequent scenes reveal that Charlie takes care of his younger brother, Fido – an adolescent whose taste for mischief recalls the escapades of the young hero of *Les Quatre cents coups* – and sleeps with the good-natured prostitute who helps look after him. One night, the pretty young waitress at Charlie's bistro, Léna, who has secretly been in love with him, manages to seduce the shy and reserved piano player. Léna soon reveals that she knows all about Charlie's past life: he was formerly a famous concert pianist with a beautiful and loving wife. Now, in a long flashback sequence narrated by Léna, we witness the details of that former existence. It turns out that his much beloved wife helped launch his career by sleeping with an important impresario. When Charlie learned of this betrayal, he treated her coldly – so coldly that, one night, his desperate and remorseful wife committed suicide by jumping from the window. It was in the wake of this suicide that Charlie gave up his career and assumed his present existence. At this point, we return to the present as the film turns into a kind of thriller, as gangsters who have had a run in with Charlie's delinquent older brothers kidnap Fido. Léna and Charlie go in search of them and end up at the home of Charlie's brothers. In the course of a shoot-out between Charlie's brothers and the gangsters, Léna is killed. As in a dream, her body rolls over in a wintry snowy landscape as Charlie looks on in despair. In the last scene of the film, he is back at the piano in a honky-tonk bar.

Even this brief summary suggests the deeply unconventional nature of *Tirez sur le pianiste*. For, as Truffaut himself remarked, his second film seemed to contain 'four or five others'. That is, it might have been a conventional *film noir* thriller (the film was, in fact, inspired by a detective story by American novelist David Goodis); a romance about Charlie and Léna or, in fact, about Charlie and his wife; a film about an adolescent – Fido – in the manner of *Les Quatre cents coups*; or even a family melodrama about Charlie and his brothers. But, instead, it was a deliberate – and disturbing – mix of all these possibilities. Attributing the failure of his film to its transgressive mixture of genres and tones, Truffaut – who was always his own best critic – insisted that the disparate nature was absolutely deliberate. Calling it a 'respectful pastiche of American B melodramas', he described what he had wanted to do:

> What I sought above all was the shattering of a genre (the detective film) by a mixture of genres (comedy, drama, melodrama, psycho-

The romantic threesome of *Une femme est une femme* (1961): Jean-Paul Belmondo (left), Anna Karina and Jean-Claude Brialy

logical film, thriller, love film, etc). I know that the public hates nothing more than changes in tone but I've always been passionate about changing tone. (1988: 112)

If, as Truffaut suggests, the public 'hates' changes in tone, it is probably because such changes undercut and frustrate audience expectations. *Tirez sur le pianiste* is no exception to this rule. For example, just when a lyrical lovemaking sequence between Charlie and Léna leads us to think that the film will bear on their romance, we are plunged into Charlie's tragic past. 'When the film went in one direction', said Truffaut, 'I cut and launched it into another ... As soon as one interpretation seemed to prevail, I destroyed it – to avoid the spectator's intellectual comfort as well as my own' (1988: 144). Moreover, the second romance – the story of Charlie's marriage – makes us uneasy about how to interpret the one that seems to be developing between Charlie and Léna. Speaking of the way he disoriented viewers by interrupting one lyrical love story with another, Truffaut observed that he broke the 'law' against 'mixing' things. 'You can't mix things', he said, 'you can't be totally in one story and [also] in another' (1988: 119). Truffaut's portrait of the gangsters also offers another important example of disturbing tonal changes. At first the gangsters seem like harmless figures of fun: for example, in the midst of a botched and semi-comical kidnapping, they engage in seemingly absurd small talk as they earnestly question whether or not women are 'magic'. In still another scene – one that would hardly have been out of place in *Les Quatre cents coups* – Fido manages to outwit them by throwing milk on the windshield of their car. They are so comical in fact that the traditional icons of *film noir* surrounding them – trench coats, car chases – assume the ironic cast of parody. But, given this aura of comedy and pastiche, it is all the more shocking when, at the end, comedy turns to tragedy with Marie's death. At the end, as Truffaut observed, everything 'seems unreal, as if we're playing, and then suddenly death is there' (1988: 115).

Even more importantly, perhaps, our feelings about Charlie – the complex figure at the centre of Truffaut's film – undergo one change after another. At first, the gifted and timid piano player seems totally sympathetic. Although his shyness is in marked contrast with the 'masculinity' of traditional *film noir* characters, it appeals to the viewer in as much as it so clearly attracts a variety of women. But, as the film progresses, we catch glimpses of a disturbing passiveness that lies beneath the surface of his timidity. Erupting, at one point, into a murderous rage, Charlie's passiveness somehow obliges the women in his life to take the initiative in every way. If this makes us uneasy so too does the final realisation that, in the end, Charlie is indirectly responsible not only for his wife's death – he refuses her comfort when she is most in need of it – but also for Léna's. His role in these deaths adds one more layer to the disturbing ambiguities and mixed emotions evoked by the film as a whole.

Like *Tirez sur le pianiste*, Godard's *Une femme est une femme* also 'shatters' the convention of genre. Whereas, however, Truffaut incorporates many different genres into *Tirez sur le pianiste*, Godard focuses on just one: American musical comedies. By exaggerating and playing off the traits of such films, he pushes what he called the 'idea' of genre to the foreground even as the film becomes, as Godard remarked of a work by Jean Renoir, both 'cinema and the explanation of cinema' (1968: 99). In contrast to the narrative intricacies of *Tirez sur le pianiste*, the plot of

Une femme est une femme could hardly be simpler. A young striptease performer, Angela (Anna Karina), who lives in the Parisian neighbourhood around St Denis with her boyfriend Emile (Jean-Claude Brialy), dreams of having a baby and getting married. But Emile is reluctant and they quarrel. Unhappiness prompts Emile to seek solace with a prostitute; the equally unhappy Angela sleeps with Alfred (Jean-Paul Belmondo), a friend who is in love with her, in order to get pregnant. But then the couple reconciles and in order to make sure that Emile might be the father of any possible baby, they make love. When it is over, Emile tells Angela that she is *'infâme'* (infamous or terrible). Punning on this word she responds that she is merely a *'une femme'* ('a woman').

From a number of perspectives, *Une femme est une femme* is one of the director's most personal films. It has a strong autobiographical dimension as it can be seen as a kind of love-letter to the film's star, Danish actress Anna Karina, who would soon become Godard's wife. (The star of Godard's previous film, *Le petit soldat*, Karina would figure in some of his most important works of the 1960s: *Vivre sa vie* (*My Life to Live*, 1962), *Alphaville* (1965) and *Pierrot le fou* (1965).) In *Une femme est une femme*, Godard films the beautiful young actress from every angle, capturing her characteristic gestures and inflections, her grace and charm. But in addition to Karina's presence, the film is also highly personal in a quite different way: as already suggested, it is a deliberate homage to the American musical comedies Godard had loved as a young critic. Ruefully acknowledging that the historical/cinematic moment of such films was over – that there was no longer any sense 'in doing remakes of *Singin' in the Rain*' – Godard went on to observe that *Une femme est une femme* 'is nostalgia for the musical comedy, as *Le petit soldat* is nostalgia for the Spanish Civil War' (1968: 301).

Even before the film begins, this nostalgia makes itself felt: *Une femme est une femme* is prefaced by titles referring to Ernst Lubitsch, to *Quatorze juillet* (René Clair's musical tribute to Paris) and so on. Paying homage to beloved films and directors, Godard also places his own film in a long tradition of light-hearted romances and musicals. And, once the film begins, there can be no doubt that we have entered the magical realm of illusion seen in, say, *An American in Paris* (1951) or *Singin' in the Rain* (1952). For *Une femme est une femme* – which was Godard's first film in colour as well as synchronous sound – presents us with the colour-coordinated world of

Hollywood musicals: here, the red of Karina's sweater and stockings are echoed by the red of the lampshade in the living room and that of the awnings on the windows. Except for a number near the beginning that is sung by Karina, the characters do not actually burst into song as they do in Hollywood musicals. But their animated and exaggerated gestures, as well as the musical soundtrack, insistently evokes the worlds of fantasy brought to life by American directors like Vincente Minnelli and Gene Kelly. 'I preferred', said Godard, 'to have the characters speak normally and to suggest the idea that they are singing through the utilisation of music' (1968: 301).

In addition to the musical soundtrack, the characters constantly give little performances that – like the musical numbers in, say, *Singin' in the Rain* – take us out of the narrative flow. For example, in a sequence composed of fixed frames, Emile and Angela strike poses associated with performers such as Gene Kelly and Cyd Charisse; in still another sequence, Angela recites a scene from a famous eighteenth-century play about love by Marivaux. As if to further underscore the sense of theatre that permeates the film, at certain moments the characters address us – or, at one point, take their bows – as if we were spectators at a live performance. Acknowledging that that these breaks in continuity may well have contributed to the failure of his film, Godard made it clear that the work was born of a desire to push one aspect of his sensibility – his taste for 'theatre' or 'spectacle' – to an extreme. In fact, alluding to the intensely theatrical tradition embodied in the Italian *commedia dell'arte*, Godard dubbed his film an example of *cinéma dell'arte*. Noting that the characters in the film 'perform and bow at the same time', he went on to say that 'they know and we know that they are performing – that they are laughing and, at the same time, crying. In sum, it's an exhibition, but that's what I wanted to do' (1968: 301).

Endings … and beginnings

While the films just discussed make clear that New Wave impulses were felt well beyond the explosion at Cannes, it is probably true, as suggested earlier, that by 1962 or 1963, the era of *la nouvelle vague* had come to an end. As the collaborative energies and exhilarating experiments of the New Wave began to fade, the leading directors associated with it embarked on the individual paths that they would follow in the coming years. As they did so, it became clear that the New Wave was, as the directors themselves had always insisted, marked by a tremendous 'diversity'. 'Each [of us] remained faithful to himself', said Truffaut in 1973, 'but, in so doing, he distanced himself from the others' (Truffaut 1988: 37). Reflecting on the highly divergent individual careers that came into focus in the early 1960s, Truffaut suggested that it was often the *third* film of a director that 'marked the beginning of a career' (1988: 119). Clearly, this paradigm is not true of all of the directors associated with the New Wave. For example, Resnais' *first* feature, *Hiroshima mon amour*, revealed the mastery that he would bring to all his films; as for Chabrol, it was not until the late 1960s that he made the films – *La femme infidèle* (*The Unfaithful Wife*, 1968), *Le boucher* (*The Butcher*, 1969) and *Que la bête meure* (*The Beast Must Die*, 1969) – that many consider the high points of his career. But, it may be true of Rohmer who hit his stride with his third feature, *Ma nuit chez Maud* (*My Night at Maud's*, 1969). (It is sometimes said that Rohmer, who continued to shoot low-budget films on location – often with unknown performers – remained the 'truest' to the New Wave aesthetic.) But, to some extent, it probably *is* true of Truffaut and Godard. As Truffaut points out, both *Tirez sur le pianiste* and *Une femme est une femme* were very personal, perhaps self-indulgent, works born of the euphoria of 1959–60. The films that followed, however, were not only 'corrections' (to use Truffaut's word) but also milestones in their careers. Truffaut's *Jules et Jim* and Godard's *Vivre sa vie* left no doubt that the directors were not only gifted young men but major directors ready to assume the mantle of Jean Vigo and Jean Renoir.

At the same time, though, these films made clear the 'distance' the two directors had travelled since their debuts. The 'amorality' of *Jules et Jim* – a tale of a woman who refuses to decide between two lovers – may have harked back to that seen in early New Wave features; still, its carefully crafted and highly literary script, period details (it is set around the time of World War I), as well as the glamorous presence of star Jeanne Moreau – all these suggested that Truffaut had embarked upon a new path. As for Godard, leaving behind what he called the film-obsessed dimension of his early films – 'our first films', he said, 'were purely the work of *cinéphiles* ... I thought in terms of attitudes that were purely cinematographic' (1968: 287) – with *Vivre sa vie* he began the series of films that would chart the rapidly changing social landscape of France in the 1960s. With the arguable exception of *Alphaville*, Godard's sole foray into the world of science-fiction, the tremendous 'nostalgia' for an earlier cinema that had fuelled the transformation of genre (thrillers, political thrillers, musical comedies) in his first three films would not return – at least in such an explicit form – until *Vent d'est* (*East Wind*, 1969). But, by that time, Godard's outlook – radicalised politically by the events of 1968 and the continuing war in Vietnam – had changed dramatically. Evoking American westerns in *Vent d'est*, he demonstrated all the fervour of a convert as he denounced the Hollywood films he had formerly loved.

René Prédal is doubtlessly correct when he observes that, by 1965, the 'New Wave was no more than a memory' (1984: 53). But if the phenomenon itself had become a 'memory' by this date, the collective energies that had fuelled the New Wave were visible on at least two occasions in the course of the 1960s. In 1965, Godard, Rohmer, Chabrol, Rouch, Jean Douchet and Jean-Daniel Pollet each contributed an episode to *Paris vu par* (*Six in Paris*), a collection of short films set in different *quartiers* of the capital. Although it is sometimes called a 'second' manifesto of the New Wave, the film seems, rather, an indication that the time of the New Wave had come and gone. While some of the episodes are amusing, taken as a whole – with the possible exception of the episode by Chabrol – *Paris vu par* seems to look backwards rather than towards the future.

Three years later, New Wave directors gathered together once again on a far more momentous occasion – one that evoked the beginnings of the phenomenon even as it underscored its end. In protest rallies often considered as a prelude to the sweeping student rebellion seen later that year, in February 1968, artists, intellectuals and filmgoers of all stripes gathered together to protest the decision of the French government (led by Minister of Culture André Malraux) to remove Henri Langlois as head of the Cinémathèque. Not surprisingly, Godard and Truffaut were on the frontline. In what Truffaut called an atmosphere of 'exceptional comaraderie', the former Young Turks were joined by directors of the preceding generation (Henri-Georges Clouzot and Marcel Carné) whose work they had so scornfully dismissed in the past. Now, of course, it was the Young Turks themselves – these 'children of the Cinémathèque' – who had joined the ranks of the nation's most respected directors. As such, they were a living testimony to the influence and importance of Langlois and his 'museum' of cinema.

If, however, these protest rallies recalled the early fervour of the Young Turks, the events of May '68 also put a more definitive end to the era of the New Wave. In the new, highly-charged political landscape that took shape in the wake of May, the intense *cinéphilie* and anarchic individualism of the New Wave seemed to belong to another era. At the same time, the events spawned a new generation of young directors. Some, like Bertrand Tavernier (who worked with Aurenche and Bost) seemed to rebel against the New Wave; others, like Philippe Garrel and Jean Eustache, are often seen as its 'sons'. But, as suggested earlier, the real legacy of the New Wave was probably more deeply felt in other countries than in France. For just as the New Wave was fading into the past in France, its influence was taking hold around the globe. In the course of the late 1960s and the 1970s, cinematic 'new waves' sprung up around the globe: young filmmakers – from Germany, Brazil and the United States to Hong Kong and Japan – saw the French example as the very symbol of a different kind of film praxis.

To further underscore the international resonance of the New Wave, I would like to conclude with remarks by two of its most far-flung 'sons'. The fact that these two filmmakers come from opposite sides of the globe, and make very different kinds of films, further attests to the profound influence of what occurred in France at the end of the 1950s. One is the prominent American director, Martin Scorsese. Observing that *la nouvelle vague* has influenced all filmmakers who have worked since that era, Scorsese declares that its 'most important contribution has been to give a visible image of liberty to every aspiring director ... The first films of Godard, Truffaut, Chabrol, Rivette, Rohmer and others gave you the feeling that you yourself could make a film anywhere, with anyone and using any story – that you didn't need expensive material, stars or powerful equipment' (Various authors 1998: 97). The second testimony comes from Iran's leading director, Abbas Kiarostami. Taking contemporary Iranian cinema as 'proof' of the lasting influence of *la nouvelle vague*, Kiarostami declares that it was the experience of the New Wave that changed his 'way of imagining or looking at cinema. Before that time, I believed that cinema belonged to superstars, to studios and elaborate sets. Afterwards, I could see myself and my neighbours in films ... It revealed a different path' (Various authors 1998: 96). It is, of course, the evolution of this 'different path' – one ardently embraced by young and fearless directors eager to break established rules – that I have tried to trace in the pages of this study.

NOTES

chapter one

1   Michel Marie (1997) is one of the few who argues that the New Wave
    was, in his words, an 'artistic school'.
2   Along with Braunberger, Anatole Dauman and Georges de Beauregard
    were instrumental in producing highly personal films by young directors.
    Underscoring the vital role played by these three men, Serge Toubiana
    observes that without them 'the New Wave would doubtlessly not have
    existed in its historical form' (Toubiana 1998: 86).

chapter two

1   In 1946 two networks of *ciné-clubs* – the *Fédération française des
    ciné-clubs* and the more Marxist *Fédération des loisirs et culture ciné-
    matographique* – were created to bring films to young people in the
    provinces as well as Paris.
2   On the right-wing dimensions of Truffaut's essay see Marie 1997: 34–38.
    The essays gathered together in Borde *et al.*, 1962, constitute attacks
    on the Young Turks by *Postif* critics.

chapter three

1   As Melville tells it, the head of the Resistance had asked Vercors never
    to sell the rights to the novel because he 'viewed with horror the idea

that this story, which had virtually served as a Bible during the war, might be made into a film'. To surmount this obstacle, Melville (who had served with the Resistance) apparently gave a written guarantee to submit the finished film to a jury composed of former members of the Resistance. Only if they agreed would the film be shown; otherwise Melville pledged to burn the negatives. See Melville 1971: 23.

2   Interestingly, although the great African director Ousmane Sembène was not happy with Rouch's films in general – Rouch, he felt, looked at Africans 'as if they were insects' – he admired *Moi, un noir*. See Cervoni 1996: 104–106.

3   Although critics usually agree that these three directors formed the core of the Left Bank group, other filmmakers – for example, Jacques Demy, Marguerite Duras and Georges Franju – are sometimes included in this group. On this issue see Alan Williams 1992: 365.

4   The sheer number of such films, and the respect they frequently gar- nered, did much to create what Alan Williams describes as a 'commu- nity of [documentary] filmmakers who were all very much aware of each other's activities' as well as 'an awareness of nonfiction film among critics and presumably among a certain number of film spectators' (Williams 1992: 363).

5   As Antoine de Baecque and Serge Toubiana remind us in their exhaus- tive biography of Truffaut, the term of 'hussards' or 'hussars' can be traced back to the late 1940s. At that time, a group of contributors to the journal *Arts*, home of the intellectual right-wing, were named 'hus- sards' for their 'rough and tumble' style. When Truffaut began writing for *Arts*, he took the opportunity to attack left-wing intellectuals for what he called their 'cultural political activism' (De Baecque/Toubiana, 2000: 80). The authors of this biography also trace Truffaut's political evolu- tion as he moved away from his initial stance as a right-wing 'dandy'.

6   Despite these labels, critics generally agree that Varda – perhaps because of her outsider status as a woman – has not really been given adequate credit for her pioneering work. For example, speak- ing of Varda's 'feminist bias', Sandy Flitterman-Lewis writes: 'There is an undeniable consistency in Varda's work in terms of what could be described as 'New Wave practice', but over and above that is a feminist consistency, which has, ironically, distinguished (if not excluded) her from that very practice' (Flitterman-Lewis 1990: 264).

7   'A woman's vocabulary exists', declared Varda, 'linked to a feminine universe. I feel this occasionally insofar as I am pulled by a certain number of attractions, of subjects, which attract me a little more than if I were a man' (Varda 1960: 7).

8   'I was so annoyed at having made a commissioned film', said Varda, 'that I consoled myself by shooting something myself in 16 millimeters. Initially, [cameraman] Sacha Vierny helped me out but after that I managed by myself' (Varda 1994: 230).

9   Before making *L'ascenseur à l'échafaud*, Malle worked on an underwater documentary with Jacques Cousteau. Eventually, he received co-directing credit for the finished film, *Le monde du silence*, which won the prize for best film at the Cannes festival of 1956.

10 Vincendeau makes the interesting point that Moreau, in 'concentrating the values of romantic love, sensuality, sensitivity and modernity ... brought a feminised surface to the New Wave which superimposed itself on its male and misogynist foundations' (Vincendeau 2000: 130).

chapter four

1   On this issue, see, for example, Wood & Walker 1970: 6–19.

2   Faced with charges of 'fascism' regarding this film, Chabrol (who did have extremely right-wing friends including the politician Jean-Marie Le Pen) felt compelled to explain that the 'German' aspect of the film reflected his attraction to German romanticism. But he went on to say that he wanted to 'show that fascism is seductive as well as disquieting and dangerous' (Braucourt 1971: 117).

3   Before making *Les quatre cents coups*, Truffaut – with the help of his father-in-law, Ignace Morgenstern, who owned a small production company, SEDIF, as well as a large distribution company – had set up a tiny production company. (Named after a film by Jean Renoir, it was called *Les films du carrosse*.) After producing *Les mistons* (*The Brats*, 1957) – a successful short that garnered Truffaut the award for best director of short films at the Festival du film mondial in Brussels in February 1958 – Morgenstern agreed to co-produce Truffaut's first feature.

4   Truffaut has said that this scene was fortuitous. Apparently, the woman who plays the psychologist was out of town when he began shooting; thinking he would film her later on, he concentrated on Antoine's

responses. But when cameraman Henri Decaë saw the sequences, he said it would be 'madness to shoot the reverse shots. You must leave it like that.' See Truffaut 1988: 92.

chapter five

1   Two films in particular seemed designed to disturb left-wing sensibilities. Godard's *Le petit soldat* depicts left-wing revolutionaries who calmly engage in torture as they read Mao and Lenin. In *Les bonnes femmes*, Chabrol seemed to cast a jaundiced eye on the proletariat by hinting at a complicity between working class shop girls and the serial killer who preys on them.

2   Richard Neupert points out that this film launched Rohmer's partnership with Barbet Schroeder (who plays the part of the male protagonist in the film) and with his small but important production company, Les Films du Losange. See Neupert 2002: 255–6.

3   The long and difficult gestation of *Paris nous appartient* – begun in 1958, the film was completed in 1960 – has become the stuff of cinematic legend. Problems stemmed not only from the lack of funds but also from Rivette's admittedly obsessive temperament.

FILMOGRAPHY

À bout de souffle (*Breathless*) (Jean-Luc Godard, 1960, France)

Alexandre Nevsky (S.M. Eisenstein, 1938, USSR)

Alphaville (Jean-Luc Godard, 1965, France)

Les amants (*The Lovers*) (Louis Malle, 1958, France)

L'année dernière à Marienbad (*Last Year at Marienbad*) (Alain Resnais, 1961, France)

L'ascenseur à l'échafaud (*Lift to the Scaffold*) (Louis Malle, 1957, France)

Le beau serge (*Handsome Serge*) (Claude Chabrol, 1957, France)

Bob le flambeur (Jean-Pierre Melville, 1955, France)

Les bonnes femmes (Claude Chabrol, 1960, France)

Le boucher (*The Butcher*) (Claude Chabrol, 1969, France)

Boudu sauvé des eaux (*Boudu Saved from Drowning*) (Jean Renoir, 1932, France)

La boulangère de Monceau (*The Girl at the Monceau Bakery*) (Eric Rohmer, 1962, France)

Un chant d'amour (Jean Genet, 1950, France)

Chronique d'un été (Chronicle of a Summer) (Jean Rouch, 1960, France)

Citizen Kane (Orson Welles, 1941, US)

Cléo de 5 à 7 (*Cleo from 5 to 7*) (Agnès Varda, 1961, France)

Le coup du berger (Jacques Rivette, 1956, France)

Les cousins (*The Cousins*) (Claude Chabrol, 1959, France)

Le dernier métro (*The Last Metro*) (François Truffaut, 1980, France)

Dimanche à Pékin (*Sunday in Peking*) (Chris Marker, 1956, France)

Du côté de la côte (Agnès Varda, 1958, France)

Et dieu créa la femme (*And God Created Woman*) (Roger Vadim, 1956, France)

Les enfants terribles (Jean-Pierre Melville, 1949, France)

La femme d'à côté (*The Woman Next Door*) (François Truffaut, 1981, France)

Une femme est une femme (*A Woman is a Woman*) (Jean-Luc Godard, 1961, France)

La femme infidèle (Claude Chabrol, 1968, France)

Fireworks (Kenneth Anger, 1947, US)

La Grande illusion (*Grand Illusion*) (Jean Renoir, 1937, France)

Guernica (Alain Resnais, 1950, France)

Hiroshima mon amour (Alain Resnais, 1959, France)

Le joli mai (Chris Marker, 1963, France)

Journal d'un curé de campagne (*Diary of a Country Priest*) (Robert Bresson, 1950, France)

Jules et Jim (*Jules and Jim*) (François Truffaut, 1961, France)

Ladri di Biciclette (*The Bicycle Thieves*) (Vittorio de Sica, 1949, Italy)

Lettre de Sibérie (*Letter from Siberia*) (Chris Marker, 1958, France)

Ma nuit chez Maud (*My Night at Maud's*) (Eric Rohmer, 1969, France)

The Magnificent Ambersons (Orson Welles, 1942, US)

La mariée était en noir (*The Bride Wore Black*) (François Truffaut, 1967, France)

Meet Me in St Louis (Vincent Minelli, 1944, US)

Le mépris (*Contempt*) (Jean-Luc Godard, 1963, France)

Moi, un noir (Jean Rouch 1958, France)

Muriel (Alain Resnais, 1963, France/Italy)

North by Northwest (Alfred Hitchcock, 1959, US)

La nuit américaine (*Day for Night*) (François Truffaut, 1973, France)

Nuit et brouillard (*Night and Fog*) (Alain Resnais, 1955, France)

O saisons, ô châteaux (Agnès Varda, 1957, France)

L'opéra-mouffe (Agnès Varda, 1958, France)

Orfeu negro (*Black Orpheus*) (Marcel Camus, 1959, France/Italy/Brazil)

Paisà (*Paisan*) (Roberto Rossellini, 1946, Italy)

Paris nous appartient (*Paris Belongs to Us*) (Jacques Rivette, 1960, France)

La peau douce (*The Soft Skin*) (François Truffaut, 1964, France)

Le petit soldat (*The Little Soldier*) (Jean-Luc Godard, 1962, France)

Pierrot le fou (Jean-Luc Godard, 1965, France)

La pointe courte (Agnès Varda, 1954, France)

Quatorze juillet (René Clair, 1932, France)

Les Quatre cents coups (*The 400 Blows*) (François Truffaut, 1959, France)

Que la bête meure (*This Man Must Die*) (Claude Chabrol, 1969, France)

La règle du jeu (*The Rules of the Game*) (Jean Renoir, 1939, France)

Roma, città aperta (*Rome, Open City*) (Roberto Rossellini, 1945, Italy)

Sait-on jamais? (*Does One Ever Know?*) (Roger Vadim, 1957, France)

Siamo donne (*Of Life and Love*) (Episodes by Gianni Franciolini, Alfredo Guarini, Robert Rossellini, Luchino Visconti and Luigi Zampa, 1953, Italy)

Le signe du lion (*The Sign of Leo*) (Eric Rohmer, 1959, France)

Le silence de la mer (Jean-Pierre Melville, 1947–1948, France)

Singin' in the Rain (Gene Kelley/Stanley Donen, 1952, US)

Les statues meurent aussi (*Statues also Die*) (Chris Marker/Alain Resnais, 1950/1953, France)

Tirez sur le pianiste (*Shoot the Piano Player*) (François Truffaut, 1960, France)

Toute la mémoire du monde (Alain Resnais, 1956, France)

Umberto D (Vittorio de Sica, 1952, Italy)

Van Gogh (Alain Resnais, 1948, France)

Vent d'est (*East Wind*) (Jean-Luc Godard, 1969, France)

Viaggio in Italia (*Journey to Italy*) (Roberto Rossellini, 1953, France/Italy)

Vivre sa vie (*My Life to Live*) (Jean-Luc Godard, 1962, France)

Zéro de conduite (*Zero for Conduct*) (Jean Vigo, 1933, France)

BIBLIOGRAPHY

Alpigiano, J.-L. (1998) 'L'ordre et le désordre des mémoires: André Bazin, Chris Marker, Alain Resnais et l'Espèce humaine', in *Les cahiers du cinéma*, special unnumbered issue, 'Nouvelle Vague: Une légende en question', 24–8.

Andrew, D. (1990) *André Bazin*. New York: Columbia University Press.

Aprà, A. (1974) 'Geografia del labirinto', in *Il cinema di Jacques Rivette*. Pesaro: Quaderno informativo, No. 62, 100–5.

Astruc, A. (1968 [1948]) 'The birth of a new avant-garde: La caméra-stylo', in P. Graham (ed.) *The New Wave*. London: Secker and Warburg/British Film Institute, 17–23.

Auzel, D. (1990) *François Truffaut: Les Mille et Une Nuits Américaines*. Paris: Henri Veyrier.

Bazin, A. (1958) *Qu'est-ce que le cinéma? Vol I*. Paris: Cerf.

_____ (1962) *Qu'est-ce que le cinéma? Vol IV*. Paris: Cerf.

_____ (1968 [1957]) 'La politique des auteurs', in P. Graham (ed.) *The New Wave*. London: Secker & Warburg/British Film Institute, 137–55.

_____ (2003 [1958]) 'Bazin on Marker', *Film Comment* (July–August), 44–5.

Benayoun, R. (1980) *Alain Resnais: Arpenteur de l'imaginaire*. Paris: Stock.

Bergala, A. (1983) 'Le vrai, le faux, le factice', in *Les cahiers du cinéma*, 351 (September), 5–9.

_____ (1998) 'Les techniques de la Nouvelle Vague', in *Les cahiers du cinéma*, special unnumbered issue, 'Nouvelle Vague: Une légende en question', 36–43.

Beylie, C. (1999) 'Le Signe du lion', in A. de Baecque and C. Tesson (*eds*) *La Nouvelle Vague: Textes et entretiens parus dans les cahiers du cinéma*. Paris: Cahiers du Cinéma, 105–111.

Billard, P. (1995) *L'âge classique du cinéma français*. Paris: Flammarion.

Bounoure, G. (1962) *Alain Resnais*. Paris: Seghers.

Borde, R., F. Buache and J. Curtelin (1962) *Nouvelle Vague*. Paris: Serdoc.

Braucourt, G. (1971) *Claude Chabrol*. Paris: Seghers.

Burch, N. (1959) 'Four Recent French Documentaries', *Film Quarterly*, 13, 1, 56–61.

Burdeau, E. (1998) 'Hold-up romanesque', in *Les cahiers du cinéma*, special unnumbered issue, 'Nouvelle Vague: Une légende en question', 67–69.

Cameron, I. (1970) *Second Wave*. New York: Praeger.

Cervoni, A. (1996) 'Une confrontation historique en 1965 entre Jean Rouch et Sembène Ousmane', *CinémAction*, 81, 104–6

Chabrol, C. (1962) 'Entretien', *Les cahiers du cinéma*, 138 (December), 2–19.

_____ (1970/71) 'Chabrol talks to Rui Nogueira and Nicoletta Zalaffi', *Sight and Sound*, 40, 1 (Winter), 2–6.

_____ (1976) *Et pourtant je tourne*. Paris: Laffont

_____ (1996) 'L'homme au Stetson', *Les cahiers du cinéma*, 507 (November), 74–5.

Clouzot, C. (1972) *Le cinéma français depuis la Nouvelle Vague*. Paris: Nathan.

Cook, D. (2004) *A History of Narrative Film*, 4th edn. New York and London: Norton.

D'Allones, F. R. (1988) 'Genèse d'une vague bien précise', in *D'un Cinéma L'autre: notes sur le cinéma français des années cinquante*. Centre Georges Pompidou, 76–98.

Daney, S. (1986) *Ciné journal 1981–1986*. Paris: Cahiers du Cinéma.

_____ (1998) 'Survivre à la Nouvelle Vague', *Les cahiers du cinéma*, special issue, 'Nouvelle Vague: une légende en question', 62–66.

De Baecque, A. (1991) *Les cahiers du cinéma: histoire d'une revue, Vol. I: à l'assaut du cinéma 1951–1959*. Paris: Editions Cahiers du Cinéma.

_____ (1998) *La Nouvelle Vague: Portrait d'une jeunesse*. Paris: Flammarion.

_____ (2003) *La Cinéphilie: Invention d'un regard, histoire d'une culture, 1944–1968*. Paris: Fayard.

De Baecque A. and C. Tesson (eds) (1999) 'Table ronde sur *Hiroshima mon amour* d'Alain Resnais', in *La Nouvelle Vague: Textes et entretiens parus dans les cahiers du cinéma*. Paris: Cahiers du Cinéma, 36–62.

Deleuze, G. (1985) *Cinema 2: L'image-temps*. Paris: Minuit.

Doniol-Valcroze, J. (1958) '*Les Amants*', in J. Douchet (1999) *French New Wave*, trans. Robert Bonnono. Paris: Editions Hazan/Cinémathèque française, 110.

_____ (1959) 'L'histoire des *Cahiers du cinéma*', *Les cahiers du cinéma*, 100 (October), 62–8.

Douchet, J. (1999) *French New Wave*, trans. Robert Bonnono. Paris: Editions Hazan/Cinémathèque française.

Douin, J-L. (1983) *La Nouvelle Vague: 25 ans après*. Paris: Editions du Cerf.

Duras, M. (1961) 'Synopsis', in *Hiroshima mon amour*. New York: Grove Press, 8–13.

Fieschi, J-A. (1973) 'Dérives de la fiction: Notes sur le cinéma de Jean Rouch', in

Cinéma: Théorie, Lectures. Paris: Klincksieck, 255–64.

Flitterman-Lewis, S. (1990) *To Desire Differently: Feminism and the French Cinema.* Chicago, IL: University of Illinois Press.

Forbes, J. (1992) *The Cinema in France After the New Wave.* Bloomington and Indianapolis: Indiana University Press.

Frodon, J-M. (1995) *L'Age Moderne du cinéma français.* Paris: Flammarion.

Gillain, A. (2000) 'The script of delinquency: François Truffaut's *Les 400 coups*', in S. Hayward and G. Vincendeau (eds.) *French Film: Texts and Contexts*, second edition. New York/London: Routledge, 142–157.

Godard, J-L. (1968) *Jean-Luc Godard par Jean-Luc Godard.* Paris: Belfond.

Harcourt, P. (1973) 'Alain Resnais: Memory is kept alive with dreams', *Film Comment* 9, 6, 47–50.

Hayward, S. (2005) *French National Cinema.* London/New York: Routledge.

Hayward, S. and G. Vincendeau (eds.) *French Film: Texts and Contexts*, second edition. New York/London: Routledge.

Hillier, J. (ed.) (1985) *Cahiers du Cinéma. The 1950s: Neo-Realism, Hollywood, New Wave.* Cambridge, MA: Harvard University Press.

____ (ed.)(1986) *Cahiers du Cinéma. 1960–1968: New Wave, New Cinema, Reevaluating Hollywood.* Cambridge, MA: Harvard University Press.

Hoveyda, F. (1986 [1960]) 'Sunspots', in J. Hillier (ed.) *Cahiers du Cinéma. 1960–1968: New Wave, New Cinema, Reevaluating Hollywood.* Cambridge, MA: Harvard University Press, 135–45.

Ishaghpour, Y. (1982) *D'une image à l'autre: La nouvelle modernité du cinéma.* Paris: Denoël/Gonthier.

Jeancolas, J-P. (1979) *Le cinéma des français: La Ve République, 1958–1978.* Paris: Stock.

Jousse, T. and S. Toubiana (1996) 'Le deuxième souffle de Melville', in *Les cahiers du cinéma*, 507 (November), 63.

Labarthe, A. (1960) *Essai sur le jeune cinéma français.* Paris. Terrain Vague.

Magny, J. (1987) *Claude Chabrol.* Paris: Cahiers du Cinéma.

Malle, L. (1993) *Malle on Malle*, ed. Philip French. London: Faber and Faber.

Marie, M. (1997) *The French New Wave: An Artistic School*, trans. Richard Neupert. Oxford: Blackwell.

____ (2000) 'It really makes you sick!': Jean Luc Godard's *À bout de souffle*', in S. Hayward and G. Vincendeau (eds.) *French Film: Texts and Contexts*, second edition. New York/London: Routledge, 158–173.

____ (2003) *The French New Wave: An Artistic School*, trans. Richard Neupert. Oxford: Blackwell.

Melville, J-P. (1971) *Melville on Melville*, ed. Rui Nogueira. New York: Viking.

Monaco, J. (1976) *The New Wave.* New York: Oxford University Press.

Neupert, R. (2002) *A History of the French New Wave Cinema*. Madison, WI: University of Wisconsin Press.

Pasolini, P.P. (1972) *Empirismo eretico*. Milan: Garzanti.

Pingaud, B. (1961) *Alain Resnais*. Lyon: SERDOC.

Powrie, P. and K. Reader (2002) *French Cinema: A Student's Guide*. London: Hodder and Stoughton Educational.

Prédal, R. (1968) *Alain Resnais*. Paris: Lettres Modernes/Minard.

____ (1984) *Le cinéma français contemporain*. Paris: Editions du Cerf.

____ (1989) *Louis Malle*. Paris: Edilig.

____ (1991) *Le cinéma français depuis 1945*. Paris: Nathan.

____ (1996) 'Ambiguité du cinéma ethnographique?', in R. Prédal (ed.) *Jean Rouch, ou, Le ciné-plaisir*. Paris: *CinémAction*, 81, 38–9.

Rauger, J.-F. (1996) 'L'attente hypnotique', in *Les cahiers du cinéma*, 507 (November), 72–3.

Rivette, J. (1954) 'L'Essentiel', in *Les cahiers du cinéma*, 32 (February), 42–5.

____ (1958) 'Mizoguchi vu d'ici', in *Les cahiers du cinéma*, 81 (March), 28–37.

____ (1985 [1955]) 'Letter on Rossellini', in J. Hillier (ed.) *Cahiers du Cinéma. The 1950s: Neo-Realism, Hollywood, New Wave*. Cambridge, MA: Harvard University Press, 192–204.

____ (1999 [1968]) 'Entretien', in A. de Baecque and C. Tesson (eds) *La Nouvelle Vague: Textes et entretiens parus dans les cahiers du cinéma*. Paris: Cahiers du Cinéma, 264–314.

Rohmer, E. (1985 [1956]) 'Ajax ou le Cid', in J. Hillier (ed.) *Cahiers du Cinéma. The 1950s: Neo-Realism, Hollywood, New Wave*. Cambridge, MA: Harvard University Press, 111–15.

____ (1989) *Le goût de la beauté*. Paris: Flammarion.

____ (1999 [1965]) 'Entretien avec Eric Rohmer: L'ancien et le nouveau', in A. de Baecque and C. Tesson (eds) *La Nouvelle Vague: Textes et entretiens parus dans les cahiers du cinéma*. Paris: Cahiers du Cinéma, 231–63.

Rohmer, E and C. Chabrol (1979 [1957]) *Hitchcock: The First Forty-Four Films*. New York: Ungar.

Ropars-Wuilleumier, M-C. (1990) 'How history begets meaning: Alain Resnais' *Hiroshima mon amour*', in S. Hayward and G. Vincendau (eds) *French Film: Texts and Contexts*. New York and London: Routledge, 173–85.

Rouch, J. (1996a) 'Interview with Eric Pauwels: Cinéma, mémoire du monde', *Nouvelles de Danse* (Brussels), 26 (Winter), 9–18.

____ (1996b) 'La camera et les hommes', in R. Prédal (ed.) *Jean Rouch, ou, Le ciné-plaisir*. Paris: *CinémAction*, 81, 42–45.

____ (2003) *Jean Rouch, Ciné-ethnography*, ed. and trans. by Steven Feld. Minneapolis: University of Minnesota Press.

Siclier, J. (1961a) *Nouvelle vague?* Paris: Editions du Cerf.

____ (1961b) 'New Wave and French Cinema', in *Sight and Sound*, 30, 1, 116–20.

Simsolo, N. (2000) *La Nouvelle Vague*. Radio broadcast. Paris, INA/Radio France.

Smith, A. (1998) *Agnès Varda*. Manchester: Manchester University Press.

Sontag, S. (1969) 'Godard', in *Styles of Radical Will*. New York: Delta, 147–189.

Tacchella, J-C. (1990 [1983]) 'André Bazin from 1945 to 1950: The Time of Struggles and Consecration', in D. Andrew (ed.) *André Bazin*. New York: Columbia University Press, 237–257.

Temple, M. (1994) 'Big Rhythm and the Power of Metamorphosis: Some Models and Precursors for *Histoire(s) du Cinéma*', in M. Temple and J. Williams (eds) *The Cinema Alone: Essays on the Work of Jean-Luc Godard 1985–2000*. Amsterdam: Amsterdam University Press, 77–95.

Toubiana, S. (1998) 'La Nouvelle Vague ou le culte du premier film', in *Les cahiers du cinéma*, special unnumbered issue, 'Nouvelle Vague: une légende en question', 85–87.

Toubiana, S. and de Baecque, A. (2000) *Truffaut: A Biography*. Paris: NFF/Gallimard.

Truffaut, F. (1955) *'Ali Baba* et la 'Politiques des Auteurs'', in *Les cahiers du cinéma*, 44 (February), 43–7.

____ (1962) 'Entretien', in *Les cahiers du cinéma*, 138 (December), 40–59.

____ (1967) *Hitchcock*. New York: Simon and Schuster.

____ (1975) *Les films de ma vie*. Paris: Flammarion.

____ (1985 [1955]) 'A Wonderful Certainty', in J. Hiller (ed.) *Cahiers du Cinéma. The 1950s: Neo-Realism, Hollywood, New Wave*. Cambridge, MA: Harvard University Press, 107–8.

____ (1987) 'Une certaine tendance du cinéma français', in F. Truffaut, *Le plaisir des yeux*. Paris: Cahiers du Cinéma, 192–224.

____ (1988) *Le cinéma selon François Truffaut*, ed. Anne Gillain. Paris: Flammarion.

Varda, A. (1960) 'Agnès Varda de A à Z', *Cinéma*, 60 (October), 4–20.

____ (1994) *Varda par Agnès*. Paris: Editions Cahiers du Cinéma.

Various authors (1959) 'Cannes 59', in *Les cahiers du cinéma*, 96 (June), 38–49.

____ (1998) 'Questionnaire' (1998), in *Les cahiers du cinéma*, special unnumbered issue, 'Nouvelle Vague: une légende en question', 96–7.

Vincendeau, G. (1996) *The Companion to French Cinema*. London: British Film Institute.

____ (2000) *Stars and Stardom in French Cinema*. London/New York: Continuum.

____ (2003) *Jean-Pierre Melville: An American in Paris*. London: British Film Institute.

Williams, A (1992) *Republic of Images: A History of French Filmmaking*. Cambridge,

MA and London: Harvard University Press.

Witt, M. (1994) 'Montage, My Beautiful Care, or Histories of the Cinematograph', in M. Temple and J. Williams (eds) *The Cinema Alone: Essays on the Work of Jean-Luc Godard 1985–2000*. Amsterdam: Amsterdam University Press, 33–50.

Witt, M. and M. Temple (2004) ' A New World', in M. Witt and M. Temple (eds) *The French Cinema Book*. British Film Institute, 183–93.

Wood, R. and M. Walker (1970) *Claude Chabrol*. New York: Praeger.

INDEX

A History of
British Publishing

John Feather

/R

ROUTLEDGE
London and New York

First published in 1988 by
Croom Helm Ltd

First published in paperback in 1988 by
Routledge
11 New Fetter Lane, London EC4P 4EE
29 West 35th Street, New York, NY 10001

Printed in Great Britain by
Biddles Ltd, Guildford and King's Lynn

British Library Cataloguing in Publication Data

Feather, John
  A history of British publishing.
  1. Great Britain. Publishing industries,
  to 1986
  I. Title
  338.4'70705'0941
ISBN 0–415–02654–7

Library of Congress Cataloging in Publication Data

ISBN 0–415–02654–7

Contents

Preface

The sonorous phrases of the Book of Common Prayer have echoed through the hearts and minds of the English people for nearly four centuries. On the three or four thousand Sundays of a lifetime, men and women have heard the priest 'publish' the banns of marriage. The dictionary definition of the verb 'to publish' is 'to make known' or 'to make public', and it is in that sense that the priest uses it. It is, however, generally understood to apply to one particular form of making known or making public: the issuing for sale of printed matter, whether books, magazines or newspapers; more recently the producers of computer software have also begun to describe themselves as publishers. What is a publisher, and what is the process of publishing? It is perhaps easier to define what a publisher does not do. He does not write books. He does not print them, or bind them. He does not sell them to those who will read them. He is essentially a middleman between author and reader, but to perform that role he must undertake many complex tasks. He commissions or accepts books from authors. He prepares their manuscripts or typescripts for printing. He arranges for the production of the book by printers and bookbinders. He organises the provision of illustrations and dust jackets. He advertises and promotes the book in his catalogue and through various media. Finally, he sells his books, not to readers, but to booksellers and distributes them through the booksellers to the individuals and institutions who are his ultimate customers. The publisher therefore is an organiser; but he is also a financier. All of the operations of publishing are funded with the publisher's money. He pays his authors, he pays editors, illustrators, printers and binders. The promotional budget is his responsibility. Moreover, almost all of this money has to be spent before a single copy of the book can be sold. The publisher is, in the most literal sense, the capitalist of the world of books.

It is comparatively easy to define what a publisher does, but perhaps rather more difficult to define what he owns. He makes little capital investment in equipment beyond that of an ordinary office. He can function with few staff, for almost all of the operations of publishing can be undertaken on his behalf by others on a freelance or agency basis. How then does this capitalist ensure that he makes a profit on his investment in a book? He does so in a way which, although not unique to publishing, is nevertheless essential to it. The publisher owns the exclusive right to publish his books. When he buys a book from an author he buys more than the paper on which the words appear. He buys the words themselves, or rather the arrangement of them which the author has made in writing his book. A property, created by the author from his intellect or imagination, is traded with the publisher on the understanding that once sold or leased it cannot be sold or leased to anyone else. Copyright is the cornerstone of publishing in a free-market economy. Without the protection which it affords, the publisher could not risk his money in a business which is, at the best of times, uncertain.

The organisational role of the publisher, and the central importance of copyright to the publishing industry, are two of the principal themes of this book. The former antedates the invention of printing, but the latter is a product of the age of the printed book. Although books had been objects of commerce before they could be printed, it was the invention of printing which created the modern publishing industry. Printing was a technology which could multiply by a factor of thousands the capacity to reproduce texts. It brought with it, however, like any new technology, its own commercial and social challenges. The production of books in large numbers meant that they had to be sold in large numbers. Markets had to be discovered and exploited, or developed where none had existed before, if the products of the printing press were to make profits for their producers. These markets had to be accessible through networks of distributors who could take the books to the customers who would be their readers. These commercial imperatives, and the mechanisms which were developed to meet them, are the third theme of this book.

The dissemination of the printed word was not, however, received as an unmixed blessing. Despite the advantages which it offered to its users, it was, and still is, often perceived as a danger by those to whom ideas seem dangerous. The censor was never far behind the printer in early modern Europe, and the fourth theme of this book is how publishers worked with or against the censors as they went about their task.

In the history of the publishing industry in Britain, these four themes have varied in importance over the centuries. The twentieth-century British publisher happily has little concern with censors, although a degree of censorship still exists. For his sixteenth- or seventeenth-century forebears it was a matter of daily concern. The modern publisher accepts the existence of the law of copyright, but rarely pauses to consider it. Yet his business is possible only because the law exists, and he can thank his predecessors in the seventeenth and eighteenth centuries for the work which they did in establishing both the validity of the concept and the law which embodies it. The market for books has undergone almost continuous change over the last five hundred years, although there are periods of comparative stability and periods of rapid development. These cannot be divorced from the wider social, political and economic developments of the society in which they took place, any more than the changes in the economic structure of the publishing industry can be understood separately from the changing nature of commerce and industry as a whole. At different times in the last five hundred years, different concerns have predominated in the publishing world. These are necessarily reflected in the emphasis given to them here. Thus in writing of the sixteenth century, much space is devoted to the control of the press by authority; it is a subject largely irrelevant to an understanding of the trade in the nineteenth and twentieth centuries. Similarly, the problems of mass distribution and sales which are fundamental to an understanding of the trade since the beginning of the nineteenth century were far less prominent in earlier periods when fewer books were produced and fewer people could read them.

One characteristic of British publishing has, however, remained largely unchanged since the fifteenth century: a small number of producers marketing their products through a large number of retailers. For the greater part of that time, those producers have been in London, either by law or by inclination. London has exercised an almost total dominance of British publishing, and however important the provincial, Scottish and Irish markets may have become since the eighteenth century, publishing activity in Britain is essentially confined to a single city. In this book, which is a history of British publishing and not a history of the book trade or of the book in Britain, that dominance is inevitably reflected on every page. My objective has been to show how British publishing has developed over the last five hundred years, and to explain why it has taken the directions in which it has travelled, in short, to show how it came to be what it is today. The publishing industry is now one of Britain's major earners of foreign exchange; for fifty years or more it has consistently exported about 40 per cent of its total output, and has carried the language, literature, culture and scholarship of Britain throughout the world. The unique cultural value of the products of the publishing industry give the industry itself a unique cultural role. Its history is therefore of concern to all who would seek to understand the development of British society, and it is in the hope of achieving that understanding that this book has been written.

John Feather
Loughborough University

Note to the paperback edition

For this reprint, I have been able to make a small number of minor corrections.

J. P. F.
Loughborough University
May 1988

Introduction
The Book Trade Before Printing

In the middle years of the fifteenth century, when the German goldsmith Johann Gutenberg was beginning the experiments which were to lead to the invention of typographic printing, the form of the book with which he was familiar was already sixteen hundred years old. The codex, folded sheets held together in a binding, had gradually displaced the scroll between the first century BC and the third century AD, until it had become the only form in which texts were normally copied.[1] The trade in manuscripts was even older than the codex itself. There is evidence for a commercial book trade in ancient Athens and its existence is well authenticated in Rome. Scribes working for booksellers made copies of texts for individual customers or for authors to distribute to their friends, or even speculatively for the bookseller to offer for sale.[2] After the fall of the Western empire at the beginning of the fifth century, the copying of manuscripts retreated into the monasteries, and it was not until the twelfth century that it emerged again into the sphere of commerce. This crucial development took place in Paris, and thereafter commercial book production developed in most of the major cities of the West.[3]

In England there was a commercial book trade in the fourteenth century, and a hundred and fifty years before printing was introduced into the country in 1476 it was sufficiently highly developed for the scribes who wrote the manuscripts to have formed their own trade gild in the City of London. The scribes were sometimes employed by wealthy individuals who wanted a copy of a particular text,[4] but they also worked for the stationers who by the middle of the fourteenth century were acting as intermediaries between the scribes and the bookbuyers. The stationers were the publishers of the late Middle Ages. They co-ordinated the work of all the craftsmen who were involved in the production of manuscript books, the scribe, the illuminator and the bookbinder, and were also the suppliers of the materials, either paper or vellum, on which the book was written.[5] Literary manuscripts were copied in considerable quantities and often to a high standard by commercial scribes. There is even evidence for a particular scribe being associated with a living author, and working under his direction as his 'publisher', preparing a

1

number of copies of a new work for circulation to patrons and friends.[6] Moreover, the crafts of book production were not confined to London. There were commercial stationers working for the universities in Oxford and Cambridge,[7] and there is evidence for a book trade in York and other cities before the invention of printing, although even at that early date there is a suggestion that for manuscripts of the highest quality the bibliophile would turn to the London book producers.[8]

Late medieval England was certainly not a bookless society. The ownership of books was not uncommon among the richer classes, both clerical and lay, and the evidence for it is abundant in inventories, wills, catalogues and incidental references.[9] Books were undoubtedly expensive,[10] but they were available and in limited circles of society they were familiar. Printing did indeed cause a revolution in the world of the book but it did not create that world. Many of the skills of the manuscript book producers were carried over into the age of print. The codex form itself was retained, and with it the binding. Of all those involved in manuscript production it was the bookbinders who suffered least from the new invention. In fact, their skills were in greater demand than ever before because of the vast increase in the number of books which was being produced.[11] In the transitional period between manuscript and print, we find the work of the same binders on both manuscripts and printed books,[12] and although the increase in the number of books forced the binders into developing cheaper and simpler forms of binding the basic principles remained unchanged.[13]

It was into this world that the printers brought their new art. The first English printer aimed his books at the traditional market of upper-class readers, but his contemporaries and successors looked elsewhere to the worlds of the law, of commerce and of education. Many of the great manuscripts of the middle ages were produced in monastic scriptoria for liturgical use, or to adorn the monastic library for the glory of God; the tradition of monastic scriptoria was still alive in the fifteenth century, and as late as 1485 carrels for copyists were included in a new cloister at Christ Church, Canterbury.[14] By the middle of the fifteenth century far more books and documents were being produced commercially for mundane reasons of administrative convenience or profit, although some monastic houses also produced manuscripts for sale.[15] It was this commercial element which was to be emphasised by the invention of printing. The monastic scriptoria, and many of the monastic manuscripts, vanished with the monasteries themselves in the 1530s, but long before that disaster overcame England's medieval bibliophilic heritage, the monasteries and other foundations had recognised that their role as book producers had come to an end. A few houses tried to use printers as they had used scribes, but the commercial difficulties were too great and the attempt was abandoned.[16] The universities, also great producers and consumers of manuscripts, began to confine themselves to licensing printers to operate within their jurisdiction, although again commercial difficulties inhibited any successful enterprises until late in the seventeenth century.[17] The future lay with the commercial stationers and their successors, but they were able to build on centuries of tradition as they became the unwitting creators of a cultural transformation and a new industry.

Part One:
The Press in Chains 1476–1695

1

The Book Revolution

The invention of typographic printing in the middle of the fifteenth century is properly recognised as one of the turning-points of world history. Within less than a century, the printed word had transformed the intellectual world of the West, and had facilitated political, religious and economic change. Western Europe's dominance of the rest of the world, built on the solid foundations of its own achievements since the fall of Rome and on the emergence of a capitalistic free market economy, would never have been fully realised without the ease and uniformity of communication and the easier interchange of ideas which was made possible by printing. Like some other technologies and ideologies now considered distinctively 'western', however, printing was not unknown outside Christian Europe. A form of printing from carved wooden blocks was in use in China and Korea in the sixth century AD, but there is no evidence that this was known in the West or that it influenced in any way the evolution of similar block books which may have been produced in Europe before the invention of printing from type.

In any case, typographic printing was based on a crucially different principle. Its inventor, Johann Gutenberg, a German goldsmith, developed his technique from the realisation that the smallest unit into which all the western languages could be divided was the individual letter. The 23 (or in some languages 26) letters of the Latin alphabet repeated in varying combinations was the basis of his invention. Each letter was cast as a single piece of type; the mould from which the cast was made could be used more or less indefinitely. Therefore he could produce vast quantities of identical type which could be combined and recombined to produce words. This is the essence of Gutenberg's invention; he had to develop the press itself and the means of using it but here there were precedents for him to follow. Type was the key because it was type which made printing comparatively simple and comparatively fast.

The immediate impact of printing should not, however, be overemphasised. Edition sizes were small for most of the fifteenth century, although even the 250 or 500 copies which were probably the norm was a number far in excess of anything which the largest existing scriptorium could have produced in a comparable time. The real problem was that of distribution and sales, a persistent theme in the history of the book trade. Printed books were soon being sold at trade fairs, but the ultimate market was a difficult one to reach. Although Western Europe had an essentially common culture and educated Europe had a common language, the direct participants in that culture were few and scattered. Small concentrations in the great cities, in Paris, Cologne, Basle or Rome, were separated by hundreds of miles of unimproved waterways and difficult or even dangerous roads. Yet, to be successful, a printer had to reach these outposts of literacy and learning. Not surprisingly, it was such cities which themselves became the centres of the new craft in the 1460s and 1470s but even they could not provide a sufficiently large local market. It was international trade which provided the basis for the early economic success, such as it was, of the printed book, and hence it was the Latin texts of the common culture which formed the bulk of the work of the fifteenth-century printers.

The printed word penetrated only slowly towards the fringes of Western Europe. One measure of this is the date of the introduction of printing. In the 1460s, printers reached Italy, the Netherlands, Switzerland and France, the heartlands of the West. Only in the next two decades, however, did they venture further. In 1473, the first printers were established in Budapest, Cracow and Barcelona. There were no printers in Scandinavia until 1482 (Denmark) and 1483 (Sweden); it was not until 1487 that a printer reached Portugal. Printing had crossed the Atlantic to Mexico in 1540 over twenty years before it was to be found in Russia in 1563. The introduction of printing into England was part of the second phase of its dissemination, for it was in 1476 that William Caxton established his press in the precincts of Westminster Abbey. England, brought low by external defeat and sapped by civil war, lay at the edge of the world, isolated both by the surrounding sea and her obscure and virtually unknown language. Even her great university at Oxford, once the equal of Paris or Bologna, had fallen into provincial obscurity, while the Englishmen who had absorbed something of the intellectual ferment which was brewing in Italy were few indeed. It was not very promising ground in which to plant a printing press.

Even so, printed culture did make its way into England, and it did so before Caxton went to Westminster. As early as 1465 an English clergyman, James Goldwell, Dean of Salisbury, is known to have bought a printed book in Hamburg;[1] he had successors and perhaps even predecessors. Indeed, in the dissemination of print, as opposed to the art of printing itself, the international trade and culture of Western Europe were central factors. It is possible that some books were commercially imported into England in the 1460s; Caxton himself, at that time a merchant in Bruges, was certainly involved in the trade in manuscripts and may also have dealt in printed books.[2] At least one Latin book was printed on the continent specifically for use in England. This was the first edition of the Breviary of the Use of Sarum, the uniquely English version of the western liturgy; it was probably printed in the southern Netherlands in about 1475, and can only have been intended for the English market.[3]

At about the same time as the Breviary, another book was printed in the Low Countries for the English market. This was Caxton's own translation of a French romance, *Recueil des histoires de Troie*, which he printed in 1474–5, under the title *Recuyell of the histories of Troy*.[4] Caxton had translated the work at the request of Margaret, Duchess of Burgundy, the sister of Edward IV and his patron at the Burgundian court where he had some sort of diplomatic status.[5] In 1475, Caxton travelled to Cologne, probably on official business, and while there he learned the art of printing from Johann Veldener. Whether this was in fact the real motive for his journey is not known, but there can be no doubt that it was a momentous consequence.[6] Veldener himself left Cologne at the same time as Caxton and settled in Louvain; it may be that they were together and that it was there, rather than at Bruges, as was traditionally supposed, that the *Recuyell* was printed.[7] Whether it was produced in Louvain or Bruges, there can be no doubt of the significance of the book; it was the first to be printed in the English language and it marks the beginning of the British publishing industry.

Caxton printed four other books in the Netherlands,[8] but in

1476 he returned to England. The exact date is uncertain, but on 30 September 1476 he paid rent for a shop in the precincts of Westminster Abbey; he was to remain there until his death in 1492.[9] He had brought home with him a supply of type, and probably some workmen including Wynkyn de Worde, who was to be his successor.[10] The press itself may have been imported, or it may have been built locally to Caxton's specifications; we do not know. We do know, however, that by 13 December 1476 he had produced the first piece of printing done on English soil, an indulgence for which the English commissary was John Gant, Abbot of Abingdon.[11] During the next fifteen years Caxton produced more than a hundred books and other items of which copies are known to be extant; it is more than likely that there were others which are now lost.[12]

As the founding father of English printing (the 'prototypo-grapher' as the Victorians loved to call him) Caxton is, of course, a major figure in the history of British publishing. On the other hand, he was far from being typical either of his successors or of the trade which he helped to create. First, Caxton was not a printer in the literal sense of operating a printing press; he was an employer of labour whose own function was as capitalist and salesman. In other words, he was primarily a publisher. By 1476 Caxton had behind him a solid record of commercial achievement. Since the 1440s he had been travelling regularly between England and the Low Countries and had been established in Bruges since about 1445. There he had become the leader of the prosperous community of English merchants who controlled the trade in cloth exports which was the most prosperous sphere of the English economy, and he had built up a large and successful import and export business.[13] By 1476, he was a wealthy man and well able to indulge his taste for literature. This is not to say that his press was a hobby. It was clearly intended as a profitable enterprise for which he carefully selected titles which would sell to a small but well-defined market.

Secondly, Caxton was not only a businessman but also a diplomat who moved in court circles both in England and in Burgundy, a fact which was central to one aspect of his publishing policy. The links between England and Burgundy were strong; commercial ties were reinforced by the Duke's marriage to the King of England's sister. This was the Duchess Margaret, Caxton's first literary patron. Through her he came into contact with the Duke of Clarence, the king's brother, and the Yorkist royal circle. When he returned to England it was the Yorkist nobility of the court who provided both patrons and customers.[14] Although his Yorkist links caused him some difficulties after the accession of Henry VII, Caxton weathered that storm and his business continued to flourish. To appeal to this courtly audience, Caxton printed many volumes of the romances and poetry which were the dominant literary amusement at the courts of Edward IV and Richard III. Many of these he translated himself from French originals, thereby exercising a decisive influence on the development of language, for it was Caxton's Kentish English which was embodied in print as the recognised form of the language.[15] He also printed the works of Gower, Chaucer and Lydgate, among others, and thus prepared the way for the English literary tradition of the Middle Ages to be transmitted to the writers of the Renaissance.

Because he was patronised by the court, it was natural for Caxton to establish himself at Westminster, the seat of the court and of Parliament, rather than in the City of London, the commercial centre of the kingdom. In addition to the vernacular works for which he is chiefly remembered, Caxton also published a number of liturgical books, devotional treatises and indulgences all of which would have been useful to the clerics who clustered around the Abbey in which his shop was situated. It was, however, the court connection which made Caxton unique and gave him unique opportunities, which he readily seized, to develop his extensive programme of publishing literary works in English. Apart from the religious books, he made little attempt to appeal to an audience outside the important but narrow circles in which he moved.

Others were neither so fortunate nor so constricted. From the high point of typographical and literary achievement which characterised the products of Caxton, the English book trade soon descended into the plains of the mundane work which was to sustain it throughout its subsequent history. Caxton soon had a competitor who, although unspectacular and virtually forgotten, was far more typical of future developments. John Lettou was, to judge from his name, of Lithuanian origin, although he learned to print in Rome. He established himself in the City of London in 1480, and printed a few indulgences and other books. In 1482 he took a partner, William de Machlinia, a native of Flanders, and together they printed the first English law book, *Tenores novelli*, in 1482. This marked the beginning of one of the most profitable fields of early publishing, for the uniqueness of the English common law meant that the Roman law books printed in great quantities on the continent were of little use in England. English law depended largely on precedent and statute; it was a field in which the changeover from manuscript to print was to be both rapid and comprehensive. The statutes from 1327 to 1483 were published by de Machlinia in 1484 or 1485; the first abridgement of them was already in print, having been published by Lettou and de Machlinia in 1482. The same publishers issued the earliest printed Year Books, the reports of judicial decisions which formed the all-important precedents of the common law, in 1482. Within a few years, and less than a decade after the first press was operated in England, the essential documents of the English law were available in print.[16]

Like Caxton's vernacular books, the law books were peculiarly English. There was no market for them outside England, and no reason why any continental printer should trouble to publish them. Indeed, the Englishness of English publishing is one of its abiding characteristics. From the beginning, it was predominantly in the English language, and predominantly literary, legal and popular. Scholarly publishing in England was a much later development, and a difficult one, for such demand as there was could easily be met by the import of continental books as had happened before 1476. Indeed, the import of books in considerable quantities is always in the background of the early history of British publishing. Moreover, it was not only books which were imported, but also materials and workmen. The early English printers, except for Caxton himself, were all foreigners,[17] and indeed an Act of 1484,[18] designed to restrict the activities of foreign merchants in England, specifically excluded 'any scrivener, alluminor, binder or printer of . . . books'. Ironically, then, it was foreigners who established the traditions of English publishing, for it was not until the 1520s that a generation of Englishmen began to dominate the new trade. Indeed it was only in 1534 that the relevant clause of the 1484 Act was repealed,[19] and foreign printers and booksellers were forbidden to practise their trades in England except, in the latter case, as wholesalers.

The import of books on a growing scale in the late fifteenth and early sixteenth centuries created in England precisely the same problem which the first European printers had faced, that of distribution and sale. The basic mechanisms of trade certainly existed through markets and fairs. We know that by the early sixteenth century books were being sold at the major fairs such as those at Stourbridge, near Cambridge, and the St Frisewide's Fair in Oxford. There is evidence that London booksellers travelled to the country fairs, but it is also clear that as booksellers established themselves in country towns they too used this method of sale.[20] The import of books, however, was a small and recent phenomenon compared with import of paper. That trade had begun in the early fourteenth century, and a hundred years later it was a major commercial enterprise. Indeed, England's paper was largely derived from foreign sources until the late seventeenth century and it was not until the 1730s that domestic production was able to meet demand.[21] Paper was imported by London merchants and distributed by them through provincial fairs where they functioned as wholesalers. In the late sixteenth century the shop began to displace the market stall as the principal channel of retail trade, but long before then paper was widely available throughout England. The paper merchants were men like Caxton in his Bruges days, merchants with large and complex businesses; books were often added to these imports, and thus found their way into the mechanisms of domestic trade.[22]

The links between the paper trade and the book trade were inevitably close, and the growth of printing increased them. The printers were among the major consumers of paper and the two trades gradually coalesced so that by the late fifteenth century the combination of printer and stationer was already a common one. When the printers moved into the City of London in the early sixteenth century, and were obliged to join a gild, it was to the gild of scriveners and 'writers of text letter' that they gravitated, a gild which was transformed in 1557 into the Company of Stationers.[23] The early importers of books therefore pioneered the development of a distribution system within England by using the existing channels of trade in association with the dealers in a closely related product. From the little evidence that exists of the sale of English books at fairs it is clear that the English printers and publishers followed their example.

The early sixteenth century was a crucial period in the history of British publishing for it was then that its basic structure was established: it was inward-looking, seeking a domestic rather than a European market; it was for that reason primarily concerned with vernacular books; and it was developing distribution mechanisms which assumed distribution from London to the rest of the country. London's predominance, which has dictated the history of British publishing, was perhaps inevitable, but it was not entirely unchallenged in the early decades of the trade. Until the middle of the sixteenth century it seemed that the trade in England might develop as it had on the continent, where printers established themselves in many cities under the patronage of a local institution such as a monastery or university. In Germany and Italy, lacking central political structures, this was a widespread phenomenon and so, briefly, it became in England.

About two years after Caxton arrived in Westminster, a second printer appeared in England, not in London but at Oxford. This was Theodoric Rood, who apparently came from Cologne, perhaps at the invitation of a group of members of the university or perhaps as a commercial venture. Certainly Oxford was precisely the sort of town to which a printer would have been attracted had it been in northern Italy, but in England the enterprise proved hopeless. Rood began work in Oxford in 1476 or 1477 and was subsequently in partnership with Thomas Hunt, one of the university stationers, but he was in no sense running a university press. He printed fewer than twenty extant items, and vanished from the scene in 1486. Most of his books were patristic or classical texts for which the English market was miniscule, and we may take it that the first Oxford press was a commercial disaster.[24]

A similar, and similarly unsuccessful, enterprise existed in the early 1480s at St Albans. The Benedictine Abbey of St Albans had been a major centre of manuscript production for centuries, had assembled a proportionately large library and had attached to it a very successful school.[25] The first St Albans printer, whose name is unknown, produced his first book, an edition of a work on rhetoric, in 1479 or 1480. Between that year and 1486 eight books were produced, including two in English for a secular market. The St Albans printer, apparently a master at the school, obviously worked as an amateur. He had no real commercial interests and was no competition for the London printers.[26] Two other monastic houses encouraged printers in the last years of their own existence. In 1525 there was a printer at Tavistock Abbey, under the patronage of a monk, Thomas Richard, who produced an edition of Boethius, and in 1528 John Scolar, already established as a printer in Oxford, printed a Breviary at the abbey in nearby Abingdon.[27]

The other early presses outside London were also associated

with towns which had a long ecclesiastical or educational tradition. In 1520 a group of humanists invited John Siberch to Cambridge where he printed a few books under their patronage before returning to his native Germany. He was as unsuccessful as Rood had been in Oxford in establishing a learned press.[28] Both Canterbury and York had presses before the middle of the sixteenth century; Frederic Freez may have been printing in York as early as 1497–8 and was certainly doing so by 1509, while there was a printer at Canterbury by 1536.[29] In Ipswich, the native town of Cardinal Wolsey who founded a college there, Anthony Skolokar may have been printing in 1547, followed in 1548 by John Oswen, who is alleged to have printed four books in the town before moving to Worcester to print religious books for distribution in Wales in 1549.[30]

It is easy to dismiss all this activity as trivial and marginal, but it would be wrong to do so. It is clear that a number of individuals and institutions did feel the need for printed books. The monastic houses, especially perhaps St Albans with its great history of book production, saw the printing press as an extension of their traditional concerns. Certainly the one consistent theme running through the history of these early provincial presses is that the printers were working for a patron as a scribe might have done in earlier times. Book production by patronage was, however, no longer viable in the age of the printed book. To produce a single copy of a printed book is a commercial and technological nonsense; to produce 500, however, or even 150, requires a distribution and marketing system which the patrons simply did not have. The monasteries and universities and cathedrals of England, great institutions as they were, could not themselves provide a sufficient market, and were not equipped to reach markets elsewhere. In retrospect, these presses can be seen not so much as the harbingers of the new age but rather as the last heirs of the medieval tradition of localised book production for local use.

The centrifugal forces which concentrated the English book trade in London had their origins in economic imperatives. The trend was, however, reinforced by political considerations. The initial impact of the printed word was on the traditionally literate classes, the clergy and the lawyers and a small group of courtiers and wealthy merchants. However great that impact may have been it was nevertheless confined to this elite; when, however, it began to be seen that the dissemination of print was beginning to disturb the very foundations of society kings and bishops began to take a closer interest in the new art.[31] This interest became closer from the 1520s onwards as the unity of western Christendom was wrenched apart by the Protestant Reformation.

Centralisation of government and closer control of all manner of activities was a policy pursued by Yorkists and Tudors alike in their attempt to restore the power and the wealth of the debilitated English monarchy. The royal prerogative was generously defined and widely exercised, a process from which printing did not escape. In 1484 Richard III's parliament had encouraged foreigners to come to England to practise the various branches of the book trades;[32] in 1528, Henry VIII issued a proclamation which strictly limited the number of aliens employed and forbade aliens to open new bookshops or printing houses, while at the same time encouraging them to take English apprentices. In 1534, the 1484 Act was repealed, printing restricted to English subjects and strict controls imposed on imports by foreigners.[33]

Superficially, this was a measure designed to protect the economic interests of the growing number of English printers and booksellers, and certainly it had this effect.[34] It also ensured, however, that all of those involved in the book trades were indisputably in the royal jurisdiction. The explicit prohibition on book imports by foreigners was undoubtedly intended to prevent the import of books, whether in English or Latin, which were politically or religiously unacceptable to the crown. It marks in fact the beginning of the restrictive controls which were to characterise the English book trade until the end of the seventeenth century and which residually survive even today.[35]

It was not only imports which were controlled. In the early 1520s, Lutheran books were publicly burned in London; in 1525 Wynkyn de Worde was brought before an ecclesiastical court for printing an unacceptable book; and in 1526, Thomas Berthelet suffered the same fate for publishing an innocuous work for which he had not sought prior permission.[36] Throughout the 1520s and 1530s the controls were made more stringent as Henry VIII and Cromwell forced their own version of the Reformation on the English church. In 1538, the king finally systematised the *ad hoc* developments of the previous twenty years; in another proclamation he required that all books should be approved by the Privy Council or designated members of it before publication. This procedure survived the further religious changes under Edward VI and the Catholic reaction under Mary I. Not until 1557 did the queen and the hard-pressed Council begin to seek an efficient but less burdensome alternative.[37]

Censorship was not the only manifestation of royal interest in the book trade; from Henry VIII's reign onwards a series of privileges, patents and monopolies was granted to various individuals within the trade for various reasons. In 1504, William Facques was appointed as King's Printer with the right and the duty to print royal proclamations, statutes and the other 'crown' books. Although the early history of the office is sometimes obscure, it is nevertheless continuous from that year. By 1508, Facques had been succeeded by Richard Pynson; on Pynson's death in 1530, it passed to Thomas Berthelet, and in 1547 from Berthelet to Richard Grafton. By that time, it was a highly lucrative position, but in 1553 Mary I took away certain of the Printer's rights and conferred them separately on others. This was an important decision, for what Mary did was to grant to Richard Tottel the sole right to print all common law books, and at the same time to forbid all others to do so. This was not entirely without precedent. In 1539, Berthelet had petitioned Henry VIII for similar privileges with regard to the Bible; the king accepted the principle, but the privilege was actually conferred upon Thomas Cromwell. After Cromwell's execution, it was transferred to Anthony Merler, a merchant who was in fact one of Grafton's financial backers. In 1543, Grafton himself was granted similar rights in service books and primers, to which the statutes were added in 1547.[38]

There was, however, an essential difference between Tottel's patent and those in Bibles, service books and statutes, for Tottel's covered a whole class of books, including any written after the granting of the privilege, whereas the earlier patents had related to specific books. It was these class privileges, or monopolies as they were to be known to their opponents by the end of the century, which multiplied in the next few years. By 1559, Tottel had the sole rights in all law books; by the late 1570s similar privileges covered not only law books, Bibles and prayer books, but also almanacs, ABCs, catechisms, Latin books, grammars and printed music. The list was to be extended yet further before 1600.

Royal censorship and royal patents both re-emphasised the concentration of the trade in London. Provincial printers were difficult to control and were discouraged; a second experiment in printing at St Albans was brought to an abrupt end when two

17

Protestant books came from that press in 1534–8.[39] Whatever geographical diversification that might have developed was effectively halted by the need to have books approved, in London, before publication, and by the concentration of the most profitable parts of the trade in fewer and fewer hands. By the late 1550s, there was a clear community of interest between the crown, with its desire to control the press, and a small group of printers eager to obtain and to defend special privileges. This was never more apparent than in 1557 when the old gild of text writers and scriveners was reconstituted as the Stationers' Company, which was to dominate the English book trade for nearly a hundred years.

2

Books in the Marketplace

When Queen Elizabeth ascended the throne in 1558, the art of printing had been practised in her kingdom for less than a century. During that comparatively short time, however, the printed book had begun to make fundamental changes in the lives of many of her subjects. The ancient crafts of book production had been virtually eradicated by the new art, and the economics of the book trade had been radically changed. The need to intervene in the free flow of printed matter, which had been felt since the reign of Henry VIII, testifies to the importance ascribed to the printing press and its products. For the printers and booksellers, however, such considerations of state were subordinate to their commercial concern with the selling of books. Printing made it comparatively easy to produce books, but exacerbated the problem of sales. The foundations for the future successes of the book trade lay in the existence and expansion of the market for books.

Caxton's publishing policy was clearly a recognition of the importance of market forces,[1] and the gradual increase in the number of printers and in the number of books which they produced can be seen as a series of explorations of the potential of the English market for printed books. It is a story of failure as well as success; the experiences of Rood in Oxford and Siberch in Cambridge both suggested that scholarly publishing along the lines developed by several printers in Venice or Froben in Basle was not viable in early modern England.[2] The success stories of the first century of English printing were all in the production of vernacular books for the English market; English printers could not compete with their continental rivals in the international trade, but they had the English market to themselves.

The size of the market was ultimately defined by the number of people who could read. It is impossible to deal in accurate statistics in considering the extent of literacy in the fifteenth and early sixteenth centuries, but some general patterns are clear. The upper classes, both nobility and gentry and both men and women, were, on the whole, literate in both English and French and frequently in Latin as well.[3] Even so, there were regional variations of some significance, and as late as the second half of the sixteenth century there was still a substantial amount of illiteracy even among the gentry in the north-east of England, although it had virtually vanished before the Civil War.[4] Lower down the social scale variations were more marked, and the degree of illiteracy generally greater. Literacy was more common in the towns, and especially in London, than it was in the countryside, and among tradesmen there were clear distinctions between trades such as vintners and grocers where literacy was normal if not universal, and those such as gardeners and thatchers where it was very unusual.[5] Clearly, there is a correlation between the complexity of the activity and the need for literacy in order to pursue it.

The extent of literacy depended on the availability of the means to acquire it, and having acquired it, of both the means and the motivation to retain it. The fifteenth century saw the foundation of many new schools, although universal education was never the objective. The function of the schools was to provide clergy and a pious laity rather than to further secular ends. Despite the fact that at least some schools, especially in the chantries, provided free education to all-comers, or offered financial assistance to poor scholars, education was in practice restricted to those whose family circumstances made it possible to spare the time for their children to be educated.[6] As in the developing countries today, for the great majority of the rural poor the need for hands, however small, to help in the fields and the cottage was far more urgent than learning the skills of a remote ruling class. Nevertheless, some progress was made in the fifteenth century, and it brought with it the partial secularisation of education. Especially in London, with its great demand for literate tradesmen, there is evidence of independent schoolmasters catering for a market which was not necessarily served by monastic or cathedral foundations.[7]

When Caxton established his press at Westminster he knew that a market existed for the sort of books which he intended to publish. His audience was the nobility, the gentry and upper tradesmen whose literary tastes were for the books which he published. It was a taste which he understood well, for this was his own class. From the beginning, English printers were marketing their books to the educated laity, as well as to the clergy, and it was the law, the greatest of the lay professions, which provided one of the greatest opportunities for the pioneers of English publishing.[8] The printers were obliged to look for their markets and to publish books which appealed to them. Caxton's market was a narrow one, and represented a passing phase of literary fashion at court. The demand for more mundane books was far more stable and of far greater long-term significance.

At the most rudimentary level, the process of learning to read offered an important opportunity to the publishers. The elementary medieval grammar texts, such as Donatus, were soon in print, but even more important were the new grammars which were written in the late fifteenth century. John Anwykyll, the first Head Master of Magdalen College School, Oxford, had been influenced by the contemporary Italian grammarians, and his *Compendium totius grammaticae*, published by Rood and Hunt at Oxford in about 1483, was the first humanist Latin grammar published in England.[9] His colleague at the school, John Stanbridge, was also a grammarian, whose *Accidence* was to become the standard introductory work for many years. Stanbridge, like his younger contemporary Robert Whittinton, was published by both Pynson and de Worde, and both produced many profitable editions of their works.[10] These early humanistic grammars were all eventually replaced by that compiled by William Lily for St Paul's School in 1513; in its final form, first published in 1542, it became the officially prescribed grammar for all schools in England, and the right to publish it was the subject of a profitable and contentious patent.[11] The rights in Lily were still valuable enough for the young Thomas Longman to acquire them in the early eighteenth century.[12]

The more advanced student of the classics had to use editions printed abroad. Few classical texts were published in England, although from Caxton's time onwards there was always a stream of translations, through which the majority of Englishmen acquired what knowledge they had of ancient culture and literature. Caxton published a translation of Cato in 1477, and others followed. Among the most popular authors were Ovid, Aesop, Vergil, Plutarch, Cicero and Seneca. These translations were perhaps more important culturally than they were commercially, but their publication in considerable numbers in the fifteenth and sixteenth centuries argues that there was a steady market for them.[13] It was not only Latin and Greek works which were translated into English. The sixteenth-century vogue for Italy was reflected in number of translations from that language, although the number fell towards the end of the century when Italian dictionaries and grammars began to be published in England and the language itself more widely studied.[14]

The output of translations, of classics and even of schoolbooks, however, seems puny when set beside the flood of religious publications which poured off the presses of London and the provincial towns in the fifteenth and early sixteenth centuries. Among the major printers of the period, Caxton, de Worde, Pynson and Berthelet all devoted about 40 per cent of their production to religious books of one sort or another. Moreover, this has to be seen in the context of the import from the continent of the majority of liturgical books intended for use in England.[15] From the beginning of printing in England, vernacular books intended for the devout layman formed an important part of the products of the press, and played a significant role in laying the foundations for an economically viable trade in printed books. The real flood, however, came with the Reformation, which provoked a vast controversial literature which in turn provoked Henry VIII and the advisers of Edward VI into stricter measures to control the press. Lutheran books were being imported in the 1520s, and a domestic controversial religious literature developed soon afterwards.[16] At the height of the English Reformation in 1548–50, the number of books published increased fivefold, and attained a level not to be equalled during the next twenty years.[17]

Despite the fact that so many books, including many entire editions, have been lost, it is clear that from its very beginning the publishing industry relied on books which could command a large market. Indeed, the economics of the production of printed books meant that it could not do otherwise. Of course, this has to be understood in the light of a small population, and restricted literacy, as well as an underdeveloped system for the sale and distribution of books, but even so it was clear that the market was there if the printers could reach it. In every field, we find evidence for books which were clearly aimed at a 'popular' market, even in subjects like law and medicine. By the middle of the sixteenth century, there were books published which would assist the local magistrate in carrying out his increasingly onerous duties, and there were 'medical' treatises which distilled the essence of centuries of folk wisdom and the lore of the herbalists.[18] The gradual spread of literacy down the social scale created a market for books on a much wider range of occupations, especially those associated with farming.[19] All of these subjects came together in the almanacs and prognostications which were to form the basis of another profitable group of patent books.

Prognostications, single sheets in which an astrologer presented his predictions for the coming year, had been familiar in manuscript before the invention of printing, and there is a number of continental examples of printed versions in the fifteenth century. The first printed prognostication in English was published in 1502, and thereafter there was a steady stream of them year by year. Gradually, the prognostication and the almanac took on a more substantial form, becoming a small book which contained not only predictions but also useful information on the weather, farming, medical and veterinary matters and similar material of general interest. By the middle of the sixteenth century, the predictions were becoming increasingly political, and indeed, despite the efforts of successive censors, the almanac continued to be a vehicle for political comment until the middle of the seventeenth century.[20] The almanacs attained an immense popularity; quite apart from their practical value, they had a strong appeal to a society in which traditional beliefs still competed with formal religion in the popular imagination.[21]

The patterns of publishing which were quickly established after Caxton's return to England remained constant for many years to come. The book trade became larger and better organised, and the number of titles published grew significantly decade by decade throughout most of the sixteenth and seventeenth centuries, but changes in the kind of books which were published came only very slowly. Above all, religious publishing lay at the very centre of the trade's success, changing only in response to the changes made in the official religion of the kingdom. The Protestant emphasis on Bible-reading and the sermon were both significant to the trade. The Bible became part of the patent of the King's Printer,[22] but sermons were open to competition, and many thousands were published, especially from the Puritan wing of the Church of England in the late sixteenth and early seventeenth centuries.[23] The printed word became the medium of religious instruction and propaganda, particularly for those denied access to the pulpit. Of no group was this more true than the Roman Catholics, whose books were banned and who responded both by surreptitious production in England and by illegal import of books printed abroad.[24] Indeed, there were times during the reign of Queen Elizabeth when the Puritans had to resort to similar tactics, most notably in the famous affair of the Marprelate Tracts in 1588–9 when large numbers of pamphlets were printed at various secret locations and widely distributed.[25]

In their different ways, the astrologers and the religious polemicists had both discovered the political potential of the printing press. It was a point which was not lost on governments. In England, in Henry VIII's reign, printing was used both for propaganda ' purposes through the publication of proclamations,[26] and as an instrument of administration. The printed form, designed to enquire into some matter of interest to the government, or to provide, for example, the basis of a tax assessment, was in use by the 1530s.[27] The publication of pamphlets to explain the government's views or actions became common during the sixteenth century; some were overtly 'official' publications, but others were given a superficial objectivity by ascribing them to 'independent' authors.[28] The importance of the press was recognised at an early date by successful governments throughout Europe, especially during times of great upheaval such as the Reformation. Although this recognition had the negative effect of provoking the development of strict and elaborate systems of censorship, it also had the opposite consequence of forcing kings and their ministers into making use of the power of the press for themselves. Through such means, the printed word gradually became not merely a part, but an essential part, of English society. The shift from an oral to a printed culture should not be overemphasised, but it was undoubtedly beginning in England in the sixteenth century. In the first phase of printing, the texts which were published were those which had been available through manuscripts to a literate elite for many centuries. In the second phase, however, which in England began in the very early sixteenth century, there were two parallel developments which laid the next layer of the foundations of a print-dependent society. On the one hand, oral traditions were put into print, and on the other, books were specifically written for printed publication.

By the end of Henry VIII's reign traditional ballads, or ballads based on traditional stories, were beginning to find their way into print as single sheets, as often sold by pedlars as by booksellers.[29] The use of medieval folk traditions in this way continued throughout the century. Just as Caxton had published the romances which appealed to the aristocracy of the late fifteenth century, so his successors transformed them into a genre which appealed to the gentry and upper tradesmen. Translations of French and Spanish romances were still popular at the end of the sixteenth century, and new versions of the old stories of Palmerin or Amadis de Gaule appeared regularly. Gradually, the anonymous stories were adapted by English authors, or imitated by them. John Lyly's *Euphues* (1578–80) was one of the first of these, and exercised a seminal influence on a whole generation of writers. Robert Greene, an early rival of Shakespeare in the theatre, was the author of *Pandosto*, a 'euphuistic' work published in 1588, whose story later formed the basis of *The Winter's Tale*. The prose romances, whether influenced as these two were by Italian originals, or derived from English traditions such as Robin Hood or Guy of Warwick, were the first substantial body of literature designed to amuse rather than to edify and demonstrated the existence of a market for light reading for leisure.[30]

By the end of the sixteenth century literature, in the broadest sense, had become a commercial commodity. The rewards of that commerce, however, were for the printer, publisher and bookseller rather than for the author. This is not entirely surprising, for it was the printer who had taken the medieval book out of the scriptorium and into the marketplace. The economic realities of printing, and of the sale of printed books, meant that it was the publisher who was financing the production and distribution of books, and that it was therefore he who principally reaped the benefits when profit was generated. The publisher, whether or not he was also the printer of the book, was, however, under pressure from the market himself. In the earliest years of printing in England, and indeed elsewhere in Europe, a small number of printers/publishers were able to survive by printing the common heritage of the Middle Ages which was freely available, sometimes in hundreds of manuscript copies.[31] The authorship of many works was unknown, or so remote as to be irrelevant; in other cases, such as the law precedents, the very concept of authorship was meaningless. The marketplace, however, created its own demands on the publishers. Printing provided a technology which was able to satisfy an existing demand for books, but the demand did not cease when the first group of texts had been made available in print. Indeed, it was self-perpetuating, for the wider availability of books made it easier for more people to learn to read and then to retain the skill of literacy. In turn, that created a demand for more books in greater numbers, and it was because of that demand that the book trade became a flourishing and profitable occupation in the sixteenth century. Endless reprints could not satisfy this growing market. Changing political and religious circumstances and changing tastes and fashions created a climate in which new books were needed, as well as more copies of the old ones. In turn, that meant that the publishers had to find authors who would write their books for them.

The professional author, like the professional publisher, is a product of the age of the printed book. By the end of the fifteenth century books were being written which would not have been written had there not been a press on which to print them and a book trade through which to sell them. It was already apparent that the long-term development of the book trade would depend upon the willingness of authors to write books which the public would wish to buy. It was to be two hundred years before the full implications of this were recognised, but even in the sixteenth century, the conditions of authorship underwent significant change. The medieval author worked for himself, for God or for a patron, or indeed for all three. The role of the patron was to provide material support for the author as he might have done for any other servant. This might take the form of appointing him to an office in the patron's gift, or direct financial reward, or some combination of the two. Whatever form patronage took, it was a means of paying the author for his book which, however, gave him no reason to expect any further payment.[32]

Such a system could not survive entirely unchanged in the commercial environment which enveloped the book world after the invention of printing. It is true that some printers were, in effect, the patrons of their authors. Froben supported Erasmus, many of whose works he published, and Aldus maintained a veritable academy of classical scholars in Venice in the early sixteenth century.[33] Nevertheless, the patronage system was inevitably modified by printing. One practice which developed in the sixteenth century was that of dedicating a book to a patron, actual or potential, in the hope of financial reward.[34] In

Elizabeth's reign, the Earl of Leicester was a munificent patron, to whom scores of books were dedicated in this way, and who used the patronage system to further his own political and religious ends.[35] Queen Elizabeth herself, however, despite her later reputation, rarely patronised authors.[36] Young authors sought a patron in or close to court circles to support them and to lend respectability, as Shakespeare did in dedicating *Venus and Adonis* to the Earl of Southampton, or, among lesser authors, George Puttenham when he dedicated his *Arte of English Poesie* (1589) to Burleigh, Elizabeth's Lord Treasurer.

Patrons, however, were unable and unwilling to lend their names to the very works which were becoming most profitable to the book trade. The trade itself became involved in the process of causing books to be written, beginning the shift away from patronage to payment. Almanacs were compiled by astrologers whose income came from other sources, such as casting the horoscopes of the wealthy,[37] but the manuals of advice on a multitude of secular subjects, and the growing number of versions and translations of popular stories, were written by men who sought their financial rewards from the printer and publisher rather than the patron. Patronage was still the most important source of support for many writers throughout the sixteenth century,[38] but gradually publishers began to pay their authors a little for the right to publish their books. It was impossible to make a living from writing,[39] except perhaps from writing for the stage,[40] but it was increasingly possible to generate some sort of income. Sometimes a publisher would give an author a number of free copies (usually 26) which he could sell for his own profit, or perhaps use to present to an existing patron or to attract a new one.[41] Despite the financial obstacles, and despite the contempt in which those who wrote for money were held by their more fortunate contemporaries, authorship was a recognisable occupation by the end of the sixteenth century. At least another century was to elapse before the professional author could take some pride in his profession, but 'writing for the booksellers' as it was to become known, was necessary for publishers, authors and readers alike if the flow of new books was to be sustained.[42]

By the middle of the sixteenth century the print revolution was visible to all who chose to see it. The transition from scriptorium to printing house was more than merely a change from one form of book production to another. So great was the difference between the two that the change provoked a profound shift in the intellectual, political and religious life of the West. It was an unplanned revolution, and one which came so stealthily that governments were sometimes slow to notice it and slower to exploit it for their own ends. Within the world of the book itself the changes were perhaps more immediate than in society at large. Above all, the rapid triumph of the printing press forced upon the book trade a new set of problems and priorities. The production problem was solved at a stroke by the invention of printing, but it brought in its wake the problem of sales. Printed books could only be commercially produced if they were to be sold in large numbers, and that meant the wider dissemination of books than had ever been possible, or even desirable, in the Middle Ages. The availability of books created the demand for more books, and for authors to write them. It created also the perception of the need to control this ever-increasing flood of words. It might seem that the interests of the producers of books and the state were inevitably to conflict, and indeed such confrontations did take place from time to time. In England, however, the book trade arrived at a compromise with the state which was to be the foundation of its prosperity. The first years of the trade in printed books in England were disorganised and even anarchic, but as the state recognised the importance of the new trade, and the printers and booksellers themselves came to recognise the need to protect their investments, it came to be accepted that some form of control was necessary for commercial as well as for political reasons. There was a growing market for the products of the press, and a growing number of authors to provide books to satisfy it. The book trade became the intermediary between the author and his audience, and it is that intermediary role which is the very essence of publishing.

3

The Foundation of an Industry

The early attempts of the crown to bring the book trade under control were not entirely unsuccessful. The various regulations issued by Henry VIII were substantially enforced but the very success of the trade made enforcement increasingly difficult. The growing demand for printed books and the consequent increase in the numbers of printers and booksellers made the task of control ever more complex. This was not only a problem for the crown; it was also a problem for the trade itself, and especially for those within it who had made substantial investments in equipment and personnel. By the middle of the sixteenth century it was clear that if the trade was to be properly regulated and organised, as contemporary opinion held that every activity should be, new mechanisms would be needed to achieve that end. The mechanism which emerged was the Stationers' Company — the Worshipful Company of Stationers of London, to give it its full title — whose history from the 1550s to the early eighteenth century is central to the wider history of British publishing and whose residual influence survived long after its legal position had been undermined.

Like the book trade itself the Company existed before the printed book. As early as 1357 the writers of legal documents and the illuminators of manuscripts had a craft gild in London; after a brief separation, they were reunited in 1403 and the reorganised gild included both booksellers and bookbinders.[1] Gilds were more than mere trade organisations; they were an integral part of the political structure of the City of London. The right to trade in the City was granted only to freemen of the gilds, but freedom itself was granted only after a period of apprenticeship in a livery company. The freedom of a gild and of the City were thus interlinked, so that it was the gilds who provided the elected officers who conducted the City's public business and defended its cherished rights.[2] Conversely, a man who was not a freeman could not trade in his own name or operate his own business, so that full membership of a gild was the necessary foundation of a commercial career in London. The situation was, however, complicated by the physical expansion of London itself. Around the City boundaries, suburbs had developed in which the City's writ did not run, and even within the City itself there were 'liberties' which were exempt from the City's jurisdiction. In the suburbs and the liberties anyone could practise a trade without any gild regulation at all.

The gild of stationers[3] could and did regulate the production and sale of books in the City, but in fact most of the early printers were outside its control in the liberties or, as in Caxton's case, at Westminster.[4] The booksellers and bookbinders inevitably became deeply involved in the trade in printed books as it developed in the early sixteenth century. The assimilation of the printers into the gild to which most of these men already belonged was a rather longer process. It was possible, but not easy, for aliens to become freemen of the City; the first printer to do so may have been Henry Jacobi, a Frenchman, at some time before 1509.[5] The first major printer in the City's jurisdiction was Julian Notary who was trading in St Paul's Churchyard by 1515 at the latest, and probably as early as 1510; he was probably not an alien.[6] His shop in the precincts of the Cathedral set a fashion which was to be followed for over two hundred years, for the area around St Paul's became the very heart of the book trade and the links were not finally broken until after World War II.

Although both the history and organisation of the gild of stationers is obscure, it is clear that by the middle of the sixteenth century it was exercising considerable influence over the economic organisation of the trade.[7] Nevertheless, the next stage of its development was as spectacular as it was unexpected; it can only be understood in the context of the trade which it came to control.

There seems little doubt that in the early fifteenth century the dominant powers in the gild were the scriveners ('writers of text letter', as they called themselves) who were responsible for the production of manuscripts and legal documents; in fact it was almost certainly the latter which provided the bulk of their trade. The activities of the scriveners were displaced from the 1470s onwards, spectacularly so in the case of the law-book scribes, but two special factors need to be considered. First, the printers did not immediately join the gild because the London printers, being aliens, could not, and Caxton, being at Westminster, did not need to do so.[8] Thus it was not until printing had been established for nearly a century that the printers were able to develop a political profile in the trade comparable with their economic and technical importance. Secondly, within the trade itself one of the first consequences of the establishment of a domestic printing industry was a vastly increased demand for paper. From the handful of books produced in the 1470s and 1480s output rose to more than 500 editions in the 1520s and more than 1,000 in the 1550s. In 1550 alone, more than 200 books were published.[9] In 1560, the earliest year for which we have even partial statistics, 26,432 reams of paper are known to have been imported, rather more than 12 million sheets.[10] Imports on this scale could only be undertaken by wealthy merchants, and the importers were the wholesale stationers who were, for the most part, citizens of London and members of the stationers' gild. It was, therefore, the stationers and not the printers who had become the dominant group in the gild by the middle of the sixteenth century through their control of the supply of the most fundamental raw material of book production. Indeed, it was not until ten years after the gild was reorganised in 1557 that the printers were able to take control of the trade which they had transformed.

The medieval gild of stationers was a City institution, but in 1557 it was granted a royal charter and thereby acquired all the advantages of corporate legal status. Most of the Charter is concerned with the minor organisational matters which are necessary to any corporate body but two provisions were crucial to the future development of the trade. These were, first, a *de facto* ban on printing outside London, and, secondly, the Company's involvement in the procedures of pre-publication licensing.

The ban on provincial printing was not explicit, but the Charter restricted the right of owning a press to members of the Company; by definition the freemen were citizens of London, and in the sixteenth and seventeenth centuries were normally resident there. In practice, this had little meaning in 1557. So far as is known, there had been no provincial printing since Oswen's venture at Worcester came to an end with the accession of Mary I in 1553,[11] and none of the early provincial enterprises had been very successful.[12] Although the provision was to be slightly modified in future years, printing was henceforth effectively confined to London until the end of the seventeenth century. The Stationers had their own reasons for supporting this policy; the English market for printed books was so small that even limited and localised competition was unwelcome. It was also a policy which was attractive to the crown; censorship was more effective if printing could be confined to London where control could most easily be exercised.

The Charter also made provision for the Company itself to become inextricably involved in the process of censorship. The preamble states that the Charter is being granted to control 'scandalous, malicious, schismatical and heretical' books,[13] although that may well have been a pretext rather than a reason, as we shall see. The Charter, however, does seem to envisage that the machinery of control resides in the rights granted to· the Company: the right to control entry into the trade by regulating apprenticeship, the prohibition on printing by non-members and the rights of search and seizure in pursuit of illegal books.

In 1559, Elizabeth I issued a series of Injunctions which clarified the definition of what could and could not be printed.[14] The most important provision refined the earlier system of licensing by requiring new books to be approved either by six Privy Councillors or by any two of the Archbishops of Canterbury and York, the Bishop of London, the Bishop and Aldermen of the place of printing, or the Vice-Chancellors of the two universities.[15] No other books are to be printed, and all subjects of the crown, 'specially the Wardens of the company of Stationers', are to obey these regulations. This is the first official recognition of the Company's explicit role in enforcing the licensing system, and the legal basis for the practices which developed during the next decade.

Before tracing those developments, however, we must return to the Charter, and consider the reasons why it was granted. There has been considerable controversy about this, essentially revolving around whether the initiative came from the crown or from the gild. There is almost no direct documentary evidence on the matter, so we can do no more than interpret the Charter itself and subsequent events.[16] Grants such as that made to the Stationers in 1557 were normally a result of a petition to the crown asking for a charter or other document; if there was such a petition it has not survived, but the one document which is extant suggests that the normal procedures, which were in any case statutory, were followed.[17] Secondly, the members of the gild had a clear commercial interest in obtaining a charter which gave them a conjoint monopoly over their increasingly profitable trade; this the Charter certainly granted them. Both of these considerations argue against a crown initiative, as indeed does the general tendency of Mary I and her advisers to ignore, somewhat foolishly perhaps, the significance of the printed word.[18] The whole line of argument is strengthened when we consider the alleged motive of the crown, the control of the press, for there was no need to create a corporation when there were existing executive decrees to the same end. Moreover, there is nothing in the Charter which grants the Company any rights of censorship or licensing, and the Injunctions make it quite clear that it was envisaged that the traditional system, somewhat modified and augmented, was to be continued. Far from being a 'master-stroke of Elizabethan policy',[19] the grant of the Charter was a perfectly regular transaction for the benefit of the gild of stationers which we may take to have been initiated by them.

If there was a 'master-stroke' it came not from the crown but from the Company itself in the early 1560s when it realised the ways in which it could exploit both the Charter and the 1559 Injunctions. The Stationers were named in the Injunctions for the obvious reason that they were more likely than anyone else to be involved in surreptitious printing. The Company, however, was already beginning to evolve its own 'licensing' system for a different purpose, to protect the interests of individual freemen. The Charter granted to the Company the right of self-regulation, and in 1559 a new set of ordinances was drafted for this purpose.[20] Among them there is the crucial requirement that 'Every book or thing [is] to be allowed by the Stationers before it is printed',[21] and it seems that it was already the custom to record this permission in a register.[22] In 1562, when the Company finally agreed and issued its Ordinances, this provision was repeated.[23]

The Company's ingenuity lay in the use of the word 'allow' which had been in use for decades to describe the permission to print granted by the censors. Within the Company, however, the word was used in a significantly different sense. It meant the right to print a particular book, or 'copy', granted by the Company to an individual Stationer on the implicit understanding that no other Stationer had previously obtained the same right. This was essential to maintain good relations within a corporation whose members were all engaged in the same highly competitive trade, but it also provided precisely the mechanism which the crown needed for the enforcement of its own control of the press, since no book was 'allowed' (in the Company's sense) until it had been 'allowed' or licensed by the royal censors.

We do not know how rigorously the regulations, especially the censorship regulations, were actually enforced,[24] but it is clear that some books did not go through the hands of the censors, and that in the 1560s the Company began to register copies which did not have the formal authority of the censor's licence. The officers were naturally very careful in doing this, and gradually they became involved in the censorship process itself. The Stationers' Company in the late sixteenth and early seventeenth centuries was indeed the agent of the crown, but it was so by its own choice, for by keeping good order in the trade and thus avoiding the need for government intervention it guaranteed both its own import-ance and the protection of its members against competition. In 1566 this was explicitly recognised in an Order-in-Council which gave additional powers to the Company to police the trade for illegal books,[25] and in 1586 in a decree of the Court of Star Chamber which fully acknowledged the Company as an equal partner with the crown in the suppression of undesirable books.[26] The 'master-stroke' was indeed complete; the Stationers, over a period of less than thirty years, had so impressed the authorities with their orthodoxy and efficiency that they had been officially accepted as an integral and essential element in the regulation of the output of the book trade.

Before considering the far-reaching implications of this achievement, we need to turn briefly to the organisation of the Company itself in so far as this affected the development of the trade. The central fact about the Stationers' Company in this period is its comprehensiveness; the Charter, the Injunctions of 1559, the Ordinances of 1562, the Order-in-Council of 1566 and the Star Chamber decree of 1586 were all aimed, from varying motives and with different approaches, at a single end: restricting the right to print to a limited number of known and reliable persons. In the Charter this was perhaps conceived as granting that right to all members of the Company, although such liberality of intention may be doubted and was certainly never practised. Almost from the beginning of the Company's chartered existence, the freemen were divided into two distinct groups, the Yeomanry and the Livery. When an apprentice was made free, he normally became a Yeoman; if he could afford it, and if he could command sufficient support, he was then eligible for election to the Livery. This was crucial, for date of election as a Liveryman determined a man's seniority in the Company which in turn determined his eligibility for office. The junior office was that of Renter Warden, who was responsible for collecting the Company's debts; two Renter Wardens were elected annually, and were thereafter eligible for election to the Court of Assistants. The Court, which was a self-elective body, was the central organ of government within the Company and the source of all power; from its members the Master and the Upper and Under Wardens were elected. A pattern was soon established; a man served his term as Under Warden, was elected Upper Warden three or four years later, and Master a few years after that. It seems that all former holders of these three offices continued to be members of the Court for the rest of their lives.[27] The Court ruled the Company, and was increasingly dominated by past office-holders. In this lay the key to the triumph of the printers in the 1560s and the resentment of that power which came close to destroying the Company some forty years later.

The first Master, in 1557, was Thomas Dockwray, a lawyer who had presumably been involved in the legal work necessary to obtain the Charter.[28] During the next ten years, only four men held the office: John Cawood (1561, 1562, 1556), Richard Waye (1558, 1563), Reyner Wolfe (1559, 1564, 1567) and Steven Kevall (1560, 1565).[29] Cawood had been Queen's Printer since 1553, survived the transition from Mary I to Elizabeth I, and was obviously a politically wise choice. Waye, Wolfe and Kevall, however, were quite different. Although Wolfe was a printer, printing was a very small part of a very large business and neither Waye nor Kevall ever printed at all. They were booksellers and stationers, both of whom were probably involved in the import of paper. Wolfe was also heavily committed to the import trade; he was a native of the Low Countries, although he had been in England for many years and had been naturalised in 1533. He made his fortune as a book importer and did not even begin to print until 1542.

In its early years, therefore, the Company was dominated by importing wholesalers not by printers, but the printers were gradually laying the foundations of their power. Richard Jugge and William Seres appear to have been responsible for this. Jugge was Upper Warden in 1560, 1563 and 1566; Seres was Upper Warden in 1561 and 1565. Behind them were two or three other printers, notably Richard Tottel (Under Warden, 1561; Upper Warden, 1567 and 1568) and John Day (Under Warden, 1564 and 1566). In 1567, after a decade of oligarchy by Cawood, Waye, Wolfe and Kevall, the printers made their move. For nine of the next ten years, Jugge and Seres shared the mastership between them; the only other Master in that decade was Wolfe in 1571. By the early 1570s a whole group of printers had served as wardens, and the Court was dominated by them; Seres was succeeded by Tottel in 1578 and Day was Master in 1580. From then until well into the next century control by the printers was secure. Their power was based on their access to the limited production facilities in an expanding trade, and by using this power they were able to reinforce it even further. By the mid-1570s, the right to own a press was confined to a small group within the Livery, called the Master Printers; there were probably never more than about 25 of them before the Civil War.[30] Their position was officially recognised in 1586, when the Star Chamber decree required that the Court of High Commission had to approve their appointments.[31] By that time the trade was firmly in the hands of the printers, both politically and economically, and they were able to entrench their position yet further by their use of the system of patents and privileges.

The patents, from their almost casual origin in the reign of Henry VIII,[32] gradually came to embrace nearly all of the most profitable areas of publishing. Day, for example, had held a patent on the *Catechism* in English since 1553, and in 1567 became patentee for the *Psalms* and the immensely valuable *ABC*, the elementary reading book prescribed for use in schools.[33] Tottel held the law book patent, and Seres that for primers. Perhaps the most valuable of all the patents was that of the Queen's Printer; when Christopher Barker was granted the office in 1583 he acquired with it sole rights not only in all official printing, but also in Bibles, service books and statutes. The patents represented a formidable concentration of economic power in a select group within the already select Master Printers, and they also represented a challenge to the evolving system of internal licensing which had been developing in the Company since the early 1560s.[34]

Protests against the patents began in the early 1570s. A number of them had been reconfirmed since 1557, notably Day's in 1560 and 1567 and the Watkins and Roberts patent for almanacs and prognostications in 1571.[35] The problem was economic; the number of freemen was increasing, but the number of Master Printers was virtually fixed and unchanging. In the early 1580s the troubles came to a head. A considerable number of printers had already been fined by the Company for infringement of the patents, and a few cases had even reached the Privy Council.[36] Day was, as the chief patentee, the first victim. A petition by the unprivileged freemen to the Privy Council in 1577 named the *ABC*, which Day owned, as a major grievance, and meanwhile piracy of it grew apace. In 1582, Day appealed to the Privy Council himself, and subsequent investigations proved that Roger Ward had printed at least 10,000 illegal copies of the *ABC*.[37] In the same year, John Wolfe also pirated both the *ABC* and the *ABC and Little Catechism* for which William Seres had the patent. Wolfe was actually imprisoned for these offences, but in fact these cases were to have far more important long-term consequences than the temporary inconveniencing of one notorious pirate.[38]

It was in fact the Day case which provoked the official investigation into the affairs of the trade and the Company which led to the 1586 decree, but even before then a different solution to the immediate problem was being evolved within the trade itself. After John Day's death in 1584, his son Richard succeeded to his business,[39] and continued to prosecute pirates. He also, however, made an agreement with Wolfe, the leader of the anti-patentee group, under which in 1584 or 1585 Wolfe became one of five assignees of the Day patents. Thereafter, and especially after the 1586 decree, John Wolfe himself was an especially vigorous prosecutor of pirates.[40] The Day patent was now a complex piece of jointly owned property and the Seres patent soon took on the same character.[41] The problems of managing these jointly owned patents were solved (or at least shelved) by allowing the Court of Assistants to play an increasingly important role. In effect, the Court regulated the operation of the patents by granting the actual printing of the patent books to various less prosperous freemen on behalf of the patentees, and then making arrangements for the disbursement of the profits. By the 1590s this operation had its own Treasurer and in 1603 it was formally incorporated as the English Stock of the Company.[42] At the same time, its financial basis was reorganised, with the agreement of the assignees of the patent; the Stock was divided into shares of a notional capital of £9,000. To satisfy the demands of the majority, while retaining control in the hands of the Court, the 105 shareholders delegated the management of the Stock to a committee consisting of the Master, the Wardens, and two representatives each of the Assistants, the Livery and the Yeomanry. The five seniors could always outvote the four representatives of the lower ranks, despite the fact that there were 60 Yeomanry shares (of £50 each) and 30 Livery shares (of £100) as against only 15 Assistants' shares (£200). Vacancies among the shareholders were filled by the Court of Assistants, and these were in much demand, for the annual dividend in the early seventeenth century ran at about 12½ per cent per annum.[43]

The creation of the English Stock out of crown patents was an achievement as noteworthy as the Company's *de facto* takeover of crown licensing. The ruling oligarchy had strengthened their hold on the trade, and even in making concessions to the poorer freemen they had evolved a system which gave the yeomanry a vested interest in maintaining the rule of their superiors. As a pragmatic solution it was ingenious, but it did not address the fundamental problem: too many men chasing too little work. By the early seventeenth century it was a common practice for the printing of a single book to be shared by two or more printers,[44] a practice which reflected an important change which had overcome the trade in the previous thirty years. The printers, who had so confidently seized power in the 1560s, now found their position challenged by a new group, the copy-owning booksellers.

The patents were one of the early forms of copyright; the other was that which developed from the record of licences in the Register, although the distinction was not absolute and the two had a common origin in crown grants of privileges to print. The Company's licence was, as we have seen, distinct from the censor's licence as early as the 1560s; the latter was a generalised permission for the book to be printed, while the former granted the specific and unique right to do so to a named person. This was regulated by the Company's Ordinances of 1562, not by any of the various official decrees. It was an internal matter under the control of the Court of Assistants, which indeed devoted much of its time to dealing with disputes about the ownership of copies. The basic principle upon which the Court operated is clear: the first person to enter a copy in the Register was the sole owner of it and had the sole right to print it, provided that no other member of the Company had a prior claim which could be properly documented.[45] Although entry was never actually required by the Company in this period, it was the only way of establishing an unchallengeable claim to a copy, for the person requesting the entry had to satisfy the Wardens of his right to do so.[46] Although failure to enter a copy was not itself an offence, it is stretching the evidence to suggest that unchallenged publication had the same effect as an entry.[47]

Licences could be granted to any freeman of the Company, but they began to accumulate in the hands of a small group of men and were handed on to their widows and children. These people included some who were printers, but more who were not, and as the number of freemen increased in the late sixteenth century the proportion who were copy-owners declined. In 1579 James Gonneld was the first Master since Steven Kevall in 1565 who was not a printer,[48] but the real harbinger of the future was his successor William Norton; Norton never printed, but he was a large-scale owner of copies.[49] During the 1580s and 1590s most Masters were printers, but the rising generation were not. Francis Coldock (Under Warden, 1580 and 1582; Upper Warden, 1587–8), Ralph Newbery (Under Warden, 1583–4; Upper Warden, 1589–90), Gabriel Cawood (Under Warden, 1589–90; Upper Warden, 1593–4) and Isaac Bing (Under Warden, 1594; Upper Warden, 1595 and 1598) were all copy-owning booksellers and all were future Masters.[50] Printers continued to hold office occasionally, but by the 1620s their former dominance had vanished; between 1620 and 1639, five Masters were printers and six were not, but the six booksellers, all copy-owners, held the office for eleven of the nineteen years.[51]

The printers' loss of their power, like their acquisition of it, was a consequence of the economic realities of the trade. Although some Master Printers were copy-owners in the early seventeenth century,[52] many were not, and the booksellers increasingly came to regard the printers as agents rather than equals. The printers had been undermined partly by the increase in their own numbers, but more importantly by the development of the licensing system. The Company licences allowed those who were not printers to accumulate a form of capital as important as printing equipment or the office of Master Printer, for the copy-owners held the rights in the copies which the public actually wanted to buy. The early decades of the seventeenth century in fact saw the beginning of the separation of the printing and publishing functions which was to be the future pattern of the trade.[53]

It was, however, only the beginning and should not be

exaggerated. In 1640, as in 1580, the Master Printers were also booksellers, most owned copies, many were Assistants and some were shareholders in the English Stock. They were still a very important group. Beneath them, however, was a growing class of journeymen who could never aspire to a Master Printer's place, or perhaps even to the Livery. In 1586, there were 21 Master Printers, who had between them 39 presses; by 1637 there seem to have been 26 active printing houses in London and perhaps 50 presses.[54] The bulk of the actual production capacity could be readily absorbed by the growing, but still modest, demand for printing; the pool of trained labour could not. The Master Printers were binding and freeing apprentices at a rate which was flooding the market. In 1580, 14 men were made free of the company, and ten years later there were 15. Thereafter, the figures rise dramatically. In 1601–10, an average of 24 men a year were freed; in 1611–20 there were 34 a year; in 1621–30 there were 29; and in 1631–40 there were no fewer than 42.[55] Not all of these new journeymen were printers, but the proportion of printers' and non-printers' apprentices in this period did not significantly change. There was not enough work to go round, and new tensions inevitably developed between the oligarchs and the majority.

The alliance between the oligarchy and the crown, upon which the power of the Court ultimately depended, received a final reinforcement in 1637 when a new decree of Star Chamber reiterated some existing regulations, strengthened others and, crucially, officially recognised some of the customs of the trade which had developed since 1586.[56] The provisions for crown licensing of books were made stricter, and to ensure proper control two copies were to be given to the licenser, one of which to be retained and one taken to Stationers' Hall for registration. For the first time, entry in the Register was required rather than encouraged, a clear victory for the copy-owners. At the same time, penalties for printing illegal books or printing by unauthorised persons were drastically increased. Like previous regulations, and like the controversy about patents, the 1637 decree has to be seen in a broader context. The whole thrust of crown policy in the 1630s, under the direction of Laud and Strafford, was centralisation and control. Laud was concerned about the growing divisions in the Church of England and the opposition to his ecclesiastical policies. Fully aware of the power of the press, he sought to control it; in secular matters, Laud's enemies in the

Church were equally the enemies of the crown's policy in the Thirty Years' War, the last of the great wars of religion, which had been raging since 1618. While the Swedes and the Dutch went to the defence of their fellow-Protestants in Germany, England stood aside, to the indignation of the growing Puritan minority within the Church. Once again, the state and the leading members of the Stationers' Company had interests in common, and the 1637 decree satisfied both parties. This happy conjunction of interests was not destined to last. In 1640, Charles I was forced to call a parliament; its successor, the Long Parliament, abolished Star Chamber, imprisoned Laud and executed Strafford. The oligarchy within the Stationers' Company was severely shaken by the beginning of what was to be two decades of revolution. The old certainties never returned, although much of what had evolved between 1557 and 1640 survived as fundamental practices in the trade.

During the eighty years when it dominated the English book trade, the Stationers' Company had obtained many remarkable benefits for its members. The trade had been recognised as an important element in the state. Its senior members had learned to work with the highest levels of government and had successfully achieved many of their own objectives. The consequences of their success were profound. The parallel evolution of crown and Company licences had laid the foundations for the practice, and later the law, of copyright. The Company takeover of the rights of the crown patentees had created a valuable source of income both for the Company itself and for its members. The trade in 1640 was more prosperous than ever before, even if the typical unit was still small. Most printers had two presses, two or three journeymen and an apprentice; the bookseller had an apprentice and his family and perhaps a journeyman. Nevertheless, the demand for books could be met, and channels of distribution were being developed which would take the products of the press to every corner of the kingdom. Already there were booksellers in the major provincial towns buying books from London and selling them locally. Internally, the trade was indeed dominated by successive oligarchies of importers, printers and copy-owning booksellers, but their very success ensured that some of results of that success were available to everyone.

The copy-owners were the men of the future. By 1640, they were firmly entrenched as the leaders of the trade; it is a position that they have never relinquished. Long-standing family businesses were beginning to develop; intermarriage between these families was not uncommon and over two or three generations dozens of valuable copies were being concentrated in a few firms. The story of the English book trade for the next 150 years is the story of these men and women who asserted their power inside the Company and outside it to retain their dominance of the trade and their own substantial share in its financial success.

4

A Taste of Freedom

The collapse of crown authority in London in 1641–2 and the subsequent outbreak of civil war had far-reaching consequences for the book trade. The oligarchs were open to many fashionable criticisms. Their control of the trade rested on the authority of the crown expressed through the courts of Star Chamber and High Commission, both abolished in the first phase of reform in 1641. Their economic power was reinforced by the Court of Assistants' effective control of the English Stock which, like other monopolies, was coming under attack. Within the trade there was a growing group of malcontents, economically disadvantaged and politically alienated, who were attracted to the anti-royalist groups which had come to dominate the House of Commons. Indeed, many livery companies experienced similar difficulties at this time.[1] In this situation, it is hardly surprising that the Assistants came under intense pressure to reform the Company.

The rumblings of discontent which had first been heard in the attack on the patents in the 1570s came out into the open again in 1641. Michael Sparke, the leader of the group, already had a history of trouble-making. He had been well known as a publisher of Puritan books in the late 1620s and throughout the 1630s, one of his publications being the notorious *Histrio-Mastix* (1632) for which both he and William Prynne, the author, had stood in the pillory.[2] Sparke was an active sympathiser with the Puritan cause in a political as well as a religious sense, and he also had good economic reasons for opposing the trade's hierarchy. He did a good business in Bibles imported from Holland, a trade conducted in defiance of the rights of the King's Printer which Sparke justified, probably accurately, on the grounds that his imports were cheaper than the legally produced domestic article. With the breakdown of royal control, Sparke seized the opportunity for a more general assault. His pamphlet *Scintilla, or a light broken into dark warehouses* (1641) was a wide-ranging attack on the Stationers' Company, the English Stock and the patents, again based on the argument that book prices were kept artificially high by the existence of the monopolies. The Court of Assistants reacted by appointing a committee; this body investigated Sparke's allegations, but it deliberated for a year and by the time that it reported Sparke himself had lost his enthusiasm for this particular cause for the time being. In 1643, he declined the office of Renter Warden, offered to him as a conciliatory gesture, and thereafter dropped out of sight for several years.[3]

Sparke's challenge to the authority of the Court was only one of several troubles which beset the trade in the early 1640s. In one sense, the political and military events of these years were beneficial to publishers. The demand for news of public events produced a huge crop of pamphlets and newsbooks, but much of the potential benefit was lost to the trade's establishment as many of them were printed without licence and sold on the streets. This outburst of publishing would not have been possible without the pool of surplus manpower in the trade, and it did at least have the effect of absorbing some of that. It was, however, anathema to the Court of Assistants and their allies. Even the semblance of control had broken down by the spring of 1642. The House of Commons had appointed a Committee for Printing in 1641 which was intended to oversee the trade, since the House suspected, rightly, that there was a number of royalist sympathisers in the upper reaches of the Stationers' Company. The Committee was wholly ineffective. Over the next two years, the situation deteriorated even further. The trade was rife with piracies, including piracies of the almanacs which were becoming the most valuable part of the English Stock; the newsbooks were out of control both in content and in production and distribution. Neither a direct order from the House of Commons to the Company in 1642, nor the Ordinance for the Regulation of Printing which the House issued in 1643 had any significant impact on the flood of printed matter.[4]

No real solution was within the power of Parliament itself, and certainly far beyond any possible action by the Court of Assistants. The licensing system existed only on paper, the English Stock was being challenged by men who might reasonably expect parliamentary support and, in practice, both sides in the Civil War were more interested in the use of printing for propaganda than in protecting the investments of the copy-owning booksellers. Even the London monopoly of printing, the ultimate basis of the trade's structure, was challenged, and that in the most formidable way. In March 1642, Christopher Barker, the grandson of the King's Printer and acting on his behalf, joined Charles I at York, and over the next seven months issued more than seventy books, pamphlets and broadsides. Although much of this output was of royal proclamations and similar documents, some of it was more overtly propagandist and was part of the war of words which preceded the outbreak of fighting between the king and some of his subjects.[5]

There was no doubt of the King's Printer's right to print the privileged material wherever he wished; indeed there was a precedent, for in 1639 John Legatt, also acting on behalf of Robert Barker, had travelled with Charles I to Newcastle-upon-Tyne during the Bishops' War, and had produced at least four items there.[6] Throughout the Civil War, Christopher Barker was with one or other of the royal armies, at Shrewsbury in 1642–3, at Bristol from then until 1645 and finally for a few months in 1646 at Exeter.[7] There is evidence to suggest that in Exeter, if not elsewhere, the presses were also used by other people for non-official work. Although this was not a major commercial danger to the London monopoly it was another breach in the defences of the trade.

Throughout the Civil War, the trade was dominated by political propaganda in various forms. In London, printing houses proliferated despite every attempt to prevent this, and the output of printed matter vastly multiplied. The bookseller George Thomason, a leader of one of the groups of malcontents within the trade and a supporter of the parliamentary cause throughout the war, collected some 23,000 newsbooks and pamphlets in the 1640s and 1650s.[8] The production of printed matter on this scale was a wholly new phenomenon not merely in quantity but in content. Proclamations, new laws and similar official documents had been printed since the early sixteenth century. The same was true of official versions of public events, which can be traced back to a pamphlet called *The trewe encountre* published shortly after the Battle of Flodden Field (1513) which it describes.[9] The periodical newsbooks, the ancestors of the modern newspaper, first appeared in England in 1621, but they were banned in 1632 and although they were revived in 1638 it was not until the political struggle intensified in 1641 that they came into their own.[10]

The newsbooks of the 1640s were quite different from their predecessors which had been generally neutral in tone and confined by the licensers to foreign news. From 1641 onwards the newsbooks were politically committed and almost entirely concerned with domestic affairs. By the summer of 1643 a newspaper war was running in parallel to the real war, co-ordinated on the royalist side by the remarkable Sir John Berkenhead, who has some claim to be regarded as the first English editor. Berkenhead's newsbook, *Mercurius Aulicus* began in January 1643 and survived until the very end of the war; the last issue appeared on 7 September 1645. It was printed in Oxford, the royalist headquarters for the whole of this period, although it may also have been reprinted in Bristol in the winter of 1643–4. It was widely circulated even in London, and was regarded as a major problem by the parliamentarians and as an important weapon by the royalists.[11] At the height of its career, *Mercurius Aulicus* may have been printed in an edition of at least 1,500 copies, compared with the 250 copies of the pre-Civil War newsbooks.[12] Even this figure falls far short of the print runs of some individual pamphlets in the 1640s, for which 10,000 copies are claimed.[13]

The parliamentary response to the success of the royalist propaganda campaign is significant, for it initially took the form of trying to reinforce the licensing system. Unlicensed news was banned by the House of Commons in March 1642, and the newsbooks were the principal target of the Ordinance of 1643.[14] It is unsurprising in the circumstances that these attempts at regulation failed, and that Parliament eventually reacted by issuing its own newsbooks. Its early efforts were rather half-hearted; throughout the summer of 1643, when Berkenhead was making a strong impact even in London, Parliament could manage only a few irregular issues of its official newsbooks and had to rely on support from privately owned enterprises. In August, however, they found their editor in Thomas Audley who, with his assistant Marchmont Needham, began to produce *Mercurius Britannicus* which never circulated more than about 500 copies but was at least regularly attacked by Berkenhead. It did have some influence although until the very end of the fighting the royalist editors won the propaganda war even when the royalist armies lost the battles.[15]

The traumatic events of the 1640s were to leave their mark on English history in many profound ways. Not the least of these was that the printing press could never again be ignored as an instrument of propaganda. The leaders of the republican regime established in 1649 were well aware of this. John Milton is only the most famous of a group of writers who put their pens to the service of the Commonwealth. In three Latin pamphlets published between 1651 and 1655, aimed at overseas opinion, Milton defended both the rebellion and the execution of the king.[16] It was Milton also who opened, in his *Areopagitica* (1644), a debate on the freedom of the press which was to continue long after the Stuarts had been restored to their throne and had lost it again. In fact, Milton argued for only a limited degree of freedom, and he envisaged that there might still be a need for a licensing system of some sort.[17] Others, especially among the Levellers, took the argument much further, and were soon demanding complete freedom of the press. There was, however, a clear continuity of thought between the Leveller approach to this question and earlier attacks on the trade. In *England's birth-right justified* (1645), almost certainly by John Lilburne, a free press is demanded on the grounds that the oligarchy of the Stationers' Company is exercising the same powers as it had under Charles I and Laud, and that the licensers are still at work.[18] The hatred of monopolies and monopolists had perhaps been the most important single factor in creating the opposition to Charles I, and it was inevitable that the Stationers' Company, as a very visible monopolist, should suffer in the general assault. The newly recognised importance of the printed word merely exacerbated the radical attack.

Throughout the war, the Court of Assistants complained bitterly to Parliament of the chaos in the trade, but Parliament was unable, even had it been willing, to take any realistic measures. Milton himself, later to be the regime's most prestigious propagandist, published pamphlet after pamphlet, including *Areopagitica*, without a licence. In this he was typical. The writers of works which would have been rejected or altered simply ignored the system altogether, and sought the services of one of the increasing number of printers who were quite outside the control of the Company and the Commons alike. The printers were indeed the trade's principal beneficiaries of the war. The booksellers, on the other hand, suffered badly.[19] In 1645, indeed, the printers only just failed to break away from the Stationers altogether and establish their own gild.[20] This was only one of the Company's internal troubles by the end of the war. In 1645, Sparke returned to the attack; with the help of Henry Fetherstone (the former master of George Thomason who was now an influential political figure in the City), John Partridge and others he proposed a new electoral system which would have given more power to the Yeomanry by increasing their representation on the Court. It was at this point that the trade began to split. Sparke's support came almost entirely from booksellers, whose trade had been so badly damaged by the war. The printers supported the Court, and when Sparke seemed likely to succeed they threatened secession. In fact, a compromise was reached which did indeed result in the election of two new Assistants, but the oligarchy, and their control of the English Stock, remained substantially intact.[21]

After the war, however, the internal problems of the Company had to take second place. Lilburne's attack on its 'tyrannical monopoly' found some sympathetic ears in the House of Commons, but the leaders of the Army, which was the last remaining credible centre of power in the kingdom, had other ideas. In 1645, the House had begun to deal in earnest with the sectaries whose influence was spreading everywhere and many of whom were very adept in their use of printed propaganda. In January, they ordered the Stationers' Company to tighten its control of the trade; later in the year, and perhaps rather more usefully, the House put its authority behind the Assistants in their struggle against Sparke and the Yeomanry.[22] From that time onwards, the new government expected, and substantially obtained, the Company's support in regulating the press and indeed a licensing system was developed which might well have justified Lilburne's earlier complaint that the Commons was becoming as tyrannical as Charles I had ever tried to be.

It was the Army which took the first initiative. Fairfax, supported by his senior officers, protested to parliament in 1647 that pamphlets attacking his Army were being published without any restraint. Underlying this was his fear that the lower ranks of the Army itself, rife with members of sects of all kinds, were becoming fertile ground for the spread of democratic ideas. Fairfax added that, despite Parliament's military victory, the number of royalist newsbooks was actually increasing, an indisputably true assertion. Berkenhead was still active, although more as a pamphleteer than as an editor,[23] and even in London a few royalist newsbooks were still being secretly printed. Their publication was irregular, and they were short-lived, but they represented a serious threat to the stability of both the Army and the regime itself.[24] In the summer of 1647 Parliament tried hard to bring the press under control. John Rushworth, the assistant Clerk of the House of Commons, who had been licenser since April 1644, was dismissed in March 1647,[25] but he was not replaced. In September, Parliament tried to put the whole business on a firmer footing, but Gilbert Mabbot, the licenser appointed under a new and stricter Ordinance, was in fact Fairfax's nominee. The Army takeover was apparently complete. After 1647, the regime increasingly tightened its hold on the press. Successive laws were even more repressive and by the mid-1650s only officially inspired newsbooks were permitted. The newsbooks of the last five years of the Interregnum are as dull and uninformative as only such newspapers can be. Lilburne's fears were now fully justified: Cromwell was indeed more tyrannical than Charles and Canterbury.[26]

The immediate effects of all this on the trade were disastrous. The mushroom growth of printers had been stopped, but this had merely increased the numbers of the unemployed or under-employed. The bookselling trade was indeed at a low ebb in the 1650s, with little to sell and few customers. Yet in some ways the trade had survived remarkably well. Despite all the problems encountered in the early 1640s, the power of the Court of Assistants was substantially intact. They had defended the English Stock until the time came when Parliament had more pressing concerns than old grievances about monopolies. The resurgent power of the printers in 1645 had proved to be a temporary phenomenon produced by the breakdown of both economic and political control. Although times were bad in the 1650s, the booksellers, especially those who owned copies, were members of the Court and owned Assistants' shares in the Stock, had the means of regaining their positions when circumstances changed. Indeed, the lesson of the 1640s was that the established powers in the trade needed the support of state regulation as much as the state needed to control the press. Only the old mechanisms of control had actually been destroyed by the Civil War; the community of interest which had sustained them had not, and when Charles II returned to his kingdom in May 1660 it seemed that the Stationers as well as the Stuarts would be restored.

5

The Licensed Press

The two decades between the summoning of the Short Parliament and the restoration of Charles II had been as difficult for
the book trade as they were for the nation as a whole. The
obvious wish to go back to at least some of the old ways in 1660
was an expression of a deeper desire for familiarity and stability.
Yet not everything was, or could be, restored. On one level, the
prerogative courts had gone for ever, and with them at least some
of the powers of the crown. At another level, however, what had
been lost was the mutual confidence of the governors and the
governed. The desire for domestic peace was not for peace at any
price; the lessons of the Great Rebellion could not be ignored, but
the ideas which it inspired were never entirely forgotten. Within
the book trade, the lesson was clear enough: the alternative to
control was chaos. This was not, however, a complete analysis,
satisfactory as it may have seemed to the Master and Wardens of
the Stationers' Company as they joined in the City's official
welcome to Charles II in the summer of his return.

The unstable political structures of the interregnum had
vanished, but the social consequences of the Civil War and its
aftermath were to determine the future course of English history.
The vast output of pamphlets and newsbooks during the war, and
the efforts of Parliament and the Army to control them after it,
was one measure of change. There could no longer be any doubt
of the power of the printed word, or of the hope (and fear) which
it could inspire. Thomason's 23,000 pamphlets are a more
enduring monument of the interregnum than any of the political
or military manœuvrings of those decades; after that experience
the book trade could never be the same again. The newsbooks
and pamphlets had bypassed the bookshops and been sold on the

streets. They had helped to create a wider market for printed matter; it was perhaps even more important that by their very existence they had reinforced the Puritan ideology of the necessity of literacy. Whatever the superficial resemblances may be, the book trade after 1660 was fundamentally different from that which had existed before 1640. The closed world of the oligarchy was on the verge of becoming a publishing industry.

The first task, however, was to sort out the organisational chaos which was the legacy of twenty years during which the Court of Assistants had first had to defend their very existence and then to succumb to the demands of an increasingly dictatorial and now wholly discredited regime. A few things could be easily and swiftly accomplished; for example, the patent of the King's Printer was confirmed to Christopher Barker in partnership with John Bill, sons of the men who had helped Charles I in the early 1640s.[1] Other things were more difficult. With the prerogative courts abolished, and all the interregnum acts and ordinances invalidated, there was no mechanism for government control of the press, although the Company itself still maintained the Register as it had throughout the 1640s and 1650s. In 1661, Parliament rejected a Bill to control the press which would have put licensing in the hands of twelve printers under the ultimate authority of the Archbishop of Canterbury. This was the last attempt to revive the ancient theory that censorship was primarily a matter for the church. When a Printing Act was passed in 1662 it was wholly secular in intention and operation.[2]

The 1662 Act revived all the essential principles of pre-1640 licensing except one. The number of master printers, presses and apprentices was to be limited; printing was confined to London, the universities and (under the supervision of the Archbishop) York; copies had to be entered on the Register to prove ownership; and every copy had to be licensed before it could be entered. The one principle which was not revived was the practice which had evolved in the 1580s of permitting the Master and Wardens of the Stationers' Company to act as *de facto* censors. A Licenser was to be appointed and he was to be subject to the authority of the Secretary of State whose office was to have a general oversight both of the press and of news.[3] The Printing Act may have seemed to be an essentially conservative measure, but this provision was a radical departure from previous practice. It confirmed, in the most blatant way, the powers of the crown over the press; at the same time, however, it brought the whole system, for the first time, into the sphere of parliamentary legislation rather than the royal prerogative, a change which was to prove of great significance.

In 1663, Roger L'Estrange was appointed Licenser and he acted quickly to exercise his powers. The printers were summoned to Stationers' Hall for an investigation of who was and who was not licensed to print; 59 men responded, as against the official figure of 20 Master Printers.[4] Arrangements were made for a period of transition, but L'Estrange was determined to reduce the number to 20 as quickly as possible. In this, as in much else, he never entirely succeeded; by 1666, there were nearly 150 men in London who had served apprenticeships as printers, and as late as 1675 there were still 20 unlicensed printers. Fundamentally, L'Estrange disliked and distrusted the Stationers, and the trade disliked him. To their complaints that there were long delays in obtaining licenses, L'Estrange could reply that several members of the Court were involved in unlicensed printing and that many in the trade did all that they could to obstruct him. Even the election in 1668 of three new Assistants who were crown nominees did not significantly improve the situation.[5] Five years earlier, L'Estrange had successfully opposed the establishment of a Company of Printers, an idea revived from 1645, not out of any love for the Stationers' Company, but because he felt that it was difficult enough to find reliable men to run one livery company in the book trade and impossible to find them for two.[6]

Moreover, the Act under which he was granted his powers was itself impermanent. Like a good deal of post-Restoration legislation it was to run for a fixed period, in this case three years, after which it had to be renewed; this ploy was designed to ensure that there could never again be any attempt by the monarch to govern for long periods without a parliament. The Act was indeed renewed in 1665, but it lapsed in 1679, and a new system of control was needed. L'Estrange was full of schemes, all of which revealed his continuing distrust of the Stationers. He had now decided that the printers were more reliable than the booksellers, and that they should, after all, be encouraged to form their own Company, through which control would be exercised; this they now declined to do. The Stationers' Company was proving a hopeless instrument for control of the press, and even during the mastership of Samuel Mearne, the King's Bookseller and Bookbinder, and one of the royal nominees to the Court of

Assistants in 1668, little could be done. The government was under intense pressure during the summer of 1679. There was a rising tide of feeling against the king's pro-French and pro-Catholic sentiments, and this manifested itself in the attempt to prevent his Catholic brother, James Duke of York, from succeeding to the throne when Charles died without a legitimate heir, as was now inevitable. The Exclusion Crisis of 1679–81 was a situation in which the control of the press was as difficult as it had been in the 1640s. The official reaction was to use the law of seditious libel, an offence derived from medieval statutes which could be interpreted to mean that any attack on the king or his ministers was an act of treason.[7] The advantage of the law was that it could be used to prosecute booksellers, and thus avoid the difficulties of finding the printers of unacceptable books. The disadvantage was the need to prove the offence to a jury. Juries could be, and were, packed but they were often reluctant to convict, especially in London where feelings against the Duke of York were running high. Not until 1681, when the third attempt to exclude the Duke of York failed and Charles II regained control of the political situation, did this policy begin to succeed. Once again, however, it had become apparent that in times of great political controversy it was virtually impossible to suppress the opposition press.[8]

The newspapers of these years taught the same lesson to the authorities. The strict control which had been successfully exercised during the last five years of the interregnum was maintained after the Restoration, although it was increasingly difficult to do so. In 1663 L'Estrange bought the only regular newspaper which had survived the transition from republic to monarchy. This was *The Kingdom's Intelligencer*, which had started life in 1659 as *The Parliamentary Intelligencer* and judiciously changed its title in the following year. The editor was Henry Muddiman, whose services L'Estrange retained for some time. In effect, the *Intelligencer* was an official newspaper, through which L'Estrange exercised the official monopoly of news granted to the Secretary of State under the Printing Act.[9] Although a few non-political unofficial newspapers were published from time to time, this monopoly was kept substantially intact until 1679,[10] but after 1665 the official organ was a new one founded for the purpose by Sir Henry Williamson, the Secretary of State. This newspaper began in 1665 as *The Oxford Gazette*, the court having retreated from London to Oxford to escape the great plague of that year.

When they returned to London, the paper was renamed *The London Gazette*, and is still published under that title. Muddiman was the first editor, although soon after the move to London he was succeeded by Charles Perrolt who held the office for many years.[11]

After the lapse of the Printing Act, a number of new newspapers appeared, many of which were opposed to government policy. L'Estrange's first reaction was to start *The Observator* as a pro-government newspaper, but when this proved unsuccessful more traditional methods were invoked. In 1680, unofficial newspapers were banned by a royal proclamation, but its implementation was only partly successful,[12] and it could be argued that the newspaper press was never again brought under full government control. The difficulty was that the newspapers had become too popular, and, from the government's point of view, this was compounded by the fact that they were read much more widely than their comparatively small circulation figures might have suggested. Since the late 1650s, the coffee houses which had become a notable feature of London life had been making newspapers available to their customers, so that a single copy might be read by dozens of people.[13] L'Estrange's efforts with *The Observator*, unsuccessful as they were, in fact pointed the way to the future, when governments would recognise that opposition propaganda had to be met on its own ground and by the same techniques.

The Exclusion Crisis had one lasting political legacy, for it was during the three exclusion parliaments that two distinct parties began to emerge and applied to each other the opprobrious terms of Whig and Tory which were to become their permanent names even when the ideas which they represented had undergone profound change. Within a surprisingly short time, the idea of the legitimacy of opposition within the framework of the law was to be accepted as a part of the constitution, although the lesson was a hard one for some politicians to learn. It was a lesson which began dramatically. In 1685, the Duke of York did indeed succeed to the throne, but within three years had been driven into exile by the combined efforts of Whigs and Tories, equally opposed to his attempts to revive the royal prerogative and to dispense both with the law and with Parliament. Immediately after his accession, however, Parliament had, at his instigation, renewed the Printing Act, and a new Licenser had been appointed. The Act was renewed again after the Revolution in

1688, and again in 1693. In 1695, however, when it was due for its next renewal, Parliament rejected it.[14] To argue that England suddenly acquired a free press in 1695 is to stretch the truth more than a little, but it was nevertheless an important turning point both for the trade and for the politicians, for pre-publication censorship was never thereafter revived.

The public history of the book trade from the Restoration to the Revolution is, however, a small part of the story, for while Charles II, James II and their ministers struggled to control the press, the trade was undergoing major commercial developments. In 1660, the trade was in a depressed state, but the booksellers still had their basic assets of copies. For twenty years there had been little scope for publishing many of them, but with the Restoration came a revival, and soon a rapid increase, of demand. It was these commercial factors which provoked the great changes which now overcame the trade. Both privately owned copyrights and the English Stock were still of great potential value, and the Stock had a particularly valuable property in the form of the almanac monopoly. Indeed, it was this which in future was to be the foundation of the Stock's prosperity. In the reign of Charles II, the Company was regularly printing and selling some 300,000 almanacs each year; in the 1660s this produced an annual profit of about £1,000, increasing to perhaps £1,500 by the end of the century.[15] No other part of the Stock was so successful, for much of what had been incorporated into it before 1640 was no longer of any great interest to the bookbuying public. The Elizabethan schoolbooks like the *ABC* had at last been abandoned in favour of more recent and unprivileged works,[16] while the Book of Common Prayer of 1662, which replaced all the previous prayer books of the Church of England, was reserved for the King's Printer and the presses of the two universities. This left the almanacs as the only substantial part of the English Stock still in regular demand, but they continued to be a profitable monopoly for the shareholders until the last quarter of the eighteenth century.

To some extent the debate about the patents and privileges survived the Restoration,[17] but in fact the more adventurous booksellers were looking in different directions for their business and were working in a very different way from their predecessors, responding to the changing tastes and interests of the reading public. Immediately after 1660, there was a good deal of reprinting of pre-1640 literary texts which had been out of favour during the interregnum. This was particularly true of plays, the *bête noire* of the Puritans since the reign of Queen Elizabeth. Plays had indeed been printed in the 1650s, but with the reopening of the theatres in the summer of 1660, many more reprints were needed, of which the most spectacular was the Shakespeare Third Folio of 1663–4.[18] Copyrights in pre-1640 books still existed, and had indeed been transferred by entries in the Register throughout the interregnum. By inheritance and purchase these were now more than ever concentrated in a few hands. The process which had begun in the 1590s was coming to fruition, for in the second half of the seventeenth century we can see the emergence of copy-owning booksellers who were consciously specialising in their chosen fields.

Literature is the most obvious of these fields, although perhaps only because it has been the most intensively studied. In 1660, three men were prominent for their ownership of literary copyrights. Humphrey Moseley had been in the trade since 1630 and had steadily accumulated literary copies throughout those thirty years. He published Milton's *Poems* (1645), Donne's *Βιαθανατοζ* (2nd edn, 1648) and *Paradoxes* (1652), and many works by lesser poets including Denham (*Cooper's Hill*, 2nd edn, 1650), Crashaw (*Steps to the Temple*, 1646, 1648; *Delights of the Muses*, 1648), Waller (*Poems*, 1645 (three editions); *Workes*, 1645) and Vaughan (*Olor Iscanus*, 1651; *Flores solitudinis*, 1654).[19] Moseley died in 1661 and most of his copies were bought from his widow by Henry Herringman who had himself already entered some seventy copies on the Register, many of them plays. From 1667 to 1678, Herringman succeeded to Moseley's position as the outstanding literary publisher of his day; copies he owned included Donne, Jonson, Waller and Cowley as well as part of the Shakespeare copyright. By 1680, Herringman was a wealthy man and from then until his death in 1704 he continued to live on the profits from the reprints of his copies.[20]

Herringman has been called 'the first publisher'[21] and certainly he ran his business in a way which gives him some claim to that title. In particular, although he was owner or part-owner of valuable older copyrights, Herringman was also much involved with the publication of contemporary literature. He was Dryden's principal publisher during the early years of the poet's career when he was at the height of his success as a popular playwright. He published, among other plays, *All for Love* (1678), *The Conquest of Granada* (1672), *The Indian Emperor* (1667), *Marriage à-la-mode*

(1673), and *The Wild Gallant* (1669), as well as some of his non-dramatic works including *Annus Mirabilis* (1667). The Dryden copies were a profitable investment for Herringman. With a few minor exceptions, all of them were reprinted several times. *The Indian Emperor*, for example, went through at least ten editions between 1667 and 1700, in all of which Herringman was involved either alone or with others.[22] This was a new kind of publishing, in which the publisher was seeking out works which would be fashionably successful, but would also, he hoped, have a long-term existence. The 'back-list' is another of the characteristics of modern publishing practice which can be traced back to the second half of the seventeenth century.

The third of the literary publishers and booksellers of the reign of Charles II was Francis Kirkman, who had been one of the first to begin the reprinting of pre-1640 plays after the Restoration, an enthusiasm which extended to the piracy of a number of plays whose copies were actually owned by Moseley. Kirkman was also an innovator in another important respect, for in 1661 he opened the first commercial circulating library, an institution which, like the coffee house, was to have a major impact in making books available to those who could not or would not buy them.[23] As well as being a publisher and a librarian, Kirkman was an author, his most notable book being *The English Rogue* (4 parts, 1665–71) which he wrote in collaboration with Richard Head.[24] *The English Rogue* was an early example of a genre which is a product of the period, the fictional prose narrative, the direct ancestor of the novel. These proto-novels introduced a new realism into fiction, and indeed many were based on actual and often recent events.[25] The novel is the only literary genre to have been invented since the invention of printing, and its literary history is inseparable from the history of its publication. In both the eighteenth and the nineteenth centuries the popularity of the novel as a form of entertainment was a factor of great economic significance for the book trade.

In the very different field of scholarly publishing there were also important developments in the late seventeenth century. The insular traditions of English publishing were hard to break, and in the first half of the seventeenth century it was still almost impossible for an English scholar to find a publisher for his work in his own country. The lack of contact between the English book trade and the continent, and the impenetrability of the English language, created almost insuperable obstacles to learned publishing. When Francis Bacon wished to address a European audience in his *Novum organum* (1620) he wrote in Latin as More had done in *Utopia* a century earlier. Two enterprises in the reign of James I illustrate the difficulties. In 1610, John Minsheu was looking for a publisher for his massive multilingual dictionary, Γλοσσον ΕτγμολογιΚον; no bookseller would touch it, and he failed to obtain help from the Stationers' Company, the universities or the Inns of Court. Eventually, Minsheu raised the money privately, by inviting pre-publication subscriptions from his customers. These advance payments covered the costs of production, and the book was indeed published in 1617. Minsheu had invented the system of subscription publication which was used occasionally during the rest of the seventeenth century, and frequently in the eighteenth, for works of scholarly importance but little commercial appeal. Other seventeenth-century examples include Brian Walton's polyglot Bible of 1657 and Edmund Castell's *Lexicon heptaglotton* in 1661–9.[26]

The second example of the difficulties of scholarly publishing is furnished by the story of Sir Henry Savile's attempts to publish an edition of the works of St John Chrysostom. Savile, Provost of Eton and Warden of Merton College, Oxford, had travelled all over Europe in pursuit of manuscripts of Chrysostom's works, which had never been published in full. When the edition was ready for the press, no English printer was willing or even able to undertake it, and eventually the work was done at Eton under Savile's direct supervision. He employed William Norton, the King's Printer, to operate a press which he installed in the College, but the first problem was to obtain a decent fount of Greek type. The fact that this could not be found in England is in itself an eloquent comment on the lack of a tradition of scholarly publishing. Eventually, a fount was obtained from Germany, through contacts which John Bill, Norton's partner, had established at the Frankfurt Book Fair at which he was one of the few regular English visitors in the early seventeenth century. The work was eventually printed in eight volumes between 1610 and 1613, but it was a commercial disaster which, in that sense, proved how right the London booksellers had been to be wary of venturing into learned publishing.[27]

Private finance or subscription made possible the publication of some works of scholarship but these were at best unsatisfactory solutions. The need to facilitate the publication of works of learning was a matter of concern to Archbishop Laud in the 1630s, and he drew up elaborate plans for a university press at

Oxford which would have embarked on a programme of scholarly publishing appropriate to his vision of a rejuvenated university.[28] These plans come to nothing, but after the Restoration the remarkable John Fell, Dean of Christ Church and later Bishop of Oxford, revived the idea. With three partners he took a lease on the university's printing privilege, which had been confirmed in the 1662 Printing Act, equipped a printing house in the newly completed Sheldonian Theatre in 1668 and began an ambitious publishing programme which gradually came to fruition over the next three decades.[29] The products of Fell's press included Anthony Wood's *Historia et antiquitates universitatis Oxoniensis*, a Greek New Testament (1675) and Fell's own edition of the works of St Cyprian (1682).[30] Cambridge lagged somewhat behind. There had been 'university' printers there since 1584 (as there had in Oxford since 1585) but they had achieved little.[31] In 1696, Richard Bentley, the great classical scholar and future Master of Trinity, persuaded the university to establish a press on a proper footing comparable with that at Oxford, so that at Cambridge too a programme of learned publishing was inaugurated.[32]

Both university presses encountered great difficulties in their operations, and especially in sales. Indeed, 'want of vent' as a contemporary called it,[33] almost brought Oxford down at a very early stage, and the problem of distribution was never satisfactorily solved. It was in fact a many-sided problem. Distribution of books since the earliest days of printing had always been undertaken by the London trade, and by the second half of the seventeenth century the mechanisms of distribution was already very complex. Distribution from a provincial printing centre was a very different matter, and required special arrangements which the London booksellers were not always prepared to make, especially against the background of disputes between the Stationers' Company and both universities about the right of the universities to print almanacs and other privileged books.[34] Another aspect of the problem of sales was the nature of the books themselves. The market was small, and prices had to be high in order to finance the short print runs which were all that could be justified. Cambridge approached the distribution problem in a more practical way than Oxford. Bentley initiated a series of well-edited texts of classical authors, and arranged for London distribution through Jacob Tonson who, by the end of the seventeenth century, had succeeded to Herringman's position as the most active literary publisher of the time.[35] These editions included Terence (1701), Horace (1701) and Catullus, Tibullus and Propertius (1702).[36] A great scholarly enterprise, similar to those which Fell encouraged at Oxford, was less successful. This was an edition of Suidas's *Lexicon* which took three years to print before it was finally published in 1705, and despite a number of reductions in price, 75 of the original 1,500 sets were still unsold as late as 1752.[37] Neither university in fact overcame the problems inherent in publishing such books, but at least the attempt had been made. The university presses did not solve their financial and distributional problems until the nineteenth century, but both had a continuous existence after the late seventeenth century, and neither entirely abandoned its work.

New enterprises and the reorganisation of old activities were both conspicuous features of the trade in the second half of the seventeenth century. In no field was this more true than in the trade's response to the growing demand for popular literature for entertainment. Broadside ballads had been published in England since the early sixteenth century, but like the almanacs they were now in greater demand than ever before in an increasingly literate society. Indeed, the ballads crossed the barriers between the literate and the illiterate, for they were sung and recited as well as read in their printed form.[38] Unlike the almanacs, the ballads had never been a part of the English Stock, but they were nevertheless controlled by a very small group of booksellers. For a period of sixty years, from the 1620s to the 1680s, the ballad copyrights were bought, sold and inherited within a group of about fifteen men and women who had no formal privilege for printing them but who actually encountered little competition. The reasons were manifold, but perhaps the most important were first, that the production of the single-sheet ballads was a rather specialised matter and secondly, that their distribution was quite different from that of other books. Although pamphlets were sold on the streets as well as in shops, the ballads were more often marketed in this way than through the bookshops. They were sold by itinerant booksellers, who were often little more than pedlars, at markets and fairs throughout the country and they were sold in huge numbers.[39] The ballad partnership in fact pioneered what were to be some of the most notable characteristics of the trade in the eighteenth century: national distribution, complex multiple ownership of copyrights, and joint production and wholesaling.

Distribution was becoming one of the most important preoccupations of the trade, another indication of its transformation into a publishing industry in which a limited number of producers were marketing their products through a much larger number of retailers. There is evidence for bookselling in the major provincial towns before the end of the sixteenth century, and indeed there had been a book trade in some cities before the invention of printing.[40] It was, however, in the late seventeenth and early eighteenth centuries that the provincial trade began to be an important consideration for the copy-owning booksellers in London. New trade practices were developed to cope with the growing demand for books which in turn created the need for the higher capital investment necessary to produce larger editions and more titles. The first requirement was for the copy-owners to ensure that the existence of their books was known to their potential customers, and it was during this period that the output of the press was, for the first time, systematically recorded. The *Term Catalogues*, first published in 1668, were quarterly lists of recently published books which were intended primarily for the use of retail booksellers both in London and in the provinces. Catalogues had been issued before, but never on a regular basis and never with any intention of being both comprehensive and continuous. Indeed, the *Term Catalogues* mark the beginning of the practice of publishing regular lists of new books which is now embodied in the *British National Bibliography* and the weekly, monthly and annual versions of *British Books in Print*. It was a very important development, which marked a major step forward in the history of the trade.[41]

The problem of distribution also impelled another significant development, that of wholesaling. Immediately after the Restoration, as had been the case since Caxton's time, the publisher sold his books at his own retail bookshop. This practice residually survived until the nineteenth century, but in the late seventeenth century it gradually began to be replaced by a system of wholesaling and general retail bookselling. The advantages to the publisher were clear: he sold a significant percentage of his edition immediately upon publication and therefore recouped a proportionate amount of his investment as soon as the book went on sale. This required a system whereby the wholesalers could also make a profit, so they marked up the price to the retailer, who marked it up again to his customer. In practice, the pricing arrangements worked the other way round: discounts were given at each stage on a notional retail price, another practice which was to be a continuing feature of the English book trade in the future.

The impetus for the development of wholesaling was not entirely commercial. Until the final lapse of the Printing Act in 1695 there was always a need to find *sub rosa* channels of distribution for unlicensed material. Most of the books of the period were published without legal problems, but at times of political crisis there was inevitably a good deal of surreptitious publishing. The practice of selling on the streets, which had been used during the Civil War and interregnum for similar material, continued after the Restoration, and it too was systematised. There emerged a group of men and women in the trade who specialised in the distribution of pamphlets, often allowing their own names to be used in the imprints rather than those of the printer or copy-owner. These people, the so-called 'trade publishers', provided an alternative system of distribution which was more likely to evade the attention of the censors and the Secretary of State's officials. They survived the lapse of the Act to become an important group of wholesalers of pamphlets, newspapers and indeed of more substantial books.[42]

When the Printing Act was not renewed in 1695 the book trade was very different from the trade which had emerged from the interregnum. It had changed direction in many important respects. New trade practices had developed, and all of them had had the effect of distancing the bulk of the trade from the traditional centre of power in the Stationers' Company. Although members of the trade continued to be freemen of the Company (as indeed they had to be for so long as the Printing Act was in force), the Company itself no longer controlled the trade. The licensing provisions of the Printing Act had removed one of the most important functions which the Company had abrogated to itself; the relative decline of the commercial value of much of the English Stock, other than the almanacs, further emphasised the Company's loss of position and prestige. The trade was more entrepreneurial than it had ever been, and was operating in a more purely commercial ethos in which competition was rampant. The growing demand for new books, and the accumulation of valuable copyrights in the hands of individuals or small groups, were creating new alliances and divisions within the trade. The copy-owners clearly had interests in common, even if they were in competition with each other. Above all, they were concerned to protect their increasingly valuable investments in copies against piracy, and to find some efficient and cost-effective means of distributing the books which they published. Thus there emerged one group of men who can only be described as publishers, and another who were wholesalers; there was still a good deal of overlap between the two, but the general trend of the trade's development could be clearly discerned by the middle of the 1690s. The lapse of the Printing Act was to provoke further developments, but the seeds of change were germinating even while the Act was still in force.

Part Two:
Licence and Liberty 1695–1800

6

Response to Freedom

The lapse of the Printing Act was by no means an unmixed blessing for the trade. Indeed, the copy-owners saw little merit in it. They were, on the whole, law-abiding men who had never been troubled by the censors, or who, when the occasion arose, had taken advantage of the services of the trade publishers to distribute any doubtful or surreptitious material. The fact that copies no longer had to be licensed was neither a benefit nor a disadvantage to them. What did concern them greatly, however, were the unintended consequences of the lapse of the Act. The comprehensive nature of the 1662 Act and its successors, effectively embodying in the statute law the customs of the trade, had provided the same protective wall around the copy-owners' privileges which their predecessors had enjoyed through their control of the Stationers' Company. The regulations which had evolved since the middle of the sixteenth century were all enshrined in the Act: controls on numbers of master printers and apprentices, the London monopoly and, above all, registration and control of copy-ownership. It was this last issue which was the most important, for without some form of protection for copies there would be, as was direly predicted throughout the 1690s, chaos in the trade.

The preservation of the London monopoly was a less immediate problem, because it was not in serious danger. Provincial printing developed only slowly over the next three or four decades, and never had an economic base from which to challenge the London trade. London was by far the largest city in the kingdom, it was the seat of government, the centre of commerce and the hub of literary culture. Not even the other capitals in the British Isles, Edinburgh and Dublin, could compete with this position, and certainly none of the English provincial towns could do so. Although printers began to establish themselves in the provinces in the decade after the lapse of the Act, they were working for a local market and generally depended almost entirely on the revenues of the weekly newspapers which were the *raisons d'être* of their businesses. The development of the provincial trade which followed in the wake of the local newspapers proved to be a major benefit to the Londoners, for the new provincial booksellers, who came into existence to distribute the local newspapers, were to provide the basis for a far wider network of distribution of London books throughout the country.[1] The pattern of central production and national distribution was actually reinforced by the lapse of the Printing Act.

National distribution on a larger scale did, however, bring some problems in its wake, for the greater demand meant that the copy-owners had to commit even more capital to the production of their books. In addition to the cost of buying the copy, there was also the need to finance long print runs and to ensure that the books could actually reach the bookshops. In the last decade of the seventeenth century the trade evolved a new mechanism of wholesaling which was designed to cope with these new problems, the problems of success. The essence of the difficulty was the same as that faced by every publisher since the invention of printing and still faced by their successors in the twentieth century. Although books are normally produced in considerable numbers (edition sizes of 1,000 or 2,000 were not unknown by the early eighteenth century), they are, unlike most other mass-produced goods, manufactured in a single series of operations. The idea of a continuous production line of identical goods, with the sales of the earlier output financing the production of the later, is wholly alien to the book trade, which does not operate on a sufficiently large scale to justify such an arrangement. A publisher invests all, or almost all, of the capital which is assigned to a particular edition before a single copy of that edition is sold. Therefore, his immediate objective must be to sell as many copies as possible immediately after publication in order to recoup his costs and move into profit. The copy-owning booksellers of the late seventeenth century did not think or talk in terms of break-even points or marginal profitability, but they had a clear empirical understanding of the principles involved. The wholesaling system·which was developed in the 1690s was aimed precisely at this central economic dilemma of publishing:

maximising sales at the time of publication.

The origins of the system can be most easily seen in the steps taken by the bookseller Richard Royston to protect his heirs after his death. Royston made his will in 1682, when the Licensing Act was not in force, bequeathing his copies (which were valuable ones) to his granddaughter on certain conditions. These included the wise provision that the girl, who was only 16 at that time, should marry a man approved by her mother and grandmother (she did: her bridegroom, in 1686, was Royston's former apprentice Luke Meredith), and also that she should take advice from his 'overseers' or executors, before embarking on new editions of any of his copies. The crucial condition, however, was that she should sell the editions she printed to 'six or eight or more Tradeing Booksellers in and about the City of London'. These 'tradeing booksellers' were the wholesalers, and Royston's will is our earliest evidence for their existence. This group, known in trade cant as the 'conger',[2] seems to have emerged in the period when the Printing Act was not in force (1679–85) as a protective device for the copy-owners. The underlying principle was a simple one of deterrence. By marketing their books through a few major booksellers, the copy-owners effectively ensured that those booksellers would not deal in piracies; if they did so there was the implicit threat of the loss of the far more profitable trade in legitimate editions. The conger system did, however, have the incidental advantage of providing income to the copy-owner in that awkward interval between his investment in publication and the arrival of revenue from the first sales, for the members of the conger were not passive distributors. They were genuine wholesalers who bought the books and then resold them to retailers at a higher price, making their own profits from the difference between the two prices. We can presume that the conger system continued to operate in some form during the last few years of licensing from 1685 to 1693; what is certain is that it reached its fullest flowering in the following decade when it proved to be the crucial weapon in the defence of the entrenched interests of the copy-owners.[3]

The wholesaling conger continued to operate until the middle of the eighteenth century, although it was in the first 20 years after the lapse of licensing that it was of central importance in the trade. By the middle of the first decade of the century the conger was handling about 20,000 books a year, to a total value of about £5,000; this was not far short of the turnover of the English

Stock.[4] In itself the conger was an ingenious and successful device which protected the investments of the copy-owners and assisted their cash flow. It was also, however, to be the pattern for other developments which all tended towards the creation of an inner circle of dominant copy-owners whose interests largely dictated the pattern of the trade as a whole. From the moment at which the crown and the Stationers' Company recognised the mutual benefits of co-operation, the leading members of the book trade had operated in collaboration as well as competition. For nearly a century, this collaboration was expressed through the Court of Assistants and its careful regulation of the trade, largely, as many saw it, for the commercial benefit of the Assistants themselves. While it was true that the Court had made concessions to the majority in the trade, by far their most significant act had been to bring together the crown patents in the English Stock. This had the effect of giving the lesser members of trade some interest in maintaining the position of their superiors, for the profits of their shareholdings were ultimately dependent upon the integrity of the Stock's copies. Thus, long before the end of the seventeenth century, there was a well-established tradition of collaboration for mutual benefit within the trade, a tradition which was particularly marked among the copy-owning booksellers who had dominated the Court since before the Civil War and were now working together in the aftermath of the lapse of the Printing Act to ensure that their position was not put in jeopardy. At the centre of this concern for self-defence was the single issue of the defence of investments in copies, and the need to discourage piracy. It was precisely this consideration which had caused Royston to recommend the wholesaling conger to his grand-daughter, and which had, indeed, caused the conger to evolve. The same concern lay at the root of other developments for which the wholesaling conger provided the model.

The key to this lay in the pattern of operation which the conger adopted at an early stage in its existence, as well as in the mere fact of its existence. The 'tradeing booksellers' were to some extent competitors as well as collaborators; the members of the conger never operated as a partnership, but rather as a group whose members worked independently of each other while also working collectively in defence of mutual interests. Not every member took copies of every book which was offered to the conger, nor did those who did take copies all take the same number. The actual process of sale was by auction, but the auction was very far from being the public sale which had been introduced into England from Holland in Charles II's reign and was already the most common means of retailing collections of second-hand books.[5] The crucial difference was that the conger sales were private, open only to invited members of the trade, and that everyone attending was as likely to be a vendor as a purchaser, for the members were copy-owners and hence publishers as well as wholesalers. The wholesaling conger had between 15 and 21 members in the first decade of the eighteenth century when it was at the height of its activities, and it was these men who were admitted to the private auctions at which its transactions were conducted. It was the private auction among a select group, first developed by the wholesaling conger, which suggested the mechanism for an even more important element in the trade's defensive actions to protect its copies in the difficult decade after the abolition of statutory controls.

Mutuality of interest in the sales of books led to mutuality of interest in their publication. In 1699, a new edition of Abel Boyer's *Royal dictionary* was published, which appears to have been printed for the members of the wholesaling conger collectively.[6] In this case, they were working together to finance the book from the beginning rather than merely collaborating in selling it when it was completed. The wholesaling conger did not repeat this experiment until 1711, but long before then other groups in the trade, also called congers by contemporaries, were regularly operating in this way. By 1706 at the latest, copy-owning congers were a recognised feature of the trade,[7] and in one form or another were destined to outlive the wholesaling conger which was probably the inspiration for their creation. Essentially, the members of a copy-owning conger were owners of shares in a group of copies, although, as with the wholesaling conger, there was not necessarily a complete overlap of interests. Although the membership of these congers was limited, it was never precisely defined; groups of booksellers often worked together on an *ad hoc* basis for particular titles. Copies were divided into shares, varying in size from one-half to fractions as small as one-sixty-fourth or even less in the case of the most valuable and desirable copies. The jointly-owned copies came to include the best properties in the trade, which further emphasised the need for the leading members of the trade to work together in defence of their common interests whatever degree of competition might exist between them.

The copy-owning congers, like the wholesaling conger, needed to find a means of keeping the shares within the group of booksellers which constituted their membership. Their difficulty was that copies had a far longer life than any particular edition; indeed, in the first decade of the eighteenth century there was no reason to differentiate between the existence of a copy and the existence of any other piece of property: it was assumed to exist for ever. If, therefore, shares began to be sold outside the conger, sooner or later the conger itself could be taken over by 'outsiders'; to prevent this, the sharers developed a form of insider trading known as the 'trade sale'.[8] Like the sales of books in the wholesaling conger, the trade sales were private auctions, to which only select booksellers were invited. Copies and shares in copies had of course changed hands many times since the Stationers' Company had evolved its own form of licensing in the 1560s, but formerly changes of ownership had taken place in more conventional ways, by inheritance, or by private treaty sale. The auction, however, offered the obvious advantage of competitive bidding to maximise the value of the shares. Since all the buyers, by definition, owned shares themselves, a general rise in the price of shares in copies was of mutual benefit, provided that books did not become so expensive as to deter the potential customer in the bookshop. With the rising tide of demand in the early eighteenth century such an outcome was in the highest degree improbable.

The first trade sale for which there is definite evidence took place on 3 April 1718, but the pattern is so close to that of the wholesaling conger, to the extent that it took place at the Queen's Head Tavern in Paternoster Row where the wholesaling sales were held, that it has to be considered at least possible that such sales had been held before that date. The evidence for the 1718 sale is the survival of a single copy of a printed catalogue, the first of a long series which continued for over a century. The rights in the copies of an astonishingly high proportion of books which went into more than one edition in that long period of time passed through a trade sale at some stage in their history,[9] and the sales became the chief mechanism for the marketing of shares and for the protection of the shareholders. The rules were strict. Although there is no extant formal statement of them before 1829,[10] it is clear that it represents the practices which had evolved over the previous hundred years, and that these practices had developed very shortly after the inauguration of the sales themselves. The fundamental rule was that shares bought at sales could only be sold at sales, thus protecting the interests of the other shareholders against 'outside' ownership. If a shareholder died (the usual reason for a sale), or went bankrupt, or left the trade or simply wanted to dispose of some or all of his copies, they had to be offered at a trade sale, which all the other shareholders could attend if they wished and at which all the bidders were necessarily committed to the maintenance of the share-book system.

The wholesaling congers, the copy-owning congers and the trade sales were devices to ensure that the historic practices of the book trade were not seriously disrupted by mere legal niceties. Nevertheless, the trade did make a serious effort to ensure that the law should once again come to their aid. When the passage of the Bill to renew the Printing Act was not completed by the end of the parliamentary session of 1694–5, no one supposed that it would not be revived in the next session.[11] So indeed it was, and this revival was accompanied by a petition from the book trade emphasising the need for order in the trade. The Stationers' Company took the lead in this, for the Court was dominated by shareholders who had most to lose by chaos; other petitions, however, came from the printers and the journeymen, both asking for the restoration of the restrictions on the numbers of printers and apprentices. Between 1695 and 1698, four Bills which would have received the Printing Act were introduced, but all were either rejected outright or lost in the byways of parliamentary procedure. Two further Bills, which started their life in the House of Lords, were rejected in 1699 and 1701. By that time, it was clear that licensing was gone beyond recall, and indeed even the politicians, who had most to gain from a controlled press, were looking elsewhere for means of exercising that control.[12] For the first time since the reign of Mary I the interests of the trade and those of the government had seriously diverged, for the trade still felt the need for the legal protection which it had always enjoyed. The key issue was that of the investments of the copy-owners, and although the trade's rapidly developing internal mechanisms offered some measure of protection, piracy was on the increase and the courts were slow, expensive and unsympathetic to the few members of the trade who went to Chancery to take civil proceedings against those who infringed their rights.[13] Statute law was needed, and in 1707 the trade began in earnest to find some way of obtaining it.

The initiative was expressed through the Stationers' Company, but the thirteen signatories of the petition which was laid on the Table of the House of Commons in February 1707 included no fewer than nine members of the wholesaling conger, a vivid demonstration of the central position in the trade which they had come to occupy during the previous ten years. Other petitioners were members of the Printing Conger, a group of printers who worked together much as the copy-owning congers did,[14] and senior partners in the English Stock. It was a formidable array of vested interest; indeed, there is probably no clearer statement in the whole of the eighteenth century of the power of a small group of men in the affairs of the trade. The 1707 petition abandoned all pretence of asking for a renewal of licensing for the good of the body politic; the petitioners asked for the protection of what they called 'literary property'. The faint cultural overtones of the word 'literary' could not disguise the fact that what they were actually asking for was legal protection for their copies. A Bill was introduced as a result of this petition, but it failed, and was not revived until the session of 1709–10, when, at last, the trade obtained the statutory protection it had sought. A Bill passed through all its stages and came into effect on 10 April 1710 as the Act for the Encouragement of Learning.[15]

The title of the 1710 Copyright Act (as it is usually known) was, like the use of the phrase 'literary property', more than a little disingenuous. In so far as learning was to be encouraged by the provisions of the Act, it was by permitting the unrestricted import of works in the classical and northern languages even if there was an edition printed in England and by appointing a committee to regulate the prices of books to ensure that there was no profiteering. The learned works were an easy concession to make; they were of no serious commercial value, for school books, which were valuable, were not covered by the definition in the Act. The committee on book prices never attempted to do anything, and indeed, so far as is known, never actually met. The essential point was that from 10 April 1710, all existing copies were confirmed to their present owners for a period of 21 years, and all new copies after that date were protected for 14 years with the possibility of a further fourteen thereafter. In both cases, protection depended upon entry in the Stationers' Register for proof of ownership. Except in the preamble, authors were not mentioned at all, and indeed a series of references to authors' rights in the first draft of the Bill was removed in committee, almost certainly under pressure from the trade.[16] In other words, the Act was a booksellers' act not an authors' act, and it seemed to represent precisely what the copy-owners were seeking. In addition to the clear statement of their rights, the copy-owners were also given statutory sanction for civil proceedings against pirates, and penalties were specified for anyone found guilty of infringement of rights. Although there was, in fact, a good deal of ambiguity in both the wording and intention of the Act, it seemed to the trade in the spring of 1710 that they had won the battle of the copies; order was restored to the trade and their investments were safe.

This did not, however, lead to major changes in trade practices. Although the wholesaling conger gradually faded away, this was more a reflection of the changing economic circumstances of the trade than of its legal position. The development of the trade sales during the decade after the Act would probably have happened anyway, for they were a logical consequence of the way in which the trade was already conducting its affairs. Indeed, although the 1710 Act was undoubtedly a great victory for the copy-owners, they saw it as little more than confirmation of their existing rights. They argued that rights in copies were simply properties, but that their property had been invaded by trespassers against whom they had no easy means of redress since their protection had been accidentally removed in 1694. They certainly did not suppose that in 1731–2, in the case of pre-1710 copies, or from 1724 onwards in the case of new copies, their property would suddenly vanish and their rights with it. The 1710 Act, however, was to prove a fruitful source of difficulties in the future; there were too many holes in it for it to be good law, and the authors whom it so conspicuously neglected soon found that they too could exploit the statutory existence of rights in copies once they realised that no such rights could exist until they created them.

The obsession with rights in copies which characterised so many of the leading members of the trade in the late seventeenth century and for the next hundred years can easily be explained in terms of their economic dependence on the income which those rights generated. It was undoubtedly the case that the recognition and protection of such rights created an ethos in which the booksellers felt that copies were a sound investment and had some confidence in the conduct of their businesses. On the other hand, there was a certain stultifying effect, for the really valuable copies were those which were reprinted year after year and for which there was a sure and apparently inexhaustible market. Even before 1710 a corpus of copies which was to dominate the trade was coming into existence. From the early seventeenth century there was Shakespeare, from the middle decades Milton, and from more recent times there were Congreve, Bunyan, Wycherley, and the new generation of writers, Swift, Addison, Defoe, Steele, Pope and Gay, as well as the less literary but equally profitable works of bishops such as Burnet, of philosophers like Locke and of theologians such as the anonymous author of the perennially popular *Whole Duty of Man*. This corpus grew steadily through the century, but it was essentially ossified; these copies were not only the favourites of the eighteenth-century reader, they were also the favourites of the eighteenth-century publisher, and there was little incentive to seek out new works or new authors. Authors needed to be paid. The 1710 Act did, even if only in the preamble, recognise their existence; there could be no doubt of the logic of the argument that if a copy was a property then the author was the maker of the property and had to be paid for it. Eighteenth-century publishers were not ungenerous to their authors on the whole, and in a few cases quite the opposite, but the economic certainties of the reprints were rather too tempting when set against the more tempestuous seas of speculative publishing. The 1710 Copyright Act was ultimately to benefit publishers and authors alike, but in the first decades of its operation it was the former who were its beneficiaries, as indeed they had been its progenitors.

The rapid growth of the trade in the eighteenth century emphasised the value of the booksellers' investments in copies. The most valuable of them, such as Shakespeare or *The Spectator*, changed hands for large sums of money at the trade sales, and even small shares in such copies became worthwhile possessions. It is hardly surprising that the sharers were as anxious to defend their rights as some others were to infringe them, and the struggle between the two sides eventually coalesced on an issue whose outcome was to transform the British publishing trade dramatically and permanently. The issue was the meaning of certain clauses in the 1710 Act. The Act was distinctly vague in several important respects; in particular, it did not define 'copy' or 'rights'. These omissions were a direct consequence of the Act's origins in the inner circles of the London book trade, where men like Tonson and Baldwin knew exactly what rights and copies were, and had no need of a law to define them. Unfortunately for their successors, the judges were less certain, for there were no legal precedents to which they could turn for enlightenment.[17]

The problems began to emerge in the 1730s, when the twenty-one year rights expired. These copies included some of the most valuable in the trade: *Pilgrim's Progress, The Spectator, The Tatler* and Burnet's *History of His Own Times* were only a few of these rich sources of regular income derived from minimal effort. Those with long memories, or who had listened to the stories of their elders, knew of the uncertainty and expense of Chancery suits to protect rights in copies, and how little such suits had actually achieved in the chaotic years after the end of licensing and registration. Consequently, they began to seek new legislation to protect their investments, looking to Parliament to amend the 1710 Act by extending the period of copyright.

In the ten years after 1695 the petitions to revive licensing had been a cover to gain statutory protection for copyrights. Similarly, the agitation for the extension of the period of copyright in the 1730s was, to some extent, also a cover for the trade's true objective. The fact was that a new danger had arisen, far more insidious than any previous infringement of booksellers' rights; this new factor was the development of reprinting outside London. So long as would-be pirates (who had always existed) were in the capital, there were moral, commercial and legal pressures which could be brought to bear upon them; they would have difficulty in finding a printer, and when their editions were produced the normal channels of wholesaling and distribution would be closed to them. Distant pirates, however, were a much greater danger, especially when they had easier access than the London booksellers to the rapidly developing provincial markets, and they could offer a cheaper product.

The printers and booksellers of Ireland (which in practice meant Dublin) and of Scotland (in Edinburgh and Glasgow) had little need to concern themselves with the Copyright Act. Indeed, the Act did not apply in Ireland, and in Scotland there was a good deal of legal opinion which was sympathetic to the idea that copyrights did not exist in Scots law. In 1710, this had not been a matter of any great importance. The Irish and Scottish book trades were far less well developed than that in London; they produced few books, and those few were almost entirely of regional interest. Moreover, the whole tenor of the Act was to maintain existing trade practices, and that essentially meant the

77

existing practices of the London trade. By the 1730s, however, this situation was changing. Both Scotland and Ireland were undergoing something of a cultural and economic renaissance, and their entrepreneurs were looking for new markets. For their book trades, the north of England, where the London trade could not yet guarantee regular supplies, represented an ideal area for expansion. Consequently, they began to reprint some of the most valuable London copies, and to sell them in England. Well-established trade routes existed to expedite this trade. From Dublin, ships sailed to the ports of north-west England, while the Scottish booksellers could use either the overland route or the even cheaper sea transport along the east coast.[18]

The Irish and Scottish incursions represented a major challenge to the London booksellers' monopoly of the English book trade. The Londoners reacted both commercially and legally. Commercially, they began to take account of provincial booksellers and provincial readers. *The Gentleman's Magazine*, after 1732, played a crucial role in this development, with its reliable and comprehensive lists of new books and its wide circulation. The provincial newspapers, which by the mid-1730s covered the greater part of the country with their local agents, provided a ready-made distribution system to which the London trade could gain access through their existing contacts with the provincial newspapers proprietors. At the same time, the London newspapers, especially the thrice-weekly evening newspapers, became generally available in the provinces, and they were full of book advertisements, epitomes and reviews. In all of these developments, the 1730s was a crucial decade, as the London booksellers responded to the dangers which beset their investments in copies by providing more information about new books and more efficient supply.[19]

The legal challenge to the Scottish and Irish booksellers was more difficult to mount. One point however, was clear: the Irish were not breaking the law merely by reprinting London books. This perfectly legal activity only became illegal when the reprints were imported into Great Britain for sale. Beyond that, the 1710 Act was difficult to interpret. It could be argued that it meant what it apparently said: that the pre-1710 copyrights expired in 1732, and the 28-year copyrights from 1739 onwards. The Act could, however, be interpreted to mean that what actually expired were the penalties for breach of copyright. This argument supposed that the rights which the Act protected were common law rights whose existence pre-dated the Act itself. It was on this point that the argument about copyrights was in turn for the next forty years.

At first, however, the trade did have a victory of sorts. In 1739, Parliament passed an Act which forbade the import of any English books into Great Britain. Although it was never wholly enforced, it did give some protection against the Irish reprinters who were increasingly invading the growing provincial market. Although the Import of Books Act appeared to be a victory, it was in the end illusory, for enforcement was difficult, and the only real protection for the copy-owner was to take a civil action after the illegal import and sale had actually taken place.

It was not until the 1750s that the leading London booksellers began to take action to protect themselves against this illicit trade. A group of copy-owners, led by John Whiston, formed a committee which raised some £8,000 from the trade to mount a campaign against the illegal imports. The success of the subscription is a measure of the importance which the London trade attached to stopping the influx of Irish reprints, but it was not matched by the success of the campaign itself. Only a permanent system of vigilance could prevent the sale of Scottish and Irish reprints, and so it was to the provincial booksellers, rather than to the Scottish and Irish publishers, that the London booksellers addressed themselves. Early in 1759 a letter was circulated to the provincial booksellers in which the London committee offered to buy at cost their existing stocks of imported reprints, or to replace them, copy for copy, with legally printed London editions. This apparently generous offer was really a recognition by the London trade of their own impotence. From the provincial booksellers' point of view, the generosity of the offer was very limited; although a bookseller who complied would have the moral comfort of knowing that he was no longer breaking an unenforceable law, when he looked to the future he would doubtless reflect on the likely consequences of the restoration of a complete London monopoly over the best-selling books of the age. The London booksellers would be able to charge any price they wished, and the provincials would have to pay since these were the books which their customers wanted to buy.

The openly intimidatory part of the letter was even more of a house built on sand. The proposal was that after 1 May 1759, the deadline for the return of illegal books, 'riding officers' would be appointed who would tour the country to inspect the stocks of the provincial booksellers. If Scottish or Irish editions were found, legal proceedings would be started under the 1739 Act, and the offending booksellers would no longer be supplied on trade terms. The latter threat was a serious one, for the provincial bookseller's livelihood was derived from the 15 to 20 per cent discount on the retail price which was the usual basis of supply in the middle of the eighteenth century.[20] Again, however, the problem was one of enforcement, exacerbated by the sheer scale of the undertaking. The £8,000 might have been enough to buy up the stocks of illegal books, but it was certainly not sufficient to sustain a long-term campaign of inspection and prosecution. It is doubtful whether this letter, and subsequent documents relating to the same scheme, was ever intended to do more than frighten the provincial booksellers into abandoning their trade in piracies. Even at that level, however, it failed completely, and once again the London copy-owners had to reconsider their position.

In some ways, that position was less critical than it had been in the 1730s when the problem first arose. Despite the trade in piracies, and the bad feeling which it had caused, the London and provincial trades were by this time indissolubly linked. A few provincial booksellers were shareholders in London books, although this was very unusual and the Londoners were not enamoured of it.[21] More important, however, was the rapid growth of the provincial trade itself. In the early 1760s, the increasingly tight interlocking of the London and provincial trades, and the highly efficient system of distribution which had been developed, seemed likely to lead to a natural atrophy of the whole problem of illegal imports of reprints. That this did not happen was almost entirely the result of the persistence of one man, the Edinburgh bookseller, Alexander Donaldson.

Donaldson had made a good career and a reasonable fortune as a pirate. He had been involved in the reprint trade for many years and his books were widely available in the north and the Midlands. In the early 1760s, however, his trade began to suffer, like that of all the reprinters, as the London and provincial booksellers worked together more closely for their mutual benefit. He therefore took it upon himself to mount a challenge to the London book trade. His motives were primarily commercial, although there is some truth in his presentation of himself as a man of principle; in the Scotland of Adam Smith, free trade was an idea whose time was rapidly coming. Donaldson decided that the offensive should be one which the Londoners could not ignore: he opened a bookshop in London. In itself, of course, that was perfectly legal; what was blatantly and provocatively illegal was that he sold there his own reprints, under the noses of the very booksellers who claimed to own the rights in the copies. When he printed Thomson's *Seasons* immediately after the expiry of the 28-year period of copyright, Andrew Millar, the owner of the copy, with the support of others in the London trade, initiated proceedings against him for infringement of common law rights of property. The alleged offence had been committed in Scotland, where the book had been reprinted, as well as in England where it had been sold. It was in a Scottish court and under Scots law that the case was to be heard.

This was Millar's first and crucial mistake. The Scottish courts had never been entirely happy in dealing with copyright cases. A number of such cases had been heard in the Court of Session in the 1750s and 1760s, but no coherent body of practice had emerged. In general the Scots judges had ruled against perpetual copyright, because there was an underlying feeling that Scots law did not recognise the existence of copyright at all. The problem was that the Roman basis of Scots law did not admit of the concept of 'incorporeal' property: to be a legal entity, a property had to have real, or physical, existence. Thus, although a book or a manuscript was certainly a piece of property, Scots lawyers were generally very doubtful whether the same could be said of the text.

By contrast, English law was more flexible. Without the strict codes of Roman law to restrain them, the English courts had gradually come round to the view that the author created a piece of property when he wrote his book. In general, however, the English judges had argued that the Act had not, and indeed could not, interfere with fundamental common law rights in property. Having recognised a copy as a property, they accepted the argument that like any property it had a perpetual existence and that its owner could do with it as he wished. The English courts, therefore, had generally upheld the booksellers' argument for the perpetual existence of copyrights under the common law of property, arguing that the 1710 Act had merely imposed some specific penalties against those who trespassed on those property rights during certain periods of time. It was only these penalties which had a time limit, not the existence of the property itself, and even after that time there was nothing to prevent the courts from penalising trespassers according to the established practices of the law. *Millar v. Donaldson* was to challenge the law in both countries, and indeed to bring about a conflict between the two jurisdictions.

The arguments on both sides had been heard many times before. In essence, the plaintiff complained that his rights had been infringed by the theft of his property by Donaldson; the latter replied that there was no case to answer because the law of Scotland did not recognise the existence of the alleged property. It was now that Millar began to suffer for the error of suing in Scotland. The Lords of Session did indeed take great trouble with the case, reviewing at length all similar cases which they and their predecessors had heard during the previous 20 or 30 years, and reaching back into the mists of history for precedents on both sides. In the end, they ruled for the defendant. This was unsurprising, for it merely confirmed the Scottish verdicts over many years. Now, however, Millar turned to Donaldon's real challenge, the London bookshop and the sale of the reprints in England. The Scots judges were, of course, wholly uninterested in that, but the English judges were not. In 1774, therefore, Millar appealed the Scottish verdict to the House of Lords.

Millar and his lawyers must have been very optimistic about the outcome of this appeal. The import of English-language books into England was an offence, and Donaldson had committed it; the English law undoubtedly recognised the existence of copyright as a property; and in general, although with a few exceptions, English judges had taken the view that as a piece of property, copyright had a perpetual existence. Once again, familiar arguments were heard on both sides, but when the peers began to give their opinions, it became clear that something unexpected might happen. A new argument was heard, which suggested that the monopoly of the London booksellers was not in the public interest, and that it maintained the price of books at an artificially high level. Doubts were expressed about exactly what kind of property copyright really was, and whether it could indeed be compared with a horse or a house. It was questioned whether the encouragement of learning, which was after all the alleged basis of the 1710 Act, was really best served by a commercial monopoly. Against the whole trend of the last thirty years, the Lords found for Donaldson, and against the existence of perpetual copyrights.

This verdict was a decisive turning-point in the history of the English book trade, for it marked the end of the long era of protectionism which had begun with the granting of the Stationers' charter in 1557. It threw the London trade into a confusion which it had not known since the lapse of the Licensing Act, the last breach in the protectionist walls. An attempt to reverse the verdict by legislation was lost in 1774 on its second reading in the House of Commons. The Lords had in fact reflected a change in the climate of opinion. The whole question had provoked a substantial pamphlet literature through the middle decades of the eighteenth century. When the issue reached its climax in the House of Lords, it was widely recognised for what it was: a challenge to the oligopoly of the small group of copy-owning booksellers who had dominated the trade since the beginning of the seventeenth century. The challenge was a success, and it was the last of a series of developments which impelled the final stage of the emergence of the publisher as the dominant figure in the trade in printed books.

7

The Trade and the Law

Copyright legislation, important as it was to the trade, was not of any great significance in the wider world of public affairs. The 1710 Act was essentially a measure granted by Parliament under pressure from a commercial group who were able to exercise enough influence to achieve a specific objective for their own purposes. From the point of view of the politicians, the end of pre-publication licensing had quite different implications. For the first time since the early sixteenth century, the men who ran the country's affairs could not control what was printed and published, and the brief experience of a comparatively uncontrolled press in the early 1640s was not a happy precedent. In 1695, the Glorious Revolution was a very recent memory, and it was far from certain that it could not be reversed. There was still a substantial Jacobite faction at home; Louis XIV of France was, for his own reasons, willing to support the Stuarts against the House of Orange; and William III was not personally popular especially among those who suspected that his principal motive for accepting the crown was so that he could use English money and English soldiers to continue this long battle against French hegemony in north-west Europe. The brief unity of 1688 was lost, and the parties which had begun to emerge during the Exclusion Crisis became a permanent feature of the parliamentary and electoral landscape. The politicians had wrested a good deal of power from the crown, but they were still learning how to handle it. Nothing in their experience had taught them how to cope with unrestrained public attacks in print, and for many decades a controlled press continued to be seen as both desirable and normal by large and powerful groups of men.

The politicians' first reaction to the lapse of licensing was to attempt to reintroduce it. A few advanced Whigs may have agreed with Locke that a free press was an integral part of a system of parliamentary government,[1] but the great majority of men in public life took the view that the press should be under stringent control for the security of the state. There was, indeed, some legal basis for this view. It had long been an accepted maxim of English law that all information about state affairs was a state secret. It was on this basis that L'Estrange had successfully maintained the crown monopoly of news for much of Charles II's reign.[2] Quite apart from this theoretical consideration there was both statute and common law which could sustain the view that an attack on the monarch or his immediate servants was an act of treason, in the form of seditious libel. Between 1695 and 1704 no fewer than nine Bills were introduced into Parliament which would have revived virtually the whole of the Licensing Act. For various reasons all were lost, but perhaps the most significant defeat was that of the 1699 Bill. It had originated in the House of Lords and passed through all its stages there, but when it reached its Second Reading in the Commons, it was lost on a division.[3] The Commons, subjected to triennial elections after 1690, were increasingly aware of the value of propaganda for electoral purposes. The desire to stifle news and opinion decreased in opposition, and in a fluid two-party House it was difficult for a politician to know when he might be in opposition himself. By 1705, the revival of licensing in its old form was a dead issue, and governments had to find other means of exercising some control over the output of the rapidly growing number of presses.

One important aspect of the growth of the trade under William and Mary and Queen Anne was the accelerated development of the newspaper. Newspapers were the most immediate beneficiaries of the end of pre-publication censorship as the political battle at home and the country's involvement in war abroad created an intense interest in public affairs. The first successful daily newspaper, *The Daily Courant*, began publication in 1702, and soon had rivals.[4] Party allegiance among newspapers had been common since before the Revolution, but in the 1690s it became even more marked. Although the pamphlet continued to be an important medium of political propaganda for the next 50 years, and on the streets the ballad and the slip-song still influenced popular views, the newspapers. were gradually becoming the principal vehicles for both fact and opinion. In a remarkably short time after *The Daily Courant* was first published, the newspapers became an integral part of the political and social fabric, and the politicians had to learn yet another lesson: how to live with a newspaper press and those who owned it and wrote for it. The first politician to do so was, significantly, the most successful of his generation, Robert Harley, later first earl of Oxford. Harley came to prominence in the Tory party in the 1690s, but reached the height of his power in Anne's reign when he dominated every ministry either by his leadership or his conspicuous absence. He was a formidable power broker and an intelligent and efficient administrator. He was also a pragmatist, and when it became clear to him in 1704–5 that the Printing Act was gone for ever, he turned to the exploitation of a press which he could no longer control. He employed Daniel Defoe as one of his several propagandists; he subsidised newspapers which supported him; he used such legislation as existed to prosecute those which opposed him. In fact, he established the pattern of relationships between governments and the newspaper press which was to persist in Britain until the reign of Queen Victoria.[5]

Harley also instituted another tradition which was to survive until the nineteenth century: the taxation of printed matter. His motives are a matter of some debate, but the facts are clear. In 1711 an Act was passed which imposed an excise duty on certain classes of printed matter. These classes were defined initially by purpose, for the first group to be taxed was the almanacs, at different rates according to their size and period of validity.[6] This was, beyond question, a measure designed to raise revenue, a matter of considerable concern after nearly 20 years of a ruinously expensive war, and merely followed a long-standing practice of taxing certain commodities.[7] Such taxes were known as 'stamp duties' because the evidence for the tax having been paid was the impression on the article in question of a printed or embossed stamp. In 1712, however, the duties on printed matter were extended to newspapers, and it is this extension which has caused Harley's motives to be called into question. The need for revenue is beyond dispute, but in view of the interest in the press which Harley had shown over the previous decade it has been suggested that the duty was also intended as a measure of censorship, since the newspaper owners would have to pass on the cost of the tax to their customers and thus double the price of their papers from 1d to 2d (or 1d to 1½d for a half-sheet newspaper).[8] If this was indeed Harley's real reason for taxing the newspapers, he was remarkably unsuccessful, for while the initial effect of the 1712 Act was to reduce the circulation of newspapers, they soon recovered, and indeed both the number of newspapers and the number of copies of each soon far exceeded the levels which had been achieved before 1712.[9]

Later in the century, however, the stamp duties were undoubtedly exploited for political purposes. The various excise duties were the principal form of indirect taxation throughout the eighteenth century and beyond, and the general level was raised continuously, except during a brief period of fiscal liberalism in the 1780s, while the duties were simultaneously extended to a vast range of goods, far beyond the luxury items which had been the original subjects of taxation. Like all taxes, the duties were unpopular, although it was not until the nineteenth century that the newspaper duty became the specific subject of attack. Nevertheless, no government could ignore the fact that newspapers and pamphlets (which were also subject to duty) were a very special commodity. The importance of the printed word in creating the political climate forced politicians to take account of it, and in times of crisis throughout the century the duties were raised. In each case it is possible to argue that the increased duties were needed to sustain the public revenue, and indeed the major increases do coincide with the frequent wars in which Britain engaged between the death of Queen Anne and the battle of Waterloo. It was during the last and greatest of these wars, that against revolutionary France, that the duties on newspapers reached their highest level, and there can be little doubt that, whatever the case may have been earlier, at that time the younger Pitt was using the level of duty to deter the potential buyers of newspapers.[10] Such duties meant that a single copy of a newspaper cost as much as the normal daily wage of a working man, and in a period when there was a good deal of sympathy with the ideals of the French Revolution, this was indeed intended to stop the flood of pro-French propaganda among the potentially revolutionary working classes of the new industrial towns.

All this, however, lay far in the future when Harley introduced the first duties on newspapers in 1712. Harley's own view of the press was a positive one. He had, through his group of journalists, mastered the arts of propaganda, and had little to fear from the comparatively ineffective efforts of the Whigs to counter him. He had recognised that direct administrative control of the press was impossible, and turned instead to other means of ensuring that his own views were not unknown to the growing band of regular readers of newspapers. The stamp duties were merely a successful politician's largely successful attempt to exploit for financial reasons a commodity whose popularity and importance he had himself helped to create. The fact that the first duties on printed matter were imposed on the almanacs supports this contention, for they were by far the largest and most popular category of books, and would therefore yield the largest revenue. Moreover, this revenue would be comparatively easy to collect, since the Stationers' monopoly of almanac publishing was still intact.[11] Harley the pragmatist sought the largest potential source of public income and the simplest means of collecting it.

This does not, however, mean that the publishers were wholly exempt from the attentions of the law. Although the only legislation of any professional concern to the great majority of eighteenth-century publishers was the Copyright Act, they had to take account of the restrictions which still existed on what could be published. The absence of specific legislation made this at once easier and more difficult, for the very vagueness of much of the law created difficulties of application and interpretation. There were essentially two areas in which governments were (and are) concerned with published matter: morals and politics. The moral area, although philosophically perhaps the more complex, is rather easier in legislative and legal terms, and can be dealt with first. Until 1857, there was no specific legislation dealing with obscene publications, although certain classes of material were deemed to be illegal from time to time. Like other moral offences, obscenity was in origin an ecclesiastical crime which had been dealt with by the church courts. During the seventeenth century, however, the secular courts had gradually taken over the supervision of moral offences committed by laymen, and this included cases dealing with allegedly obscene publications. The basis for the secular offence of obscene libel was that obscenity was a breach of the King's Peace, or likely to cause such a breach. The problem, as always, was to define what actually fell into this category, and indeed which courts were to try alleged offenders. In the second half of the seventeenth century, a number of cases was tried by the City of London magistrates at the Guildhall Sessions, but in 1707 all outstanding cases were transferred to the Court of King's Bench, a higher court where there was trial by jury before a judge.[12] No case was successfully prosecuted until

1725–6 when Edmund Curll was found guilty of publishing *Venus in the Cloister*, a translation of a famous French pornographic work. The legal basis for the judgment was that Curll had committed a common law offence because, it was argued, such a book 'tends to corrupt the morals of the king's subjects, and is against the peace of the king'.[13] During the rest of the century, there were occasional campaigns against pornography, notably in 1745[14] and in the late 1780s.[15] Obviously, this was of small consequence for the great majority of publishers, although it did establish the pattern, which survives to the present day, of the courts trying to reflect prevailing public attitudes to morality in reaching decisions on cases of alleged obscenity.

The common law of obscene libel, like that of blasphemy,[16] derived from the fact that the English law made Christian assumptions in dealing with moral and religious cases. The control of the press for political reasons was based on the rather different assumptions which underlay the medieval law of *scandalum magnatum*, or libels which reflected directly on the monarch. This had some statutory basis although, in its eighteenth-century manifestation, seditious libel like obscene libel was essentially a matter for the common law drawing on the practices of the courts and the decisions of the judges, both of which were, to some degree, subject to the general influence of public opinion. In the seventeenth century, juries had occasionally accepted that an attack on the king's immediate servants or ministers was to be treated as if it were an attack on the king himself, but this interpretation could not and did not survive the Revolution and the transfer of so much effective political power from the crown to Parliament and ministers responsible to it. Nevertheless, seditious libel did survive as an offence, and was indeed the principal legal means of prosecuting authors, printers, publishers and booksellers throughout the eighteenth century. The problem, however, was to define precisely what constituted such a libel, and it was only after a series of cases in the reign of George I that the courts assembled a sufficient body of precedents upon which they could draw. Briefly, all of these revolved around the monarch himself, which was indeed the original intention of the law of *scandalum magnatum*. The cases in George I's reign established that it was illegal to question the legitimacy of the Hanoverian succession or to support the claims of the Stuarts; that it was illegal to make personal attacks on the king or the immediate members of the royal family; and that it was, in some circumstances, and especially in time of war, illegal to make extreme attacks on the conduct of foreign or military policy.[17] Within these very broad limits there was indeed substantial freedom of the press, and certainly for the greater part of the eighteenth century the United Kingdom had a press which was less controlled than that of any other major power in Europe.

This freedom was materially assisted by the need to prove cases to the satisfaction of the jury, and this crucial issue was the subject of the one major piece of eighteenth-century legislation which directly affected the freedom of the press. In the early seventeenth century it had been established that the rights of the jury in cases of seditious libel were very limited. Indeed, they were empowered only to decide whether the accused had actually published the offending words. This was, in practice, a serious limitation, for the interpretation of the word 'publish' was very broad. The publisher of a libel could be the author, printer, distributor, wholesaler or bookseller. Although there were cases when it was very difficult to pin down personal responsibility for any of these activities,[18] and the actual machinery of control was severely limited by the very small numbers of officers available for investigation of alleged offences,[19] it was nevertheless an important consideration when a case did come to court. The Libel Act of 1792, however, gave to juries the very important additional right of deciding whether or not the words cited in the indictment were indeed libellous.[20] Ironically, this liberalising law came at a time when the general trend of policy was more repressive than at any time since 1714, and it was to prove of great importance over the next 20 or 30 years in protecting some vestiges of the freedom of the press from the increasingly virulent attacks of an increasingly reactionary establishment.[21]

The comparatively free climate in which British publishers were able to operate in the eighteenth century, like the greater restrictions which had preceded it, was a reflection of attitudes in society at large. It was no longer assumed that the crown had sole rights over information, or that the crown or its representatives should involve themselves in every sphere of economic life. Indeed, there was a growing body of influential opinion which held that governments had no business to be interfering in commercial matters at all, a view which was most authoritatively expressed by Adam Smith in his *Wealth of Nations* (1776). At the same time, there was a growing confidence about the stability of Britain and the excellence of her political institutions. Foreigners saw in Britain a constitutional monarchy which they hoped to emulate in their own countries, and the British saw their peculiar constitutional arrangements giving their country sufficient strength to expand her influence and her empire across the globe and even to survive the traumatic loss of the American colonies. The constitutional stasis which had evolved after the Revolution seemed in little danger, and his freedom became an important birthright to the Briton. The freedom to read a book or a newspaper, and to read there a vitriolic attack on the ministers of the crown and their policies, was soon seen as an integral part of that birthright. Taken together with the idea of free trade, untrammelled by gild regulation and outmoded protective legislation, the idea of a free press created a situation in which the book trade could flourish as never before. Comparatively prosperous, in a period of domestic peace disturbed only by the two abortive Jacobite rebellions, the country could enjoy the luxury of liberty. When that liberty was apparently challenged, however, the shallowness of its roots, both ideological and legal, were to be starkly revealed.

The difficulty was that the law itself had not evolved as quickly as the way in which it was applied. The flexibility of the common law, and the unpredictability of juries, could as easily work against freedom as in its favour for so long as the law itself was unchanged. The crisis came after the outbreak of revolution in France in 1789. Although the French Revolution was initially welcomed in England, even at the official level, as heralding a constitutional monarchy along British lines, the abolition of the French monarchy, the execution of the royal family and the eventual outbreak of war between the two countries soon brought about a dramatic change of attitudes. A few continued to support the French Revolution even in its most extreme manifestations, but the general mood was compounded of genuine distaste for the excesses of revolutionary zeal across the Channel and atavistic folk memories of generations of enmity between Britain and France. In this atmosphere, much that had been won since 1714 was rapidly lost. This was the background to the penal increases in Stamp Duty designed to deprive the working man of news and opinion. Despite the effects of the 1792 Libel Act, juries showed an increased willingness to convict for seditious libel. The law itself was pushed to its limits, until even the mildest aspersions on the policies of the government were prosecuted, often success-fully. The press which had proliferated in nearly a century of freedom from control was now seen as a danger to the very foundations of the state. In the late 1790s, Pitt's government armed itself with a weapon which was, in its way, as draconian as any of the laws of the Tudors or the Stuarts. This was the Seditious Societies Act of 1799, which required, *inter alia*, the registration of all presses and printing types, the inclusion of the printer's name on all printed matter and the maintenance by each printer of a complete file of all his products which the Justices of the Peace could inspect on demand.[22] It was a climax to the eighteenth century which was as untypical as it was unexpected, and unlike so many previous attempts it did actually succeed in controlling the press to a very considerable extent. Indeed, the opposition newspaper press, at least in London, was virtually eliminated by the end of the century.

During most of the eighteenth century publishers operated in a free market and in an intellectual and political atmosphere which generally favoured freedom of expression. Even so, their activities were hedged about by restrictions. The laws of obscene and seditious libel may have affected only a few, but the stamp duties impinged on the whole trade, either directly, as with the newspaper tax, or indirectly, through the taxes on all blank paper. The great output of newspapers and political pamphlets was, to a substantial extent, subsidised by successive governments, either openly or by using money from the Secret Vote. In general, the burden of proof had passed from the publisher to the government, and in that sense the end of pre-publication censorship did make a tangible difference to the way in which publishers could conduct their affairs. Nevertheless, the undercurrent of control remained, and in looking at British publishing in the eighteenth century it is important to remember that we are never looking at a press which was wholly or even substantially 'free'.

8

The Expanding Trade

The formal changes in the book trade in the eighteenth century were only one aspect of its development. The direct effects of the end of pre-publication censorship, and of the *ad hoc* system of control which evolved in its absence, were felt by few members of the trade. The copyright question was important to the major booksellers, and dominated the affairs of the trade more than once during the century, but even this great issue was of only intermittent concern to the majority. Of far greater significance were the incidental effects of the broader social and political changes which underlay the changes within the book trade itself. Eighteenth-century England was, on the whole, peaceful and prosperous. Britain's wars, after the upheavals of the seventeenth century, were fought on remote foreign soil; even the two Jacobite rebellions had little effect on the mainstream of British life. From the 1730s onwards there began that expansion of the economy which was to reach its climax during the Napoleonic Wars when Britain became the world's first industrial capitalist society. Economic expansion and broad political harmony created a climate in which the arts of peace flourished, and leisure became, for the first time, a commercial commodity.

Although books were not the only constituent of the new commercial leisure market, they were an important competitor to the theatres, concert halls, assembly rooms and sporting events which were attracting ever more patronage.[1] Moreover, the printed word was often a part of other leisure activities. Indeed, there were few parts of the eighteenth-century leisure industry which did not in some way benefit the book trade directly or indirectly, whether in the form of guide books for travellers or bloodstock books for horse-breeders. The demand-led expansion of the trade, however, was not only to be found in fields of leisure and culture, but also in practical books, assisting the reader in every activity from accountancy to navigation. Such manuals had, of course, existed since the sixteenth century, but the number of them greatly increased during the eighteenth century.

The scale of the book trade's response to market demand was perhaps most obvious in printing, where the small printing-houses of the sixteenth and seventeenth centuries were displaced by firms which were family owned but which operated with large workforces of paid employees. Tonson and Watts were employing about 50 men in 1730,[2] and Samuel Richardson had three printing-houses and more than 40 employees in the 1750s.[3] Although the typical 'publishing' firm was much smaller than the large printing businesses, the number of publishing booksellers increased, and the total output of the London trade rose quite dramatically during the century. Edition sizes, which had been restricted to 1,250 by the Stationers' Company in the early seventeenth century, and had rarely reached even that level, now increased substantially. Although many eighteenth-century editions were probably of 1,000 or 1,500 copies, editions of up to 10,000 were not unknown, and some popular books, especially schoolbooks, chapbooks and almanacs, were regularly reprinted in such numbers.[4]

The success of the book trade in the eighteenth century depended on three related factors: the existence of a growing and prosperous market, the availability of books which could meet the demands of that market and the efficiency of the distribution system which took the books from producer to customer. An understanding of these factors is essential to an understanding of the structural changes within the trade, and of its collective concern with the copyright issue.

The size of the market is difficult to define and impossible to quantify. The fundamental consideration is literacy, although that presents many problems. First, illiteracy was not necessarily an obstacle to participation in a printed culture. The oral tradition was still strong, and there is ample evidence for the singing of printed ballads and public reading from newspapers.[5] Secondly, our knowledge of the extent of literacy is both limited and controversial.[6] The controversy turns essentially on three points: the percentage of the population which was literate to a reading level, the relative increase and decrease in literacy in different parts of the country at different times in the century and the means and motives for the acquisition of literacy. One school of thought can be briefly summarised as holding that literacy was widespread and that it was acquired at home, even in quite humble families, in the same way as other traditional occupational skills. To some extent domestic teaching was supplemented by formal schooling in private schools, but the important factor was the existence of an essentially literate tradition even among the poor.[7] The opposite view holds that literacy, even at the simplest level of the ability to sign one's name, was limited, especially among women, and that, with some regional variations, there was actually a decrease in literacy towards the end of the century after a period of improvement.[8]

The apparently irreconcilable divergence of these two views arises largely from the nature of the evidence which underlies them. The 'optimistic' school, which considers that there was something approaching mass literacy even among the rural poor, is derived from a consideration of the availability of educational provision, and of the evidence afforded by the existence of large numbers of books which were clearly aimed at the lower classes of society. The 'pessimistic' school, arguing for low and perhaps decreasing levels of literacy, bases its case on statistical studies of such documents as marriage registers and the number of brides and bridegrooms who were able to sign the register rather than make their marks.[9] Neither methodology is perfect as the proponents of each admit, but the problem really arises from the different nature of the evidence which is being considered. The ability to sign one's name is not a measure of ability to read even simple continuous prose. Illiteracy was becoming a social stigma and it is at least possible that some young people learned to sign specifically to avoid the humiliation of making a mark on their wedding days. On the other hand, the existence of books and schools, and the evidence for informal teaching, is necessarily more subjective than statistical evidence derived from essentially objective and factual documents. Nevertheless, there is evidence for book ownership among the comparatively humble, even if the books were only the Bible and *Pilgrim's Progress*, and there is also evidence that children of humble families could and did learn to read them. Perhaps the most that we can say in the present state of our knowledge is that while educational provision was inadequate by modern standards, it was certainly not wholly lacking, and that there was a degree of literacy which was not negligible. To err on the conservative side, it may be that about 50–60 per cent of men and a somewhat smaller number of women had attained functional literacy by the middle of the eighteenth century. It seems that there was a percentage decline among the urban workers in the new industrial towns in the 1780s and 1790s, although in absolute terms the number of literates may actually have increased. Moreover, these considerations apply only in England. In Scotland, with its far superior system of education, the literacy rate was certainly higher.

For the majority of people, literacy was essentially a social and recreational skill rather than an occupational necessity. Despite the growing number of occupations which required technical skills, especially in the industrial areas in the second half of the century, literacy remained a necessity only for the practitioners of the learned professions and of the newer service occupations, such as accountancy, auctioneering and banking, which were developing to sustain the developing industrial economy. Market demand was largely for leisure reading, although it did not follow that this was 'light' reading. Indeed, the largest single category of books produced by British publishers in the eighteenth century was in the field of religion,[10] although other genres were growing in significance. Apart from the vast corpus of political literature generated by a comparatively open system of government, public affairs in the broader sense also created a demand for information. This is perhaps most obvious in the development of the newspaper side of the trade,[11] but many thousands of books were published to meet public demand for facts. Many of these reflect the Briton's growing interest in the wider world, which was increasingly seen as Britain's destiny. The wars of the mid-eighteenth century were fought in remote places — India and North America, most obviously — and British navigators were opening the southern oceans, the last substantial unexplored area of the seas. It is hardly surprising that books of voyages and travels were among the most popular of the century, and that history, both domestic and foreign, was also in heavy demand.

The most significant new development, however, was in the emergence of a whole new literary genre, the only one to have been invented since the invention of printing itself: the novel. Prose fiction had been published on a small scale since the middle of the seventeenth century,[12] and literary scholars argue about which book was the first 'true' novel.[13] Nevertheless, in essence, the novel is a product of the eighteenth century. Despite the example of Defoe, or before him of Richard Head, the novel really came of age with the publication of Richardson's *Clarissa* in 1740, and in Richardson and his contemporary, Fielding, we have the first great English novelists. Richardson and Fielding, however, together with Smollett and Sterne, are far from typical of eighteenth-century novelists. Conscious and successful literary artists, although always attuned to the financial benefits to be derived from their work, they are outstanding as major writers. The great majority of eighteenth-century novels was produced by far lesser authors whose motives were entirely commercial. Many of these thousands of novels are (perhaps fortunately) anonymous, and many are (perhaps mercifully) no longer extant.[14] From the trade's point of view, the significance of the novel lay not in its literary merit but in its essential triviality. It was seen as an ephemeral production to be read once and then forgotten. This meant that, once the demand had been created, a continuous supply of new novels was needed to fill it. Waves of fashion swept over the novel. Richardson's moralising and Fielding's bluff comedy were succeeded by the Gothic fantasies of Walpole and Beckford and their scores of lesser imitators, and the 'sentiment' of Fanny Burney and hers.

The customer and the product both existed. The remaining problem was to bring them together. The late seventeenth-century developments in wholesaling and distribution provided a solid foundation upon which the trade could build.[15] That system, however, was based on the assumption that all books were printed and published in London, and that most of them were subsequently sold there. The dominance of London publishing was unbroken in the eighteenth century because it was so strongly entrenched. The provincial trade did indeed undergo revolutionary developments, and was to be of great importance to the London publishers, but it provided a distribution system rather than becoming a rival producer. The advantages of the Londoners were too great for any real competition to be possible: they owned the copyrights in the most valuable books and they had the capital to buy more; they had access to the most efficient printing houses; and above all they had each other, for the leading members of the trade, despite the competition between them, always worked together when their oligopoly seemed to be in danger. Nevertheless, they could not ignore the growing provincial market. The country towns may not have had the metropolitan advantages of London, but they were certainly not cultural deserts, and from the beginning of the century the book trade developed rapidly throughout England and Wales.[16]

By about 1730, printers were established in most major towns throughout the country. These printers were not engaged in book production, but in newspaper and jobbing work. The provincial newspapers, throughout the eighteenth century and beyond, were little more than pale imitations of the London papers which were the principal source of their news. Although some became more truly 'local' towards the end of the century, their real local or regional significance was as an advertising medium rather than as a source of news.[17] For the book trade as a whole, the significance of the provincial newspapers lay in the system of distribution which their owners evolved. The provincial newspapers were often circulated over very wide areas, perhaps two or three counties, although these areas tended to contract after the middle of the century as more towns proved able to support a paper of their own. Even then, however, the essential feature of the distribution system remained unchanged: the existence of a chain of agents in all the communities, even down to the level of the larger villages, which the newspaper sought to serve. These agents arranged for local delivery through newsboys who took the paper to individual subscribers. The agent was the crucial link in the chain of supply, for he took orders and advertisements and transmitted them regularly to the newspaper owner. The owners themselves were in regular contact with London, because London was the only source of supply of the stamped paper which, after 1712, was required for all newspapers. Thus the provincial newspaper owners established contacts and, crucially, lines of credit, with the London paper merchants, and through them were able to develop links with the London book trade. From the point of view of the London publishers, the provincial newspaper owners represented a means of deep penetration of the provincial market; the newspaper owners themselves, and many of their agents, became booksellers, and by the middle of the eighteenth century there was no town of any significance which did not have at least one 'bookseller'. Their stocks were limited, but through the chain of contacts which the newspaper distribution system provided, they could order books from the London publishers, which, through the same system, the Londoners were able to supply.

The opening of the provincial market was one of the most important changes in the book trade in the eighteenth century. It is impossible to calculate what percentage of books was actually sold outside London, but the existence of a flourishing provincial book trade itself suggests that the market was significant. It provided the London trade with a national market which enabled them to increase their edition sizes (and thus reduce the unit cost of production) and which consequently increased both their profits and their cash-flow. Moreover, the provincial bookshops did not only sell books; many, perhaps most, of them were also lenders of books through their circulating libraries. These libraries, both in London and the provinces, were of particular importance to the publishers of novels, for far more novels were borrowed than were bought, but the libraries were also significant for other publishers. By the end of the eighteenth century, the library market was another important new addition to the trade's customers, and its importance has never decreased since its establishment.[18]

The distribution system, however, would have been of no avail if it had not been supported by an adequate system of information about what books were available. Again, the achievements of the late seventeenth century were the starting-point for further advances.[19] Although the *Term Catalogues* came to an end in 1709, various individuals within the trade attempted to provide acceptable substitutes. The problem was basically economic; a list of new books might be useful, but it was certainly not likely to be a best-seller. As publicity material it was too expensive for the wide distribution which alone could have justified that expense. The problem was neatly resolved by Edward Cave when he began to include lists of new books in *The Gentleman's Magazine* from its first publication in 1732.[20] *The Gentleman's Magazine* and many of its less successful imitators became the most important source of information about recent publications for customers and booksellers alike. For fifty years *The Gentleman's Magazine* was the trade's only source of such information, until in 1773 William Bent published his *London Catalogue of Books* which purported to list all books published in London since 1700. It did not, but it was the first of a series of such catalogues which Bent published until his death in 1823. His name survived in *Bent's Literary Advertiser* (from 1832), a weekly listing of new books, and the direct ancestor of the lists now published in *The Bookseller* and cumulated in *British Books in Print*.[21]

Catalogues, however, important as they are within the trade, are essentially the occupational tools of the publisher and the bookseller. To attract the customer, something else was needed. Advertising became an important characteristic of many trades in the eighteenth century, but for the book trade, with its centralised production and national distribution, it was of particular importance. Some publishers began to use otherwise blank pages at the end of a book to advertise other titles, but at best this reached a limited audience.[22] Fortunately, there was a more general advertising medium to which the trade had uniquely easy access: the newspapers. The London newspapers, in the course of the eighteenth century, became national newspapers, widely available throughout the country. As with books, the key factor was distribution, although the distribution of the London newspapers was in fact quite independent of the book trade. It depended upon the Post Office, which carried the papers as part of the mail, and whose local officials often acted as agents for the London newspaper owners. By the end of the eighteenth century, millions of copies of newspapers were leaving London for the provinces every year,[23] and for most of these papers advertising revenue was a major constituent of their profits. Eighteenth-century newspapers are full of advertisements for books, because the London newspapers, like books, were nationally distributed. Advertising on a considerable scale became an important part of a publisher's costs, and although the advertisements were sober and factual they represented the beginnings of the vast publicity machine by which the publishing industry now seeks to attract its customers.

Advertisements are by definition favourable to products which they seek to sell. Reviews, on the other hand, are usually somewhat more objective. The reviewing of books in newspapers and magazines is another development of the eighteenth century. Although the earliest 'reviews' were really little more than summaries of the books which they noticed, by the middle of the century a more critical style of reviewing was being evolved largely under the influence of Ralph Griffiths and Tobias Smollett. Griffiths in *The Monthly Review* (from 1749) and Smollett in *The Critical Review* (from 1756) approached their task in a different way from their predecessors; they made assessments of the books they reviewed, and although they often used the occasion to make a political point or to pursue a literary quarrel, they nevertheless pioneered book reviewing of the kind which is now familiar.[24] It was a long time before all reviewers adopted this approach, and epitomes which would not have been out of place in the 1730s were still to be found in some newspapers in the late nineteenth century and sometimes even today. Nevertheless, the emergence of this new style of reviewing was important to the trade: it offered more or less objective assessments of books, and it was not long before 'puffs' derived from favourable reviews began to take their place in the publishers' advertisements in the newspapers.

With the exception of reviewing, these developments within the trade took place in the first half of the century. Indeed, by the end of the 1730s, its operations were different in several significant respects from those of 30 or 40 years earlier. The newly opened provincial market, the existence of good sources of information about new books, and an effective distribution system all pointed the way towards the future pattern of publishing in Britain. It was based in London but depended for its success on a national market. This in its turn created the mutual interdependence of London publishers and provincial booksellers, each seeking to maximise his own profits without alienating the other. Within the London trade itself, change was perhaps less obvious, although the growth of the market did have the important consequence of increasing yet further the value of the publishers' investments in copyrights. Eighteenth-century publishing was, however, essentially a conglomeration of small-scale family businesses, a characteristic which the trade has retained to some extent to the present day. The typical 'publishing house' was small; the owner and his immediate family were the usual participants in it, and all of the publishers were still retail booksellers at least of their own books and often of those of other houses as well.

Small as they were by later standards, the leading publishing houses of the eighteenth century were stable and prosperous businesses. This was perhaps nowhere more apparent than in the three generations of Tonsons who dominated the London book trade. The first Tonson was Dryden's publisher, and one of the pioneers of literary publishing at the end of the seventeenth century. He and his son acquired shares in the copyrights of Shakespeare, Milton, Congreve, Otway, Addison, Steele, Prior and a host of lesser writers. Indeed by the 1730s Jacob (III) Tonson could survive, and live well, entirely on reprints of these old copies.[25]

The success of the Tonsons during a period of over half a century spelt out a clear message for others. The Tonsons' prosperity was based on their ownership of copies, and on the reprinting of the old favourites at regular intervals. For newcomers, the problem was how to acquire the copies which would make this possible, and how to break into the inner circles of the trade at which they were bought and sold. Marrying the master's daughter was one traditional means of entry into any trade; for Thomas Longman and his descendants through six generations it proved to be the road to very great prosperity indeed.[26] For other aspirants there was the harder road of taking the risk of acquiring new copies and testing them in the market. In the expanding trade of the eighteenth century, this route was always possible, and a number of new entrants to the trade made their fame and fortune. Robert Dodsley was one of these, and with the initial help of Alexander Pope, he built up a literary list almost as distinguished as that of the Tonsons themselves.[27]

The trade was, however, giving hostages to fortune. Those who were successful depended essentially on the long-term demand for reprints which were cheap to produce and had a ready-made market. Innovation was not a conspicuous feature of eighteenth-century publishing, and indeed success was more often based on the lack of it. While Dodsley's career showed that it was possible to build up a business based on literary publishing, many turned to the mundane but profitable world of publishing for the newly developing market for practical and instructional books. Longman recognised this at a very early stage in his career, and began the specialisation in schoolbooks which has characterised the house ever since. He had barely gone into business for himself when he acquired the privilege for Lily's *Latin Grammar*, and one of his first new publications was Ainsworth's *Latin Dictionary* (1736). This began a tradition which culminated in the publication of Kennedy's *Primer* which, as *The Revised Latin Primer* (1888), seems likely to survive for as long as the teaching of Latin itself. In the 150 years from Lily to Kennedy, the Longmans built a large part of their business on the publication of schoolbooks.[28]

The demand for books, and especially the demand for new books, created a further demand for writers. Even literary authorship, although it was atypical, was not unaffected by the changes within the trade and expansion of its markets. For the most part, writers no longer even pretended to an indifference to the financial rewards for their labours. The gentleman-poets of the Renaissance had been replaced by the professional writers who looked to Dryden and later to Pope as their model.[29] To make a living from literary writing was a good deal easier in the eighteenth century than it had been before. Many of the major literary figures of the century, including Pope himself, Johnson and Goldsmith, were dependent upon the popularity of their writing for their incomes.[30] Others, of course, had other sources of income; Addison, Steele and Sheridan were all politicians, Richardson was a very successful printer and Gray was a Cambridge don. Nevertheless, for even a few literary writers to survive by their pens was an advance on previous centuries. With the exception of the dramatists, no earlier writers had been able to do so. Pope was probably the first writer ever to make a comfortable living from poetry alone.

This was no accident. Pope was very conscious of his artistry and of the rewards which he felt were his due for employing it. He had an intimate knowledge of the book trade, and disliked much of what he knew. In particular, he sought to exploit the 1710 Copyright Act to his own advantage. He used the law to defend his copyrights, and had a crucial role in establishing that after the first 14-year term of protection the rights in a copy reverted to the author, although in fact few if any other authors followed his example.[31] To protect the artistic integrity of his work, as well as his own income, Pope retained as much control as possible over the publication of his poems. He even intervened directly in the trade; he was certainly responsible for helping Dodsley to establish his business,[32] and probably also established two lesser figures, Lawton Gilliver, the first publisher of *The Dunciad*, and John Wright, the printer of that and many other works by Pope and members of his circle.[33]

No other author was in a position to follow Pope's example of direct involvement in the trade, but Johnson knew the trade at least as well as he. The son of a bookseller, and, despite some of his more famous comments on the subject, the friend of booksellers throughout his life, Johnson always worked for the trade. Almost everything he wrote was written on commission for one or more booksellers, and in that sense he was far more typical than Pope of the majority of eighteenth-century British authors. He was not, however, the first to live in this way. There had been authors who wrote to order since at least the early seventeenth century; an early example was the prolific Gervase Markham, who in the reigns of James I and Charles I had churned out indifferent plays, dreadful poetry and an important group of practical treatises on farming and animal husbandry.[34] By the beginning of the eighteenth century, Markham's successors were the source of almost all the new books that were published.

Much nonsense has been written about Grub Street and the

hacks. In fact, most of them were reasonably well paid, and certainly few if any starved; if they lived in garrets they did so of choice. Moreover, many of them were also reasonably well educated, and although their occupation may not have commanded much respect, it was recognised as one for which payment was both expected and offered.[35] The victims of *The Dunciad* were for the most part paid political writers, who wrote to order not for the booksellers but for their political patrons. It was, however, out of this group that there developed the tradition of writing to order, and it was to such men that an eighteenth-century publisher turned when he wanted a new book on a particular subject. Many of these writers had other occupations: some were clergymen, some were schoolmasters, others had less elevated callings. All of them, however, were professional writers whose motive for writing was money. The development of authorship as a profession in the eighteenth century, under pressure from publishers who were themselves under pressure from customers and competitors alike, was a very important change in the affairs of the trade. The publishers were operating in a sellers' market, but so too were the authors, and gradually the payments made to authors increased, and they began to command rather more respect if only for their growing economic power. Typically, an author was paid by the sheet, that is by the number of printed sheets which his work would fill. It was a one-off payment: he sold the copyright to the bookseller, who could then do with it as he wished. Extant agreements, however, do show some variations, and by the middle of the century there were already a few which show primitive forms of profit sharing or royalty payments, with the author's payment linked to the commercial success of his book.[36]

In some respects, however, the trade had not changed. It was still, as it had been in England since the fifteenth century, insular in outlook. In seeking to defend their copyrights, the trade in 1739 succeeded in persuading Parliament to ban the import of all books in the English language,[37] although the Latin trade from the continent continued, and an increasing number of French books was imported during the century. Exports, however, did grow in importance during the eighteenth century, although, at least as far as exports to Europe were concerned, this was accidental rather than the result of any deliberate actions by the trade.[38] Indeed, English books began to be printed abroad as knowledge of the language spread, and it began to establish itself as a competitor with French as one of the major languages of European culture.[39] The most valuable export markets, however, were in the growing English-speaking communities overseas, especially in North America. Although the American book trade was developing throughout the century, even after 1776 it stood in essentially the same relationship to the London trade as did the provincial booksellers in England itself. Large quantities of books were exported to the American colonies and, partly as a result, the publishing industry both in the colonies and in newly conquered Canada developed late and slowly.[40]

By the middle of the eighteenth century, the British book trade had taken on many of the characteristics which continue to distinguish it. It was dominated by a small group of copyright-owning publishers, whose risk capital lay at the heart of the trade. They were, almost without exception, in London; they were well known to each other and, despite the competitive atmosphere in which they operated, they co-operated whenever their joint interests were threatened. The printers were essentially their paid agents and the retail booksellers, in London and the provinces alike, were their primary customers. The private bookbuyer dealt principally with retail booksellers, and booksellers and customers alike were able to draw on information from catalogues, advertisements and reviews to discover what books were available. The books themselves were a combination of reprints of old favourites and new books on a wide variety of topics, most of which were written by men (and a very few women) for whom writing was an important source of income. It was a situation which is familiar enough to Thomas Longman's successors.

It would, however, have been very strange to his predecessors as little as 50 years before Longman set up shop at the Sign of the Ship. The ending of official controls over publishing had opened the floodgates. The waters which poured out, however, were not those of sedition and blasphemy which had been the nightmare of Tudor and Stuart monarchs, but a highly developed free-enterprise trade, working to the demand of a diverse and growing market, and generating substantial profits for the many who were involved in the long chain of supply from author to reader.

9

Periodicals and Part Books

British publishing in the first half of the eighteenth century was generally characterised by growth and prosperity rather than by innovation. There were, however, three significant exceptions to the generally conservative approach of most members of the trade. The first was the development of the novel. The second was the beginnings of leisure publishing for children. The third, which marked a radical departure from previous practices, was in the field of serial publications. Like some of the trade practices which seem to be characteristic of the eighteenth century, however, serial publishing had its origins in the last decades of the previous century. Indeed, one very important group of serials, the newspapers, had existed since before the Civil War.[1] The second half of the seventeenth century, however, saw the beginnings of a different kind of serial publication, which was not directly concerned with the reporting of current events. These new serials were of two kinds: publications intended to be published at regular intervals for the foreseeable future, and books published in parts. These two kinds of serial, the magazine and the part book, were both of great importance to the trade in the eighteenth century, for each, in its own way, opened up new areas of the market and provided regular incomes for publishers, booksellers and authors alike.

The tradition of periodical publishing was French rather than English in its origins, although when introduced into Britain it soon took on a distinctively British format. The first periodical other than a newspaper is generally considered to be the *Journal des Sçavans* published in Paris from 1665.[2] This was a monthly review of new books, with perhaps a slight bias towards the natural sciences. It was the inspiration for the *Philosophical*

Transactions of the Royal Society which began publication in the same year. *Philosophical Transactions*, until the nineteenth century, was far from being a purely scientific periodical, and the early issues certainly reflected the very broad interests of the early members of the Royal Society itself.[3] Even so, it could hardly command a popular market, but in the 1680s a number of more popular periodicals began to appear which were loosely based on the format of the *Journal des Sçavans* and *The Philosophical Transactions*, but which were deliberately more popular in approach. One of these, *Weekly Memorials for the Ingenious*, was a conscious imitation of its French predecessors, and like the *Journal des Sçavans* was primarily a reviewing periodical.[4] Similar journals, most notably *The History of the Works of the Learned*, maintained their popularity well into the eighteenth century.

These periodicals appealed to a limited market, although a less restricted one, in terms of seventeenth-century readership, than do their modern successors, the learned and scientific journals. The first British magazine which aimed to capture a wider market was *The Athenian Gazette*, published by John Dunton from 17 March 1691, and issued at various intervals between weekly and four times weekly until it closed in 1697.[5] Dunton was a bookseller with a long and colourful history behind him when he started this enterprise, one of several by which he hoped to make his fortune. *The Athenian Gazette* (called *The Athenian Mercury* after its twelfth issue) took the form of a question-and-answer journal. Questions on a wide variety of topics, allegedly submitted by readers, were answered by the 'Society of Gentlemen' (in fact, Dunton himself) who were the 'authors' of the magazine. The question-and-answer journal remained popular for a number of years, and *The Athenian Mercury* found a number of imitators, such as *The British Apollo* (1708–11);[6] indeed, in the late nineteenth century, the young George Newnes revived the form for one of his first forays into popular journalism, *Tit-Bits*.[7] The real significance of Dunton's enterprise, however, lay in the demonstration that there was a market for publications which contained a wide range of miscellaneous information. Dunton himself operated on the fringes of the booktrade; he was, to his chagrin, excluded from the developing inner circle of the conger,[8] and both the peripheral position of the publisher and the anonymity of the magazine itself were typical of much that was to follow.

The Athenian Gazette was very obviously different from its rather sober predecessors and contemporaries in the periodical field, although the most direct ancestor of the typical miscellany magazine of the eighteenth century was *The Gentleman's Journal*, started by Peter Anthony Motteux in 1692. Motteux, as his surname suggests, was a Frenchman, and before coming to England he had known some of the French periodicals, especially the *Mercure Galant*, published in Paris between 1673 and 1674 and again in 1678–9.[9] *The Gentleman's Journal* was unlike either *The Athenian Gazette* or the reviewing periodicals, although it had some of the characteristics of both. It retained the epistolatory convention for certain articles, and it carried some epitomes of new books. The wide range of its coverage was defined by Motteux himself in the first issue: 'News, History, Philosophy, Poetry, Musick, Translations, &c.'. On the whole, Motteux kept this promise of variety. Although the news content was minimal, he did include a number of works by leading poets of the day, including Prior and Sedley, songs (with music), and essays on a wide variety of subjects, as well as fiction some of which was original and some translated from contemporary French romances. In all, *The Gentleman's Journal* was both innovative and interesting.

The Gentleman's Journal, which survived until 1694, was the first example of one of the favourite periodical genres of the eighteenth century, the general magazine with a miscellany of contents in prose and verse, intended as light reading but not devoid of some more serious matter. In that sense, it is indeed the precursor of the general-interest magazine of today such as *The Illustrated London News*. Another tradition of eighteenth-century periodical journalism, however, equally significant in its time, has now entirely vanished, the so-called essay periodical. This tradition started with Defoe, who in 1704 began his *Review*.[10] In its final form, the *Review* consisted of a single essay of several thousand words, covering both sides of a broadside half-sheet, almost invariably on a political theme. Later writers were not so dedicated to politics as was Defoe, and the essay periodical became an important feature of the literary as well as the publishing landscape of the first half of the eighteenth century. Five such periodicals are outstanding. Steele's *Tatler*, and its successor, *The Spectator* in which Steele and Addison collaborated, were both immensely successful. *The Tatler* was published thrice-weekly for nearly three years, and although it maintained to some extent the fiction of a club dealing with the queries of correspondents, it was really a platform for Steele's own views on politics, literature, culture and society.[11] *The Spectator* was, if anything, an even greater success than *The Tatler*. For over 500 issues in 1711–12, it was published on a daily basis, and seems to have sold up to 4,000 copies a day, although its circulation fell after the Stamp Act forced it to increase its price.[12] The most immediate imitator of *The Tatler* and *The Spectator* was *The Guardian*, published daily between March and October 1713, but it never attained he same circulation as its two predecessors.[13] Later in the century, the form was revived by Johnson, whose *Rambler* and *Idler* were conscious imitations of the work of Addison and Steele, although they never achieved comparable popularity. *The Rambler*, for example, was published twice-weekly, and sold about 500 copies.[14]

Circulation figures of even 500 copies on a twice-weekly basis made the magazines into valuable commercial propositions, while *The Spectator* was one of the most spectacular best-sellers of the early eighteenth century. Not surprisingly, the leading members of the book trade were soon very interested in the whole business of periodical publishing, and they played a particularly important role in the publication and distribution of the essay periodicals. The problem for the publisher of a magazine was the need to produce large numbers of copies at regular intervals, since any interruption to the periodicity would be disastrous for sales. There was only one group of men in the trade who could do this, the newspaper printers, and among them there was really only one who was accustomed to working on the scale, and at the speed, which the success of *The Spectator* demanded. This was Samuel Buckley, the publisher of *The Daily Courant*, the first successful daily newspaper, which was selling 800 copies a day as early as 1704.[15] Buckley duly became the first publisher of *The Spectator*. One of the two distributors was Abigail Baldwin, whose late husband, Richard, had been the distributor of *The Gentleman's Journal* in the previous decade.[16] Abigail Baldwin was a trade publisher which suggests that these magazines were sold through unconventional channels as well as through the bookshops of the 'respectable' trade. So successful was *The Spectator* that Tonson himself was attracted to it; he became the publisher with issue no. 499,[17] and in due course he and Buckley each paid Addison and Steele £575 for a half-share each in the copyright of the paper. This was after weekly publication had ended, and Tonson and Buckley re-issued the *Spectator* essays in book form; the four volumes, published between 1711 and 1713, were the first of a whole series of reprints of *The Spectator*, which, like *The Tatler*, was to become one of the most valuable of eighteenth-century copyrights.[18] Tonson was impressed by this success. He was the publisher of *The Guardian*, once again distributed by Baldwin. Despite the comparative failure of this periodical, a collected edition was issued in book form in 1713, and reprints continued for many years.[19] Once again, *The Rambler* and *The Idler* followed this pattern, as indeed did many lesser essay periodicals throughout the century.

Although the essay periodicals were a major commercial and literary success in Queen Anne's reign, it was the less prestigious *Athenian Gazette* and *Gentleman's Journal* which really set the pattern for the future as far as content was concerned. The importance of the essay periodicals in the history of publishing derives from the trade patterns which they established. Indeed, it has been argued that the discipline of producing a weekly or daily publication, whether of a magazine or a newspaper, was responsible for enlarging the management skills of those members of the trade who were involved in their production and sale.[20] The fundamental problem, however, was not production, it was distribution, for important as the metropolitan market was, it was the provincial market which expanded so dramatically during the eighteenth century.[21] Here the periodicals came into their own, and it was this ground that Edward Cave, with his *Gentleman's Magazine*, was to claim for himself. *The Gentleman's Magazine* was by far the most successful of the general magazines of the eighteenth century, and that success was largely built on the vast circulation which it achieved through provincial distribution. Significantly, Cave himself came from a provincial background. He had been involved in the formative years of provincial newspaper journalism, and had also been an official of the Post Office. From these two vantage points, he could see both the growing market for reading matter among the gentry and the urban tradesmen of the provinces, and the means of reaching them directly and comparatively easily.[22]

The Gentleman's Magazine was not as innovative as is sometimes supposed. Indeed, its mixture of contents was not unlike that of the defunct *Gentleman's Journal* which may well have influenced the choice of title. The first issue appeared in January 1732, and the pattern which it was to follow for many years rapidly established itself. It included essays on a wide variety of subjects, poetry, a digest of recent news, columns of births, marriages and deaths and lists of new books. None of this was new in itself, although the listings of both books and personal information were far more accurate than those in competing journals. Most of the information however was avowedly drawn from the newspapers, and even the essays were often reprinted from elsewhere. Cave did, however, make one important innovation. From May 1731 onwards, he began to include reports of proceedings in Parliament. Again there were precedents, but parliamentary reporting was still illegal, being regarded by the House of Commons as a breach of privilege. Those suspected of it were brought to the bar of the House, and it was not unknown for them to be committed to prison until the end of the session. By 1732, the reports of debates were being printed as a major feature of *The Gentleman's Magazine*, using various disingenuous devices, such as disguising names by anagrams, or reporting the Proceedings of the Senate of Lilliput, to disguise the true nature of the articles.[23]

In this, Cave was an important pioneer, although he did not escape parliamentary censure himself;[24] moreover, there is no doubt that the printing of the debates was significant to the success of the magazine. Cave managed to recruit a band of highly talented contributors to *The Gentleman's Magazine*, including Samuel Johnson, who was one of his parliamentary reporters.[25] In fact, Johnson was only one of many writers who benefited from the existence of *The Gentleman's Magazine* and its competitors. The magazines, as they grew both in numbers and popularity, were always in need of material to publish, and they needed writers who could be trusted to meet a deadline. Although the newspapers had produced the first generation of journalists in Queen Anne's reign, it was the magazines which provided an outlet for the talents, great and small, of writers who could not support themselves by writing for the booksellers. These writers, contributing essays, reviews, epitomes, news reports and the like, were able to support themselves by their periodical writing, and the magazines thus played a crucial role in helping authors to establish a stronger position *vis-à-vis* the book publishers in the middle of the eighteenth century.[26]

With the important exceptions of the parliamentary reports and the comprehensive and accurate lists of new books,[27] Cave was doing little that had not been done before, at least in terms of the contents of his magazine. What was revolutionary, however, was his recognition of the importance of the provincial market, and his exploitation of it. His own provincial background explains why he realised the importance of the market, although it is also relevant that Cave came from outside the inner circles of the book trade. He had never been apprenticed to a bookseller, and until he bought his printing house when he established *The Gentleman's Magazine* he had never worked in the trade in London at all. Distribution and sales of periodicals had always been a problem. The more successful magazines, especially the essay periodicals, had been associated with the newspaper proprietors or with major booksellers, while others which had not had these advantages had suffered accordingly.[28] Cave, however, circumvented the traditional mechanisms of distribution. He used the growing number of provincial booksellers; he used his contacts in the Post Office; and he accepted direct subscriptions from customers. All of this laid the foundations for the long-term success of his magazine, and set the pattern for the future. Success brought other rewards too, especially in the form of advertising revenue. Although this is not well documented, it is clear that advertisements represented an important part of the income of *The Gentleman's Magazine* from a very early date, and it was Cave who instituted the practice, soon followed by others, of printing the advertisements on blue paper as part of the wrappers which were removed before the annual volumes were bound.[29]

Cave had many imitators, but the magazine which he founded dominated the market for general magazines for the rest of the eighteenth century, although there was strong competition such as *The London Magazine* (1732–85) and other later titles. In general, however, the other magazines which were successful were those which appealed to a different market from that of *The Gentleman's Magazine*. A number of authors followed the example of Johnson in attempting essay periodicals, and many writers were involved with magazines at various stages in their careers. Fielding was one of these, making a number of excursions into journalism. He was the co-founder of *The Champion* in 1739, and later founded *The True Patriot* (1745) and *The Covent Garden Journal* (1752), although like many authors he tended to use his essay as an opportunity to pursue literary quarrels or to make political points.[30] Smollett was also a periodical journalist, not least as the founder of the influential *Critical Review* (1756), which set new standards of book reviewing in the magazines.[31] Most of these magazines were overtly political, in a way which *The Gentleman's Magazine* was not, although it was the latter which was the exception, a fact which may help to explain its popularity.

Gradually, magazines began to be published for more specialised areas of the market, and towards the end of the century even *The Gentleman's Magazine* began to specialise in antiquarian matters under the direction of Cave's successor, the printer and antiquary John Nichols.[32] It was a sign of the times that magazines for women, which had existed sporadically since the late seventeenth century, proliferated after 1750, as publishers began to realise that the growing literacy of women was providing a whole new market ripe for exploitation.[33] The businessman also needed information, and in the rapidly changing economy of the late eighteenth century he was served by a number of specialised journals, of which the most famous, although by no means the only, example was *Lloyd's List*.[34] Other areas, however, were less well covered. Despite the lively musical culture of eighteenth-century England, no musical periodical was published,[35] and British scientific publishing was as woefully behind that of Germany as was British science itself, although the situation was somewhat alleviated by the development of scientific societies in the last quarter of the century.[36]

The magazines also became a medium for the publication of fiction, and were an important ancillary to the development of the book-form novel from the 1740s onwards. Fiction had been serialised in the magazines and newspapers since the end of the seventeenth century, but in the last third of the eighteenth century this form of publication assumed a new importance. A number of works by major authors were published in serial form, of which the first of any literary significance was Smollett's *Sir Lancelot Greaves*, published in 25 parts in *The British Magazine* between January 1760 and December 1761. Although fiction had been published serially for many years, Smollett was the first author to write a long work specifically for magazine publication, and he had numerous successors.[37] The use of the magazine for fiction was only one of many ways in which serial publication was used to attract purchasers who might be deterred from buying a book for several shillings but who were prepared to spend sixpence on a weekly or monthly basis.

By the middle of the eighteenth century, the periodical was as familiar in the publishing world as it is today, and was of great economic importance to publishers and booksellers alike. To their readers, the magazines offered a great range of miscellaneous information and entertainment and did so cheaply. Indeed the very word 'magazine' sometimes had a very different meaning from that implied by Cave and his successors and imitators. One interesting example is *Martin's Magazine*, published between 1755 and 1765, which was not in the usual sense a magazine at all, but a series of books on philosophy, manners, philology, mathematics and history by Benjamin Martin, published serially. Each issue of the 'magazine' simply consisted of the next part of whichever book was being serialised at the time.[38] *Martin's Magazine* was, in fact, closer to another phenomenon of eighteenth-century periodical publishing, the part book or number book. The part book differed from the magazine in that, although it was issued serially, it was intended to come to an end when a single complete work had been published. This form of publishing had its origins in the late seventeenth century, but it became a major factor in the publishing world only in the mid-1720s when the success of the essay periodicals had demonstrated the existence of the market for serial publications.[39]

It was, however, in the year 1732 that the fashion for part books really began, with rival editions both of the works of Josephus and of Rapin's *History of England*.[40] For the next twenty years, the part books were important to the trade, not least because they appealed to the provincial market. The publishers of the part books, like Cave, had recognised the growing importance of provincial bookbuyers in the economics of the trade. The part books, issued weekly or monthly, physically resembled the magazines, and, like them, could easily be distributed both through the Post Office and through the provincial booksellers. They allowed the impecunious bookbuyer to spread his expenditure over a period of several months or years, and at the same time they allowed the publisher to spread his investment as well. The purchaser normally committed himself to buy the whole series, and to pay by instalments. The publisher therefore only had to fund the printing and distribution of one part at a time, but had often collected the payment for several parts to come. It was a system of publication as beneficial to the trade as it was convenient to the customer. Indeed, part books were perhaps the first publications to be the subject of national advertising campaigns in the book trade, and it is clear that they were a great financial success.[41]

Serial publication, which had barely existed before the Civil War, and was in its infancy when Queen Anne came to the throne, was a permanent and important feature of the publishing scene by the second quarter of the eighteenth century. The wide variety of serial publications — newspapers, essay periodicals, weekly and monthly magazines of all kinds and part books — were increasingly significant in the economics of the publishing industry. They reached a vastly larger audience than any conventional books had ever done in such numbers, and thus both responded to and encouraged the growing literacy of the British public, especially outside London. These early serials are important both as a cultural and as an economic phenomenon, for they provided a regular flow of news, opinion, information, and entertainment throughout the country, and helped to create a common culture and a shared view of the world. Although in later years book publishing and magazine publishing were to become more distinct from each other than they were in the eighteenth century, and the newspapers were to become an entirely separate industry, all three went together for much of the eighteenth century. Thus the serial publications helped to provide the regular income which book publishers needed to provide the risk capital with which they could publish new books, and in that sense the history of magazine and newspaper publishing, and of the part books, is integral to an understanding of the book trade in England in the middle years of the eighteenth century.

10

Publishers and Booksellers

In the middle of the second half of the eighteenth century the British book trade still bore many of the characteristics of 60 or 70 years earlier. Despite important developments, especially in the quantity and variety of material which was being published, the trade was still organised in the way which had been evolved in the twenty years following the lapse of the Licensing Act. This organisation depended essentially on the continuity of the copyrights in which the leading copy-owning booksellers had invested so much of their capital. New books were seen as another addition to a copy-owner's permanent stock of copies, in which, in due course, shares might be made available to others through the trade sales. The system was familiar, safe and successful, all of which made it attractive to the trade. It was not even as exclusive as it might sometimes have seemed. New men did make their way into the trade, although sometimes with difficulty. Despite the rapid growth of the trade, however, it was essentially stable; the momentous events of the 1770s transformed, if they did not entirely destroy, that stability which the trade had enjoyed for so long. The Stationers' Company, whose leading members were already reeling from the Lords' decision in *Millar* v. *Donaldson*, suffered another blow in June 1775 when the Lords ruled that the English Stock's almanac monopoly was also illegal.[1] This marked the end of another long battle against 'piracy', and another victory for the 'pirates'. The almanac monopoly had been under challenge intermittently since the late seventeenth century, but it was Thomas Carnan, who had been in business in London since 1744, who mounted the final assault. He had openly printed almanacs for many years, but in 1773 he virtually challenged the Company to prosecute him. It did, and

Carnan won. Although the English Stock continued to derive considerable revenue from the almanacs until the early nineteenth century, these events reinforced the feeling that the mid-1770s were the end of an era in the formerly ordered world of London publishing.[2]

Although the break with the past should not be overemphasised, new developments came from every direction in the last quarter of the eighteenth century. The ending of 'perpetual' copyrights threw into public domain the profitable copies on which the London trade had depended for nearly a century. New reprint series abounded, and, in real terms, the price of books probably fell under the stimulus of competition. The most famous of the reprint series began as a direct response to the loss of perpetual copyright. John Bell, an enterprising and innovative publisher who had founded *The Morning Post* in 1772, announced his intention to publish a series called *The Poets of Great Britain* in collaboration with the Apollo Press of Edinburgh. This series, which began to appear in 1777, was to include all those popular poets whose works were no longer protected. Bell had already published an edition of Shakespeare (1774), and had initiated a series of reprints of plays under the title of *The British Theatre* (21 vols., in weekly parts, 1776–8). The former copyright owners felt obliged to reply.[3]

Led by Edward Dilly, who was still writing mournfully about the 'invasion' of his 'literary property', some 36 booksellers combined to produce their own edition of the poets. In the end, it was more modest than Bell's, for the booksellers confined themselves to poets working after 1660, did not begin to publish until 1779, and finally produced only 10 volumes by 1781; Bell published 109 volumes between 1777 and 1782. Dilly's trump card was Samuel Johnson whose *Lives of the Poets* were written as the prefaces to the London booksellers' series. Despite its undoubted place in literary history, however, in the history of publishing this series represented the past, while Bell represented the future. Dilly and his associates were merely trying to avoid the inevitable consequences of *Millar* v. *Donaldson*.[4] Bell had discovered, as many after him were also to realise, that reprinting works in the public domain could be a highly profitable activity. There were no authors to be paid (or indeed to be cajoled for copy) and for so long as the book was in demand there was a large and reliable market. There is a direct line of descent from Bell's *British Poets* to Everyman's Library and the Penguin English Classics, for the reprint series and the back-list were destined to become the economic pillars of the British publishing industry.

Having lost the virtually guaranteed income provided by continual reprinting of old favourites under the protection of the law, publishers were forced into new attitudes. If copies were to be protected, at best, for 28 years, then it was necessary to generate new and protected copies. In turn, this meant that the booksellers needed authors to write books for them, advertisements to publicise the books when they were published, and booksellers to sell them to the public. The trade became more specialised than it had ever been before. Dilly himself was an interesting example of this trend. An ardent Whig, he had for many years been involved in publishing political pamphlets as well as in general trade publishing. Wilkes, Hollis and Franklin were among his friends and authors, and after the outbreak of the American War of Independence in 1776, he came to have a near-monopoly of pro-American books in London and even continued to develop his profitable trade with the rebel colonies.[5]

Innovation had never been a notable characteristic of the trade in the eighteenth century, although there had been some developments. One of these, which can now be seen to have pointed towards the future, was in the publishing of children's books. Significantly, the innovator came from outside the charmed circles at the centre of the London book trade. Although John Newbery had family connections with the trade, be began his career in Reading, and only subsequently moved to London. The obvious parallel is with that other great pioneer, Edward Cave,[6] and it is not without interest that Newbery was apprenticed to William Carnan, father of the destroyer of the almanac monopoly. Newbery moved to London in 1743–4 and began to build up a modest but successful general publishing business. His authors included Johnson, Goldsmith and Smollett, of whom the latter edited *The British Magazine* for him.[7] His real fortune, however, came initially from an enterprise outside the book trade, although strangely connected with it. In 1746, he acquired the patent in Dr James's Fever Powder, a proprietary remedy which was an immediate success and which was still on sale in the twentieth century.[8] This was not as eccentric, or as irrelevant, as it might seem. There had been links between the trades in books and patent medicines since the seventeenth century,[9] because the two trades shared a characteristic with each other which differentiated them from almost all other trades: they dealt in products which were centrally produced and nationally distributed. This called for national advertising as well as national distribution, in both of which the book trade had an important role to play. The London newspapers provided the only national advertising medium, and the owners of the medicine patents were quick to recognise the advantages of making use of them.[10] The book trade was even more essential for distribution. The trade's unique pattern of nationwide distribution through local booksellers offered a system from which the medicine owners could clearly benefit. Many provincial booksellers were agents for patent medicines, and a number of members of the London book trade were themselves involved in the medicine trade.[11] Newbery's purchase of Dr James's Fever Powder was a very good investment, but not quite so odd as might be superficially supposed.

It was from the profits of his powders, as much as from his publishing, that Newbery made a good living, but he nevertheless has an important place in the history of publishing for a number of reasons. First, he learned from his experience of promoting the Fever Powder that advertising sold goods, and he applied the lesson to his publishing work.[12] Secondly, he was the first publisher who began to issue his books in an 'edition' binding, in which all copies were uniformly bound before sale as part of the wholesale or retail price.[13] Thirdly, he was the first publisher who made something of a specialism of books intended to amuse children rather than to educate them. He commissioned Goldsmith to write his *History of England* (1764) for the children's market, but his first real children's publication was *The Lilliputian Magazine* (1751). It was issued in monthly parts, and was a juvenile version of the general-interest magazine which is so typical of the mid-eighteenth century.[14] His most famous children's book was *Goody Two-Shoes* (1765), but it was by no means alone.[15] After Newbery's death in 1767, the business was carried on by others,[16] and there were to be many later publishers who found children's books a very profitable aspect of the trade. It is doubtful whether the well-established copy-owning booksellers thought that they had anything to learn from the interloper from Reading, but in fact he had taught them, if they were willing to learn, that there were new markets to be conquered and new means of making money even in an old trade.

Others moved in other directions, and not all of them were new entrants to the trade like Newbery. John Rivington, whose father had taken over the long-established business of Richard Chiswell in 1711, had succeeded to the family firm in 1742. His father, James, had been a member of the New Conger in 1736,[17] but had gradually withdrawn from the collective publishing which characterised the trade in the mid-eighteenth century. The break was not complete, for John was involved with the share books until the 1770s, and was indeed to be Master of the Stationers' Company in 1775.[18] Nevertheless, John Rivington took an increasingly independent line; he became, to his great profit, official printer to the Society for the Propagation of Christian Knowledge in 1760, and was increasingly the sole publisher of the new titles which he issued. When John died in 1792, he bequeathed to his sons, Francis and Charles, a well-established business with a long history of successful publishing. He did not, however, leave them a comparably large bookselling business. Although they continued to sell by retail from their shop in Paternoster Row, the Rivingtons were primarily publishers, perhaps the first firm which can truly be described by that word.[19]

Another old-established business which was revolutionised at the end of the century was that of the Longman family. The first Thomas Longman bought the bookshop of his former master, John Osborn, in 1724,[20] and with it some valuable shares in copies including *Robinson Crusoe*. Both he and his son, also Thomas, who succeeded in 1755, were involved with the congers, active at the trade sales and in the very heart of the trade's affairs. In the last two decades of the century, however, the Longman business began to undergo significant change. When Thomas Norton Longman took over in 1797 he continued and accelerated the process which had been begun by his father of withdrawing from joint publishing enterprises. This proved to present some problems, for although the Longmans could now retain all the profits from their books, they also needed larger amounts of capital to invest in new books. In 1797, T. N. Longman brought in a new partner, Owen Rees, a Welshman who had been a bookseller in Bristol, and others from outside the family followed in due course. Soon the firm employed clerks who were neither family nor partners, established a separate wholesale department and virtually abandoned their retail bookshop. By 1810, Longmans was recognisably a 'modern' publishing house, whose senior partner no longer lived 'over the shop' but had established himself in genteel *rus in urbe* at Hampstead.[21]

Longmans and Rivingtons survived to take their place among the giants of Victorian publishing because they adapted to changing circumstances, abandoning long-standing practices and learning to work in the harsher climate of free-market capitalism. Even so, both remained essentially family firms, Longmans rather less so than Rivingtons, but both had been fortunate in having energetic young men who took over at the end of the old century. Others were less fortunate and less enterprising, and clung on to the old ways for too long. This left the field open for new men like John Bell, and, perhaps most famous of all, John Murray.

The first John Murray, after a brief career in the navy, became a bookseller in 1768, observing that 'many blockheads in the trade are making a fortune'.[22] He bought the stock and copies of William Sandby for about £400, but, like Longman, he now needed more capital. He took a bank into partnership to provide it, in itself a testimony to a more general perception that the book trade could be a profitable investment. In 1771, Murray inherited money from an uncle,[23] and began to publish more adventurously, so that by the 1790s he was regarded as the leading publisher of *belles-lettres*. He had cultivated good relations with booksellers in Ireland and Edinburgh, as well as in London and the English provincial towns, and recruited authors, especially from the Scottish universities, by using these contacts.[24] This was a new way of publishing by a man untrammelled by the traditions of the trade. When Murray died in 1793, he left the business to his son, also John, and a partner, Samuel Highley. As soon as the younger Murray came of age, he bought out the unenterprising Highley, and embarked on the same process as his contemporaries and rivals, Longman and Rivington. He disposed of his retail stock and concentrated entirely on publishing; his authors were to include Scott and Byron and probably no publisher reaped greater profits from the literary revolution of the early nineteenth century.[25]

These dramatic changes in the trade flowed ultimately from *Millar* v. *Donaldson*, although much depended on the personalities of the men involved, and the direction of change might have been somewhat different had it not been for the other factors which were also at work to force the bookseller/publishers of the eighteenth century to change or perish. Far away from the comfortable world of Paternoster Row, the British economy and indeed British society were undergoing radical change. Although technological change came late to the book trade, the effects of the industrial revolution and associated social developments were being felt in the trade during the last quarter of the eighteenth century. Competition was rampant in a period of massive and largely uncontrolled economic growth. New towns grew up around new industries, and created new markets which were demographically vibrant and geographically compact. Service trades flourished in this new economy, and services for education and leisure, which the book trade could provide, were in increasing demand. Self-improvement by self-education was encouraged, and only the book trade could facilitate it. It was a period of great opportunity for those who could grasp it.[26]

In this climate, the provincial trade was of greater importance than ever before and the provinces were beginning to exert a far greater influence on all forms of economic activity. Carnan, the man who had wrecked the almanac monopoly, was not a Londoner. Longman brought Rees from Bristol to inject capital into his business. Above all, the energy and enterprise of the Scots were brought to bear on the London trade. The links between the London trade and Scotland had been strong for some time. Andrew Millar and William Strahan were only two of the most distinguished of the many Scots who were active in the London trade in the eighteenth century.[27] Murray was a Scot, and his link with Scott was in fact through Constables of Edinburgh, as his earlier links with Edinburgh University had been established through Creech and Eliot, the largest booksellers in the Scottish capital.[28] A newer development, however, was that of real competition from the provincial and Scottish publishers, and especially from the latter. In the first two decades of the nineteenth century, four Scottish houses, Constables, A. and C. Black (1807),[29] Blackie (1809)[30] and Collins (1819),[31] represented the first serious and sustained challenge to London's domination of British publishing.

This competitive ethos created an even greater need for an efficient system of marketing and distribution. The first of the great wholesaling houses was, like the first of the true publishing houses, a product of the late eighteenth century. George Robinson was a Cumbrian by birth, went to London in 1755 and worked for John Rivington. With some financial help from Thomas Longman he set up his own business in the 1760s and began to buy shares in copies during the 1770s. By the 1780s, however, he was largely a wholesale bookseller, buying from the publishers and selling to the retailers, especially those in the provincial trade. He soon had by far the biggest business of this kind, which represented another revolution in the book trade.[32] Joint wholesaling had lain at the heart of the conger system which had preceded and prefigured the development of share-book publishing. As the share-book system began to disintegrate in the face of aggressively individualistic publishers like Murray, Longman and Rivington, joint wholesaling also came to an end. Indeed, it had been dying for decades, but the emergence of a large and prosperous wholesale house, benefiting (and profiting from) the entire trade, was a new and significant development, for this was to be the pattern of distribution in the British book trade until after World War II.[33]

The retail trade also underwent changes, although they were perhaps less dramatic. The emergent publishing houses abandoned their retail business for many reasons. By far the most important factor was the sound business practice of specialisation, but in London there was a more specific additional reason related to the changing social geography of the capital. Throughout the eighteenth century there was a westward movement of London's wealthier and more fashionable inhabitants. They left the City for Covent Garden and the adjacent parish of St Giles-in-the-Fields and then went further to St James's, Piccadilly, Marylebone and even Chelsea. Whole areas of the West End, as it came to be known, were redeveloped, as fine houses were built in the new squares: Grosvenor, St James's and Hanover.[34] Among the many far-reaching consequences of the flight from the City (which, for the poor, was in an easterly direction) was the movement of shops to the west, in pursuit of their customers.

The customers of the bookshops were among those who moved in the fashionable world. When Dodsley had established his shop in Pall Mall in 1735, he was among the first to follow them, although Andrew Millar had previously made the move as far as The Strand.[35] Others followed, until by the end of the century Piccadilly, Pall Mall and St James's Street were the centres of the London retail book trade. There were at least seven bookshops in Pall Mall, five in Piccadilly, and three in St James's Street, with others in York Street and Old Bond Street.[36]

If Rivington, Longman and Murray were the first of the new publishers, and Robinson revolutionised the wholesale trade, the pioneer of the new fashion in bookselling was their contemporary John Hatchard. After his apprenticeship, Hatchard had worked, from 1798, for Thomas Payne, the greatest antiquarian bookseller of the day, at his shop in Mews Gate. In 1797, however, he struck out on his own and opened a bookshop in Piccadilly, having chosen the street because it was in the heart of fashionable London. He did a little publishing, but he was primarily a bookseller, and within four years he had the largest conventional retail bookshop in London.[37] The pattern which was to prevail throughout the nineteenth century was now firmly established. The publishers injected risk capital into new books, wholesalers distributed them, and at the end of the chain the retail booksellers laid them before the public.

Hatchard sought his customers from what came to be called the 'carriage trade', but, at the opposite end of the social scale, the 1790s saw another development of great significance for the future: remaindering. The inventor of remaindering was another outsider, James Lackington.[38] He came from a poor and virtually bookless background in the west of England, and after various adventures he established himself in the London retail book trade in 1774. He approached the trade with a philosophy which was very different from that of his predecessors and contemporaries. Lackington claimed, with some justification, an interest in reducing the price of books for cultural and religious reasons, but he also recognised that selling large numbers of books at marginal profits could in the long term generate more income than selling fewer books at higher prices. He gained access to the auctions at which publishers sold slow-moving stock, bought in quantity and proceeded to sell off the books to the public at greatly reduced prices which nevertheless still left him with a small profit on each copy sold. At first, this practice outraged the more conventional members of the trade, not least by its manifest success. Lackington's bookshop, which with typical immodesty he called 'The Temple of the Muses', was soon the largest in London and possibly in the world. Despite trade opposition he was successful, not least because gradually the publishers came to realise the advantage of selling off old stock *en bloc* and thus recouping at least some of their own investments.

By the end of the eighteenth century, the British book trade was recognisably a modern publishing industry. The process of gradual separation of the several functions of the printer, the publisher and the bookseller, which had been evolving since the seventeenth century, was complete. Within each group special-isms were being developed. There were printers who worked on books, and others who produced principally newspapers, just as there were booksellers who catered for different areas of the market. Above all, however, there were publishers who had established their reptutations and developed their expertise in different fields, and whose names were coming to be associated with books on particular subjects or of particular genres. Despite the fears expressed by some in 1774–5, the trade came to the end of the century in a far better condition than it had been at the beginning. Change was in the air, not least a technological revolution in the production of books, but there were those in the London book trade in 1800 to whom change was welcome. That was perhaps the most revolutionary change of all.

Part Three:

The First of the Mass Media
1800–1900

11

The Book Trade and
the Industrial Revolution

The eighteenth century had witnessed an unprecedented rate of growth in demand for the printed word, and had seen the beginnings of the final stages of the transformation of Britain into a print-dependent society. The initial impact of print in the fifteenth and sixteenth centuries had been on the cultural elites already accustomed to the use of the written word. Although the vastly greater number of books, and the much lower cost of buying them, were of great significance, the real importance of the printed word was essentially for a small group. The Reformation broadened this group, and in Britain the political revolutions of the seventeenth century expanded it yet further, but the mass impact of the printed word still lay in the future.

During the eighteenth century, however, the position changed. The development of the provincial trade, and of more efficient mechanisms of supply and distribution of London books throughout the country, both exploited and helped to create a market. Provincial readers shared many tastes with their London counterparts, and indeed the two groups overlapped at the upper end of the social scale, but there were some distinctive trends in the trade which can be attributed to the growing importance of bookbuyers outside London in the economy of the trade as a whole. The thrice-weekly evening newspapers, intended almost entirely for provincial distribution, are perhaps the most obvious example. Another is that of the part books which were principally intended for the provincial market; the form itself had been evolved to overcome the considerable distribution problems which existed in the first two or three decades of the century. It is no accident that the part books came to an end in the 1750s when the trade had developed adequate mechanisms for the distribution of conventional books. Despite their brief life, however, the part books offer a vivid insight into the tastes of provincial readers, and it is particularly noticeable how many of them are books with a practical bias. Instructional manuals in accountancy, simple legal procedures, business practices and the like bear testimony to the awakening economy of the provinces, and of the essentially practical concerns of many provincial readers.[1]

At the same time, the spread of printing through the provincial towns, although it presented no threat to the established book printers in London, gave ready access to printing facilities on a far greater scale. Provincial printers did a little book work, but their real profits were from jobbing printing and, in a few cases, newspapers. Jobbing work was the economic cornerstone of the provincial printing trade in the eighteenth century, and provided the great flood of material which enmeshed the printed word into the fabric of everyday life. Tickets, handbills, advertisements, catalogues, posters and a mountain of other ephemeral productions became familiar to the mass of the people for the first time. As the pace of economic change increased, so too did the dependence on print. More sophisticated marketing techniques, which accompanied the development of new technologies in many basic industries, demanded printed documents of many kinds for packaging and selling alike. In such a society, illiteracy was no longer merely a social stigma, it was a fundamental economic disadvantage.

For the book trade as a whole these developments were to have profound consequences. The deeper penetration of print into society created a greater demand for literacy and for the education which precedes it; but a literate population creates further demand for printed matter for business and pleasure alike. It was from this cycle of development and change that there grew the great edifice of the Victorian publishing industry when the trade reached unprecedented, and perhaps still unequalled, heights of prosperity. The growth in demand for reading matter provoked a search for technical innovations which would facilitate the fulfilment of that demand, although there was also a circular effect: technological innovations which made book production faster and easier, and thus .cheaper, stimulated a further demand-led growth in publishing. The printing process at the beginning of the nineteenth century was essentially unchanged from the methods which Gutenberg had invented 350 years before. Typesetting, printing and binding were all handcraft processes, as were papermaking and typefounding. Within a hundred years this was transformed, although change came slowly, and in some cases very tardily.

The need for mechanisation both of book production itself and of the manufacture of the materials of book production was widely felt in the trade at the end of the eighteenth century. The first changes came to the most fundamental of all the materials of book making, paper. It has been argued that the growth of the papermaking trade in Europe in the fourteenth and fifteenth centuries was an essential precondition to the success of printing itself,[2] but by the middle of the eighteenth century, the paper trade was facing a serious problem. Paper had traditionally been made from linen rags, and the supply of rags could no longer keep up with the demand for paper. Books were absorbing more and more of the available supply; the publishers of the *Encyclopédie* disrupted the entire European paper industry in the 1780s by the sheer quantity of their needs.[3] Inevitably, the price of paper went up, and with it the price of all printed materials. Quantity, however, was not the only problem; as the supply of good rags diminished, so did the supply of good paper since inferior materials were, inevitably, substituted.[4] In England, both Whatman and Baskerville experimented with high-quality papermaking, and Whatman developed a new papermaking method which certainly produced a very high quality of paper,[5] but this was the exception, not the rule. There was a marked decline in the quality of paper towards the end of the eighteenth century as chemical additives began to be used to compensate for the low quality of the only rags which were available in sufficient quantities. Indeed, the quality of ordinary printing and writing paper continued to decline throughout the nineteenth century, and has only recently recovered.

Quantity, however, was the really urgent problem. The age-old method of papermaking by hand was slow and expensive, and could produce only comparatively small sheets. Experiments in the mechanisation of papermaking began in the 1780s, and in 1798 Nicholas-Louis Robert succeeded in building a papermaking machine, driven by water power. He and his designs were brought to England by two London wholesale stationers, Henry and Sealy Fourdrinier, and they built the first commercially viable machine in 1807.[6] The Fourdrinier machines, as they came to be known, revolutionised the paper industry, and indeed the design has never been fundamentally modified. In due course, steam power was substituted for water power, which further increased the speed of the process and reduced the cost of the product. The industrial-scale use of the Fourdrinier machines made paper plentiful and cheap, and transformed the whole paper trade. Formerly paper had been manufactured on a small scale by a large number of mills; in the nineteenth century the paper industry was characterised by the development of a few very large businesses producing huge quantities of paper and marketing it through a small number of specialised wholesalers.[7] The transformation of the paper trade was the first direct impact of industrialisation on the book trades.

Printers had long since lost the central role in the book trade which they had played in the sixteenth century. The economic power was with the publishers, for whom the printers were little more than paid agents; except for the two universities, no major publisher was his own printer. On the other hand, printers had many customers other than the book publishers. Jobbing printing, the production of all the printed paper needed by a sophisticated industrial economy, was the mainstay of the printing trade by the end of the eighteenth century.[8] Book printing was already the specialised concern of a few major houses, another trend which was to strengthen throughout the nineteenth and twentieth centuries. The jobbing printers and the book printers had many problems in common, problems of speed, durability of equipment and ever-increasing print runs, but nowhere were these problems more acute than in the most specialised area of all, newspaper printing.

There were two separate but related problems which were exaggerated in the peculiar conditions of newspaper production. The first was the speed of typesetting, a matter of particular concern to the printer of a daily newspaper, for which many columns of type must be set to an unalterable deadline. The mechanisation of typesetting was to prove the most difficult of all the technical problems facing the printers. Early attempts to reduce the work of the compositors, such as logography, proved to be unmanageably cumbersome.[9] It was not until 1884 that the first successful mechanical system was developed by Ottmar Mergenthaler, an American engineer. His line-casting system, marketed as Linotype, was introduced into Britain in about 1890, and became the norm for newspaper work until it was displaced by computer-based systems in the late 1970s. For book work, however, mechanical typesetting came even later; it was not until after Tolbert Lanston had produced the Monotype system in 1887 that the British book printers began to mechanise their composing rooms. This process started in 1897, and Monotype survived until long after World War II.[10] Thus, for virtually the whole of the nineteenth century, typesetting was done as it had been since the middle of the fifteenth century. Almost the only technical development which affected the great majority of printers was the invention (or more accurately, re-invention) of stereotyping in the first decade of the nineteenth century.[11] Composing rooms were the major source of cost in the book production process, and the compositors found themselves in an increasingly strong position to bargain with their masters. Training was still by apprenticeship,[12] unionisation came early to the composing rooms, and grew strong roots there.[13] As early as 1785, the major London book printers agreed the first version of the London Scale of Prices by which the compositors were paid standard piece-rate wages.[14] The cost of paying higher wages was, of course, passed on to the printers' customers, and ultimately to the book-buying public.

While the composing room remained essentially unchanged, the printing shop was transformed in less than thirty years. The first iron press was built to the designs of Earl Stanhope for the Oxford University Press shortly after 1800.[15] Various other designs followed, most notably the Albion, first made by G. W. Cope in the 1820s, which was to be the standard British book press for decades.[16] As with typesetting, however, the real pressure for change came from the newspaper trade, where speed of production was as important as speed of composition. In 1814, John Walter installed a steam-driven press at *The Times*, the first which had ever been in commercial use.[17] Steam printing was for some decades largely confined to newspaper printing, but gradually books too began to be printed by steam. Long high-speed print runs were now possible for the first time, and, while this reduced unit costs, it also forced publishers to look at the economies of scale which they could obtain from larger editions. For smaller editions, steam printing offered few advantages, and could actually cost more than using an Albion. Many books were still being printed by hand in the middle of the century, although the great bulk of printed matter was, by that time, printed by steam. As time went on, ever more sophisticated presses were designed, which could cope with multiple feeding of sheets, and rolls (or webs) of paper. At every stage, it was the newspaper printers who took the first step,[18] but the book printers eventually followed. Those printers who wished to compete for large jobs were forced to invest in expensive equipment, and the number of printing firms which had the latest and most efficient machines available was small indeed. As in the paper industry this had the effect of creating large-scale businesses. The Victorian printing industry was made up of a few firms using the latest equipment and thousands of small family businesses which were still setting and printing small jobs by hand when the Queen died.

The technical innovations in the printing industry were not confined to papermaking, typesetting and printing itself. In 1798 the process of lithography was invented by Alois Senefelder in Germany. It was introduced into England in 1801, and ultimately revolutionised music printing as well as providing a high-quality, although very expensive, graphic process for illustrations.[19] The more conventional illustration processes were also transformed, first by the development of new versions of traditional techniques, such as plates engraved in hardened steel rather than the softer copper which had formerly been the usual material,[20] then by the invention of new processes for colour reproduction,[21] and finally, and most dramatically, by the evolution of a technology which permitted the printed reproduction of photographs.[22] Lastly, the mechanisation of book binding began in the 1820s, although it was not completed until after the turn of the twentieth century.[23]

All of these changes have to be seen in the broader context of the gradual mechanisation of British industry. Book production was not in the forefront of change, although it was able to take advantage of many innovations made elsewhere, notably in the harnessing of new forms of motive power, such as water, steam, coal gas and, later, electricity. It was not, however, only in technical matters that the industrial revolution had a profound effect on the British publishing industry. Quite apart from the new business practices which were developed in the nineteenth century, which led to a greater regularity in the keeping of accounts and the recording of orders and sales for example, the trade's market also underwent a dramatic transformation as did the means of reaching it.

The industrial revolution created a new kind of urban environment, the modern city. The pre-industrial city, although it was often a centre of production, was in essence a place of commerce and services. The new cities, such as Manchester,

Glasgow and Birmingham depended for their very existence on manufacturing rather than mere trading. The production methods demanded large workforces and thus created the great urban conglomerations of intermingled housing and factories which characterised the cities of mid-Victorian Britain. In turn, this provided a wholly different kind of market for the producers of both goods and services. Rapid population growth increased the number of potential consumers, and at the same time their concentration in large towns made them easier to reach. In turn, this created sufficient business to justify the development of specialised retail and wholesale outlets for many goods. The book trade was not exempt from any of these developments. Indeed, the trade was better placed than many to survive, and benefit from, these changes, for it had pioneered the disseminated retailing of centrally produced goods, as the owners of medicine patents had recognised over a hundred years earlier.[24] Books had always come from few sources and been distributed through many outlets. By the end of the century there were at least 1,000 bookshops in England and Wales, and few towns of any size which had no shop at which books and magazines could be bought. In the major cities there were many bookshops, some of which were large and well-stocked.[25]

Distribution, however, was a different problem. Again it was one which the book trade had always faced, and with which it had coped surprisingly well in the eighteenth century, when sophisticated systems of supply had been developed despite poor transport facilities and primitive credit transfer arrangements.[26] The existing distribution system, however, was transformed by the building of the railways, a process which began in the 1830s and had resulted in the creation of a national network within twenty years. Indeed, the railways have had a central role in the history of British publishing in the nineteenth century in two ways. First, and most importantly, the virtual completion of the railway system in the 1850s gave the publishers rapid and reliable access to the whole United Kingdom market, at comparatively low cost. One of the fundamental economic problems of publishing is the very low value to weight ratio of books. Carriage charges on the railways were low, and for bulk transportation they were ideal, both economically and physically.[27] Improvements in the postal services, which were in part a consequence of the greater speed made possible by the railways, simplified the whole process of ordering and payment, while the latter was also materially assisted by the development of modern banking practices.[28] The second great effect of the railways on the trade cannot be so precisely defined, but it certainly existed. Early railway journeys were long and tedious. Reading on the train became a common pastime among travellers, and spawned a whole family of 'railway' books, cheap books designed to be sold at the station, read on the train and perhaps left behind at the end of the journey. At least one major publisher, George Routledge, made his first fortune from such a series.[29] These series are the true ancestors of the modern paperback bought at the airport bookstall and abandoned at the end of the flight. They proved to be a major economic boon to the publishing trade.

Nowhere is the significance of the railways in the history of the book industry more apparent than in the story of W. H. Smith. At the end of the eighteenth century, Henry Smith was a wholesale newsagent and stationer in a small way of business in the East End of London. His son, William Henry, took over the business in 1812, and developed it considerably over the next few years, especially on the wholesaling side. The dramatic expansion, however, began in 1848 when Smith negotiated with the London and North Western Railway an exclusive contract for bookstalls on that company's stations. The first was opened at Euston in the same year, and over the next twenty years Smith made similar arrangements with almost all the major railway companies. By the end of the 1860s, the number of Smith's station bookstalls exceeded five hundred.[30]

It was not, however, only as retailers that Smith's came to dominate a large part of the retail book trade in Victorian England. W. H. Smith also negotiated contracts with the railway companies for the carriage of newspapers, often on special trains timed to ensure that the papers were available for early morning distribution in the major provincial cities. The firm came to be as dominant in newspaper and magazine wholesaling as it was in railway bookselling, and a very potent force in the publishing industry of the nineteenth century. When Smith's added town shops (as opposed to station shops) and circulating libraries to their armoury, they were well on their way towards a near-monopoly position in bookselling in many smaller provincial towns.[31] For W. H. Smith himself, the reward was a Victorian apotheosis: he was one of the best-respected businessmen of the age, a Member of Parliament and First Lord of the Admiralty, for which latter distinction he was immortalised by W. S. Gilbert as 'the ruler of Queen's navee'. It was a long way from a stationer's shop in the East End.

Smith's, however, were not alone in the field of wholesaling. Indeed, their wholesaling activities were largely confined to the field of newspapers; for books the dominant firm was Simpkin, Marshall and Company. Again, it was a company with humble origins which became one of the giants of the trade. Simpkin and Marshall, however, were unlike Smith in that they were imitators rather than innovators. They began by following the example of Lackington in buying large quantities of books from publishers at low prices.[32] This was in the 1820s when the trade was going through a period of depression; publishers needed to recoup their investments even if the long-term profits were slightly reduced as a consequence. Simpkin and Marshall began to build up contacts in the provincial trade, through which they could dispose of their growing stock of remainders, and they thus established themselves as wholesalers, following the pattern established by Robinson in the last quarter of the eighteenth century.[33] From that point, the business took off, and by the middle of the century. Simpkin, Marshall and Co. was synonymous with book supply for the great majority of retailers in the provinces, and indeed for many in London. When the firm went out of business after the destruction of its warehouse and stock in the Blitz in 1941, it was a major disaster from which the trade never entirely recovered.[34]

The British book trade in the nineteenth century was a modern industry in every way. It took advantage of mechanised systems of production, developed highly efficient distribution arrangements based on the most up-to-date means of transport, and evolved a division of labour both between and within its various branches. Many firms were still family businesses, but they were large and well-organised, and many of their owners were employers of labour on a substantial scale. Millions of pounds of capital investment poured into the trade, much of it generated directly from profit. It was inevitable that attitudes within the industry also underwent a profound change. The parochialism of the battle for literary property and the restrictive practices of the congers and the trade sales vanished into history; the trade was in the marketplace, and the first consideration was economic success in the face of competition.

12

The Organisation of the Trade in the Nineteenth Century

During the first three hundred years of its history, the trade in printed books in Britain was both centralised and organised. This situation was not unique to the book trade. All economic activities were subject to state control, either directly or, more often, through trade gilds and similar bodies. As formal control broke down in the seventeenth century, the protectionist and mercantilist policies developed under the early Stuarts and essentially followed by all governments until very late in the eighteenth century maintained the same tradition. The evolution of the theory and practice of free trade, which was to be the dominant economic theory of Victorian Britain, represented a profound change in the organisation both of the economy as a whole and of trading practices within it. The book trade was not exempt from this change of attitude, and as a consequence its formal organisation in the nineteenth century was far less rigid than it had been previously.

The Lords' decision in *Millar v. Donaldson* can be seen in retrospect as the moment at which the book trade had to confront the problem of competition in its fullest sense. Competition between copy-owning booksellers in the seventeenth and eighteenth centuries had always, in the last analysis, been restrained by their need to work together to protect the very idea of copy ownership. The share books, and the wholesaling congers from which the share book system developed, were only the outward manifestations of the trade's general recognition of the need to modify competition by co-operation. In the last quarter of the eighteenth century, however, this situation changed, and publishers found themselves operating in a harsher climate in which success or failure was apparently a matter for individual firms rather than for the trade as a whole. Those who survived the transition, such as Longman and Rivington, did so by adaptation to the new ways, so that they could compete with newcomers like Murray who knew nothing and perhaps cared less about the traditions and customs of the trade. Longmans and Rivingtons were among the few houses which succeeded in bridging the gap between the old system and the new. Both were fortunate in their family circumstances, but commercial acumen and both the ability to spot new markets and a willingness to deal in them were equally important factors. In mid-nineteenth-century Britain, individual enterprise and achievement were as highly prized in publishing as in all other aspects of economic life.

As names which had been familiar for a century or more vanished from the trade, new names, some of them still familiar today, began to dominate the publishing scene. No firm exemplifies this more than the house of Macmillan, founded in 1843 by Alexander and Daniel Macmillan; the sons of a Scottish crofter, they had been booksellers first in Cambridge and then in London before they began to publish books. The Macmillans imposed their own personalities on their company in many ways. They were careful businessmen who ran an efficient and profitable business. They were also, however, capable of being adventurous publishers. Among their first books were some of F. D. Maurice's controversial works on Christian Socialism, and through Maurice, whom they had known in Cambridge, Charles Kingsley came to Macmillans. They published *Westward Ho!* in 1855, the first of a long series of eminently respectable novels which was to characterise the firm.[1]

Macmillans, however, never confined themselves to a single genre. Indeed, the firm is the archetype of the 'general trade publisher' which is so typical of the British publishing industry in the nineteenth and twentieth centuries. They dealt in both fiction and non-fiction, never too specialised, but never wholly devoted to the popular best-seller while not despising the books which sold well. After Daniel Macmillan's death in 1857,[2] Alexander led the firm in the same direction for the next 40 years. His authors ranged from Kingsley to Kipling, and subjects from theology to travel, but all were characterised by their essential seriousness of purpose. By the last quarter of the century, John Morley, a Macmillan author himself but even more important as a vastly influential reader for the house, felt he could detect, even if he could not define, 'a Macmillan book'.[3]

In the final analysis, the Macmillans were committed to publishing serious books as a serious business proposition. Although Daniel, Alexander and Alexander's son Frederick, who succeeded to the business, all had strongly-held political and religious opinions,[4] they never allowed these to prevent them from publishing worthwhile books which could make a profit, even while they resisted the instrinsically unworthy however personally sympathetic they might be to the author, his argument or his subject. Merit was all, for merit was seen as the key to success in the market.

The Macmillans were not unique in taking this approach to publishing, but there were others in the trade whose editorial policies were based on their own political and social opinions. John Cassell was such a man. He was a committed advocate of the teetotal cause before he became a publisher. Like William Collins and William Chambers, both of whom were publishers and temperance leaders, he combined his two interests.[5] Unlike them, however, Cassell entered the trade, almost accidentally, to promote his views. After a period as a tea merchant, he began to publish *The Teetotal Times* in 1846, and it was from this that he built up his publishing business.[6] Even when he tried to diversify from this somewhat narrow approach, he never abandoned the first principles on which he had founded the firm. He recognised, as did other advocates of the teetotal cause, that the working man had to be lured from the public house by means other than exhortation. Alternative entertainment, and, above all, the means of self-improvement, had to be provided, and much of Cassell's publishing was aimed at precisely this end. He published a number of cheap periodicals aimed at the working-class market, as well as part-books on improving subjects.[7] He also ventured into conventional book publishing, where his list included an early (and arguably pirated) edition of *Uncle Tom's Cabin* in 1852, and a Latin dictionary (1854) whose successor is still in print.[8]

Despite his attempt to extend the range of his business, Cassell ultimately failed in publishing; although his name survived as Cassell and Company, the family connection actually ended in 1864 with John Cassell's death, and in reality he had lost control of the business as early as 1855.[9] A cause alone was not enough. Commercial astuteness was the essential precondition of survival in the capitalist ethos of Victorian publishing, and John Cassell was too eager to promote his cause rather than to attend to the wider demands of the reading public.

The marketplace was the master, and the successful publishers were those who recognised how the market was developing. At one end of the scale, there was a genuine demand from people of all classes for leisure reading. There were few other commercially available leisure activities before the last two decades of the century, when the music halls and spectator sports began to make some inroads into the working-class leisure market. The giants of Victorian publishing may have thought in terms of improving literature, but much of the most financially successful publishing of the nineteenth century was very far from the ideals of Samuel Smiles. Publishers like Edward Lloyd, employing such authors as G. W. M. Reynolds, churned out popular fiction and periodicals for a working-class audience and sold them at a penny a part.[10] Some of this verged on the pornographic, although more was as respectable as it was dull. The mainstream publishers, solid middle-class men who sought a solid middle-class audience, had little sympathy with, or understanding of, the real tastes of the majority of the working class.

The middle-class publishers did, however, recognise and exploit the more respectable market for self-improvement. The cheap reprint series, whose development had been one of the first consequences of the ending of perpetual copyright, was prominent in the trade throughout the nineteenth century. Although much of the publication of improving works for the lower classes was undertaken by charitable and religious societies, it was a segment of the market which was too important for commercial publishers to ignore. By exploiting cheaper methods of production, cheaper materials and cheaper and more efficient systems of distribution, it was possible to sell books in far greater numbers than at any previous time in the history of the trade. Bell's immediate successors in the cheap reprint field included John Cooke[11] and Charles Whittingham.[12] The latter's reprint series included *The British Poets* in 100 volumes (1822), and if that evoked memories of Bell so did the Chiswick Press, Whittingham's imprint, which had exceptionally high standards of production and was a major beneficial influence on early nineteenth-century British book printing. The cheap reprint series had become a fixture in the landscape of British publishing.

Perhaps the greatest innovator in the field was John Murray, son of the founder of the house,[13] whose *Family Library* was inaugurated in 1829. Between that year and 1834, when the series came to an end, some 47 volumes were published, together with 6 others in an associated 'Dramatic Series'. Murray made use of the technological innovations of the previous thirty years, especially stereotyping, to hold down both costs and prices. This was an important innovation in itself, but the *Family Library* is also notable for its contents. Unlike Bell, Whittingham, Cooke and others, Murray did not simply reprint the favourites of earlier generations. *The Family Library* included Southey's *Life of Nelson* (1830), several books by Washington Irving and Milman's *History of the Jews* (3 vols., 1829). Consequently, Murray was paying copyright fees, unlike the earlier reprinters, and this contributed substantially to his expenses. In the end, the *Family Library* failed, partly because the books were perhaps a little too serious for the popular market for which they were intended, and partly because of the comparatively high costs incurred by Murray's standards. Nevertheless, the *Family Library* was a significant short episode in British publishing, for it showed that major publishing houses would have to learn the ways of their lesser competitors if they were to compete in this growing area of the market. It was a lesson which was not to be lost on others.[14]

Murray was perhaps never entirely comfortable with the reprint series. Others revelled in it, none more so than George Routledge. Routledge had trained as a bookseller's assistant, established his own business in 1836 and begun to specialise in remaindering. His great competitor was Henry Bohn,[15] a German refugee who dominated the remainder market in the 1830s as much as Lackington had at the turn of the century and Simpkin and Marshall in the 1820s.[16] Routledge displaced Bohn, as the latter acknowledged, but he soon came to realise that in the midst of the spate of cheap publications made possible by the adoption of steam printing, remaindering was no longer the profitable activity which it had once been. Routledge turned to publishing. He was one of the first publishers to recognise the potential of the 'railway' market; his *Railway Library*, which he started in 1848 (the very year ín which Smith opened the bookstall at Euston), was the foundation of the firm's subsequent good fortune.[17] Routledge was no Scottish Puritan in the tradition of Murray or Macmillan. His business dealings were not always above suspicion, and he found himself on the wrong side of the law of copyright on more than one occasion.[18] On the other hand, some authors, including Disraeli and Bulwer-Lytton,[19] benefited very considerably from the inclusion of their books in the *Railway Library*, and the final impression is that of an astute operator who was always sharp and sometimes a little too sharp for his own good. Certainly the firm was successful; the *Railway Library*, only one of several such cheap series which Routledge published, ran to over 1,000 volumes. At the end of the century a series of mergers led to the creation of the eminently proper house of Routledge and Kegan Paul which still flourishes.

Successful publishers in nineteenth-century Britain were those who stayed ahead of the market and helped in its evolution. Perhaps this was never more obvious than when the 1870 Education Act suddenly created a vast new market for elementary textbooks for the newly established Board Schools. The number of elementary schools increased by 50 per cent in the first four years after the passage of the Act, and the number of attendances rose by half a million.[20] Quantity, however, was not the only requirement. Matthew Arnold was only the most eloquent of the many critics of the elementary readers and other schoolbooks available in the late 1860s.[21] It was clear that a field of publishing which promised vast profits was rapidly opening, although Longmans and Murrays had both already discovered that publishing for schools was not without problems of its own when they had tried to win the contracts to provide books for the National Schools in Ireland in the late 1840s and early 1850s.[22] Longmans, with their long tradition of educational publishing, were nevertheless quick off the mark. Macmillans soon followed. More surprisingly, perhaps, so did Cambridge University Press, trying to rescue itself from financial chaos, and sensibly taking advice from experienced publishers about new trends which the Syndics would be well advised to follow.[23]

The Victorian publishing house existed very much in the image of its owner. It reflected his interests, his religious and political beliefs and his social and economic priorities. In their turn, the books which the publishers produced reflect the concerns and interests of the liberal traditions of the mid-Victorian middle class, paternalistic and exploitative by turns. Anything remotely resembling the seventeenth- and eighteenth-century structures of the trade would have been wholly inappropriate to this lively and prosperous industry. Yet the competing publishers did have interests in common. All needed to produce and to sell their books, and with the newly developed divisions of labour within the trade this meant that they were dealing with printers on the one hand and booksellers on the other.[24]

The printers were well organised, but the booksellers experienced serious problems throughout the nineteenth century, and it was they who were largely responsible for attempts to form strong central organisations. The development of clear lines of demarcation between the publisher and bookseller, a process which had begun in the late seventeenth century, but which was not complete until after 1800, necessarily created a certain conflict of interest between the two sides of the trade. Publishers sold books to booksellers, but it was the booksellers who had to sell them to the public. As publishers sought ever wider markets, and sought to reach them by cheap books printed in large editions, the booksellers found themselves facing a serious economic problem. For a publisher, the sale of say 10,000 copies of a cheap book brought a substantial income, even if part of the edition was ultimately remaindered; for the bookseller, however, the retail sale of perhaps a few dozen copies of any one title brought a profit which might seem acceptable when expressed in percentage terms, but which simply did not generate the cash-flow necessary to sustain a business. The cash-flow problem bedevilled nineteenth-century bookselling, as did the related problem of price-based competition between booksellers. As a consequence, the booksellers, despite their competitiveness, found themselves forced to act in concert with each other in the hope of imposing terms on the publishers which would enable them to survive. The internal history of the trade in the nineteenth century is largely concerned with the efforts of the booksellers to work together, and to reach agreements with the publishers to protect both their profits and their cash-flow.

From the beginning, the solution was fully understood: that publishers should fix a retail price for their books and then allow a generous discount to booksellers provided that the booksellers agreed to sell the book at not less than the publisher's fixed price. The problem was not to invent a solution, but to enforce it. The first serious attempt was made in 1829 when a group of major publishers and booksellers came together to develop the Bookselling Regulations, which had the effect of fixing both trade and retail prices, and thus guaranteeing the booksellers' profit margins. This was a time of serious crisis in the trade. In 1826, the bankruptcy of Constables of Edinburgh, publishers of Scott's novels and much else, brought down half the London trade. Some did not panic, and a few like Henry Colburn actually emerged from the year in a stronger position, but for most publishers it was a terrible time.[25] It was a good time for the booksellers to exert themselves, for the publishers, at least temporarily, had little power to resist. Unfortunately, the committee which evolved the Bookselling Regulations was not fully representative of the retail trade, and the Regulations proved impossible to enforce. By the late 1830s, when the trade was buoyant again despite the general economic depression, the system broke down completely, and even before then had never been universally accepted.[26]

There was a problem even more fundamental than reaching enforceable agreements within the trade. The whole economic philosophy of the mid-nineteenth century favoured free trade; the repeal of the Corn Laws in 1846 was the effective end of protectionist economic policies, and the dominant Liberalism of late Victorian Britain favoured the minimalist state. Indeed, the trade benefited from this in one significant way, for the repeal of the remaining paper duties in 1861 was, in part, a consequence of the application of that same philosophy.[27] It was in the immediate aftermath of the greatest triumph of the free traders that, in the autumn of 1848, the booksellers once again tried to develop a general system of fixed prices for books. It was a very ill-timed initiative. There was a storm of opposition from the establishment. From Macaulay to the editor of *The Times*, influential men attacked the trade for what they saw as a concerted attempt to impose high prices on the bookbuying public. The Booksellers' Association, which had grown out of the committee which had supervised the 1829 Regulations, submitted to public pressure and agreed to abide by the results of independent arbitration. An *ad hoc* committee was established under the chairmanship of Lord Campbell, a distinguished lawyer and politician, and a future Lord Chief Justice of Queen's Bench and Lord Chancellor. With him sat the historian George Grote, and the Dean of St Paul's, the prolific author H. H. Milman. The trade broke ranks, and the growing number of booksellers who openly defended free trade in books won the day, not least by recruiting the help of a number of authors who supported their case; these included Dickens, Carlyle, who was always a fervent advocate of cheap books and something of an enemy of the trade,[28] and Tennyson. The Campbell committee reported against fixed prices, and in 1852 the Booksellers' Association dissolved itself, inaugurating a period of unrestricted competition in the book trade.[29]

The abandonment of any attempt to enforce a fixed-price agreement was ultimately disastrous for the trade. By the 1860s, the trade press was full of sad stories of failed booksellers, and even of failed remainder merchants, for whom market forces had led to bankruptcy. By the late 1880s, the trade was in a state of serious crisis, and the publishers were faced with the prospect of being cut off from their market by a lack of stockholding booksellers. The reason was a simple one; with intensive price competition, booksellers could only afford to stock the most popular and fast selling books, and had no space on the shelves for the larger, and perhaps more worthwhile, works which would sell slowly and in smaller numbers. The bookshops, the only public shop-window for the publishers, were being squeezed out of business as a market mechanism for serious literature. Indeed, it was eventually from the publishers and not from the booksellers that there came the initiative which was to solve the problem or at least to shelve it for the better part of a century.

The lead was taken by Frederick Macmillan, who had inherited the now venerable house in 1890.[30] In that very year, he proposed that books should be published with a fixed, or 'net', retail price; the bookseller would be given a discount which made it impossible for him to sell the book to less than the net price, but which would nevertheless guarantee him a reasonable margin of profit. No books would be supplied to any bookseller who broke the rules.[31] The proposal was not popular with Macmillan's fellow publishers, but the booksellers recognised its merits, and, led by Simpkin Marshall, the great wholesaling house,[32] they supported the plan.[33] During the 1890s, Macmillans published a number of net books, and were actively supported by the newly formed London Booksellers' Society, which indeed devoted much of its effort to promoting the idea of net books throughout the trade. In 1895, the Society transformed itself into the Associated Booksellers of Great Britain and Ireland, with the avowed objective of persuading publishers to issue books at net prices and to guarantee trade discounts.[34]

Other publishers could not ignore the booksellers' enthusiastic response to Macmillan's proposal, and they formed an organisation of their own which could act as a representative body in negotiations with the booksellers. This organisation, the Publishers' Association,[35] finally agreed to experiment with net books throughout the trade, when they found that not only the booksellers, but also the authors, were generally favourable to the idea.[36] The authors were represented by the Society of Authors, founded by Walter Besant in 1883,[37] and in 1898 all three bodies met and reached a preliminary agreement. This agreement was finalised in 1899, and came into force on 1 January 1900. The Net Book Agreement, which in a slightly modified form still operates throughout the trade,[38] essentially followed Macmillan's proposal of ten years earlier. The publisher had the right (but not the obligation) to fix a price for every book published. The bookseller was then obliged to sell the book at not less than that price, in return for a trade discount. Any bookseller who infringed the rules would not be supplied on trade terms by any publisher of net books. It was a draconian measure, but it was thought to be necessary to save the trade, and it certainly worked. Individual initiative had ultimately failed, and by the end of the nineteenth century publishers, booksellers and authors alike recognised their mutual interdependence. Although the Net Book Agreement was to be severely challenged during its first few years, it survived to be the economic cornerstone of the whole structure of British publishing in the twentieth century.[39]

The absence of formal structures or of any form of central control made the British publishing industry in the nineteenth century quite different from what it had been during the previous three hundred years of its existence. The trade was a far less tightly-knit group than it had ever been before, and publishers saw themselves as competitors rather than collaborators. They could work together if it became essential, but for the most part publishing was a highly individualistic enterprise. Publishing houses of all kinds reflected the commercial, cultural and political interests of their owners. Nevertheless, a pattern of development can be seen. The crisis of the 1820s produced not only the abortive Bookselling Regulations, but also the first serious attempts to find new directions in which publishing might go in search of profit. The next decade saw many important developments as the use of steam presses for book printing brought the fruits of technological change to the publishers for the first time. By then, the structural changes which had flowed from the events of 1774–5 were complete, and the time was ripe for innovation. It came from two directions: in the world of fiction, the rediscovery of the appeal of the part book brought a new generation of novelists into the bookshops, and at the same time cheap materials and production methods began to be used for the great mission of bringing high culture to the lower classes. The story of British publishing for the rest of the nineteenth century centres around these themes. The financial troubles which beset the trade in the 1880s and 1890s were genuine enough, but they were, in a sense, the troubles of success. The printed word was unchallenged as a medium of mass communication; free competition, an expanding market and more efficient technologies combined to give enterprising publishers the greatest opportunities in the history of the trade. It was, above all, in the publication of fiction that this opportunity was seized with enthusiasm and optimistic fervour.

13

The Age of the Novel

The novel was the dominant literary form of the nineteenth century, and it was therefore a genre of the utmost importance to the publishing industry. Indeed, because the novel was a product of the age of printed publication,[1] the relationship between form and text, and between author and publisher, was unusually close. While the dramatist wrote for the stage, the essayist for the editor and the poet for a small literary elite, and the novelist wrote for his publisher. It was the publishers who exploited the mass market which the novel could command, to the extent that they even allowed market forces to dictate the physical form in which novels were produced. Throughout the century, from Scott at the beginning to Hardy at the end, the great novelists commanded a large popular audience, reached through a multitude of channels. Not only the bookshop but also the circulating library was crucial to the commercial success of the Victorian novel, and the various forms in which it was published — single-volume, multi-volume, three-volume, serialised in parts or serialised in magazines — reflected changing tastes, changing outlets and changing market demands.

The story begins with Scott whose popular successes with the Waverley novels transformed the publication of fiction. Previously novels had been published in editions as small as 500, largely for the circulating libraries, but with *Waverley* (1814) Scott and his publisher, Archibald Constable, made the breakthrough to the mass market. The book was a best-seller, perhaps the first work of English fiction which can be meaningfully described by that term. Constable sold the first edition of 1,000 copies within a few weeks, and reprinted 2,000 within three months of publication. Cheap editions followed, and by 1829 some 40,000 copies had been sold in this form. Scott's later novels repeated this early success. In 1816, *The Antiquary* was published in a first edition of 6,000 copies, and Scott and his publishers looked forward to the profits both of that edition and of the inevitable cheap reprints. The financial troubles of 1826, which ruined Constable and whose after-effects broke Scott's health, were partly a consequence of events extraneous to the publishing industry, but they did emphasise the other side of the coin of success. The huge editions, and the massive distribution problem which they created, required unprecedented scales of investment before publication. With Scott and Constable, we can see for the first time the fundamental economics of modern publishing: heavy investment in a first edition, not least in advertising and marketing, in the hope of reaping profits from reprints once the title was established as a steady seller on the back-list.[2]

The failure of Constable, however, made publishers in general very cautious about the publication of fiction, especially of new novels by unknown novelists. John Murray was one who was worried about this, and both Henry Colburn and Richard Bentley, although they were arguably the most prolific fiction publishers of the 1820s, were also reluctant to experiment with the unknown.[3] When the revival came, in the 1830s, it was largely the work of a new generation of publishers, notably Chapman and Hall, Bradbury and Evans, Smith Elder and John Blackwood. Macmillan followed the trend, although somewhat reluctantly and in very special circumstances; of the old-established houses only Longmans made any real impact on the publishing of novels in the middle years of the century.[4]

Despite the doubts and concerns of the older publishers, however, the success of Scott had demonstrated the existence of a market for novels on a hitherto unsuspected scale. So influential was the example of Scott that even the physical form which had been convenient for *Waverley* became the normal form of the novel for the greater part of the century. *Waverley* was originally published in three volumes, for no reason other than the fact that three volumes were needed for the length of book which Scott had written. Many of Scott's subsequent books were also in three volumes, and by the end of the 1820s, the 'three-decker' was established as the correct way to publish a new novel. Even the price was standardised. This again originated with Scott and Constable; in 1821, Constable priced *Kenilworth* at 10s 6d per volume, and one-and-a-half guineas (31s 6d) was the price of the three-decker until the end of its long reign.[5] Throughout the late 1820s and early 1830s, quantities of three-deckers were published, although none of them equalled the success of Scott.

The three-decker with its virtually fixed price was an essentially conservative component of mid-Victorian publishing. With its safe market in the circulating libraries it generated profits for author and publisher alike. Nevertheless, some of the greatest and most successful novels of the century were published in a very different form, the serial. The serial publication of books had been known to the trade since the late seventeenth century, and had been something of a craze for a period in the first half of the eighteenth century.[6] The application of the principle to fiction was not entirely without precedent either, for many novels had been serialised in magazines at the end of the eighteenth century.[7] There were a few more occasional examples in the 1820s, when Colburn published some serial novels under the general title of *Colburn's Modern Novelists*.[8] Even so, the remarkable success of the serial as a form of publication for fiction could hardly have been predicted when Edward Chapman and William Hall approached the young Charles Dickens in 1836 and asked him to write a text to illustrate a series of comic engravings which they proposed to publish over the next year or so.

The success of *Pickwick Papers*, the book which Chapman and Hall found that they were publishing, is one of the legends of the history of literature and the book trade alike. After initially slow sales, and a reduction of the print run from 1,000 copies to 500 between the first and second of the monthly parts, *Pickwick Papers* became the first best-seller since the death of Scott, and its author's popularity hardly wavered until his death over thirty years later, or indeed since then. This very success has tended to obscure the originality of the exercise, and the extent to which Chapman and Hall exploited newly available technologies and distribution mechanisms. As sales rose rapidly from the fourth part onwards, the young publishers (barely older than their new author), were forced into using the latest printing techniques, into stereotyping to produce multiple editions, into wide advertising and into distribution by the barely opened railways. They reaped the fruits of their enterprise, for the popular success of *Pickwick* was as crucial to the establishment of their business as it was to that of Dickens' reputation.[9]

Dickens continued to publish in parts for the rest of his life, and this fact has perhaps led to an overemphasis on the importance of the part-issue novel in the nineteenth century. Among the major novelists, only Thackeray followed the example of Dickens in using monthly parts, although George Eliot used a modified form of serial publication for *Middlemarch*, by publishing in eight bi-monthly parts which made up four volumes. This arrangement, painfully negotiated between the novelist, G. H. Lewes and John Blackwood, was unique, although Blackwood had suggested something similar to Bulwer-Lytton for *My Novel* in 1849.[10] There was, however, another form of serialisation which had a limited popularity in the middle of the century: publication in a magazine. Again, Dickens was active in this field; *The Old Curiosity Shop* was originally published in *Master Humphrey's Clock*, a magazine edited by Dickens himself. This, however, was a rather unusual example, for by that time Dickens was firmly in command of his relationships with his publishers and so great was his success that they had to do as he wished.[11] Dickens also published the work of other novelists in his magazines; Mrs Gaskell's *Cranford*, for example, was first published in his *Household Words* in 1851–3.[12] *The Cornhill Magazine*, however, was a different matter. Edited by Thackeray, whom the publishers Smith Elder paid very generously to confer his name on their magazine,[13] its serialised novels included George Eliot's *Romola* (1862–3), for which George Smith had paid no less than £7,000.[14] Indeed, George Eliot rather favoured this form of publication, for her *Scenes of Clerical Life* was first issued in *Blackwood's Magazine* in 1857.[15]

Despite the serials, however, the three-decker was the dominant format of the Victorian novel. The reason for this provides a valuable insight into the world of nineteenth-century publishing in which the marketplace was the most vital force. Three-deckers were undoubtedly expensive; while a Dickens novel in parts cost the subscriber about £1 for a completed novel, over a period of nineteen months, the purchase of a three-decker, usually with a somewhat shorter text, involved the outlay of over 50 per cent more all at once. This was not so close to the economics of the madhouse as it might seem, for the publishers of the three-deckers had a captive market to whom the three-volume novel was meat and drink. That market was the circulating libraries whose influence on the Victorian novel, in both form and content, was paramount perhaps even above that of the publishers themselves. The first circulating libraries had been opened soon after the Restoration, and during the eighteenth century they had spread throughout the country until amost every bookshop had a few books available for hire. By the last quarter of the eighteenth century the circulating libraries were perhaps the normal source from which most readers obtained their fiction, and it could be argued that the whole craze for the Gothick novel was sustained by circulating library demand. Formula fiction was born long before Mills and Boon.[16]

The circulating library, however, was transformed in the nineteenth century from being the province of the small-town bookseller to that of the national businessman. This was the achievement largely of one remarkable man, Charles Edward Mudie. Mudie started his career in 1842 as a stationer and newsagent in Bloomsbury. In the following year, he opened a circulating library, and thereafter the company grew without interruption for 50 years. By 1875, Mudie had 125 branches throughout the kingdom, and was regularly ordering new books in quantities as great as 2,500 copies.[17] Such an enterprise could not be ignored by the publishers, and for so long as Mudie wanted three-volume novels, they continued to publish them. Mudie did want three-volume novels, for he could charge his customers three times as much for them as he could for novels in a single volume. One-volume novels were less well advertised by Mudie and not so prominently displayed in his libraries; since he was regularly taking more than half of the print run of a middle-range novel, his wishes could not be ignored.[18] Even W. H. Smith, who had founded his own libraries in competition with Mudie in 1860, could not counteract Mudie in this preference for the three-decker. Although Smith never entirely shared Mudie's prejudice, and gave far greater prominence to one-volume novels, including cheap reprints, it was not until Mudie came to agree with him that Smith was able to take steps to end three-volume publication.[19]

No episode illustrates more forcefully the influence of the circulating libraries than the story of the ending of the long reign of the three-decker. In the summer of 1894, the libraries were suffering financially from a decline in membership and use, partly perhaps because of the competition which was emerging from the public libraries established in many towns under the 1850 Public Libraries Act. The owners of the major circulating libraries demanded that the publishers should reduce the price of novels to 4s 0d per volume, and wait for a year before issuing cheap editions. Mudie's announced publicly that they would refuse to buy books from any publisher which did not co-operate. This unrealistic demand was designed to disguise Mudie's real motives. Privately, he indicated that he thought that the real solution to the crisis lay in abandoning the three-decker and publishing new novels in a single volume.[20] Smiths, who had never been as attached to the form as Mudie's, took a similar line,[21] and, despite objections from the Society of Authors,[22] the pressure on the publishers was irresistible. They were already under pressure from the booksellers about underselling, and indeed from some of their own number about net books.[23] Within a matter of weeks the major publishers were announcing their novels for the 1894–5 season in single-volume form.[24] The end came quickly. In 1894, 184 three-deckers were published; in 1895 this fell to 52, and in 1897 there were only four.[25] The three-decker was dead, and it had been killed by the circulating libraries which had sustained it for so long.

The three-volume novel had always been intended primarily for the circulating libraries, although never entirely so; Disraeli's *Endymion*, for example, the only avowedly fictional work ever published by an author resident in 10 Downing Street, was a massive popular success in its three-volume form.[26] That was, however, something of an exception. In general, it was in single-volume form that novels achieved mass sales if they achieved them at all. Typically, the one-volume novel was priced at 6s 0d as against the 31s 6d of the three-decker, although many were actually reprints of books which had already been published either in three volumes or serially. The reprint series was particularly favoured by some publishers. In a sense Routledge's *Railway Library* falls into this category, although it also included a good deal of non-fiction,[27] but more typical was Bentley's *Standard Novels*, which eventually ran to 126 volumes published between 1831 and 1856.[28] An equally remarkable, and perhaps even more imaginative enterprise, was the single-volume reprint series of one author's works. In 1844, Smith Elder re-issued the novels of G. P. R. James in this form, followed by Chapman and Hall's 'Cheap' editions of Dickens and Bulwer-Lytton (both 1847).[29] Indeed, many of Dickens' later novels were issued in cheap one-volume form after the initial part-publication and single-volume reprints from the plates of the parts. *David Copperfield*, for example, was published in parts in 1849–50, and subsequently in Bradbury and Evans's 'Cheap' edition (at 5s 0d) and in their 'Library' edition (2 vols. at 6s 0d per volume).[30] Such devices kept books in the shops and on the bookstalls in a convenient form at prices which customers could afford to pay. They were also immensely profitable; Chapman and Hall sold 612,000 volumes of their 'Charles Dickens Edition' of the novelist's work in 1867–70.[31]

The one-volume novel, whether a reprint or an original work, reached a wider market than the three-decker, and was a more permanent feature of the scene than the comparatively transitory serialised or part-issue work. Even so, there was a market which the great Victorian novelists, for all their popular success, could never reach. In a society which was rapidly achieving something very close to total adult literacy there was an ever-increasing number of potential readers for whom the social niceties of Thackeray or the moral power of George Eliot was of little interest. For these readers, the genuine mass market in terms of their numbers, publishers also provided vast quantities of fiction. It is forgotten, perhaps deservedly so, by literary critics, but for the publishing industry it was of crucial importance. It is not too far short of the truth to distinguish between 'middle-class' and 'working-class' fiction in this context. The dividing lines were as sharp on the printed page as they were in the social reality of mid-nineteenth-century Britain.

The popular fiction of the 1840s grew out of earlier traditions of popular publishing. The ballad and the chapbook are both among the ancestors of the penny-a-part novel. Its literary antecedents include the Gothick horror stories which were the staple fare of the working-class reader long after the middle classes had moved on to a very different type of fiction, and the immensely popular accounts of crimes, executions and other real-life horrors which sold in tens of thousands. A new development of the late 1830s was the publication of plagiarisms of middle-class fiction, especially of Dickens, and despite attempts to use the law of copyright against the publishers of such works, they were issued in great numbers.[32] Stories of domestic life, often with overtones which could not have been so innocently presented in a post-Freudian age, were another feature of popular fiction which appealed to a mass audience. These books, almost invariably issued in weekly parts at 1d each, were not the province of the giants of Victorian publishing who brought out the works of Dickens or Trollope. Very little is known of these publishers beyond their names,[33] although one of them, Edward Lloyd, is slightly less obscure. He was later to become a semi-respectable publisher of cheap newspapers, and in 1876 bought the eminently respectable *Daily Chronicle*.[34] He was a self-educated man from a slum background who fully understood the market which he was so successful in exploiting.[35]

Lloyd normally avoided outright pornography, but others were not so fastidious. Despite the moral façade of nineteenth-century Britain, more pornography was published in Queen Victoria's reign than during any previous period. The trade in pornography was by definition *sub rosa*, but no account of Victorian publishing is complete without it, if only because of the long-term effects of the reaction to it. [36] John Camden Hotten was only one of several men who straddled the worlds of respectable and pornographic publishing. He published a good deal of American literature in London in the 1860s, and wrote lives of Dickens and Thackeray which he published himself. At the same time, he was also a prolific publisher of books which his contemporaries considered to be pornographic.[37] By the middle of the century there was a sufficient degree of concern about pornography to provoke the first legislation which had ever attempted to deal with the subject. In 1857, an Obscene Publications Bill was introduced into the House of Lords by Lord Campbell, and it became law in the same year. The 1857 Act gave the authorities new powers to continue to do what they had been trying to do for 50 years: to suppress the trade in pornography. These powers included the right of the magistrates to issue warrants to the police to search premises for suspected obscene material, and to destroy any that was found. In itself, this was useful to the police, but it was the judicial interpretation of the Act which was crucial in establishing the law. In 1868 a bookseller in Wolverhampton was prosecuted for selling obscene material, and Mr. Justice Cockburn ruled in Queen's Bench that 'the test of obscenity is whether the tendency of the matter charged . . .is to deprave and corrupt'.[38] This was to remain the law until 1959, when a new Act permitted, for the first time, a defence on the grounds of literary merit. Until that time it was possible to ban books regardless of the motives of their authors in writing them if the magistrates decided that they tended to deprave or corrupt the reader. The 1857 Act and the Cockburn Judgement were the most lasting legacy of the Victorian pornographers. Among many examples of prosecutions under the 1857 Act were those of Henry Vitzelly for publishing translations of Zola in 1888,[39] and of Jonathan Cape for Radclyffe Hall's *Well of Loneliness* in 1928.[40]

The three-decker, the cheap reprint, the working-class novel and even pornographic publications all serve to emphasise the extent to which the market for popular entertainment in the nineteenth century was dominated by books, and particularly by the novel, at least until the development of the music hall and of spectator sports. Nevertheless, other forms of literature did flourish. Scott, the first of the best-selling novelists, had been a poet before he ever wrote a word of prose fiction. His *Lay of the Last Minstrel* (1805) sold 27,000 copies in ten years, while *Marmion* surpassed even that by selling 28,000 in only four years.[41] Of course, no poet ever attained, or could hope to attain, the popularity and mass sales of the novelists, and publishers always experienced some difficulties in selling verse. *Lyrical Ballads*, for example, was a commercial disaster when it was first published in 1798, although it was taken over by Longmans soon after publication, and gradually became a steady seller.[42] The scale of poetry publishing, however, can be judged by comparing the sales figures of the novels with John Taylor's delight when 160 copies of Keats's *Lamia* were ordered before publication in 1820.[43] Only Byron among the Romantics equalled the popular success of Scott. *Childe Harold* sold many thousands, but even Byron never repeated this success; the much-vaunted publication of *Don Juan* only yielded the sales of a few thousand copies.[44] Nevertheless, the poets of the first two decades of the century gradually became classics and were steadily reprinted to the benefit of their publishers if not always that of the poets themselves. In the middle of the century, Tennyson attained great fame and considerable popularity. For much of his life, Tennyson's publisher was Edward Moxon, who was delighted to sell 100 copies of *Poems* (1833) within two days of publication.[45] In fact, Moxon was, in general, markedly suspicious of poetry as a commercial commodity, but Tennyson was successful enough to confound his worst fears. The *Poems* of 1842 sold well from the beginning;[46] after that the poet became something of a national institution, and his sales increased with each successive work. By the end of his life, Macmillan was prepared to offer him substantial inducements to change his allegiance and become a Macmillan author.[47]

Anthologies were, however, generally far more profitable than new poetry. The most famous of all, Palgrave's *Golden Treasury*, was published by Macmillan in 1861, and was indeed a source of gold for both the editor and the publisher for many years to come;

it had sold 61,000 copies by 1884.[48] Selected verse, for gift books or for educational purposes, was popular throughout the century, and it was again the case that the spread of mass education, and especially of formal education after 1870, increased the market. No doubt many anthologies were bought for reluctant recipients or by reluctant school children, but they provided a steady income for their publishers and made at least some of the work of the major poets more widely available at very reasonable prices.

The publication of works of literature of permanent cultural value has never been, and will never be, the most profitable area of publishing. Nevertheless, such books are published, and there was perhaps a brief period in the middle of the nineteenth century when literary merit and popular success coincided. Dickens, one of the greatest Victorian best-sellers, was a genuinely popular entertainer as well as a major novelist. No other living novelist sold on anything like a comparable scale in Victoria's reign, but the success of Dickens symbolises the success of the novel itself. In its multitude of forms it dominated the market for imaginative literature and was the foundation stone of several successful publishing houses as well as the great enterprise of Mudie's libraries. Even so, the apparent dominance of the novel should not blind us to the fact that, although fiction was one of the most profitable forms of publishing, it was never the only one,[49] and the mass market which was discovered and exploited by men as different as Alexander Macmillan and Edward Lloyd was also open to others who approached from a very different angle. The Victorians were serious-minded men and women, who believed profoundly in the improving value of the printed word. It was in the attempt to impose a middle-class printed culture on the working classes that we can best see the publishing industry of Victorian England at work.

14

The Diffusion of Knowledge

The Victorian novel was not merely a form of entertainment; it often also had the high moral purpose exemplified in the work of George Eliot, or the political and social function perhaps best seen in Dickens. Dickens and George Eliot, however, created literary masterpieces out of moral and social concerns. In the far larger ranks of the lesser novelists there were many for whom literature was subordinated to outright polemics. A few of these are remembered for other reasons: Cardinal Newman's fictional works, *Loss and Gain* (1848) and *Callista* (1856), are of interest for their author rather than their intrinsic merit, and indeed the Oxford Movement spawned a whole family of novels even less memorable than these.[1] Edward Jenkins, radical MP and social reformer, was another who exploited the power of the novel to make points which were perhaps more acceptable, and certainly more forceful, by their embodiment in fictional form.[2] These, however, were the middle classes talking to each other; the polemical purpose of fiction and non-fiction alike was at its most intense in the great battle for the hearts and minds of the working classes, above all in the attempt to teach them middle-class values which would divert them from the lurking danger of revolutionary ideologies.

The power of the printed word to effect the moral improvement of the working class was a fundamental tenet of the nineteenth-century philanthropists. The pages of Samuel Smiles are full of autodidacts whose road to self-help and success began with literacy; the same belief underlay John Cassell's transformation from temperance campaigner to publisher in the 1840s.[3] By that time, however, the belief in the fundamental importance of literacy was a creed with a long history behind it. Arguably, it could be traced back to the sixteenth century, when the Protestant reformers had argued that since salvation was to be attained only by a personal understanding of religion, and this could be acquired only by reading the Bible, literacy was an essential element of religious faith. To a greater or lesser extent all the Protestant churches followed through the implications of this belief. The more extreme Protestant churches seriously engaged the education question; in Scotland, the Presbyterian Church developed what was probably the best general education system in Europe, so that there was widespread literacy north of the border long before it was achieved in England.[4] The Church of England had, in theory, required the clergy to teach the children of the parish since 1604, but in practice their efforts were at best intermittent and more often non-existent.[5] From time to time individuals attempted to fill the gaps. At the end of the seventeenth century, Thomas Bray provided the inspiration and the money to found parish libraries in England and Wales, a movement which achieved some degree of success and was imitated by James Kirkwood in Scotland.[6] The eighteenth-century charity schools, especially those of the Society for the Propagation of Christian Knowledge, grew out of the same educational impulsion as the Bray libraries, but the SPCK, Bray and Kirkwood, had only limited success.[7] It was not until the creation of the industrial cities brought together a potentially dangerous mass of illiterates that the middle classes responded with their full force to the need to educate the poor.

Despite the absence of a properly organised system of basic education, a remarkable number of the children of the poor did learn to read in the eighteenth century,[8] but in the industrial towns whatever provision there had been for ecclesiastical or charitable education was collapsing by the 1780s. It is from that decade that we can date the beginnings of the new and more forceful philanthropic education movement which was to be of importance for much of the nineteenth century. The story begins with the Sunday Schools, and in particular with Robert Raikes, a newspaper proprietor in Gloucester who founded a Sunday School in that city in 1780, and used his own newspaper and his connections in the London book trade to create a national movement.[9] One of his followers was Hannah More, who founded not only Sunday Schools, but also the Religious Tract Society which was designed to produce suitable reading matter for the newly literate children of the poor. The *Cheap Repository*

Tracts, which the Society published, were sold largely to the middle classes who gave them to the poor. A combination of straightforward exhortation, Biblical instruction and moral exemplars, they were intended to provide a religious substitute for the secular chapbooks and children's books which Mrs More regarded as being, at best, amoral. Like the chapbooks, they were written in simple and direct language for the benefit not only of children but also of partially literate adults. The RTS was a major commercial success; indeed, so overwhelming was it, that Mrs More was forced to adopt not only the style of the chapbooks, but also their methods of production and distribution. The great chapbook factory in Aldermary Churchyard was virtually turned over to the RTS in the 1790s, and the tracts were produced there in tens of thousands.[10] The secular chapbook survived in the provinces, and in Scotland they were still being printed in the 1840s, but Mrs More had sounded their death-knell, and with it the death-knell of much of the folk tradition of the working class.

The Religious Tract Society consisted of a group of middle-class philanthropists who wrote and published literature which they deemed suitable for the working class. This was a pattern which was to be widely followed during the next hundred years. Unwittingly, however, the RTS had also demonstrated the existence of a vast potential market, and of the financial rewards to be reaped from it. The lesson was not lost on publishers whose interests were far from the high-flown moral principles of Mrs More. The penny-a-part novel of the 1840s, and the yellowback of the 1870s, are both direct descendants of the Religious Tracts of Hannah More.

The RTS was essentially an offspring of the Sunday School Movement, the latter providing the means to acquire literacy and the former the means to use it. Once acquired, however, the use of literacy could not be controlled, and throughout the nineteenth century publishers and philanthropists alike competed to provide literature which would appeal to the mass market. Tracts were to be a common feature of Victorian working-class life, although from the satire of Wilkie Collins, and from the factual investigations of Mayhew, it is clear that they were not always appreciated by those whom they were intended to 'improve'.[11] Commercial publishers were, of course, involved in the production of the tracts, but indeed some of the societies became major publishers in their own right. The SPCK, for example, was printing eight million tracts a year in the 1860s,[12] and the publishing organisation of the Wesleyan Methodists issued over a million copies of their tracts in the single year of 1841.[13] These tracts were never entirely restricted to religious subjects, although there was always, of course, a Christian moral to be drawn. Nevertheless, they contributed a good deal to the general education of the working class.

The practices of the religious societies were imitated by secular philanthropists who considered that the education of the poor was a worthwhile objective for economic and cultural reasons. Perhaps the most important of these organisations was the Society for the Diffusion of Useful Knowledge founded in 1827 by Henry Brougham, a radical lawyer who was to be Lord Chancellor in the reforming Whig government of 1830.[14] The SDUK issued a *Library of Useful Knowledge* in fortnightly parts at 6d per part. It covered a wide range of practical knowledge, chiefly scientific and mathematical, and was soon selling nearly 30,000 copies of each part. The editor, and often the author, was Charles Knight, who was himself a self-educated working man.[15] In 1829 Knight branched out into a more ambitious project with his *Library of Entertaining Knowledge*, covering topics as diverse as vegetables and the Elgin Marbles. Although the SDUK ultimately failed for financial reasons, it had proved that a demand could be created for something other than cheap popular fiction or the cloying morality of the tracts. With the final establishment of steam printing of books in the 1840s the publishers were at last able to exploit fully the vast potential markets which the popular educators had unwittingly created.

The commercial publishers who sought to exploit the new markets no doubt had motives which were less pure than those of the philanthropists, but from the reader's point of view they did at least have the advantage of having to publish what the market demanded. No doubt as a consequence, much of their output was fictional or sensational or both, as can be seen, for example, in the so-called execution broadsides.[16] For the publishing industry, the development of mass literacy and a mass market could only be an advantage, for it had the effect of creating a large number of potential book buyers. Indeed, it could be argued that the Victorian publishing industry was underpinned by the mass market, for it enabled it to exploit new technologies of both production and distribution by providing potential sales which were large enough to justify the capital costs involved.

Nevertheless, some obstacles remained. Although it was clear that a mass market did exist, books and other reading matter had to be produced at a price which that market would tolerate. One important problem was the cost of paper which, despite the new production techniques, was kept artificially high by the continued existence of the excise duties which tended to counteract the falling costs of paper production as the industry mechanised its production methods and began to use cheaper materials. Brougham claimed that in order to sell the parts of the *Library of Useful Knowledge* at 6d, the highest price which he felt that the market would bear, each part had to be limited to 32 pages because of the tax on paper.[17] This tax was reduced by 50 per cent in 1836, but not finally abolished until 1861.[18] Even more burdensome, and certainly more politically contentious, was the tax on newspapers. This had been deliberately raised to almost penal levels during the Napoleonic Wars to restrict the circulation of radical newspapers for working-class readers, and despite reductions, it survived to be a major issue in the 1830s.[19] The duty was reduced further in 1836, but not finally abolished until 1855 when abolition was rapidly followed by the establishment of cheap newspapers for the mass market.[20]

The newspapers were an important factor in sustaining the hard-won literacy of the working class. Prices fell steadily during the 1840s, and dramatically after 1861. *The Times*, which had cost 5d in 1855, was sold for 3d in 1870.[21] The abolition of the paper duties also brought with it a proliferation of cheap newspapers, especially in the provinces, so that by 1870 Liverpool, for example, had five daily papers, and even a comparatively small town like Exeter had three.[22] Moreover, newspapers were not the only periodicals which flourished in the late second half of the century. Magazines of all kinds proliferated, some of them aimed at particular market sectors such as children,[23] and others catering for special interest groups such as sports enthusiasts.[24] These magazines were not only cheap, but also widely available thanks to a highly efficient system of wholesaling and distribution, largely provided by W. H. Smith's. They provided an important source of both education and amusement for a large number of people, many of whose grandparents had been on the borderline of illiteracy.

The magazines and newspapers were no longer entirely a part of the book publishing industry. Although some publishing houses had their own monthlies or quarterlies, as Macmillan did after 1859,[25] the mass circulation journals were generally in the hands of companies which specialised in publishing them and which often combined the processes of publishing and printing. Certainly in the newspaper industry this was almost universally the case. For many of the book publishers the profits of mass literacy were to be found in the general expansion of the market which was inevitable in a literate society, and above all in educational publishing. At every level, educational publishing became a major industry in its own right during the nineteenth century. Although it was the schools which provided the largest market, the expansion of adult and higher education also had important consequences for the trade. At the elementary level, the real boom came after 1870, when the Education Act of that year made primary education compulsory in the United Kingdom for the first time. This required the production of large quantities of elementary books, especially basic reading books, in a wide variety of subjects. The whole matter was entirely in the hands of the publishers. An earlier experiment with Irish education had shown that publishers, educational authorities and the government made uneasy bedfellows,[26] and no attempt was made to impose a uniform curriculum on the new Board Schools, although they were required to meet certain basic standards.

Among the established publishers, Longmans, with their tradition of schoolbook publishing, entered this new market with enthusiasm; they developed many series of books for the Board Schools, not only in reading and literature, but also in history, geography and science.[27] Macmillans also acted swiftly, and such series as *Teaching to Read* became important to the financial stability of the house.[28] Both the English university presses were also recruits to schoolbook publishing. At Oxford, a Schoolbook Committee was formed by the Delegates of the Press in 1863, and began to publish the Clarendon Press Series in 1866. At first the books were aimed primarily at the public schools, then approaching the zenith of their achievements, but many of the books were intended for use outside the confines of the classical curriculum.[29] Cambridge University Press was rather later into the field, but equally successful when it arrived. In the late 1860s, it was undergoing a major reform which rescued it from near bankruptcy, and one of the new directions in which it was pointed was that of publishing for schools. Much of the Cambridge publishing was for secondary rather than elementary education, and in that sector the *Cambridge Bible for Schools* and the Pitt Press

Series of well-edited literary texts were both of considerable educational importance. The Pitt Press Series, which began publication in 1870, was particularly significant, for it was specifically aimed at providing texts which would be useful to candidates for the Cambridge Local Examinations, the ancestor of the General Certificate of Education, which the university had been administering since 1858.[30] Successful educational publishing proved to be highly profitable; Nelson's *Royal Readers*, a series used in many Board Schools, produced a profit of nearly £50,000 in just three years.[31] It is hardly surprising that publishers were anxious to exploit the growing school market. Blackie's, a long-established but rather staid Scottish house, became a major force in the publishing world because of the 1870 Act, and other houses, notably E. J. Arnold, depended for their very existence on the Board Schools.[32]

It was not only at the school level, however, that publishers were able to exploit the ever-growing market for educational books. The reform of the older universities and the establishment of new ones in the middle decades of the century had the effect not only of changing the existing curricula but also of introducing wholly new subjects. Modern history, languages and literature and, above all, the sciences, became an established part of English higher education for the first time. All of these new subjects required textbooks of one kind or another, and both the university presses and some commercial publishers were able to break into this market. Again, Longmans and Macmillans were conspicuous among the commercial houses, and both Oxford and Cambridge, not surprisingly, were very active. Once a book became a 'set' text, success was assured. The *Anglo-Saxon Reader* by Henry Sweet, which Oxford University Press first published in 1876, became a required text for undergraduates reading English almost at once, and is still so at Oxford to this day. It is still in print, having gone through several revisions over the decades. The university presses, however, never had the field to themselves; E. A. Abbott's *Shakespearian Grammar*, for example, was published by Macmillan in 1870, and is still the standard work on its subject.[33] Moreover, it was not only in the universities that there was a new spirit of professionalism in higher education. The ancient professions also changed their attitudes to training, and specialist publishers developed to meet their needs. A striking example was that of the firm founded by Henry Butterworth in 1818, which soon came to dominate English legal publishing through its massive output of guides and textbooks of the highest authority.[34]

The professionalisation of scholarship which followed from the changes in the universities in the nineteenth century brought with it many benefits for the publishing industry. Learned journals although never popular best-sellers, could, if successful, be steady generators of income over many decades. After a slow start, Macmillans had a major long-term success with *Nature*,[35] although many of the journals were, inevitably, published by the university presses or by learned societies. The later decades of the century saw the foundation of many journals, some of which still survive; *The English Historical Review*, first issued in 1886, is a notable example, and there are many others. Scholarly and scientific monographs were also not without their attraction for publishers, although sales were small and perhaps slow. Two of the greatest of all British publishing enterprises date from the last decades of the nineteenth century: Leslie Stephen's *Dictionary of National Biography* and Murray's *New English Dictionary*. They reflect, no doubt, the confidence of the Victorians in their ability to undertake anything, but they also reflect the buoyant state of . scholarly publishing in England at the end of the century. The *DNB* made a massive loss for Smith Elder, the original publishers, but the profits of Thackeray and George Eliot had provided the foundations on which they could build their great *succès d'estime*. Indeed, the original idea for the work had come from the publisher not from the editor.[36] Murray's great dictionary might also have had a commercial publisher, for Macmillans were for a time very interested in publishing in it, and would probably have done so had not the impossible James Furnivall, the Secretary of the Philological Society, Murray's sponsor, wrecked the negotiations by making too many demands.[37] Eventually the *NED* was published by Oxford University Press, who were later to take over the *DNB* as well. Both are still in print, and are still being revised, augmented and updated.

The publishing of non-fiction took many forms in the nineteenth century from the school textbook and the popular magazine to the scholarly monograph, the learned journal and the reference book. The boundaries between them were not always clear-cut. While both university and commercial houses produced works of scholarship, many of those published by the latter also achieved sales outside the academic world. The concept of general trade non-fiction, the mainstay of many houses today, was perhaps at one time in danger of being swamped by the flood of specialist books aimed at particular markets. It became apparent, however, that an educated people seeks intelligent reading matter; despite the growing specialisation of some houses, there were enough firms in the industry to ensure not merely the preservation but the multiplication of diversity. The philanthropic belief in the value of education had been transformed into a public policy, and its success created whole new markets for the publishing industry. The mass market for leisure reading and for newspapers was as profitable as that for schoolbooks, as Newnes and Harmsworth discovered with their 'new journalism' in the 1880s. The tabloid newspaper may not have been quite what Mrs More would have liked, but it was, like the penny dreadful and the yellowback, one of the fruits of her labours.

15

The Publishers and the Authors

The development of the publishing industry into the first of the mass media brought great benefits not only to the publishers but also to those who made their success possible: the authors. The author is too often the forgotten figure in the history of the book trade. It is, after all, he who writes what the publisher publishes, and the two are dependent upon each other. By the end of the eighteenth century, this mutual interdependence was already recognised to some extent. Authorship had become an established occupation largely because the newspapers and magazines provided a source of regular, if limited, income for those who could write to a deadline. In the nineteenth century, the vast increase in the output of the press created an army of writers and journalists who, unlike so many of their predecessors, could live by their pens. A successful author could expect rewards which put him among the best-paid in the land. Scott set the pattern in this as in much else. Even as a poet he had made a good deal of money,[1] but with the success of the Waverley novels he made a fortune. Almost all the major Victorian novelists, a few poets and many minor authors found themselves very wealthy indeed by the end of their careers. This created new tensions within the trade, and between the publishers and the authors, if only because there was so much more to discuss than there had been in earlier days.

This tension was most obvious in the arrangements which were made for the payment of authors. In the earliest days of printing, authors, if they were paid at all, received a single payment for their copy. During the eighteenth century, however, more complex arrangements emerged, notably Pope's device of leasing his copyrights to a publisher for a specific edition.[2] Pope, however, was in an unusually strong position because of his own involvement in the trade, and for most eighteenth-century authors the single payment for an outright sale of his copyright remained the usual practice. By the middle of the century, however, more complex arrangements, often more beneficial to the author, were becoming more common. Typically, an author would agree to write a book on a specified subject and of a specified length in return for a fixed fee. The agreement might also, however, specify the number of copies in the edition, with provisions for additional payments in the event of a reprint and perhaps with some arrangements for revisions, paid or unpaid, for editions subsequent to the first.[3] Gradually, the typical contract became a little more generous and a few of the more enterprising publishers began to make speculative investments in books which they considered to have commercial potential. The younger Murray, for example, offered the dramatist Colman £300 for *John Bull* immediately after he saw it acted.[4] It was by such enterprise that the new publishers of the late eighteenth and early nineteenth centuries developed their lists and their businesses.

Popular authors, however, especially those who had a reasonable prospect of reprints after the first edition, were no longer so attracted by the outright sale of their copyrights. Scott insisted from the beginning of his career as a novelist on 'half-profits' agreements, by which he and his publisher shared equally in the profits of an edition. Moreover, Scott would allow a publisher the rights only to one edition at a time, and renegotiated for reprints.[5] Of course, Scott was in a uniquely strong position among authors of his generation, but later writers followed his example. Dickens became something of an expert in exploiting his own commercial value, again often using the half-profits system,[6] although other authors, such as Mrs Gaskell, continued with the older practice of selling their copyrights outright to their publishers.[7]

These manipulations inevitably provoked a renewed interest in the law of copyright which made them possible. By the beginning of the nineteenth century, the 1710 Act, designed by the trade as a protection for itself, was increasingly seen as a tool to be used by authors, and they began to take an interest in the law and in strengthening it to their own advantage. There were two important strands of development in copyright law in the nineteenth century, one in the domestic sphere and the other concerned with protection abroad.

After the House of Lords decision in 1774, and the vain attempt to reverse it in 1774,[8] no action was taken for many years to reform the law of copyright. In 1814, however, a new Copyright Act specifically acknowledged the rights of authors for the first time. The term of copyright, fixed at 14 years with the possibility of a 14-year renewal since 1710, was extended to 28 years or the life of the author, whichever was the longer.[9] This was an important advance, for it was the first time that the law had made a specific connection between the lifespan of the author and that of the copyright in his works. It was an important principle which was extended further when the Copyright Act of 1842 gave protection for 42 years or until seven years after the author's death, whichever was the longer.[10] This represented a significant improvement in the position of the author, for the protection was now not only for himself but also for his family after his death.

The real significance of these legislative developments lies in their source. In 1709–10, and again throughout the middle years of the eighteenth century, it had been the copy-owning booksellers who were concerned with the law of copyright. It was their interests and their actions which had provoked change and development. The situation was now completely different. The 1842 Act, which was to remain unchanged until 1911, was essentially a product of agitation by authors, including authors as distinguished as Dickens and Carlyle. Indeed, immediately after the 1814 Act, the authors began to ask for more. Southey and Wordsworth were both active in this, and Wordsworth was directly involved in lobbying for a Bill in 1838 which was to be the basis of the 1842 Act.[11] The MP with whom they dealt was T. N. Talfourd, a distinguished lawyer who was also an author himself, as well as being a member of the literary circle which included Lamb,[12] and a friend of Dickens.[13] Talfourd had to make five attempts in successive sessions of Parliament before new legislation was passed, for he encountered a good deal of opposition to his proposals. The objectors included Murray and Longman, as well as Macaulay who regarded copyright as merely another form of taxation on knowledge. By a series of well-conceived compromises, however, the opponents were won over, and it was essentially Talfourd's Bill which became law in 1842, although by that time he himself was no longer a Member of Parliament. The Bill's sponsors in both Houses had worked closely with authors throughout, and as a consequence the 1842 Act was a much an author's law as its predecessor had been a publishers' law.[14]

Domestic law, however, was only one part of the problem, and perhaps the less important part, for the importation of foreign reprints into Britain was becoming a major problem for authors and publishers alike in the second quarter of the nineteenth century. After Waterloo, English books, and especially English novels, became something of a fashion on the continent, and continental publishers were quick to exploit the market. The Paris firm of A. and W. Galignani had been publishing a series of reprints of popular English novels as early as 1800, but when trade with France restarted in 1815 a new difficulty emerged as the French reprints began to be imported into England in large quantities. G. P. R. James, an immensely popular novelist, was among the first to raise the alarm, but it was not until the middle of the 1830s that some action was taken against the Paris piracies.[15] Richard Bentley employed agents to search out reprints of his books on sale in London, and when they did so he sued in Chancery. He was successful in rooting out the reprints of his own books, but others also suffered, and costly Chancery suits were clearly not a long-term solution to the loss of revenue caused by the import of foreign editions of copyright British books.[16]

James continued to be active in the fight against foreign reprints of British books, and his efforts met with some success. In 1838, Parliament reacted by passing the first International Copyright Act, which made it possible to reach reciprocal agreements with foreign states on copyright protection. In fact, it was not until 1846 that this law was first used, when an agreement was signed with the Prussian government under which British books in Prussia and Prussian books in Britain were fully protected under the terms of each country's domestic copyright legislation.[17] The 1842 Act, which was so important in the development of copyright law in Britain, was largely impotent in protecting authors against foreign publishers, since any unilateral legislation would necessarily be meaningless and international agreements were difficult to reach. The provisions of the Act did, however, extend to British dominions overseas, forbidding colonial reprints of books copyright in the United Kingdom, and the import into either the United Kingdom or the colonies of any foreign reprint of a British copyright book. In practice, however, this merely gave additional powers to the officers of the Customs, which they were unable to enforce to any significant extent.[18]

Nevertheless, there was some progress in the battle against foreign reprints. Reciprocal agreements were signed with a number of European states in the 1840s and 1850s,[19] and one very important continental publisher became an ally of the British authors in their attempts to reap reasonable rewards from their work. This was Christian Bernard Tauchnitz of Leipzig, who in 1841 began to issue his *Collection of British Authors*, a series which was to continue for a hundred years.[20] Tauchnitz was fastidious in his dealings with his British (and later American) authors. He bought from them, or their publishers, the right to publish their books for sale outside the United Kingdom, and this attitude created business associations which blossomed into friendships with Dickens, Harrison Ainsworth, G. H. Lewes and others. The Tauchnitz editions could not be imported into the United Kingdom or the British Empire,[21] but Tauchnitz made no attempt to do so, for he sought his market among British and American travellers on the continent and the growing number of European anglophiles. Although the success of Tauchnitz virtually excluded British publishers from the European market for their most popular titles, it was of great benefit to British authors, and provided them with the ammunition to fight the longer and more difficult battle in the other great market for English books, the United States.

The battle for recognition of British copyright in the United States will always be associated with the name of Dickens, whose relations with America and Americans were never entirely happy. Despite the great success of his books in that country and his own personal triumphs during his tours there, he was often angered by the American 'piracies' of his works from which he obtained no income. The difficulties were largely the responsibility of the Americans, for the British government made desultory efforts to use the 1838 Act at the same time as the various European agreements were being negotiated. A treaty between the British and American governments was indeed signed in 1853, but it failed to obtain the necessary majority for ratification in the US Senate, partly because the British authors and publishers did not understand the need to spend large sums of money on the Washington lobbying system.[22] Reprinting of British books in the United States and of American books in Britain continued to be a major problem until almost the very end of the century, when in 1891 Congress at last passed an Act which made arrangements, albeit limited, for the American registration of copyright in works by non-residents and non-citizens.[23] Essentially, the Chace Act (so-called after its sponsor,

Senator Chace) was protectionist legislation, designed to ensure that books copyrighted in America were typeset and printed there, but it did afford some measure of relief to the grievances of the British authors.

Before the Chace Act had passed into law, however, the European countries had already taken an important step towards the general regulation of international copyright. In 1887, many of them had signed the Berne Convention which essentially followed the principles established in the Anglo-Prussian agreement forty years earlier. Briefly, the Berne Convention states that a book which is copyright in any signatory state is also copyright in all the other signatory states under exactly the same conditions (except legal deposit) as a book first published in that country. It is on this basis that international copyright law now rests, and it ensures that authors receive a fair income from foreign reprints and translations of their works.[24]

The concern with copyright law, both domestically and internationally, was one measure of the ever-increasing sums of money which could be generated by successful books, both for the author and for the publisher. Dickens, who had been paid £14 3s 6d for each part of *Pickwick Papers*, made a profit of nearly £10,000 from *Dombey and Son* in 1846–8.[25] The executors of Mrs Henry Wood, one of the most successful novelists of the century, received over £35,000 in three years from a collected edition published by Bentley after her death, and she had already made many thousands during her lifetime.[26] Of course, not all novelists were so fortunate. With a half-profits agreement, Trollope had the princely income of £9 8s 8d from the first edition of *The Warden*, published by Longman in 1855, and £100 from *Barchester Towers* two years later.[27] On the other hand, it was not only novelists who made great sums of money; Macaulay received a single cheque for £20,000 as part of his share of the profits in volumes 3 and 4 of his *History of England* in 1856,[28] while in 1856 Chapman and Hall paid Carlyle £2,800 for the right to publish 5,000 copies of the first two volumes of *Frederick the Great*.[29]

In such circumstances, relations between authors and publishers became of central importance in the trade. Publishers found themselves in a highly competitive market, which was always seeking new books, if not novelty for its own sake. At a time when Mudie was adding anything up to 100,000 volumes a year to his circulating libraries,[30] as he was in the 1850s and 1860s, the publishers needed authors who could write them. This put the authors in a stronger position, and there were many who felt that they were not exploiting their advantages. It was easy for Dickens to manipulate his copyrights and his profits; it was a more difficult proposition for the middle-ranking writers who filled the columns of the monthly magazines or the three volumes of the circulating library novels. Since the early eighteenth century, when they first began to recognise their potential power, authors had been suspicious of publishers. They had even tried to circumvent them with their own publishing organisations such as the Society for the Encouragement of Learning, or by using the subscription system.[31] By the second half of the nineteenth century, however, it was clear that if authors were to improve their position, it would have to be done in relation to the existing structure of the publishing industry. The publishers had established and successful businesses, and to establish a new house was no small undertaking. It would be better for the authors to work together, and speak to the publishers with a single voice, rather than try to do the publishers' work for them.

The first successful attempt at founding a representative body for authors was largely a consequence of the growing feeling that there was an urgent need to enforce and extend international copyright protection. It is, perhaps, equally significant that the leading lights of the organisation were comparatively minor authors. The strongest force was Walter Besant, a novelist and journalist; at first, his associates included none of the major writers of the period. In 1883, Besant called a meeting which resulted in the establishment of the Society of Authors in the following year. Besant now proved a master of propaganda; his first great stroke was to persuade Tennyson, by that time Poet Laureate and a peer, to be the Society's President, and he was then able to recruit a number of other important and successful authors as active members. The Society of Authors soon established itself as a major force in the British book world, as it has remained. Its foundation coincided with the negotiations which were to lead to the signing of the Berne Convention, so that copyright questions inevitably played a large part in its activities in the early years. This was not, however, the Society's only concern. In the 1890s, the Society was involved in the discussions of the publishers and booksellers which were to lead to the signing of the Net Book Agreement, and through its journal, *The Author*, founded in 1890, it gave a collective voice to professional writers for the first time.[32]

In the long term, however, the most significant role of the Society of Authors was to be in forcing publishers to reconsider their literary and financial relationships with their authors. In the late nineteenth century, there were three contentious issues in this area in which the Society was to play some part: the role of the publisher's reader, the role of the literary agent and the crucial question of the division of profits between author and publisher.

The publisher's reader was a product of the more professional attitudes which came to characterise the publishing industry in the nineteenth century. Before that time, publishers had reached their own decisions, perhaps with advice from literary friends, but more often on their own. It was thus, for example, that Dodsley declined *Tristram Shandy* and forced Sterne into semi-private publication.[33] In the last two decades of the eighteenth century, however, when a more adventurous approach towards new books was forced on the publishers, it became necessary for them to consider far more manuscripts, often from authors quite unknown to them. Although publishers continued, as they still do, to commission much of their non-fiction from authors whom they already knew, the publisher of imaginative literature cannot work in this way if he is to extend his list. All publishers have to take risks and the function of the reader is to reduce that risk by assessing both the literary and commercial value of the work.

The emergence of readers as employees or paid agents of the publisher is obscure, although it seems that they existed in the 1830s.[34] Their real influence, however, dates from the middle of the century, and is particularly associated with two people, Geraldine Jewsbury, who read for Bentley from 1860 to 1875,[35] and John Morley who was reader for Macmillan from the 1860s to 1914.[36] Bentley was indeed something of a pioneer in the use of readers; as a major publisher of fiction, where personal judgement is of such importance, he had little choice, for he could not possibly read for himself the torrents of unsolicited manuscripts which poured into the house. The reader is, by definition, an anonymous and somewhat elusive figure in the history of publishing, although there can be no doubt of the importance which some of them have attained. Above all, they advise on those aspects of publishing which are so important to success and which yet are beyond the competence of so many authors. By being in regular contact with the publishing world, the reader knows what will sell and what will not; he or she can advise on length, on the suitability of vocabulary and even on plot or characterisation. Geraldine Jewsbury, for example, immediately recognised the commercial potential of Mrs Henry Wood's *East Lynne*, which was indeed destined to be a best-seller, but she insisted on many revisions to Mrs Wood's indifferent grammar.[37] Morley was undoubtedly influential in Macmillan's initially cautious attitude to Thomas Hardy, which resulted in his taking his first novel, *Desperate Remedies*, elsewhere, although Morley helped the young novelist in other ways, and he later became a Macmillan author.[38]

The reader was working for the publisher, but the literary agent, another intermediary, was working for the author. Like the origins of the reader, the origins of the agent are somewhat obscure, but there seems little doubt that the first of them who was of any importance was A. P. Watt; he seems to have begun his business in about 1875 after a modestly successful career in both publishing and bookselling.[39] He established a pattern which others followed, notably J. B. Pinker (from 1896) and Curtis Brown (from 1899). He undertook all the negotiations between the author and the publisher, in return for a proportion, usually 10 per cent, of the author's income from any book for which he was the agent. It was another aspect of the professionalisation of publishing. Authors were writers, not businessmen, and the role of the agent was, and is, to bring to bear on the author's behalf the business acumen which a good publisher will certainly employ in his own dealings. Although there was initial hostility within the trade, notably from William Heinemann who refused to deal with agents for many years,[40] they soon proved to be useful, and even influential in transferring important authors from one house to another. Watt performed this service for Kipling, whom he persuaded to move from Heinemann (which may well have been the origin of his dislike of agents) to Macmillan in the 1890s.[41]

It was to the agent's advantage to win the best possible contract for his authors, since his own income was directly dependent upon theirs. It was also, however, essential for him to ensure that he submitted to publishers only those manuscripts which seemed to have a good chance of acceptance. This indeed has become the crucial role of the agent in British publishing; from his knowledge of the trade, and of those in key positions within it, he is able to direct an author to an appropriate house, and at the same time he gives the author, especially the new author, the advantage of the reputation which he has earned from his earlier successes.

The agency system developed only very slowly in the late nineteenth and early twentieth centuries, and indeed there are still many authors, especially of non-fiction, who prefer to deal directly with their publishers. Nevertheless, the development of agency was beneficial to all authors, for the agents joined their voices with that of the Society of Authors in an attempt to find a more equitable means of paying writers in a way which reflected their commercial success. Neither half-profits (which was often unfair to the publisher) nor outright sale of copyright (which was nearly always unfair to the author) could do this. At the end of the nineteenth century, authors and their agents increasingly pressed for royalty agreements, under which the author received a fixed percentage of the selling price of each copy sold, thus linking the author's income directly to the commercial success of his work. The problem was to decide the basis on which the percentage should be calculated, but this was eased by the gradual acceptance of the Net Book Agreement which, because it fixed prices, provided a basis on which royalties could be paid. The ideal for an author was 10 per cent (or possibly even more) of the net price of each copy sold, with the author himself retaining the copyright and the overseas and translation rights. It was an ideal which was rarely attained, and relations between authors and publishers can still be uneasy, but nevertheless the acceptance of agents and royalties by the publishers represented a major advance in the acceptance of the author as a crucial figure in the work and success of the trade.[42]

The changing nature of the relationship between publisher and his author is symptomatic of the changing nature of publishing itself in nineteenth-century Britain. There was still room for innovation and individual flair, and indeed some of the finest publishers of the twentieth century were to show both of those characteristics. On the other hand, publishing was firmly enmeshed within the wider world of business and industry, and it had to follow conventional business practices if it was to survive. For some nineteenth-century publishers books were a crusade or a cultural duty; for others, however, and perhaps they were the majority, books were a product, and authors were suppliers just as booksellers were customers. The publisher who was high-minded but incompetent could not survive in such an ethos, however good and noble his books might be. The Net Book

Agreement was a recognition of the commercial realities of the book world: publishers and booksellers needed each other and both needed to make adequate profits if they were to continue trading. Similarly, the willingness, however reluctant, to deal through agents was an acknowledgement that the author too was part of this commercial world. The supplier needed his profits, just as the producer needed his, and it was unreasonable to expect regular supplies of acceptable goods unless the supplier was adequately and regularly recompensed for his work. The law of copyright merely provided a framework within which this could happen. The real revolution in British publishing in the reign of Queen Victoria was that it became a fully fledged industry, turning over millions of pounds, conducting its affairs in a businesslike manner and dealing fairly with the different interest groups within it and around it. By the year 1900, the publishing industry had equipped itself with the means of survival for the new century. The first trial of strength was to be whether that means could itself survive. The Net Book Agreement was designed as a rock upon which the house of publishing could be rebuilt. It remained to be seen whether the rock would, after all, prove to be sand.

Part Four:
The Trade in the Twentieth Century

16

The Customs of the Trade

'The customs of the trade' had been a phrase familiar to publishers, printers and booksellers alike since the eighteenth century, but in the twentieth century it has taken on a distinctively different meaning. Above all, it refers to the Net Book Agreement and its operation, which has become the principal support upon which the whole structure of the industry rests. Macmillan's concept was a good one for its day and achieved precisely the objective for which it was designed: the stabilisation of prices and the regulation of profit margins to guarantee a reasonable income to both publisher and bookseller. Nevertheless, the Agreement has never been without its critics, and any account of the British publishing industry since 1900 must begin with the story of the acceptance, defence and working of the Net Book Agreement.

The first serious challenge to the Net Book Agreement came from an unlikely source. In the first few years of the twentieth century, *The Times* was in serious financial difficulties. Although the paper which John Walter had started as an advertising sheet for a new and improbable typesetting process in 1785 had become the voice of the Victorian establishment, it had suffered badly from competition in the 1890s. There were many reasons for this; unfortunate libel suits had cost a great deal of money, *The Times* was unable or unwilling to invest in new printing technology, its price was high and its style was distinctly old-fashioned in a world in which Newnes, Harmsworth and Pearson were creating a new kind of journalism which was affecting even *The Times's* rivals among the serious newspapers such as *The Daily Telegraph*.[1] In an attempt to overcome these problems, John Walter, the owner of *The Times*, installed Moberley Bell as manager at Printing House Square. He had many ideas for the revival of the newspaper's fortunes; these included *The Times Literary Supplement*, one of his abiding successes, and The Times Book Club, which almost brought total disaster.[2] The origin of the Book Club can be traced to two American booksellers, Horace Hooper and W. M. Jackson, whom Bell met in 1897.[3] They had their background in the very different book trade traditions which had developed in the United States, where direct selling by mail was almost a necessity given the vast distances between cities in that country and the great difficulty of travel between them. They also brought with them a knowledge of the advertising techniques which had been developed in the USA to support mail-order operations.[4] It was quite unlike the staid world of British publishing, and to Bell it spelled the salvation of *The Times*.

In 1904, *The Times* reduced its annual subscription to £3 0s 0d in an attempt to win back lost readers; in the following year it raised it again to £3 18s 0d, but this new price included automatic membership of The Times Book Club, a combination of circulating library and postal bookseller. The principle on which the Club operated was a simple one: members could borrow books from the Club, but they could also buy, at greatly reduced prices, books which had been withdrawn from the Club's lending stock. It was this latter point which was to be the bone of contention with the trade, for in practice virtually new books were thus made available for public sale at huge discounts on their net prices.[5]

Bell himself was a keen supporter of the Book Club, not only because of the immediate advantages which it seemed to offer to *The Times*, but also because he believed that the trade was keeping the prices of books artificially high by use of the Net Book Agreement.[6] He and Hooper succeeded in negotiating a number of favourable agreements with major publishers to supply books to *The Times* at massive discounts, partly because some publishers believed that *The Times* had actually signed the Net Book Agreement.[7] It was soon apparent, however, that whatever may have been tacitly understood, the Club was actually selling books which were only a month old at a 33⅓ per cent discount on net, and Edward Bell, the President of the Publishers' Association met with Moberley Bell in May 1906 to discuss the matter.[8] The response of *The Times* was to increase its advertising for the 'second-hand' books, and to publish a series of articles attacking the trade for its attitude to cheap books. Edward Bell claimed that the publishers even then were ready to reach an agreement, but that *The Times* refused to co-operate with them.⁹ Whatever the truth of the matter, it is certain that in October 1906, the publishers agreed among themselves not to supply any more books to *The Times*, either for the Book Club or for review in the *Literary Supplement*.¹⁰

Throughout the winter of 1906–7, there was a bitter struggle between the publisher and the proprietors of *The Times*. The trade accused *The Times* of bad faith, and of subterfuge in obtaining books. *The Times*, with a good deal of public support, reiterated its view that book prices were too high, and that the publishers were making excessive profits. When John Murray refused to supply the Club with *The Letters of Queen Victoria*, which he published in the autumn of 1907, *The Times* printed a vitriolic attack on him. He sued for libel and was awarded damages of £7,500;¹¹ this was a serious blow to the ailing newspaper and its increasingly concerned proprietor. Walter now decided that he had to sell *The Times*, and he looked around for a suitable purchaser. After several months of secret negotiations, he sold it to Alfred Harmsworth, one of the pioneers of popular journalism and recently raised to the peerage as Lord Northcliffe.¹² Northcliffe knew that in order to restore the profitability of *The Times* he had to modernise both its management and its production, and extraneous diversions like quarrels with the publishers were the last thing he needed as he faced this unenviable task. In October 1908, *The Times* signed the Net Book Agreement, and the Book War was over.¹³

The Book War was a strange episode in the history of the trade. It arose largely out of the efforts of Moberley Bell and his American colleagues to rescue *The Times* without letting it slip from the hands of the Walter family. From the trade's point of view, however, the results of the War could not have been better. The Net Book Agreement had successfully survived what was to prove to be its most serious challenge until after World War II. At crucial moments in the fight, the publishers had held together, and the benefits of using the Publishers' Association as a collective voice for the trade were visible to all. As it happened, 1907 was the first year in which more net than non-net books were published, and by 1914 over two-thirds of new books were published on net terms.¹⁴ Gradually, the Agreement spread throughout the trade. Two important developments were to recruit HMSO to the scheme in 1917, and the netting of most fiction before the end of World War I.¹⁵

Nevertheless, there were other challenges to be faced. The Net Book Agreement was (and is) a contract between publisher and bookseller. By agreeing to buy his books according to 'the standard conditions of sale of net books',[16] the bookseller agrees not to sell them at less than the net price. The only sanction which the publishers can actually use against offending booksellers is to refuse to supply on trade terms. While this works perfectly well with the smaller shops, and even with the major retail chains (who, in any case, have their own interest in maintaining order in the trade), it cannot so easily be applied to major groups of customers whom the trade cannot afford to lose. For this reason, the Publishers' Association found itself forced to confront a number of issues in the inter-war years, and to modify the Net Book Agreement to take account of the realities of the industry.

The first challenge came from the libraries.[17] As early as 1902, the Library Association began to seek means whereby public libraries could obtain discounts on their purchases of net books. After somewhat dilatory negotiations, the publishers finally refused their request in 1908. The subject was reopened after World War I, when the situation on both sides had changed considerably. In 1919, county councils had, for the first time, been empowered to run rate-supported libraries, and they quickly followed the example of the urban areas which had long since taken advantage of their similar powers under the Public Libraries Act of 1850.[18] The number of libraries, and consequently their importance as buyers of books, had thus substantially increased by the middle of the 1920s. From the trade's point of view, the mid-1920s were not a happy time. World War I and the years immediately following had seen something of a boom in book sales,[19] but this was over by 1924–5,[20] and the publishers could not afford to alienate such an important market sector. Thus, when the Library Association made a new approach to the trade in 1925, they found themselves having a much more sympathetic hearing than they had experienced twenty years earlier. Nothing was achieved immediately, but in 1929 the Library Association succeeded in persuading a joint committee of the Publishers' Association and the Associated Booksellers to sign the Library Agreement. In substance, this still substantially regulates the relationships between the trade and public libraries. Under the Agreement, a library authority could obtain a licence from the Publishers' Association which granted it a 10 per cent discount on its book purchases from named suppliers, provided that it transacted business to a minimum value of £100 per annum with that supplier. It was a compromise which laid the foundations for many years of co-operation between the trade and its most important single group of customers, for by the 1970s public library purchases were to represent about a quarter of all domestic sales of British books, and far more than that of much fiction.[21]

Public libraries were important customers of the trade, but they were not, at least directly, its competitors. The case with book clubs was quite different. Like the techniques which had provoked the Book War, book clubs were American in origin. A few had existed in the USA in the nineteenth century,[22] but it was with the foundation of The Book of the Month Club in 1926 that their modern history began.[23] The Book of the Month Club, and its rival The Literary Guild which was founded in the same year, were quite different from the co-operative book-buying schemes which had existed in Britain during the eighteenth and nineteenth centuries.[24] They were publishing organisations, who bought from copyright-owners the right to issue an edition whose sale was restricted to registered members of the Club. Distribution was by post, and indeed the book clubs themselves grew out of the American tradition of mail-order bookselling. Club editions were considerably cheaper than the publishers' (or 'trade') editions, but members were obliged to take a specified number of books during their membership, and they had little choice of titles. The selection was made by a panel of literary experts. In the USA the book clubs were firmly established by 1930, and it was perhaps inevitable that they would be imitated in Britain.

The first British book club, The Book Society, was founded in 1929. It followed the American example to some extent, most notably in the appointment of a panel of literary experts to select the books; this panel included J. B. Priestley and Hugh Walpole.[25] There was an immediate and strong reaction in the trade. Quite apart from publishers like Harrap who objected on cultural grounds to panels of authors telling readers what to read,[26] there was general opposition among the booksellers to this new form of competition. In the year in which the Book Society was founded, the Associated Booksellers voiced their objections at their annual conference.[27] The publishers, however, did not take the same line. The Book Society was a retailing rather than a publishing organisation unlike its American progenitors. It bought new books from their publishers, often in large quantities, for sale to its members. Provided these were then sold at the net price, which they were, the Society was given the usual trade terms. The publisher benefited considerably from the transaction, for he had sold a substantial proportion of the edition at the time of publication, and thus eased the age-old problem of beginning to recoup his pre-publication investment as quickly as possible.

The publishers were always reluctant to interfere with the book clubs in the 1930s, for they saw them as a valuable source of income. Indeed, several leapt on the bandwagon themselves, led by Victor Gollancz, one of the most remarkable of inter-war British publishers. Gollancz, who had founded his business in 1928, had two great passions in his publishing life: detective fiction, of which he published some of the best examples in the golden age of the British detective story, and left-wing politics. In 1935 he founded The Left Book Club, which was to become something of a legend in British life and has more than once been credited with having had a significant influence on the Labour Party's victory in the 1945 general election.[28] The Left Book Club was crucially different from The Book Society, and not merely in making its appeal to a particular interest group. Its books were specially published for members of the Club, and available only to members directly, and not through the bookshops. This principle was followed two years later by a new general book club, Reader's Union, which, with permission, reprinted books for sale to members at a far lower price than the net price of the trade edition.[29] Again, the Associated Booksellers protested, but the publishers were lukewarm in their response, and it was not until the very eve of the outbreak of World War II that they finally agreed to regulations to control the operation of the clubs. By that time, however, another general club had been founded, the Reprint Society; this was actually a consortium of five publishers. The extent to which the publishers had welcomed the development of the clubs can be measured by the fact that one of the five was Jonathan Cape, who was never a radical in his attitude to the affairs of the trade.[30]

The Book Club Regulations of 1939 represented a compromise acceptable to both sides of the trade.[31] The most important clause regulated the time which must elapse between the publication of the trade and club editions; this was to be not less than one year, except for political or religious clubs. It is difficult to judge what effect the Regulations of 1939, and their rather less draconian successors,[32] have had on the growth of book clubs in Britain. Certainly, the clubs greatly expanded in the 1960s, when W. H. Smith added a whole stable of them to their many other enterprises,[33] but, even so, no more than about 5 per cent of bookbuying has ever been through book clubs. Probably they would never have developed beyond that point even without the somewhat restrictive Regulations, for so long as the Net Book Agreement helped to maintain a good network of bookshops there was never a demand in Britain for postal bookselling on the scale on which it had developed in the United States.

The Book Club Regulations were agreed in the summer which was to end with the outbreak of World War II. During the next ten years the publishing industry was to suffer, as was the rest of the country, from the privations of total war and austere peace.[34] Although the picture was never one of unrelieved gloom, there was little time to worry about the internal affairs of the trade when its very survival seemed to be at stake. Indeed, throughout the 1950s, the trade was organised much as it had been in the 1930s, with the Net Book Agreement and its various subsidiaries providing a buffer against the worst of the economic storms. In these quiet circumstances, the change of name of the Associated Booksellers to the Booksellers' Association in 1948 seems like a momentous event. In the 1960s, however, the trade was fearful of chaos, for once again the Net Book Agreement was under threat. This time there was perhaps even more to fear than there had been in 1906, not least perhaps because only the very oldest in the trade could remember the days of underselling. This time the threat came from the law. The law in question was the Restrictive Trade Practices Act of 1956, a well-intentioned measure designed to protect consumers from price-fixing cartels. A special court was established in which the Registrar of Restrictive Trading Agreements, appointed under the Act, would present the case against any organisation which he suspected of operating in restraint of trade against the public interest. The first response to this Act in the book trade was to revise the Net Book Agreement of 1900 into a form which seemed to conform with the new law. At the same time, the opportunity was taken to incorporate a number of the practices which had developed over the years, and to clarify the application of the Agreement to certain special fields of publishing such as maps.[35]

The Publishers' Association and the Booksellers' Association decided to defend the Net Book Agreement if necessary, and eventually the trade as a whole was to subscribe over £45,000 to defray the expenses of legal action. In the summer of 1959 the Registrar did indeed refer the Agreement to the Restrictive Practices Court, but over three years passed before the case finally came on in June 1962. It lasted for twenty-four days, during which elaborate arguments were heard on both sides from publishers, booksellers and academic experts and economists. In essence, the trade's line of defence was that publishing was different from any other trade because each book was competing with every other book, including other books from the same publisher. Moreover, it was argued that because of the special educational and cultural value of books, there was a strong social argument for their wide availability through a network of stockholding bookshops. It was alleged that if their profit margins were not protected, and underselling were to be permitted, stockholding bookshops would disappear in favour of glorified stationers' shops which would stock only paperbacks and a few best-sellers. In turn this would cause a decline in both the quality and quantity of books published, and adversely affect not only the domestic market, but also Britain's flourishing export trade in books. The Registrar argued that, on the contrary, the effect of the Agreement was an illegal price-fixing cartel which operated against the public interest.[36]

In October, the Court finally gave its verdict, in a judgement written by its Chairman, Mr Justice Buckley.[37] In this document, the court analysed in superb detail the working practices of the trade before considering the arguments which had been heard. In fact, the trade's arguments were accepted almost as they had been presented, and sometimes in the very words of the witnesses and documents. The court's summary of the likely consequences of the abolition of the Net Book Agreement was music to the trade's ears: '(1) fewer and less-well-equipped stockholding bookshops; (2) more expensive books; (3) fewer published titles'.[38] Buckley concluded that such consequences would be against the public interest, and rejected the legal argument of the Registrar that the Agreement was an illegal restraint of trade. He referred to the importance of the export trade, and accepted that books were not only of cultural importance, but also a uniquely difficult product in which to trade. When he said that 'it seems almost as hard to discern whether a new book will catch the public fancy and so be a commercial success as it is notoriously difficult to foretell whether a theatrical production will succeed',[39] he had touched on the very heart of the problem which all speculative publishers have always faced. The Court found against the Registrar, and the Net Book Agreement was not merely saved but fully vindicated as having achieved all that had been claimed for it by its advocates since Frederick Macmillan had first proposed the net book system.

The trade had emerged successfully from its defence of the Net Book Agreement, but nevertheless some changes were inevitable. The great growth of book clubs in the 1960s inevitably led to demands for revisions in the Book Club Regulations, and the new Regulations of 1974–5 were substantially modified in favour of the Clubs, especially in allowing their members a greater freedom of choice, including the right not to take any books at all after a minimum period of membership.[40] In 1968, the Publishers' Association and Booksellers' Association were forced to agree to the principle of the 'simultaneous' book club, which is permitted to publish an edition for its members at the same time as the trade edition is published for sale through the bookshops. The Literary Guild, the chief beneficiary of this decision, grew rapidly in the late 1960s, and eventually achieved a membership of some 350,000 although it is doubtful whether this actually made serious inroads into sales through bookshops.[41] Even so, the bookshops were suffering, and there was a general recognition in the trade of the need to promote the whole idea of books and bookbuying.

This thought was not entirely new. As early as 1925 the National Book Council was formed to promote books and to encourage the habit of leisure reading. The Publishers' Association was lukewarm at first and for many years to come,[42] but after World War II there was a little more enthusiasm. In 1944 the Council became the National Book League, and although it was still not officially recognised by the Publishers' Association, two leading publishers, Sir Robert Lusty and Mark Longman, gave it a real presence in the book world in the 1950s.[43] The National Book League, however, was merely generating goodwill by acting as an unofficial link between the trade and public. Promotional exercises needed something with more teeth, and out of this need there grew such bodies as the Book Marketing Council and the Book Development Council, promoting books at home and abroad respectively.[44]

As a consequence of all these developments, the British book trade has what is probably the strongest institutional structure of any publishing industry in the free world. Elsewhere, fixed prices have been abolished, as in France, Australia and Sweden, or have never existed, as in the United States where such a price-fixing agreement would be illegal under the anti-trust laws. The Net Book Agreement is still criticised from time to time for maintaining artificially high price levels, although most of the arguments which appealed to Mr Justice Buckley in 1962 are as valid now as they were then. If only to operate the Net Book Agreement, the publishers have to work with each other and with the booksellers. This co-operation, which is such a surprising feature of this intensely competitive industry, is a product of the industry's history. The Stationers' Company in its heyday was belaboured by its opponents as a monopolist, and their successors would doubtless call it a cartel. In one form or another, however, whether as the Stationers' Company, or as a conger, or as a group of copy-owning shareholders or as the Publishers' Association, British publishers have always worked together so that they could survive to compete against each other. The customs of the trade as it looks towards the twenty-first century would not be wholly unfamiliar to the Court of Assistants of four hundred years ago.

17

Old Ways and New Directions

The institutional structures which British publishing has developed during the twentieth century have been, to a considerable extent, intended to preserve rather than to change. The Net Book Agreement was, and is, an essentially conservative instrument designed to counteract a specific problem of the late nineteenth century and used to maintain a stable structure in the twentieth. In itself, the Net Book Agreement had little effect on what was published, despite the later argument that it allowed publishers to be more adventurous than they might have been in a wholly unprotected market.[1] Indeed, its principal effect, as Macmillan and its other early promoters had intended, was to allow the trade to 'continue in familiar ways; the suspicion of innovation, and of innovators, was to be a characteristic of the industry throughout the first seven decades of the century.

In the inevitable spirit of self-examination which followed from the beginning of both a new century and a new reign, the latter as unfamiliar as the former in 1901, businessmen in many fields began to reassess their methods and their performance. Publishers were no exception, but with the new power of the Net Book Agreement to protect them, and the developing collective strength of the Publishers' Association to sustain them, few felt the need for innovation. The trends which had been apparent in the late nineteenth century continued up to 1914. The separation of the various functions of the book trade was almost complete. One of the few printers which still had a publishing division retreated into its own field in 1909, when Bemrose of Derby, a pioneer of high-quality colour printing, sold its small publishing division to the rising star of George Allen.[2] Bemroses were quite clear that the reason for this was that publishing was not an appropriate activity for a printer.[3] Some of the late nineteenth-century developments continued to attract suspicion in the trade. Arthur Waugh, then an employee and later Managing Director of Chapman and Hall, was still unhappy about literary agents in the years before World War I, considering that it was the agent who now 'called the tune' in relations between author and publisher. Waugh, unlike Heinemann, dealt with agents, but there is a clear suggestion that he found it distasteful to do so.[4]

Although there was a steady increase in the number of books published each year between 1900 and 1914, many were reprints, and most came from firms which were doing what they had always done.[5] It was a recipe for steady success. Publishers who sought out and followed the taste of the reading public could not fail. Ward Lock, an unexciting and modestly successful house founded in 1854, began to concentrate on solidly middlebrow books in the first decade of the new century. Among their authors was Rider Haggard; they published his *Ayesha* (1905) when he was at the height of his fame, and later took on Edgar Wallace, E. Phillips Oppenheim, Leslie Charteris and other popular novelists.[6] Like any successful house, they also had their steady sellers from the back list; in Ward Lock's case this included the hardy perennial of Mrs Beeton's *Household Management*, first published in 1861, and still popular in the 1920s.[7] To support the whole enterprise there was the famous series of red-covered guides which survived both the turn of the century and two world wars.[8]

The move to the middle, the appeal to the popular taste of the educated middle class and its upper and lower borderlands, lay at the heart of the success of J. M. Dent in one of the first publishing experiments of the new century. Everyman's Library had its origins in 1904, when Dent conceived the idea of a series of reprints of classic texts with introductions by leading experts, to be retailed at the lowest possible price.[9] Dent always claimed that this was a wholly original idea, but in fact he had many predecessors in the field. Everyman's Library was, in one sense, just another reprint series of the kind which had been familiar since the late eighteenth century. Even among his own contemporaries, Dent was not alone, for most of the major publishers had some sort of reprint series, and Grant Richards had already been publishing his World's Classics for some time.[10] Dent's new series differed somewhat from the others in the quality of the introductions (although even that was very variable in the early years), and perhaps also in the high moral tone with which he imbued the enterprise. Everyman's Library was undoubtedly a great success, to the extent that Dent ran into production problems and had to establish his own production facilities in the new garden city at Letchworth to meet the demand. By 1906, 152 volumes were in print, and Everyman's Library was clearly a major triumph for its publisher.[11] Others inevitably followed. Humphrey Milford, charged by the Delegates of the Oxford University Press with establishing a commercial branch of the Press's publishing business in London, bought World's Classics from the bankrupt Richards, and began to publish them under the OUP imprint in 1906. The series was the foundation of the Press's successful venture into the competitive world of London publishing, and, like Everyman's Library, was important both educationally and culturally.[12]

Innovation, however, was a minority activity, as it has always been in the book trade. The steady seller is always more attractive than the risky investment, especially when the author is safely dead and the copyright expired. The inertia which underlies such publishing is perhaps more apparent in the years before World War I than at any other time since the end of the eighteenth century. When Waugh arrived at Chapman and Hall in 1901, he found that the house depended almost entirely on continuing sales of Dickens and Carlyle, both of whom they had published in their heyday. He recognised the need for new authors, and indeed new staff, but neither was easily found.[13] A. and C. Black, which had moved to London from its native Glasgow in 1891, published no fiction other than Scott, and largely survived on the profits of the *Encyclopaedia Brittanica*. Even that asset was sold in 1897, and by 1900 the firm was surviving on little more than its past earnings.[14] For both of these houses, and for others, what was needed was rescue rather than revival. Waugh saved Chapman and Hall by overcoming his dislike of agents and using them to recruit new authors, most notably H. G. Wells who came through J. B. Pinker.[15] Black was saved by the purchase of the rights in the title of the almost defunct *Who's Who* at one of the last of the trade sales in 1896, and by a subsequent venture into publishing illustrated books for the gift market.[16]

The sorry state of British publishing on the eve of World War I is at least partly explained by the trade's absorption in its own affairs. The Book War took its toll, and when the very survival of the trade seemed in doubt innovation was hardly a prudent course. The outbreak of war in the autumn of 1914 merely exacerbated this trend, and presented many additional difficulties. Paper supply was a problem, but the value of having a collective voice through the Publishers' Association soon became apparent. The Board of Trade, which was responsible for the allocation of paper, ignored many of the trade's arguments, but on one crucial issue the publishers were victorious, when the Board conceded the absolute necessity of a continuous supply of paper on which to print schoolbooks. Nothing, however, could prevent the rise in the price of paper, which was inevitably reflected in an upward movement of the prices of books themselves.[17]

Raw materials were not the only difficulty; both production and distribution facilities were interrupted by war production and war transport. Black's had to abandon their new and successful venture into colour books,[18] and like all firms they lost many key employees to the services, in many cases permanently. Despite the efforts of the Publishers' Association, publishing was not classified as a trade of national importance whose employees were exempt from military service, and both in the initial enthusiasm for voluntary recruitment in 1914–15, and in the later conscription to the forces, many good and essential men were lost. Batsfords, for example, found themselves with only two of their permanent staff remaining, and the firm inevitably suffered.[19] Stanley Unwin, who had recently bought out George Allen and established Allen and Unwin, had lost three of his fellow directors to war service by 1918.[20] The whole trade found itself in difficulties. Sales fell, and profits fell even more heavily in the face of wartime inflation.[21] For an industry whose state in 1914 had been less healthy than many had assumed, the post-war world would not be easy.

In 1918, unlike 1945, it was assumed that there would be a rapid reversion to the conditions of 'pre-war'. The land fit for heroes sounded remarkably like an idealised vision of the England of Edward VII and Queen Victoria. The reality was to prove very different from the dream, for Britain, and indeed the whole industrialised world, was about to enter two dreadful decades in which a brief period of prosperity was followed by a catastrophic economic and political crisis. The overwhelming victory for the wartime coalition at the 1919 election set the tone. Despite the continued presence of Lloyd George as Prime Minister it was in all but name a Conservative government, and conservatism was the dominant trend of the period. This was as true in the publishing industry as it was elsewhere in national life.

For much of the inter-war period, British publishing was as similar as it could be to the pre-war years. There were, of course, some institutional developments, both through partial modification of the Net Book Agreement and the beginnings of the collective promotion of books.[22] Both of these were, in part, a recognition of the changing world in which the publishers were working. For the first time, the printed word was no longer the only means of mass communication or mass entertainment. The cinema had been increasingly familiar in Britain since before the turn of the century, but its real popularity is a phenomenon of the 1920s. After the further boost of the introduction of sound in 1927 cinema attendances went up rapidly. In 1935, there were nearly 4,500 cinemas in Britain and 907 million tickets were sold.[23] Although to some extent the 'film of the book' could stimulate sales of the book itself, as certain kinds of television programmes were later to do,[24] the cinema was nevertheless a challenge to the book industry. It made inroads into both the time and the money available for leisure. Other social changes tended in the same direction, as a greater variety of leisure activities became available to more people. The motor car, and all that it implied in taking families out of their homes, was not really available to the majority until the 1960s, but there was one threat within the home itself which the publishers could not ignore. Radio broadcasting began in Britain in 1922, but came of age with the establishment of the BBC in 1926. In that year, 2.1 million licences were issued; the number had risen to over 9 million by 1939, and as early as 1935 98 per cent of the population had access to a radio set.[25] Even newspapers suffered from the incursions of the radio, for news broadcasts of a very high standard were a feature of the BBC from its earliest years.

Alternative leisure activities were a threat to the publishing industry; some other developments worked in its favour. The generally higher standard of lighting in most homes, as electricity replaced gas, made reading easier for those who wanted to read. Educational standards were rising, and almost total adult literacy had been attained. Public library provision, although still inadequate by later standards, was improving, bringing more people into contact with books and creating more libraries which had to buy them. The problem for the publishers was how to meet these challenges and how to exploit the opportunities which they offered.

One factor which should not be forgotten is that both the cinema and the radio, and later television, brought additional direct revenue into the book trade through sales of rights. As early as 1922, the Society of Authors proposed a scheme for recompensing authors whose works were read or dramatised on the radio, and they reached an agreement with the BBC. The authors were not happy with it, but it did represent an acknowledgement of the need to pay authors whose works were used at second hand.[26] In 1938, a further agreement included the publishers as represented by the Publishers' Association; in addition to increasing the levels of payment, it proposed that the BBC should mention the publisher as well as the author when a book was broadcast or referred to in a broadcast. Negotiations on the latter point were still not concluded when war broke out in 1939, but the publishers were not dissatisfied with their efforts.[27] In the cinema, it was the invention of the 'talkies' which really provoked the crisis. The production companies needed script-writers, and many authors were able to supplement their incomes from that source; in 1937 a British Screenwriters' Association was formed under the auspices of the Society of Authors.[28] For a lucky few there was another source of revenue: the sale of the film rights in their books. In 1933, for example, Hugh Walpole was able to sell the rights in his *Vanessa* to MGM for $12,500.[29]

The sale of subsidiary rights became an important source of revenue for some publishers in the inter-war years; these included not only the broadcasting and film rights, but also rights to translations or reprints in specified languages or overseas territories, and to serialisation in magazines and newspapers.[30] Such sales were dependent on the availability of saleable products, and the possibility of selling subsidiary rights was becoming a factor for some publishers in the selection and commissioning of books.

Despite the general conservatism, which sometimes seemed like inertia, not all publishers in the 1920s and 1930s were afraid of risk-taking, and there were a few who were notable innovators. Like their Victorian predecessors, they were individualistic and sometimes highly idiosyncratic, but the most successful of them were able to break into the charmed circles of the publishing world and to make their marks on it. Three men are outstanding in the history of British publishing in the first half of the twentieth century, and each of them demonstrates how an innovative publisher could succeed even against a background of general economic gloom. These three were Stanley Unwin, Victor Gollancz and Allen Lane.

They were in many ways very different from each other, but they have some intriguing characteristics in common. All of them began their careers in comparatively conventional publishing houses. Unwin indeed came from a book trade family. His grandfather, Jacob Unwin, had founded a printing house in 1826, which was to become one of the few major book printers of the late nineteenth and twentieth centuries.[31] His uncle, Thomas Fisher Unwin, had branched out on his own as a publisher in the late 1870s, having been apprenticed to Hodder and Stoughton. T. Fisher Unwin ran a notable house; his early authors included Conrad and Yeats, and his willingness to support profitable new writers rarely deserted him. He was later to be the first publisher of both Ethel M. Dell and Dorothy Sayers.[32] Conrad and Dell were both discoveries of Edward Garnett, his reader; Unwin's talent was for taking risks when he felt that they were a worthwhile commercial or literary proposition. Stanley Unwin joined his uncle in 1904, and was later to claim for himself much of the credit for the firm's success in the ten years before World War I.[33] Be that as it may, there is no doubt that the younger Unwin showed both a talent for his new profession and an impatience with his uncle's methods of pursuing it. He learned the trade from Fisher Unwin, and was to put his lessons to good use.

Unwin might well have felt that he had chosen an unpropitious moment for his leap to freedom, for it was in 1914 that he began his career as an independent publisher. He did not start entirely from scratch; his first action was to buy the ailing house of George Allen. Allens had a strange history. It had been founded in 1871, largely at the instigation of Ruskin to publish his own works. Although Allen expanded his list, it was the Ruskin copyrights which were its only real strength.[34] In the early years of the twentieth century, Allen's sons bought a number of other small houses, including Swan, Sonnenschein, a modestly successful publisher of social science and philosophy books, who are chiefly remembered as the publishers of the first English edition of *Das Kapital* in 1887.[35] By 1913, Allens was bankrupt, and it was this company which Unwin bought, renaming it Allen and Unwin, which it has remained ever since.[36]

From the beginning of his independent career, Unwin proved adept at attracting authors and at selling serious books. An early recruit was Bertrand Russell, who was an Allen and Unwin author for the rest of his long life.[37] At a later date he published both Gandhi and Harold Laski, building his list on a solid foundation of contemporary non-fiction, while at the same time exploiting his growing back-list, including, of course, the still valuable Ruskin.[38] Unwin was always active in the general affairs of the trade. He was President of the Publishers' Association in 1933–5, and involved in most of its many initiatives in the 1920s and 1930s, especially in relation to the ever-increasing complexities of subsidiary rights.

Gollancz began his career in an even more conventional house than did Unwin, and at an even less propitious time. After a short time as a schoolmaster, he joined Benn Brothers in 1921, where he found the formidable Sir Ernest Benn at the height of his considerable powers. Benns published magazines and technical books. It was in the latter department that Gollancz chiefly worked, and he transformed it by his adventurous policy of publishing books for collectors as well as technical manuals. Benns developed a large general list and increased their turnover tenfold. This was largely due to Gollancz, but eventually he and Benn quarrelled, and he left to form his own house where he could follow his own interests.[39]

Gollancz left Benns in 1928, when the book trade, like the country as a whole, was about to plunge into the Great Depression. The economic crisis took its toll on the publishing industry as much as it did elsewhere. Between 1930 and 1937 the number of new titles published each year fell consistently, while the number of reprints rose dramatically.[40] The record of a single house vividly illustrates the problem: in 1928, Hodder and Stoughton had sales worth £637,770; by 1939 this figure had fallen to £289,375.[41] The message was, apparently, clear. New books did not sell, and publishers could survive only on a flourishing back-list. It was not a good start for a firm which had no back-list, whose founder had a commitment to publishing large numbers of new books. In a sense, however, it was the economic crisis which was the making of Gollancz, for with it came the revival of the left in Britain, a revival which was further impelled by the establishment of a Nazi government in Germany in 1933. From the beginning, Gollancz, who had always been a political animal, had intended to publish political books, but he can never have imagined that they would form so important a part of his business.

In the early 1930s, Gollancz had already published a number of important books by left-wing writers. John Strachey's *The Coming Struggle for Power* and G. D. H. Cole's *What Marx Really Meant* were both published in 1932, but it was Hitler's accession to power which provided the impetus for the next development. Gollancz himself was involved in the agitation for a Popular Front, and it was out of this that there emerged his idea for the Left Book Club. The Club started in 1936 with a membership of 9,000; by 1939 it had reached 50,000 and its publications included some of the classics of modern polemics. In fact, it was never a straightforward enterprise, and not always commercially successful. It is still unclear to what extent it was dominated by communists; certainly Gollancz himself was remarkably naïve about communist influence in left-wing organisations in the mid-1930s. There were some titles which barely covered their costs even at the height of the Club's success, and the various ancillary activities, such as public meetings and newsletters, took up not only a great deal of Gollancz's time, but also a great deal of money. There is no doubt of Gollancz's sincerity in his political and charitable activities. What might be doubted, however, is his business acumen. He was rescued from the possible consequences by a loyal staff, and by the unfailing instinct for success which he had displayed during the first eight years of his firm's existence.[42]

It would, however, be quite wrong to think of Gollancz only as a publisher of political propaganda. The publisher who based his business on a cause had always found himself in commercial difficulties, as John Cassell had discovered a hundred years earlier.[43] Gollancz was far too good a publisher to make any such mistake. He was an inspired selector of both books and authors. His first best-seller, in the firm's first year, was the autobiography of the ballerina Isadora Duncan,[44] and he had brought with him a number of 'his' authors from Benns. These included Dorothy Sayers, whose contract with Fisher Unwin had gone to Benns when the latter bought the former in 1926.[45] Detective fiction became something of a feature of Gollancz lists, as did middle-brow fiction in general. Gollancz, however, recognised that there was more to publishing than choosing good books. They had to be sold. In this aspect of publishing he was a genius, and it is perhaps here that his true originality lies. All Gollancz books had a distinctive yellow and black cover, and the firm's logo became familiar through regular newspaper advertisements. He took advice from the great typographer Stanley Morison,[46] who ensured that Gollancz's books, as well as his advertisements, were always decently designed and printed.[47] By the outbreak of World War II, Gollancz had built a list and a firm which could survive the vagaries of its founder. He had revolutionised the advertising of books, and demonstrated that the popular wisdom of the trade, which was that newspaper advertising was a waste of money, was wrong. He had shown that even in the straitened circumstances of the 1930s a publisher of genius could carve out a new way for the trade.

Unwin and Gollancz were not the only new publishers of the 1920s and 1930s, although, with Lane, they were probably the most influential. Others included Jonathan Cape, who started his own business in 1921,[48] Frederic Warburg, who revived the fortunes of Martin Secker as Secker and Warburg,[49] Geoffrey Faber, who distinguished himself by publishing poetry without going bankrupt and by employing T. S. Eliot to edit the list,[50] and Michael Joseph. The difficulties of breaking into the trade are well illustrated by Joseph. His early career was quite different from that of either Unwin or Gollancz. He was a moderately successful and very prolific author who, in 1924, left Hutchinsons, where he had worked as advertising manager, to join the literary agents, Curtis Brown. Here he rapidly made a name for himself as a shrewd and perceptive judge of a book, gaining the respect of authors and publishers alike.[51] His ambition, however, was to be a publisher himself, and in 1935 he left Curtis Brown to set up his own house. Gollancz was one of the many publishers who had benefited from Joseph's work at Curtis Brown, and he willingly invested in the new firm.[52] Although three years later, Gollancz left the Michael Joseph board under rather acerbic circumstances, by then Joseph was reasonably well established, with a growing back-list and a few successes. His individuality was shown by his first catalogue, which was the first publisher's list ever to have had colour illustrations.[53] Ironically, the great publicist Gollancz was unhappy about Joseph's advertising policy, and more particularly the cost of it, but Joseph had one great talent without which no publisher can succeed: his ability to spot a book. Despite this, however, the firm was never prosperous in the pre-war period, although it published some important books, and a few best-sellers.[54]

Unwin, Gollancz and Joseph were connected in many ways,

through their firms, their authors and, above all, through their attitudes. They were all willing to take risks, both literary and commercial, and they were all somewhat iconoclastic in their attitude to the trade. Unwin and Gollancz are particularly prominent in the story of British publishing between the wars, because so much that was new and exciting was happening because of them. On a broader scale, however, the fact is that very little was happening that was either new or exciting. The older houses went on much as they always had. Small firms which could no longer compete in a more cut-throat market were bought up by larger ones, for the process of amalgamation which has created the giants of contemporary British publishing was already happening before 1939. American money also began to influence the British publishing scene. This process had begun even before World War I. In about 1895, Chapman and Hall became sole European agents for the New York firm of Wiley, publishers of scientific and technical books. At first, Chapman and Hall may have seen this as little more than a profitable agency, but in fact the success of the Wiley books began to influence their own publishing policy, and by 1914 the Wiley connection was an essential element in the financial stability of the house.[55] After the war, some firms found themselves even more deeply enmeshed with American partners. Doubleday Page and Company of New York bought Heinemanns in 1920, although they continued to run the English side of the business as a separate operation.[56] Dent's Everyman's Library was also a beneficiary of American willingness to invest in British publishing; E. P. Dutton and Co. were Dent's partner, and had a contractual obligation to take 2,000 copies of every title issued.[57] In difficult times, the need to find money to invest in new books was often paramount. The hard-pressed directors of Cassells sold their company to the Berry brothers, the newspaper magnates who were later to be Lords Camrose and Kemsley. The sale was necessary because the effects of the General Strike of 1926 brought Cassells close to bankruptcy, although in fact the book publishing side of the business was re-established as an independent entity, and achieved perhaps its greatest period under the brilliant direction of Newman Flower in the 1930s.[58]

The involvement of newspaper groups in book publishing and working arrangements with American companies were both attempts to find capital from which to fund the increasingly costly business of book publishing. There was also a constant effort by many publishers to find overseas markets, especially in the United States and the British Commonwealth and Empire. The importance of the United States as a consumer of British books had been recognised in the mid-nineteenth century when British publishers and authors had devoted so much effort to trying to obtain equitable arrangements for copyright registration in the United States.[59] Once this problem was solved, the way lay open to agency agreements, amalgamations, rights deals and other explorations of the vast American market. Indeed, some of the links antedated the conclusion of the copyright disputes. Macmillans had had a branch in New York since 1869, which in 1896 was reorganised as the Macmillan Company of New York and began to publish on its own account as well as being the American representative of the parent company.[60] In the same year, 1896, Oxford University Press, abandoning a former arrangement for American distribution, opened its own New York business, which, like Macmillans, soon began to assume a considerable degree of independence.[61] Lesser houses were equally attracted to the United States. Ward Lock opened a branch in New York in 1882,[62] and those who could not afford that step could at least use British publishers who were established across the Atlantic as their sole agents, as Black's used Macmillan until they established their own agency in 1893.[63]

Within the British Empire there was an open market for British publishers. The 1842 and 1911 Copyright Acts applied throughout the colonies, while the dominions either had similar legislation or were signatories of the Berne Convention. Macmillans opened branches in Toronto in 1904 and in Melbourne in 1905,[64] and many other firms followed their example until it was not unusual for a British publisher to have a base not only in London and New York, but also in Canada, Australia, South Africa and India. In the inter-war period, the Indian market was particularly important for a number of major publishers. The subcontinent was, in the contemporary phrase, being 'prepared for self-government', and education was seen as an essential prerequisite. Most of the books which supported this came from Britain, for it was an essentially British system of education to which the future rulers of India were to be subjected. Longmans were particularly involved in this aspect of the trade, using their long experience of educational publishing to produce series with such titles as 'Longmans' Readers for Burma' and 'Longmans'

English Reading Books for Indian Students'.[65] Others were not far behind. Macmillans also had strong Indian connections, with branches in Bombay, Calcutta and Madras before World War I, and an enlightened policy of trying to publish books which made some concessions to Indian culture and even Indian languages.[66] Oxford University Press's Indian branch, opened in 1919, was a great success, and proved to be the entreé to an important market for Bibles as well as for educational books and literary texts.[67] In fact, some of the major houses, especially those involved in educational publishing, became heavily dependent on their Indian and colonial markets, with results that were to be distinctly uncomfortable when those markets began to shrink after 1945.

British publishing during the first forty years of the twentieth century offered many contrasts. On the one hand, it reflected Britain's dominance of a world far beyond her own shores, and even in 1939 the impermanence of that domination was still not generally recognised. On the other hand, it was as insular as it had been in Caxton's day. Victor Gollancz, one of the giants of the modern British publishing industry, made his name and his fortune by publishing two archetypally English genres: detective fiction, and mild and humane left-wing politics. The great houses which could trace their names back to the reign of Queen Victoria and beyond still seemed to dominate the publishing world. The newcomers were noisy and brash, and were perhaps doing some things right, but the established houses felt no need to imitate them. All of this was to change. Some of the change came from great geo-political forces far beyond the scope of the industry itself, but at least one, which was revolutionary in its own way, came from within. One man was to recognise that there was a need to find new markets which had never been explored before: a market of those who went to the cinema, who listened to the radio, who used the libraries and who read newspapers, but who never bought a book. His idea was simple: publish cheap and attractive books, but publish good books, and sell them where people bought other goods. He was the third of the great innovators, and, beyond question, the most influential of all of them; his name was Allen Lane.

18

Allen Lane's Idea

The 1930s was not a propitious decade for new enterprise in Britain, and the publishing world was certainly not exempt from the general economic malaise. Despite the achievements of Unwin and Gollancz, the general ethos was conservative rather than radical, and favoured retrenchment rather than expansion. It is therefore startling to find that perhaps the greatest single innovation in twentieth-century publishing should have emerged during this discouraging time: the mass-market paperback, which has revolutionised the commercial world of books and has taken books to places and to people which they had never previously reached.

Paper-covered books have a much longer history than the modern paperback. Indeed, books were being issued stitched in paper covers in the late seventeenth century, and to protect the trade of the bookbinders the Stationers' Company had attempted to define a maximum size for such books and to regulate their publication.[1] Paper covers were normal in France for almost all books in the nineteenth century (and to some extent still are), while in Germany paper covers were used by Tauchnitz from the beginning of his series,[2] and by many other publishers. The Tauchnitz example is indeed of some significance in the development of the modern paperback, for it both familiarised some British bookbuyers with the concept of the paperback book, and through one of its German competitors directly influenced the format and design of the first modern British paperbacks. In addition to these continental examples, however, there were both British and American precedents for books having been published in paper covers in the nineteenth century. Indeed, in the United States paper-covered books were a familiar sight on the bookstalls by the 1850s, and a few were issued in Britain before the end of the nineteenth century.[3]

The significance of the modern paperback, however, is not solely in its physical form. To some extent, the use of paper rather than boards and cloth saves money, and the intention was indeed to use the paper cover to ensure cheapness. This in turn links the paperback with one of the great traditions of British publishing, the reprint series. This can be traced back to Bell's *British Poets* and its late eighteenth-century competitors,[4] and it was a tradition which was continued with vigour throughout the nineteenth century, especially after the railways provided a whole new market of travellers who wanted cheap light reading for their journeys.[5] In the early years of the twentieth century there were many such series in existence; Everyman's Library and World's Classics were among the more high-minded examples,[6] but there were few publishers who did not have a series of cheap reprints of their own books, especially of novels or of works whose copyright was in public domain. It was out of these two traditions, the paper-covered book and the cheap reprint series, that the modern paperback was born.

The progenitor of the 'paperback revolution' was Allen Lane, who, like Gollancz and Unwin, had been brought up in the trade before he broke away to form his own house. Lane, however, learned his trade from someone very different from Fisher Unwin or Sir Ernest Benn. His uncle, John Lane, had been the *enfant terrible* of British publishing in the 1890s. The elder Lane, with his partner Elkin Matthews, had established a bookshop at the sign of The Bodley Head in Mayfair in 1887, and they soon turned to publishing. Bodley Head's early publications included the notorious *Yellow Book*, with contributions from, among others, Wilde, Beardsley and Le Gallienne. Lane broke with Matthews before the end of the century, and established his own house; in the years before World War I he continued to publish with some success and often in the vanguard of literary taste. Unlike most British publishers, Lane was not afraid to publish foreign writers, for his authors included both André Maurois and Anatole France.[7] Allen Lane joined his uncle at The Bodley Head in 1919,[8] and soon became an essential part of the firm. He learned his trade there, and inherited the house when John Lane died in 1925. By that time, however, The Bodley Head had declined from its former eminence. Although its books were still elegantly produced, as Lane had always insisted that they should be, they were no longer in the forefront of the literary and artistic world. Allen Lane had inherited a house with a great tradition but apparently little future.

Lane revived the decaying fortunes of The Bodley Head in a most remarkable way. In a sense, he reverted to the traditions which his uncle had established in the 1890s, and added his own talent for publicity. Perhaps the most remarkable episode was that of the publication of the first British edition of Joyce's *Ulysses* in 1936. Lane had been trying to obtain the British rights for some years, and eventually succeeded after T. S. Eliot had declined the offer on behalf of Faber and Faber. *Ulysses* was duly published by The Bodley Head, and no prosecution ensued, despite the long-standing practice of British customs officers of seizing copies of the book which were brought into the country.[9] It was a major triumph for Lane, and brought him, not for the first time, wide public attention.

By that time, however, Lane had embarked on his greatest enterprise. Despite a few successes, and despite the vigour of both Allen Lane himself and his brothers, who were with him in the business, The Bodley Head was in trouble. Although in later years Lane was always to maintain that the paperbacks grew out of popular demand for cheap books,[10] the fact is that the Lanes were trying to find a way to save their publishing house. To do so, Lane looked to the tradition of cheap reprints, but decided to go even further than his predecessors by adopting a new physical format and looking for unconventional channels of sales. Lane's plan was to issue a series of cheap reprints of good books under The Bodley Head imprint, but he decided that to make his series different from the others he would use a different format. There can be little doubt that this decision was influenced by the form of the Albatross series, issued in Germany from 1932. Albatross was the brainchild of John Holroyd-Reece, an Englishman who had worked in publishing on the continent. Holroyd-Reece had set out to compete with Tauchnitz, now nearly a century old and beginning to look distinctly old-fashioned. He designed a new format for the books, slightly taller and less broad than Tauchnitz, and essentially the same size and shape as the familiar mass-market paperback of today. It was the first use of the format. His books had brightly coloured covers which were made of paper slightly thicker than that used by Tauchnitz, and using a different colour for different subjects and genres.[11] This was the source of Lane's physical conception of Penguins, and perhaps even the inspiration for the title of the series.

Lane's true originality lay in his confidence that good books could be sold in large numbers, and in his willingness, at least at first, to use unconventional channels of distribution in order to achieve this. The plan was to publish ten titles, and to sell them through chain stores and any other outlet which would accept them. The book trade was generally very sceptical, not least because to hold the price down to 6d, Lane had to produce print runs of at least 20,000 copies,[12] which presented a serious problem of distribution and sales. Jonathan Cape was one of those who doubted the viability of Lane's plans. Lane had in fact discussed the whole matter with Cape before deciding to proceed; the latter's attitude was that the young man was welcome to bankrupt himself in any way he chose. He sold the cheap-reprint rights in some of his books to Lane, and in fact six of the first ten Penguins came from the Cape list. Cape soon recognised the danger which paperbacks might present to conventional publishing; he welcomed the rights income, but he later told Lane that 'You're the bugger that has ruined this trade.' Subsequently, Cape was generally rather reluctant to sell paperback rights until long after World War II.[13] Unwin was equally convinced that Lane would fail,[14] but Gollancz was a little more perceptive. He saw the possibility of real competition from Penguin if Lane made a success of it, and his reaction was to refuse to allow any of his books to be published in paperback at all.[15] His own *Mundamus* series, a very small collection of paperbacks issued in 1930 and 1931, had been a failure precisely because he was not willing to take the same risks as Lane, especially in ordering long print runs.[16]

Ironically, Gollancz failed with *Mundamus* because he was too conventional. He saw it as a series in which he would publish novels of which he owned the copyright, whereas Lane sought to buy rights specifically for a paperback edition. This established an important pattern in modern paperback publishing. Although some houses are linked to a parent company, most of the great mass-market imprints buy rights from the original publisher or direct from the author or through his agent. Lane of course had the example of both Tauchnitz and Albatross for this approach, but he was the first publisher to work with such a system in Britain. At first he succeeded because, like Cape, many believed that it could do no harm, although they had little faith in Penguin; later both Lane and his competitors found that other publishers were only too anxious to reap the great, and sometimes vast, rewards of successful paperback publication.

The success of Penguins, as Lane knew, would depend on choosing the right books and making the right impact when the first books were launched. He chose well. Lane was a man of middlebrow tastes, and he published books for people like himself. The first ten Penguins, published simultaneously in July 1935, included novels by Mary Webb, Compton Mackenzie and Dorothy Sayers. On the other hand, like any good publisher, Lane was also looking for titles which would have some permanent value. Also among the ten were *Ariel*, André Maurois's life of Shelley, and Hemingway's *Farewell to Arms*. Within a year the list also included Butler's *Erewhon* and George Moore's *Esther Waters*, which mark the beginning of Penguin's long and continuing policy of providing cheap and accessible editions of neglected classics.[17] Whether consciously or not, Lane had created a house which was to be one of the major cultural influences on mid-twentieth-century Britain.

Selecting titles, buying rights and producing the books was, however, only the beginning. These unfamiliar and often unwelcome objects now had to be sold, and the booksellers were as sceptical as the publishers. Some of them certainly feared that the sixpenny books would sell better than more expensive, and hence more profitable, hardbacks, but not in sufficient quantity to generate comparable cash-flows. To break even, Lane had to sell 17,500 copies of each of his ten titles as soon as possible after publication, but he had collected an average of only 7,000 orders after a prolonged effort in salesmanship.[18] Orders were beginning to come in, but it was distinctly possible that Penguin was heading for disaster even before it was launched. In June 1935, however, Lane persuaded Woolworth's to place a large order. A good deal of legend has accumulated around this episode, and in particular about the part played by the wife of Woolworth's chief buyer. She is alleged to have been attracted by the books which her husband had rejected, and to have encouraged him to change his mind. The truth seems to be that Lane had been negotiating with Woolworth's for some time, and this was only one of a number of factors which made the negotiations successful.[19] The order was important, however, for it ensured that Penguin survived its first few weeks. The books then rapidly became a favourite with a far wider public than had ever bought books before. The paperback revolution had begun.

Lane had taken the first crucial steps in making this revolution possible, for in three ways he had discovered how very cheap books could be made both attractive to the mass market and profitable to the publisher: visually distinctive covers, unconventional sales outlets and rights bought from hardback publishers by a house which was involved only in paperback publishing. Lane himself was to deviate from all three in later years. He resisted pictorial covers long after they had been adopted by his rivals;[20] he withdrew into the bookshop, and in later years even opened his own;[21] and towards the end of his life he started publishing original hardbacks.[22] Nevertheless, Penguin dominated the British paperback market for twenty years, and 'penguin' itself became a synonym for 'paperback'.

It was, however, on the other side of the Atlantic that most of the later developments in paperback publishing originated. Even before Lane opened an American branch, he had an American competitor. Pocket Books was founded by Robert de Graaf in 1939, partly influenced by what he had seen of the success of Penguin during a visit to England. De Graaf, however, extended Lane's principle of marketing outside the bookshops. From 1941 he worked through the independent wholesalers who dominated book distribution in the USA, especially to department stores and news-stands.[23] By that time Penguin was established in the United States, but American experiences were unhappy for Lane. Penguin Books Inc. of New York was a separate company, owned jointly by Lane and Ian Ballantine, an American economics graduate who had been impressed by the success of Penguins while he was studying in London in the late 1930s. The American business was established in 1939, but the war caused many difficulties, and, when there were personality clashes between Ballantine and Lane, the former resigned. In his place, Lane installed Kurt Enoch, who had been involved in Albatross before leaving Germany as a refugee.[24] The later history of Penguin Books Inc. (and to some extent that of the parent company as well) is a sad story of Lane's inability to work with others or to trust them, but in fact it was the brasher approach of de Graaf at Pocket Books which was to point the way to the future.

Pocket Books, and other imprints which followed in its wake in the mid-1940s, set the pace for the development of the paperback industry in the United States, and soon found imitators in Britain. For some years, Penguin had the field to itself, but during the war two other paperback imprints were started in Britain,

Pan and Panther.[25] Pan grew out of the consortium of publishers which had founded the Reprint Society in 1939; this consisted of Macmillan, Collins, Heinemann and Hodder and Stoughton. Pan began publishing in 1944, and soon captured a substantial share of the popular market. In the early 1970s, its annual sales were estimated at some 17 million books.[26] By contrast, Panther was started by two ex-servicemen with no previous experience of the book trade. In the mid-1960s, they had succeeded to such an extent that they were able to sell the company to the Granada group for over £500,000.[27] Other companies learned from these examples, and by the early 1950s the British paperback industry had begun to develop the patterns which it has retained ever since.

On the one hand, there are the paperback houses which follow the Penguin pattern of buying rights in books published by others, often after highly competitive 'auctions' at which they bid large sums for the rights in potential best-sellers.[28] These imprints may be a part of a larger publishing organisation (as indeed is Penguin itself since it became part of the Pearson Longman Group in 1970),[29] but they essentially operate as independent entities so far as their publishing and marketing policies are concerned. The alternative arrangement is that a paperback imprint is part of a single house, and is essentially involved in the paperback publication of that house's books. Much of this paperback publishing is not mass-market publishing at all. The 'trade paperback' is really no more than sets of the printed sheets of the hardback edition bound in soft covers, and hence sold at a slightly cheaper price. It is a ploy which has proved attractive to publishers of academic books hoping to attract a student market, and indeed in the United States trade paperbacks have come to be known as ELHI (ELementary to HIgh School books) or 'egghead' paperbacks. The practice became common in Britain during the 1960s, when there were few houses, even among such giants of the trade as Macmillans, who did not have their own paperback series for their own books. Even Oxford University Press went into this market, when in 1960 twelve books were experimentally published in paperback. The venture was extremely successful, and rapidly expanded to become an important part of Oxford's business.[30]

The paperback revolution has taken books into far more homes than ever had them before. Paperbacks are cheap by comparison with hardbacks, and although Lane's sixpenny books are a distant and faded memory, even today there are mass-market paperbacks which sell for around one pound. Above all, they sell in huge quantities. In 1985, some 48 million mass-market paperbacks were produced in Britain, generating a turnover of more than £50 million.[31] They are distributed through news-agents, bookstalls at airports and railway stations and a host of other 'non-bookshop' outlets. The distribution of paperbacks, unlike that of any other substantial part of the British book trade, is dominated by wholesalers. Although wholesaling of hardback books has virtually ceased to exist in Britain since the end of World War II,[32] it is central to the distribution of mass-market paperbacks. Bookwise of Godalming, for example, one of the most important of the wholesaling houses, claims to stock all the titles of the major paperback publishers, and, like the other wholesalers, is the link between the publishers and the non-bookshop outlets which sustain the paperback industry.[33] These outlets, largely stationers and newsagents, are responsible for about 20 per cent of all book sales in Britain, and nearly all these sales are of paperbacks.[34]

The paperback, despised by some and deplored by many when it was first introduced, has come a long way since Allen Lane devised it as a means to solve the financial difficulties of his publishing house. It is now the basis of a sub-industry within publishing, linked to the major houses, but with its own traditions and its own marketing and distribution arrangements. The mass-market paperback houses have brought into the trade new techniques of selling and promotion which, although they have perhaps not always seemed attractive to some of the more staid publishers, have nevertheless put books into the hands of many who would otherwise never buy or read a book at all. They have brought customers into the bookshops, and in doing that they have proved to be a major benefit to the whole trade. Allen Lane's idea was not only profoundly influential, it was also, as it turned out, very timely. Just four years elapsed between the foundation of Penguin Books and the outbreak of World War II. That war and its aftermath wrought profound changes on the trade; these changes were to bring about the abandonment of many cherished customs, and to take the publishing industry into a new and harsher world.

19

The Trade in War and Peace

The triumphant progress of Penguin Books through its first four years shows how accurate Lane's instincts had been. There was a market to be tapped quite outside the limited range of those who normally bought books. Far from being a dying art in the age of cinema and radio, reading was still a form of entertainment and enlightenment which could command a mass audience. The underlying power of the attraction of the printed word was to be graphically demonstrated during the five years of World War II, when the demand for books rose to an unprecedented level, and the difficulties of supplying them were equally unprecedented.

Stanley Unwin was later to record that World War II was a good time for publishers; demand increased, and almost any book would succeed because demand far outstretched supply.[1] In fact, it seems that in the first two years of the war demand actually fell somewhat, and it was only in 1941 that it began to recover;[2] from then onwards, however, there was certainly a steady increase. The problem was on the supply side of the equation. In 1937, some 11,300 new titles had been published; by 1943, the annual figure had fallen to 7,500.[3] In some categories there was an increase which reflected the exingencies of war. Books on naval and military matters were, not surprisingly, popular: only 62 had been published in 1937, but there were no fewer than 229 in 1943. Books on wireless (19 in 1937; 34 in 1943) showed a similar trend, while the number of books on veterinary science, animal husbandry and agriculture which was published nearly doubled as Britain dug for victory. Later in the war, general publishing revived, as it began to be realised that people wanted to read about something other than the battle which was being fought all around them every day. From 1943, when victory seemed certain if still distant, books about the post-war world came to be as popular as books about the war itself and its origins.[4] Some other categories, however, collapsed; the lavishly illustrated gift books, which had been a feature of the Christmas market since before World War I, vanished and were never really revived.[5] The trade found itself able to sell everything it could produce, and yet ironically unable to produce enough.

As in World War I, the publishers had to cope with both shortage of materials and loss of staff; unlike World War I, however, there was the additional problem of the destruction of existing stocks of books, and of offices and records, because of enemy action in the United Kingdom itself. It was the materials problem which arose first. Britain imported much of her paper, and almost all of her raw materials for domestic papermaking. From April 1940, paper was rationed, and imports of foreign paper were banned in the November of the same year.[6] Supplies were allocated to publishers on the basis of their use of paper during the last full year of peace from September 1938 to August 1939. The ration was initially 60 per cent of consumption during that period, and the Publishers' Association's initial hopes that this would be eased proved to be optimistic when the invasion of Norway in the late spring of 1940 closed the principal source of supply of the paper industry's wood pulp imports.[7] The paper rationing scheme was intended to reflect as fairly as possible the likely demands from individual houses. Inevitably this caused a good deal of resentment in the trade, some of it directed towards HMSO which was partially exempted from the regulations,[8] but rather more towards Allen Lane. Penguin was in a uniquely favourable position because of the way in which the regulations were framed. The publisher's allocation was based not on the number of books produced, but on the tonnage of paper consumed in the designated period in 1938–9. It so happened that this had been a very successful time for Penguins, especially in the massive sales achieved by the first Penguin Specials on various subjects of topical interest. Consequently, Penguin had a very generous allocation, and since the production methods used for paperbacks were far more economical of paper than those used for hardbacks, the rate of production of Penguins could be maintained almost unchecked throughout the war.[9]

Paper rationing was only the beginning of government intervention in the publishing industry, although the Publishers' Association achieved a number of successes in restraining the government from acting on some of its more extreme proposals.

The Association prevented both the halving of the paper ration and the attempt to impose Purchase Tax on books in the summer of 1940.[10] In the following year, the trade negotiated the Book Production War Economy Agreement, under which both the quality of the paper and the size of type was reduced in order to achieve savings. The books which were produced were hideous, but they were at least produced.[11] Despite all these efforts, however, the publishers could not meet the demands of the public, and soon there were real shortages even in such crucial areas as educational books.[12] The problem of controlling the use of paper, as opposed to its distribution to publishers, was not solved until after the end of the war.[13]

The critical shortage of the most basic raw material of the publishing industry would have been bad enough in itself, but the position was made far worse by the destruction of large quantities of books which already existed. Most publishers were still based in the City of London, and stored their books in warehouses there. During the Blitz they shared in the general misery of that orgy of destruction. Unwin was later to estimate that some twenty million books were destroyed by enemy action during the War.[14] His own company lost its stock in 1940,[15] and they were not alone. Some twenty houses lost everything, many of them on the night of 29–30 December 1940, when the losses included Ward Lock.[16] Throughout the winter of 1940–1, losses mounted; Hodder and Stoughton and Harraps both went in 1941, as did innumerable bookshops not only in London but throughout the country.[17] Some escaped by evacuating their operations to the country; Batsfords, for example, went to Malvern, but it did not make their work easier, since they still had to face the problems of distribution through a disrupted transport network.[18] Others remained in London on principle, and were lucky; Macmillans was one of these.[19] Stationers' Hall was destroyed in October 1940,[20] and with it the historic heart of the book trade. Worst of all, Simpkin Marshall was hit, and with their warehouse was lost not only a substantial part of the trade's stocks, but also, as it was to turn out, the wholesaling and distribution arrangements which had sustained the trade for a century.[21] Provincial cities were almost as badly hit as London; in the autumn of 1940, most of Michael Joseph's stock was destroyed when his printer's warehouse in Plymouth was destroyed during a raid on that city.[22] By the end of the war, some 52,000 titles were waiting for reprinting to replace lost stock.[23]

The end of the war did not bring with it the end of the trade's problems, for recovery was to prove slow and difficult. The wartime controls remained intact as the newly elected Labour government struggled with the appalling task of restoring Britain's shattered economy and battered infrastructure. The publishing industry was not in the forefront of the government's priorities. Paper rationing continued until 1949, although the supply situation had gradually eased before then,[24] and a higher percentage of the quota was earmarked for the educational books which were by that time in disastrously short supply.[25] There was a gradual recovery in publisher's output; from 5,800 new books in 1945, the total rose to 11,600 in 1950, and, in addition, many of those 52,000 lost titles were reprinted.[26] The trade was recovering, and in the early 1950s something like normality was restored. The controls had gone, and some firms began to register successes.

The post-war recovery, however, took place in a very different world from that of 1939. The war had seen the final establishment of the paperback as a cheap and convenient form of reading, and publishers who had once doubted its capacity to survive Lane's first list of ten titles were now forced to issue their own.[27] Another and even more serious rival loomed over the horizon when BBC television reopened in June 1946; by 1951, over one million licences were current.[28] The publishers thus had to face new forms of competition in a situation which was already difficult for them. Domestically, not the least of these difficulties arose directly out of the Blitz. When Simpkin Marshall had been destroyed in 1941, more had gone than their stocks. Immediately after the disaster, the directors of Simpkins made it clear that their only course was to seek voluntary liquidation; it was impossible for them in wartime conditions to raise the capital which would have been necessary to rebuild their stocks, and rebuilding the warehouse was an even less practical proposition. The trade reacted immediately to protect its established wholesaling routines. A new company, Simpkin Marshall (1941) Ltd, was formed by a consortium of publishers, operating through the Economic Relations Committee of the Publishers' Association. In fact, this company was not a wholesale house at all; it was a non-profit organisation which, it was envisaged, would function as a central distribution house for the trade. Many publishers were not convinced that the scheme was viable, and, although its new owners persevered until 1951, it was never a success. In 1951, the company was sold to Robert Maxwell, but even his great energy failed to save Simpkins, and in 1955 it finally went into the voluntary liquidation which had been threatened fourteen years earlier.[29]

The end of Simpkin Marshall was not merely the end of a great institution; it was the end of an era, and it left the trade with a distribution problem which it has never fully solved. It proved impossible either to revive Simpkins or to establish another wholesale house, because of the vast capital investment which would have been required. A wholesale house made sense only if it could do what Simpkins had done for a century and keep in stock enough books to satisfy all but the most esoteric orders from booksellers as soon as they were placed. As the output of books rose throughout the 1950s, the possibility of large-scale wholesaling receded even further, and publishers were forced to develop their own arrangements. The failure of Simpkin Mashall (1941) Ltd forced the trade to recognise the need to look for new systems of distribution rather than to revive old ones.[30] Out of this recognition, there arose a number of distribution organisations, which were really joint warehousing arrangements between groups of publishers. Such organisations proved to be useful intermediaries between the publishers and the booksellers, but many difficulties remained. Gradually these difficulties were eased by the introduction of clearing house services for booksellers' orders, so that at least the bookseller was spared from having to send his orders to dozens of different destinations, and in the 1960s a consortium of major booksellers established a clearing house of their own, Bookseller's Order Distribution, which worked reasonably well.[31] In the late 1970s, the first experiments began with the use of computers to expedite ordering by booksellers, but the first 'Teleordering' scheme ran into financial difficulties, and only in the 1980s did the use of computer-based links become a significant factor in communications between publishers and major booksellers.[32] Distribution remains one of the most serious problems of the British book trade, and as the number of titles published annually continues to rise, it seems unlikely that it will be significantly alleviated. Typically, two weeks elapse between the bookseller placing an order and the arrival of the books in his shop, and in some cases it can be much longer.[33]

Distribution, however, has not been the only problem which the trade has encountered since the end of World War II, although it is one which seems to exercise an almost obsessive fascination for publishers and booksellers alike. Perhaps even more significant have been changes in the social and economic structures of Britain which have profoundly affected the publishing world. The leisure market, where publishers of books, magazines and newspapers once held unchallenged sway, has been transformed both by affluence and by technology, and the process of change is not yet complete. In 1980, 58 per cent of the population still claimed to read books regularly, but 98 per cent were regular television viewers,[34] and the hours per week devoted to television were substantially greater than those devoted to reading, even when the reading of newspapers and magazines is included.[35] Television, however, is not the only competitor; while many spectator sports have declined in popularity, active participation in sport has massively increased, especially among the young. Videos, home computers, the growth of new social habits such as eating in restaurants, and, of course, the mobility offered by the ubiquitous motor car, have all taken their toll on the publishing industry.

In the face of these challenges to its very existence, the publishing industry has begun to analyse its markets more closely than ever before. As a result, we have a clearer picture of the British reading public in the decades since World War II than at any previous time in its history. These findings can be very briefly summarised: British book readers are predominantly middle class and well educated, which in itself is hardly surprising. More alarming is the fact that over one-third of the population never read books at all, and that, of those who do read, nearly half obtain their books from libraries rather than bookshops; the libraries do of course make a substantial contribution to the financial health of the trade, but this tends to be through the specialist library supply companies rather than the retail bookshops.[36] The trade's reactions to such findings has been to make attempts to promote the very idea of reading and buying books.[37] It has also been to continue to produce books in ever-increasing numbers, and indeed the continuous rise in output has been one of the most striking characteristics of the British publishing industry since the early 1950s.

In 1950, the number of new titles exceeded 10,000 for the first time since before the war; by 1960 production was running at over 17,000, by 1970 at 23,500, and in 1980 no fewer than 37,382 new titles were published, and over 10,000 reprints.[38] By the mid-

1980s, the annual output was in excess of 40,000 titles, and still increasing; in 1984–5, some 412 million books were sold by British publishers at home and overseas.[39] Despite the competition, the British publishing industry seems to be surviving, but it has achieved survival by making major adjustments to its practices.

In the immediate aftermath of the war, the government was concerned to encourage exports across the whole range of British goods. Foreign exchange was desperately needed to replenish Britain's funds after she had paid for her war effort. Publishers who had looked abroad for markets for decades before 1939 now found themselves encouraged to revive their contacts. Unfortunately, this was to prove to be difficult. A substantial part of the traditional market for British books was now open to competition from new sources. India, which had so often generated money for Longmans, Macmillans, Oxford University Press and others, attained her independence in 1947, and an indigenous publishing industry was developed. Offices which had once been dependent branches of the parent company began to turn into semi-independent houses, following the pattern which many British firms had already experienced with their American companies.[40] This happened to Oxford University Press in India, and later elsewhere.[41] Moreover, first in India, and then in many of Britain's African colonies as they gained their independence in the 1960s, nationalist sentiment naturally preferred that there should be a substantial infusion of local ownership and local expertise into these publishing operations.[42] The developing nations of the Third World provided a vast potential market, especially for school textbooks and English-language teaching materials, but political pressures gradually began to eliminate British publishers from much of this market.[43]

Such pressures came not only from the developing countries, but also from the United States. In 1947, when the state of the trade was still parlous, British publishers had agreed among themselves to abide by the British Commonwealth Market Agreement. In essence, this Agreement stated that when a British publisher sold US rights to an American publisher, he would retain for himself the rights to sales and editions within the British Commonwealth. Furthermore, a British publisher who acquired rights in an American book would do so for the whole of the Commonwealth, and not just for the United Kingdom. The agreement worked well so far as the British trade was concerned.[44] Within the Commonwealth, the Australian and New Zealand booksellers were not always happy about being tied to buying British rather than American editions, especially when, in the 1960s, high wages and other costs in the British printing industry made the British edition more expensive than its American equivalent. The end of the Agreement, however, came when the Americans themselves effectively withdrew their tacit consent to it. In 1976, the US Department of Justice indicated that it considered the Agreement to be illegal under the anti-trust laws, and the British collapsed.[45] With that collapse came the end of protected British rights in the Commonwealth, and consequent loss of sales especially in Australasia.

Even so, exports continued to be very important to the British publishing industry. Despite the loss of some Third World markets, and part of that in the Commonwealth, British books were still being exported in large numbers throughout the 1970s and early 1980s. In 1984–5, some 30 per cent of the total value of British book sales came from exports,[46] although this actually represented a decrease from the high-points in the 1970s, when it was quite normal for well over 40 per cent of the trade's income to be derived from overseas sales.[47] Underlying the foundation of the Book Development Council was the urgent need to develop new export markets,[48] especially in such rapidly developing countries as China and Indonesia, which, it was hoped, would replace those which had been lost in 'traditional' British territories.

The response of the trade to economic and political change has inevitably been diverse, and the trade press of the last thirty years sometimes seems to suggest a continual state of crisis. There is indeed some evidence for this. Sales are not increasing at the same rate as the number of publications, and in terms of real value when measured against the rate of inflation there were steady decreases in almost all categories in the 1970s.[49] The decline continued into the 1980s, even in such critical fields as schoolbooks, where publishers were badly hit by the simultaneous loss of their Third World markets and drastic reductions in the education budget at home.[50] At the same time, public library expenditure on books fell, in real terms, at a rate of about 20 per cent per annum.[51] Even so, the number of titles published continued to increase, an apparent paradox which can best be explained by considering the trade's response to the more buoyant economy of the late 1950s and early 1960s.

The successful defence of the Net Book Agreement helped to sustain the stockholding booksellers, but other markets and other outlets were developing rapidly. Book clubs multiplied in the 1960s,[52] especially after W. H. Smiths, in association with Doubledays of New York, formed Book Club Associates in 1966. The Publishers' Association was forced to amend the Book Club Regulations, and to permit the existence of simultaneous book clubs in Britain for the first time.[53] The book clubs were a threat to the bookshops, especially perhaps in the paperback industry, for book club editions were comparable in price with the more expensive paperbacks, and very similar in their choice of material. At the same time, the booksellers were subject to other pressures. Many lost their public library business in the 1960s, as large library supply companies proved better able to meet the demands of the librarians.[54] It was a trend which was exacerbated by the formation of new and much larger library authorities in 1973, and by the libraries' increasing use of centralised computer systems for their acquisitions operations.

On the other hand, new markets developed, especially as a result of the great expansion of tertiary education in the ten years after 1963. Both booksellers and publishers were affected by this, and a number of new publishing houses was founded specifically to cater for this new and important market.[55] The general trade, however, faced serious difficulties. In the period 1968–78, despite a sixfold increase in turnover, stockholding booksellers could rarely achieve net trading profits in excess of about 3 per cent of total sales value,[56] a return which made the trade very unattractive. There were some gains, however. The paperback industry continued to grow, and television, which some had seen as sounding the death-knell of the printed word, proved to be beneficial to the trade. 'Spin-off' books, both fiction and non-fiction, became best-sellers, and indeed by the mid-1970s such books had come to dominate the best-seller lists, as they still do. It seemed that in a wealthy and literate society there was still a place for the book.

Inevitably, however, changing markets and the uncertain state of the economy wrought great changes, both structurally and editorially. The influence of American business practice had been felt before 1939,[57] but from the late 1960s onwards the American example was closely, sometimes almost slavishly, followed. Great conglomerates, such as the International Publishing Corporation, Granada, Pearson-Longman and Associated Book Publishers were created, all of them owning many imprints. Some of these were old and revered names in the trade; others were newcomers who had reached a point at which they were successful but not successful enough to capitalise further expansion. It was, of course, the benefits of corporate finance which these small firms obtained from the mergers and takeovers, but they were also subjected to the pressures of corporate profit seeking. Smaller houses do survive, often working in specialised fields, but British publishing is increasingly dominated by the conglomerates, many of them multinational in both ownership and operations.[58]

It is difficult to judge to what extent editorial policies and practices have changed under these pressures. The subject is better documented for the American publishing industry, where the evidence suggests that the individual judgement of editors is still highly valued despite the even greater financial pressures which subsist there.[59] One product of these pressures, however, has arrived in Britain; the 'created' book has come to play a part in the economy of the British publishing industry almost as great as that of the creative writer. Genre fiction, which is what many of these books are, can trace its origins back to the Gothick novels of the late eighteenth century.[60] The modern successors of The Minerva Press novels have come to dominate the fiction best-seller lists, especially among paperbacks.[61] The non-fiction equivalent is the coffee-table book, lavishly illustrated in colour thanks to new and cheaper printing techniques. It became the mainstay of some houses in the 1960s and 1970s, and also heralded the arrival of the BBC as a major popular publisher, with spin-offs from some of its more prestigious series.

There have indeed been great changes, and yet much that is familiar remains and continues to be successful. Although British publishing is now dominated by about twenty major houses, many of them linked through the conglomerates, diversity is assured by the existence of some 20,000 publishing organisations in the United Kingdom, ranging from multinational giants to tiny local societies. Some familiar problems also remain; markets have to be defined and reached, and the economics of printing and publishing are timeless. Despite competition from other media and other activities, reading in some form continues to be a part of the life of almost all of the British people, many of whom read books even when their enforced contact with them ends when their education is complete. As it enters its sixth century, the British publishing industry may indeed see itself in a state of permanent crisis, but it is difficult to find a time in the last five hundred years when that would not have been true. Yet the industry has faced the challenges which these crises presented. Expansion and innovation have been the solutions, and perhaps they will be so again. The creation of the English Stock in the late sixteenth century, the evolution of the congers and share books in the late seventeenth century, the emergence of the reprint series and the risk-taking publishing house in the late eighteenth century, the creative use of new print technology in the nineteenth century, and the invention of the modern paperback little more than fifty years ago, were all adventurous and successful responses to changing circumstances. If the Group Accountant now seems to rule where once the Editor held sway, he does so because once again the industry is looking for new ways to ensure its own future, and so to continue to do what it has done so well for half a millennium: to produce an ever-rising tide of books, good, bad and indifferent, which have amused, educated and enlightened their readers.

Notes

The following abbreviations are used throughout the Notes and Bibliography:

Ariz. Q.	*Arizona Quarterly*
BC	*The Book Collector*
Bibl.	*The Bibliotheck*
BIHR	*Bulletin of the Institute of Historical Research*
BJECS	*British Journal of Eighteenth-century Studies*
BMQ	*British Museum Quarterly*
DNB	*Dictionary of National Biography*
EEH	*Explorations in Economic History*
EHR	*English Historical Review*
GJ	*Gutenberg Jahrbuch*
Hist.	*History*
HLQ	*Huntington Library Quarterly*
J. Libr.	*Journal of Librarianship*
JPHS	*Journal of the Printing Historical Society*
JRSA	*Journal of the Royal Society of Arts*
Libr.	*The Library*
MLR	*Modern Language Review*
OBSP	*Oxford Bibliographical Society Papers*
ORE	*Oxford Review of Education*
PAAS	*Proceedings of the American Antiquarian Society*
PBSA	*Papers of the Bibliographical Society of America*
PH	*Publishing History*
PP	*Past and Present*
PSIANH	*Proceedings of the Suffolk Institute of Archaeology and Natural History*
SB	*Studies in Bibliography*
SEEC	*Studies in Eighteenth-century Culture*
Soc. Hist.	*Social History*
STC	K. F. Pantzer (ed.). *Short-Title Catalogue . . . 1476–1640.* 2 vols. (The Bibliographical Society, London, 1976–86).
SVEC	*Studies on Voltaire and the Eighteenth Century*
TAAS	*Transactions of the American Antiquarian Society*
TBS	*Transactions of the Bibliographical Society*
TCBS	*Transactions of the Cambridge Bibliographical Society*

Introduction: The Book Trade before Printing

1. Colin H. Roberts and T.C. Skeat. *The Birth of the Codex* (British Academy, London, 1983).

2. Sir Frederic Kenyon. *Books and Readers in Ancient Greece and Rome* (Clarendon Press, Oxford, 1932), pp. 82–3.

3. Christopher de Hamel. *Glossed Books of the Bible and the Origins of the Paris Book Trade* (Brewer, Cambridge, 1984). For later French developments, which were similar to those in England, see Pascale Bourgain. 'L'édition des manuscrits', in Henri-Jean Martin and Roger Chartier. *Histoire de l'édition française.* 3 vols. (Promodis, Paris, 1982–5), vol. 1, pp. 49–75.

4. Graham Pollard. 'The Company of Stationers before 1557', *Libr.*, 4th ser., 18 (1937–8), pp. 2–5; and H.S. Bennett. 'The production and dissemination of vernacular manuscripts in the fifteenth century', *Libr.*, 5th ser., 1 (1946–7), pp. 167–78.

5. For examples of stationers' co-ordinating work, see A.I. Doyle and M.B. Parkes. 'The production of copies of the *Canterbury Tales* and the *Confessio amantis* in the early fifteenth century', in M.B. Parkes and Andrew G. Watson (eds.). *Medieval Scribes, Manuscripts & Libraries. Essays Presented to N.R. Ker* (Scolar Press, London, 1979), pp. 163–210.

6. See A.S.G. Edwards. 'Lydgate manuscripts: some directions for future research', in Derek Pearsall (ed.). *Manuscripts and Readers in Fifteenth-century England* (Brewer, Cambridge, 1983), pp. 17–19.

7. For university book production, see Graham Pollard. 'The *pecia* system in the medieval universities', in M.B. Parkes and Andrew G. Watson (eds). *Medieval Scribes, Manuscripts & Libraries. Essays Presented to N.R. Ker* (Scolar Press, London, 1979), pp. 145–61.

8. Thorlac Turville-Petre. 'Some medieval English manuscripts in the north-east Midlands', in Derek Pearsall (ed.). *Manuscripts and Readers in Fifteenth-century England* (Brewer, Cambridge, 1983), pp. 125–41.

9. Generally, see E.Ph. Goldschmidt. *Medieval Texts and their First Appearance in Print* (The Bibliographical Society, Suppl. to The Bibliographical Society's Transactions, 16, London, 1943), pp. 13–15. For some examples, see K.W. Humphreys. 'Distribution of books in the English West Midlands in the later middle ages', *Libri*, 17 (1967), pp. 1–12; Jo Ann Hoeppner Moran. *The Growth of English Schooling 1340–1548* (Princeton University Press, Princeton, N.J., 1985), pp. 185–220; and N.R. Ker. 'Oxford college libraries before 1500', in J. Ijsewijn and J. Paquet (eds.). *The Universities in the Later Middle Ages* (Louvain University Press, Louvain, 1978), pp. 293–311.

10. See H.E. Bell. 'The price of books in medieval England', *Libr.*, 4th ser., 17 (1936–7), pp. 311–32.

11. See Edith Diehl. *Bookbinding. Its Background and Techniques.* 2 vols. Repr. (Hacker, New York, 1979), vol. 1, pp. 45–58.

12. See Graham Pollard. 'The names of some English fifteenth-century binders', *Libr.*, 5th ser., 25 (1970), pp. 193–218; and Howard M.

Nixon. 'William Caxton and bookbinding', *JPHS*, 11 (1975/6), pp. 92–113.

13. Graham Pollard. 'Changes in the style of bookbindings, 1550–1830', *Libr.*, 5th ser., 11 (1956), pp. 71–94.

14. Ernest A. Savage. *Old English Libraries* (Methuen, London, 1911), p. 76.

15. Ibid., p. 87.

16. See below, p. 14.

17. See below, pp. 14–15, 58–60.

Part One: The Press in Chains

Chapter 1

1. Elizabeth Armstrong. 'English purchases of printed books from the continent 1465–1526', *EHR*, 94 (1979), pp. 268–90.

2. Nellie J.M. Kerling. 'Caxton and the trade in printed books', *BC*, 4 (1955), pp. 190–9.

3. *STC* 15794. Only fragments survive, but the dating and location are reasonably certain.

4. George D. Painter. *William Caxton* (Chatto and Windus, London, 1976), pp. 59–63.

5. Ibid., pp. 32–42.

6. See Severin Corsten. 'Caxton in Cologne', *JPHS*, 11 (1976/7), pp. 1–18.

7. See Lotte and Wytze Hellinga. 'Caxton in the Low Countries', *JPHS*, 11 (1976/7), pp. 19–32.

8. Painter, *William Caxton*, p. 211.

9. Ibid., p. 82; and Howard M. Nixon. 'Caxton, his contemporaries and successors in the book trade from Westminster documents', *Libr.*, 5th ser., 31 (1976), pp. 305–26.

10. For de Worde, see N.F. Blake. 'Wynkyn de Worde: the early years', *GJ*, 1971, pp. 62–9; and N.F. Blake. 'Wynkyn de Worde: the later years', *GJ*, 1972, pp. 128–38.

11. See Alfred W. Pollard. 'The new Caxton indulgence', *Libr.*, 4th ser., 11 (1928–9), pp. 86–9; and Painter, *William Caxton*, pp. 83–4.

12. For a list and the traditional chronology, see Painter, *William Caxton*, pp. 211–15. The current researches of Dr Lotte Hellinga and Dr Paul Needham will almost certainly change, perhaps radically, the accepted chronology of Caxton's output.

13. See Painter, *William Caxton*, pp. 16–31.

14. Ibid., pp. 59–71, 108–20.

15. For Caxton's literary importance, see Curt F. Bühler. *William Caxton and his Critics* (Syracuse University Press, Syracuse, N.Y., 1960).

16. There is no general history of law printing. I am indebted for this section to a dissertation by my former student Simon H. Eade, 'English Legal Printing, 1476–1550' (Loughborough University MLS thesis, 1982). On technical aspects, see Katherine F. Pantzer. 'Printing the

English statutes, 1484–1640: some historical implications', in Kenneth E. Carpenter (ed.). *Books and Society in History* (Bowker, New York, 1983), pp. 69–114.

17. The first who was certainly English was Robert Copland, who had his own business from about 1515, although it is unclear whether Julian Notary, who is first recorded *c*.1496, was a native of England or France. See Colin Clair. *A History of Printing in Britain* (Cassell, London, 1965), pp. 40–2, 47–8; and E. Gordon Duff. *A Century of the English Book Trade* (The Bibliographical Society, London, 1905), pp. 31–2, 112–14.

18. 1 Richard III c. 9.

19. 25 Henry VIII c. 15.

20. See Graham Pollard. 'The English market for printed books', *PH*, 4 (1978), pp. 12–13.

21. D.C. Coleman. *The British Paper Industry 1495–1860* (Oxford University Press, Oxford, 1958), pp. 3–23.

22. See Sylvia L. Thrupp. *The Merchant Class of Medieval London 1300–1500* (University of Michigan Press, Ann Arbor, Mich., 1968), p. 161.

23. See below, pp. 29–32.

24. See Harry Carter. *A History of Oxford University Press. Vol. 1. To the year 1780* (Clarendon Press, Oxford, 1975), pp. 4–12.

25. See David Knowles. *The Religious Orders in England*. 3 vols. (Cambridge University Press, Cambridge, 1948–59), vol. 1, pp. 291–6; vol. 2, pp. 264–8. See also David Knowles and R. Neville Hadock. *Medieval Religious Houses in England and Wales* (Longman, London, 1971), pp. 74–5; and N.R. Ker. *Medieval Libraries of Great Britain*. 2nd edn. (Royal Historical Society, London, 1964), pp. 164–8.

26. The whole story of the St Albans press in obscure; see Knowles, *Religious Orders*, vol. 3, pp. 24–5. The only recent study is Nicolas Barker. 'The St Albans press: the first punch-cutter in England and the first native typefounder?', *TCBS*, 7 (1979), pp. 257–78. Barker argues that there were in fact two printers, one operating in 1480–1 and the second in 1486.

27. Knowles, *Religious Orders*, vol. 3, pp. 25–7.

28. See Otto Treptow. *John Siberch. Johann Lair von Siegburg*. Tr. by Trevor Jones, abridged and ed. by John Morris and Trevor Jones (Cambridge Bibliographical Society, monograph 6, Cambridge, 1970).

29. See William K. and E. Margaret Sessions. *Printing in York* (William Sessions Ltd, York, 1976) pp. 2–5; and Michael L. Zell. 'An early press in Canterbury?', *Libr.*, 5th ser., 32 (1977), pp. 155–6.

30. See S.F. Watson. 'Some materials for a history of printing and publishing in Ipswich', *PSIANH*, 24 (1946–8), pp. 184–7; and Duff, *Century*, p. 116. The Skolokar and Oswen books have Ipswich imprints, but it has been cogently argued that these are false. All are distinctively Protestant in tone. The case for rejecting their authenticity was made by H.A.N. Hallam in a paper printed in P.C.G. Isaac (ed.). *Third Seminar on the British Book Trade. Report* (British Book Trade Index [Newcastle-upon-Tyne], 1985), pp. 2–4.

31. See Elizabeth L. Eisenstein. *The Printing Press as an Agent of Change*. 2 vols. (Cambridge University Press, Cambridge, 1979).

32. See above, p. 12.

33. Frederick C. Avis. 'Book smuggling into England during the sixteenth century', *GJ*, 1972, pp. 180–7.

34. Frederick Seaton Siebert. *Freedom of the Press in England 1476–1776* (University of Illinois Press, Urbana, Ill., 1965), pp. 30–2.

35. Arthur W. Reed. 'The regulation of the book trade before the proclamation of 1538', *TBS*, 15 (1919), pp. 157–84.

36. Siebert, *Freedom of the Press*, pp. 48–51.

37. See below, pp. 32–4.

38. The early history of the privileges is still obscure. For some guidance, see Siebert, *Freedom of the Press*, pp. 38–9; and Marjorie Plant. *The English Book Trade*. 2nd edn (Allen and Unwin, London, 1965), pp. 100–1.

39. Knowles, *Religious Orders*, vol. 3, p. 25.

Chapter 2

1. See above, pp. 10–11.

2. See above, p. 14 for Rood, and p. 15 for Siberch. For the Venetians, see Leonardas Vyantas Gerulaitas. *Printing and Publishing in Fifteenth-century Venice* (Mansell, London, 1976), pp. 66–127; and for Froben, see Charles W. Heckethorn. *The Printers of Basle in the XV and XVI Centuries* (Fisher Unwin, London, 1897), pp. 86–112.

3. Jo Ann Hoeppner Moran. *The Growth of English Schooling. 1340–1548* (Princeton University Press, Princeton, N.J., 1985), pp. 150–61.

4. Davis Cressy. *Literacy and the Social Order. Reading and Writing in Tudor and Stuart England* (Cambridge University Press, Cambridge, 1980), p. 143.

5. Ibid., pp. 132–5.

6. See Nicholas Orme. *English Schools in the Middle Ages* (Methuen, London, 1973), pp. 194–223.

7. See Joan Simon. *Education and Society in Tudor England* (Cambridge University Press, Cambridge, 1967), pp. 25–7.

8. See above, pp. 11–12.

9. Harry Carter. *A History of the Oxford University Press. Vol. 1. To the year 1780* (Clarendon Press, Oxford, 1975), pp. 7–9; and Orme, *English Schools*, p. 107.

10. Ibid., pp. 107–9; and H.S. Bennett. *English Books & Readers 1475 to 1557*. 2nd edn (Cambridge University Press, Cambridge, 1969), pp. 86–7. For lists of editions of these texts see *STC* 695–696.7 (Anwykyll); 23139.5–23199 (Stanbridge); and 25443.2–25579 (Whittington).

11. Bennett, *English Book & Readers 1475–1557*, pp. 87–9. For the patent, see below, pp. 36–7.

12. See below, p. 102.

13. Generally, see Henry B. Lathrop. *Translations from the Classics into English from Caxton to Chapman 1477–1610* (University of Wisconsin Press, Madison, Wis., 1932). There is a list of translations on pp. 311–18.

14. See John L. Lievsay. *The Englishman's Italian Books 1550–1700* (University of Pennsylvania Press, Philadelphia, Pa., 1969), pp. 5–31. For an exhaustive list of translations and adaptations of Italian works,

see Mary A. Scott. *Elizabethan Translations from the Italian.* Repr. (Franklin, New York, 1969).

15. Bennett, *English Books & Readers 1475 to 1557*, pp. 65–6.

16. Ibid., pp. 70–5.

17. John N. King. *English Reformation Literature. The Tudor Origins of the Protestant Tradition* (Princeton University Press, Princeton, N.J., 1982), pp. 88–9.

18. Bennett, *English Books & Readers 1475–1557*, pp. 84–5, 97–100.

19. Ibid., pp. 111–12.

20. Bernard Capp. *Astrology and the Popular Press. English Almanacs 1500–1800* (Faber and Faber, London, 1979), pp. 25–30. On pp. 347–86 Capp has a list of English almanacs before 1700; for the same purpose, and in more detail, E.F. Bosanquet. *English Printed Almanacks and Prognostications. A Bibliographical History to the Year 1600* (The Bibliographical Society, London, 1917) is still useful, but all earlier listings for the period up to 1640 are superseded by that in *STC* 385.3–532.11.

21. Keith Thomas. *Religion and the Decline of Magic* (Penguin, Harmondsworth, 1978), pp. 347–56.

22. See below, p. 36.

23. H.S. Bennett. *English Books & Readers 1558 to 1603* (Cambridge University Press, Cambridge, 1965), pp. 148–56; and H.S. Bennett. *English Books & Readers 1603 to 1640* (Cambridge University Press, Cambridge, 1970), pp. 107–17.

24. See A.F. Allison and D.M. Rogers. *A Catalogue of Catholic Books in English Printed Abroad or Secretly in England 1558–1640* (Catholic Record Society, Biographical Studies 3:3,4, Bognor Regis, 1956). For a study of the Catholic books, see A.C. Southern. *Elizabethan Recusant Prose 1559–1582* (Sands, London, 1950), pp. 338–63. Denis B. Woodfield. *Surreptitious Printing in England 1550–1640* (Bibliographical Society of America, New York, 1973) is, despite its comprehensive title, concerned only with books in contemporary foreign langauges. These, however, include a number of religious and political works which would not have been acceptable to the censors in England.

25. Bennett, *English Books & Readers 1558 to 1603*, pp. 81–6.

26. Bennett, *English Books & Readers 1475 to 1557*, pp. 135–45.

27. On this matter, see two papers by Arthur J. Slavin. 'The Tudor revolution and the devil's art: Bishop Bonner's printed forms', in D.J. Guth and J.W. McKenna (eds). *Tudor Rule and Revolution* (Cambridge University Press, Cambridge, 1982), pp. 3–23; and 'The Gutenberg galaxy and the Tudor revolution', in Gerald P. Tyson and Sylvia S. Wagonheim (eds). *Print and Culture in the Renaissance. Essays on the Advent of Printing in Europe* (University of Delaware Press, Newark, N.J., 1986), pp. 90–109.

28. For examples of both, see Bennett, *English Books & Readers 1558 to 1603*, pp. 224–39.

29. See Victor E. Neuburg. *Popular Literature* (Penguin, Harmondsworth, 1977), pp. 19–22; and J.J. Jusserand. *The English Novel in the Time of Shakespeare.* Tr. Elizabeth Lee (Fisher Unwin, London, 1890), pp. 52–68.

30. For Lyly, see Jusserand, *The English Novel in the Time of Shakespeare*,

pp. 103–42; and generally, Louis B. Wright. *Middle-class Culture in Elizabethan England* (University of North Carolina Press, Chapel Hill, N.C., 1935), pp. 375–91.

31. Generally, see Lucien Febvre and Henri-Jean Martin. *The Coming of the Book. The Impact of Printing 1450–1800.* Tr. David Gerard. (NLB, London, 1976), pp. 159–62; and E.Ph. Goldschmidt. *Medieval Texts and their First Appearance in Print* (The Bibliographical Society, Suppl. to The Bibliographical Society's Transactions, 16, London, 1943), *passim.* For a specific example of a much printed medieval text, see C.W.R.D. Moseley. 'The availability of *Mandeville's Travels* in England, 1356–1750', *Libr.*, 5th ser., 30 (1975), pp. 125–33.

32. For a wide-ranging study, see Peter J. Lucas. 'The growth and development of English literary patronage in the later Middle Ages and early Renaissance', *Libr.*, 6th ser., 4 (1982), pp. 218–48.

33. For the importance of certain continental printers as patrons, see Elizabeth L. Eisenstein. *The Printing Press as an Agent of Change.* 2 vols. (Cambridge University Press, Cambridge, 1979), pp. 75–6.

34. For a list of dedications of this period see Franklin B. Williams, Jr. *Index of Dedications and Commendatory Verses in English Books Before 1641* (The Bibliographical Society, London, 1962), and the same author's *Dedications and Verses through 1640* (The Bibliographical Society, Suppl. to *Libr.*, 30:1, London, 1975).

35. For an exhaustive study of this subject, see Eleanor Rosenberg. *Leicester. Patron of Letters* (Columbia University Press, New York, 1955).

36. See B.B. Gamzue. 'Elizabeth and literary patronage', *PMLA*, 49 (1934), pp. 1041–9.

37. For the various occupations of the almanac writers, many of whom were physicians, see Capp, *Astrology and the Popular Press*, pp. 293–340.

38. See Phoebe Shearyn. *The Literary Profession in the Elizabethan Age.* 2nd edn, rev. by J.W. Saunders (Manchester University Press, Manchester, 1967), pp. 8–38; Bennett, *English Books & Readers 1558 to 1603*, pp. 30–55; and Edwin H. Miller. *The Professional Writer in Elizabethan England* (Harvard University Press, Cambridge, Mass., 1959), pp. 94–136.

39. Miller, *The Professional Writer*, pp. 139–40.

40. On this specialised matter, which has (perhaps inevitably) been more thoroughly researched than more general aspects of the subject, see Gerald Eades Bentley. *The Profession of Dramatist of Shakespeare's Time 1590–1642* (Princeton University Press, Princeton, N.J., 1971), pp. 88–110.

41. Miller, *The Professional Writer*, pp. 160–2.

42. For a general study, see J.W. Saunders. *The Profession of English Letters* (Routledge and Kegan Paul, London, 1964), pp. 49–67.

Chapter 3

1. Graham Pollard. 'The Company of Stationers before 1557', *Libr*,

4th ser., 18 (1937–8), pp. 5–9.

2. See George Unwin. *Gilds and Companies of the City of London* (Methuen, London, 1908), for a general account of the gilds.

3. I use this phrase to distinguish it from the Stationers' Company incorporated in 1557 which was its successor. There is no generally accepted name for the pre-1557 gild.

4. Pollard, 'Company of Stationers', pp. 21–3.

5. See E. Gordon Duff. *A Century of the English Book Trade* (The Bibliographical Society, London, 1905), pp. 79–80; and Pollard, 'Company of Stationers', p. 23.

6. Duff, *Century*, pp. 112–14.

7. See Pollard, 'Company of Stationers'; Graham Pollard. 'The early constitution of the Stationers' Company', *Libr.*, 4th ser., 18 (1937–8), pp. 235–60; and Cyprian Blagden *The Stationer's Company. A History 1403–1959* (Allen and Unwin, London, 1960), pp. 21–33.

8. Caxton was already a freeman of the more prestigious Mercers' Company.

9. These figures are from H.S. Bennett. *English Books & Readers 1475 to 1557*. 2nd edn (Cambridge University Press, Cambridge, 1969) pp. 29, 194, and are based on his chronological analysis of *STC*. The revised *STC* has added about 20 per cent and perhaps rather more in the earlier years than in the later. But the precise statistics do not materially affect the point being made here.

10. D.C. Coleman. *The British Paper Industry 1495–1860* (Oxford University Press, Oxford, 1958), p. 13. One ream = 480 sheets in the sixteenth century, giving a figure of 12,697,360. See also Edward Heawood. 'Sources of early English paper supply', *Libr.*, 4th ser., 10 (1929–30), pp. 282–307, 427–54.

11. William K. Sessions. *A Printer's Dozen. The First British Printing Centres to 1557 outside Westminster and London* (Ebor Press, York, 1983), p. 96.

12. See above, pp. 14–15.

13. The Charter is printed in Edward Arber. *Transcript of the Registers of the Company of Stationers of London (1554–1640)*. 5 vols. (The Editor, Birmingham, 1875–94), vol. 1, pp. xxviii–xxxii.

14. Printed in Alfred W. Pollard. *Shakespeare's Fight with the Pirates*. 2nd edn (Cambridge University Press, Cambridge, 1920), pp. 13–14.

15. See W.W. Greg. *Some Aspects and Problems of London Publishing Between 1550 and 1650* (Clarendon Press, Oxford, 1956), pp. 5–6. The last two provisions seem to envisage the possibility of printing at Oxford and Cambridge and outside the diocese of London. For Oxford and Cambridge printing before 1640, see above, pp. 14–15, and below, pp. 58–9.

16. For this matter, see Arber, *Transcript*, vol. 1, p. xxvi; Pollard, *Shakespeare's Fight*, pp. 10–12; W.W. Greg and E. Boswell (eds). *Records of the Court of the Stationers' Company 1576 to 1602 from Register B* (The Bibliographical Society, London, 1930), pp. lx–lxi; and Pollard, 'Company of Stationers', pp. 29–36.

17. Pollard, 'Company of Stationers', pp. 32–3.

18. On this point, see J.W. Martin. 'The Marian regime's failure to

understand the importance of printing', *HLQ*, 44 (1980–1), pp. 231–47.

19. The phrase is Greg's in Greg and Boswell, *Records*, p. 1x.

20. See Blagden, *Stationer's Company*, pp. 40–1.

21. Quoted by Greg, *Aspects and Problems*, p. 4.

22. See Arber, *Transcript*, vol. 1, p. 74, for the list of 'suche Copyes as be lycensed to be prynted' in 1557–8.

23. Blagden, *Stationers' Company*, pp. 42–5.

24. For the gaps in the evidence, see Greg, *Aspects and Problems*, pp. 41–4.

25. See Frederick Seaton Siebert. *Freedom of the Press in England 1476–1776* (University of Illinois Press, Urbana, Ill., 1965), pp. 58–9.

26. Ibid., pp. 61–2.

27. Again the records are sketchy, but the procedures are outlined as far as possible by Greg in Greg and Boswell, *Records*, pp. xxi–xxv. Masters and Upper and Under Wardens from 1557 to 1625 are listed in ibid., pp. 95–6; and from 1605 to 1800, together with the Renter Wardens, in D.F. McKenzie (ed.). *Stationers' Company Apprentices 1701–1800* (Oxford Bibliographical Society, new ser., 19, Oxford, 1978), pp. 397–407.

28. Duff, *Century*, p. 40.

29. Ibid., pp. 23, 167, 171–2 and 85 respectively.

30. Greg and Boswell, *Records*, pp. xxxix–xli. In a recent conference paper, due to be published in 1987, Michael Treadwell has analysed the number of presses and Master Printers in detail, and has corrected earlier accounts. My figures are based on his findings.

31. Siebert, *Freedom of the Press*, p. 69.

32. See above, p. 17.

33. See C.L. Oastler. *John Day, the Elizabethan Printer* (Oxford Bibliographical Society, occ. publ. 10, Oxford, 1975), pp. 22–5, 70.

34. Siebert, *Freedom of the Press*, p. 54.

35. See Oastler, *John Day*, p. 70; and Bernard Capp. *Astrology and the Popular Press. English Almanacs 1500–1800* (Faber and Faber, London, 1979), p. 29.

36. Frederick C. Avis. 'An enquiry into English privilege printing, 1582', *GJ*, 1975, pp. 150–5.

37. H. Anders. 'The Elizabethan *ABC* with The Catechism', *Libr.*, 4th ser., 16 (1935–6), pp. 32–48.

38. See Harry R. Hoppe. 'John Wolfe, printer and publisher, 1579–1601', *Libr.*, 4th ser., 14 (1933–4), pp. 241–88.

39. Oastler, *John Day*, pp. 65–9.

40. Anders, 'Elizabethan *ABC*', pp. 36–7.

41. Ibid., p. 37; and Hoppe, 'John Wolfe', pp. 259–65.

42. See Cyprian Blagden. 'The English Stock of the Stationers' Company. An Account of its origins', *Libr.*, 5th ser. 10 (1955). pp. 163–85.

43. See Cyprian Blagden. 'The English Stock of the Stationers' Company in the time of the Stuarts', *Libr.*, 5th ser., 12 (1957), pp. 167–86.

44. Peter W.M. Blayney. 'The prevalance of shared printing in the early seventeenth century', *PBSA*, 67 (1973), pp. 437–42; and D.F. McKenzie. *The London Book Trade in the Later Seventeenth Century* (Privately

printed, Cambridge, 1976), pp. 20–3.

45. Greg and Boswell, *Records*, pp. lxix–lxxvii.

46. C.J. Sisson. 'The laws of Elizabethan copyright: the Stationers' view', *Libr.*, 5th ser., 15 (1960), pp. 17–18.

47. Greg, *Aspects and Problems*, pp. 63–81, argues forcefully that rights could only be established by entry; this is undoubtedly the position enunciated in the Company's Ordinances of 1562. But by the end of the sixteenth century there is evidence that unchallenged publication was an acceptable substitute. Leo Kirschbaum. 'The copyright of Elizabethan plays', *Libr.*, 5th ser., 14 (1959), pp. 231–50, has a number of pertinent examples of unentered copies being transferred without difficulty from their first publisher to another Stationer. Greg's argument on this point (*Aspects and Problems*, pp. 80–1) is weak and perhaps even specious.

48. Duff, *Century*, pp. 57–8.

49. Ibid., p. 112.

50. In 1591 (Coldock), 1598 and 1601 (Newbery), 1597 (Cawood) and 1603 (Bing). For these men, see R.B. McKerrow. *A Dictionary of the Printers and Booksellers in England, Scotland and Ireland, and of Foreign Printers of English Books 1557–1640* (The Bibliographical Society, London, 1910), pp. 72, 199, 65 and 33–4 respectively.

51. For lists of office-holders, see n. 27 above.

52. Including all those who were Master between 1620 and 1639.

53. For examples of lesser members of the trade who were non-printing copy-owners, see two papers by Gerald D. Johnson. 'Nicholas Ling, publisher, 1580–1607', *SB*, 38 (1985), pp. 203–14; and 'John Trundle and the book-trade 1603–1626', *SB*, 39 (1986), pp. 177–99.

54. See David W. Rude and Lloyd E. Berry. 'Tanner manuscript no. 33: new light on the Stationers' Company in the early seventeenth century', *PBSA*, 66 (1972), pp. 105–34.

55. The figures are based on those in Blagden, *Stationers' Company*, pp. 284–6.

56. The decree is printed in Arber, *Transcript*, vol. 4, pp. 529–36.

Chapter 4

1. E. Lipson. *The Economic History of England*. 3 vols. 5th edn (A. & C. Black, London, 1929–48), vol. 3, pp. 333–4.

2. Frederick Seaton Siebert. *Freedom of the Press in England 1476–1776* (University of Illinois Press, Urbana, Ill., 1965), pp. 140–1.

3. Cyrian Blagden. 'The Stationers' Company in the Civil War period', *Libr.*, 5th ser., 13 (1958), pp. 1–17.

4. See W.M. Clyde. 'Parliament and the press, 1643–7', *Libr.*, 4th ser., 13 (1932–3), pp. 399–424.

5. William K. Sessions. *A World of Mischiefe. The King's Printer in York in 1642 and in Shrewsbury 1642–1643* (The Ebor Press, York, 1981), pp. 1–10, 45–55, 66–126.

6. William K. Sessions. *The King's Printer at Newcastle-upon-Tyne in 1639, at Bristol in 1643–1645 and at Exeter in 1645–1646* (The Ebor Press, York, 1982), pp. 2–25.

7. Ibid., pp. 68–71.

8. These are now in the British Library. See G.K. Fortescue. *Catalogue of the Pamphlets, Books, Newspapers and Manuscripts . . . Collected by G. Thomason 1640–1661.* 2 vols. (British Museum, London, 1908); Lois Spencer. 'The professional and literary connexions of George Thomason', *Libr.*, 5th ser., 13 (1958), pp. 102–18; and Lois Spencer, 'The politics of George Thomason', *Libr.*, 5th ser., 14 (1959), pp. 11–27.

9. See J.C.T. Oates. '*The trewe encountre*: a pamphlet on Flodden Field', *TCBS*, 1 (1950), pp. 126–9.

10. Joseph Frank, *The Beginnings of the English Newspaper 1620–1660* (Harvard University Press, Cambridge, Mass., 1961), pp. 2–16.

11. See P.W. Thomas. *Sir John Berkenhead 1617–1679. A Royalist Career in Politics and Polemics* (Clarendon Press, Oxford, 1969), pp. 28–64.

12. Ibid., p. 52.

13. Frank, *Beginnings*, pp. 57, 314.

14. Siebert, *Freedom of the Press*, pp. 205, 207.

15. Frank, *Beginnings*, pp. 48–72.

16. *Pro populo anglicano defensio* (1651); *Pro populo anglicano defensio secunda* (1654); *Pro se defensio contra Alexandrum Morum* (1655).

17. Se Don M. Wolfe. *Milton in the Puritan Revolution* (Humanities Press, New York, N.Y., 1963), pp. 120–38.

18. See Pauline Gregg. *Free-born John. A Biography of John Lilburne* (Harrap, London, 1961), pp. 126–32.

19. Blagden, 'Stationers' Company in the Civil War', pp. 16–17.

20. Cyprian Blagden. 'The "Company" of printers', *SB*, 13 (1960), pp. 1–15.

21. Cyprian Blagden. *The Stationers' Company. A History, 1403–1959* (Allen and Unwin, London, 1960), pp. 134–8.

22. W.M. Clyde. 'Parliament and the press, II', *Libr.*, 4th ser., 14 (1933–4), pp. 39–58.

23. Thomas, *Sir John Berkenhead*, pp. 145–50.

24. One example is *Mercurius Britannicus* (a very different product from that mentioned on p. 46 above), an unlicensed newsbook of which three issues were published in June and July 1647; see R.S. Crane and F.B. Kaye. *A Census of British Newspapers and Periodicals 1620–1800* (University of North Carolina Press, Chapel Hill, N.C., 1927), p. 150 (no. 1603a). This was one of the newsbooks suppressed by Parliament under pressure from the Army; see Siebert, *Freedom of the Press*, p. 213.

25. Siebert, *Freedom of the Press*, pp. 209, 213.

26. For these developments, see Frank, *Beginnings*, pp. 199–267.

Chapter 5

1. A.F. Johnson. 'The King's Printers, 1660–1742', *Libr.*, 5th ser., 3 (1949), pp. 33–8.

2. J. Walker. 'The censorship of the press during the reign of Charles II', *Hist.*, 25 (1950), pp. 219–38, is a useful summary of these matters.

3. Ibid. For the powers of the Secretary of State in these matters, see Peter Fraser. *The Intelligence of the Secretaries of State and Their Monopoly of*

Licensed News 1660–1688 (Cambridge University Press, Cambridge, 1956).

4. Cyprian Blagden, 'The "Company" of Printers', *SB*, 13 (1960), pp. 1–15. Treadwell (see above, Chapter 3, note 30) argued that Blagden misinterpreted some of the documents which he used for this paper. He showed that in late 1661 there were 34 or 35 unlicensed printing houses in London.

5. Walker, 'Censorship of the press'.

6. Blagden, 'The "Company" of Printers'.

7. For the law of seditious libel, see John Feather. 'The English book trade and the law 1695–1799', *PH*, 12 (1982), pp. 62–3; and Donald Thomas. *A Long Time Burning* (Routledge and Kegan Paul, London, 1969), pp. 43–56, 61–2.

8. For this period, see Timothy Crist. 'Government control of the press after the expiration of the Printing Act in 1679', *PH*, 5 (1979), pp. 49–77.

9. Joseph Frank. *The Beginnings of the English Newspaper 1620–1660* (Harvard University Press, Cambridge, Mass., 1961), pp. 35–6.

10. Frederick Seaton Siebert. *Freedom of the Press in England 1476–1776* (University of Illinois Press, Urbana, Ill., 1965), p. 295.

11. P.M. Handover. *A History of 'The London Gazette' 1665–1965* (HMSO, London, 1965), pp. 9–18.

12. Frank, *Beginnings*, pp. 121–3.

13. Aytoun Ellis. *The Penny Universities. A History of the Coffee-houses* (Secker and Warburg, London, 1956), pp. 30–42.

14. Raymond Astbury. 'The renewal of the Licensing Act in 1693 and its lapse in 1695', *Libr.*, 5th ser., 33 (1978), pp. 291–322.

15. Cyprian Blagden. 'The distribution of almanacs in the second half of the seventeenth century', *SB*, 11 (1958), pp. 107–16.

16. James Bowen. *A History of Western Education. Vol. 3. The Modern West* (Methuen, London, 1981), pp. 91–104.

17. Siebert, *Freedom of the Press*, pp. 244–9.

18. See W.W. Greg. *A Bibliography of the English Printed Drama to the Restoration.* 4 vols. (The Bibliographical Society, London, 1939–59), vol. 3, pp. 1116–18. The previous edition was that of 1632.

19. See Henry R. Plomer. *A Dictionary of the Booksellers and Printers who were at work in England, Scotland and Ireland from 1641 to 1667* (The Bibliographical Society, London, 1908), pp. 132–3.

20. C. William Miller. 'Henry Herringman, Restoration bookseller–publisher', *PBSA*, 42 (1948), pp. 292–306.

21. By Arber, quoted in ibid., p. 292.

22. Hugh Macdonald. *John Dryden. A Bibliography of Early Editions* (Clarendon Press, Oxford, 1939), pp. 92–5.

23. Strickland Gibson. 'A bibliography of Francis Kirkman', *OBSP*, new ser., 1 (1947), pp. 58–62.

24. Ibid., pp. 119–26.

25. See Lennard J. Davis. *Factual Fictions. The Origins of the English Novel* (Columbia University Press, New York, 1983), pp. 42–84.

26. See John Feather. *English Book Prospectuses. An Illustrated History* (Bird and Bull Press, Newton, Pa., 1984), pp. 27–33.

27. The best narrative account of this enterprise is that in the life of

Savile in *DNB*, but on the technical aspects see Robert Proctor, 'The French Royal Greek types and the Eton *Chrysostom*', in A.W. Pollard (ed.). *Bibliographical Essays by Robert Proctor*. Repr. (Franklin, New York, 1969), pp. 110–14.

28. Harry Carter. *A History of the Oxford University Press. Vol. 1. To the year 1780* (Clarendon Press, Oxford, 1975), pp. 26–36.

29. Ibid., pp. 45–73.

30. Ibid., pp. 74–6, 81–3, 113–16.

31. M.H. Black. *Cambridge University Press 1584–1984* (Cambridge University Press, Cambridge, 1984), pp. 37–38.

32. D.F. McKenzie. *The Cambridge University Press 1696–1712*. 2 vols (Cambridge University Press, Cambridge, 1966), vol. 1, pp. 6–15.

33. Carter, *History*, p. 61.

34. Ibid., pp. 157–66; and Black, *Cambridge University Press*, pp. 79–80.

35. For Tonson, see below, pp. 101–2.

36. McKenzie, *Cambridge University Press*, vol. 1, pp. 185–7, 196–7, 199–200. The Terence was successful enough to be reprinted in the same year (Ibid., vol. 1, pp. 206–7).

37. Ibid., vol. 1, pp. 224–33; and S.C. Roberts. *The Evolution of Cambridge Publishing* (Cambridge University Press, Cambridge, 1956), pp. 8, 13–4.

38. Margaret Spufford. *Small Books and Pleasant Histories* (Cambridge University Press, Cambridge, 1985), pp. 1–15.

39. Cyprian Blagden. 'Notes on the ballad market in the second half of the seventeenth century', *SB*, 6 (1954), pp. 161–80.

40. John Feather. *The Provincial Book Trade in Eighteenth-century England* (Cambridge University Press, Cambridge, 1985), p. 1.

41. Ibid., p. 45; and Graham Pollard. 'Bibliographical aids to research. IV. General lists of books printed in England', *BIHR*, 12 (1934–5), pp. 164–74.

42. Michael Treadwell. 'London trade publishers 1675–1750', *Libr.*, 6th ser., 4 (1982), pp. 99–134.

Part Two: Licence and Liberty

Chapter 6

1. See below, pp. 97–9.

2. The word was first used in print by the maverick bookseller John Dunton in 1691, as a derogatory term for an organisation from which he had been excluded; see Stephen Parks. *John Dunton and the English Book Trade* (Garland Publishing, New York, 1976), p. 207. It is perfectly possible, however, that this is merely the first record of a common usage of the trade.

3. For the origin of the conger, see Norma Hodgson and Cyprian Blagden. *The Notebook of Thomas Bennet and Henry Clements (1686–1719)* (Oxford Bibliographical Society, new ser., 6, Oxford, 1956), pp. 78–9.

4. Ibid., p. 84.

5. For the origin of the auction sale, see John Lawlor. *Book Auctions in England in the Seventeenth Century, 1676–1700* (Elliot Stock, London, 1898).

6. Hodgson and Blagden, *Notebook*, pp. 82–4.

7. Ibid., pp. 85–6.

8. See Cyprian Blagden. 'Booksellers' trade sales 1718–1768', *Libr.*, 5th ser., 5 (1950–1), pp. 243–57; and Terry Belanger. 'Booksellers' trade sales, 1718–1768', *Libr.*, 5th ser., 30 (1975), pp. 281–302.

9. An index to the copies sold at the trade sales would be a major undertaking, but well worthwhile.

10. Printed in Joseph Shaylor. *The Fascination of Books* (Simpkin, Marshall, London, 1912), pp. 165–9.

11. John Feather. 'The book trade in politics: the making of the Copyright Act of 1710', *PH*, 8 (1980), p. 22.

12. See below, pp. 89–91.

13. R.C. Bald. 'Early copyright litigation and its bibliographical interest', *PBSA*, 36 (1942), pp. 81–96.

14. For the Printing Conger, see Hodgson and Blagden, *Notebook*, pp. 89–91.

15. Feather, 'Book trade in politics', pp. 30–9.

16. Ibid., pp. 35–6.

17. I have discussed the developments in copyright law between 1710 and 1775 in 'The publishers and the pirates: British copyright law in theory and practice 1710–1775', *PH*, 22 (1987), pp. 5–32. The reader is referred to this paper for detailed references for the rest of the chapter.

18. John Feather. *The Provincial Book Trade in Eighteenth-Century England* (Cambridge University Press, Cambridge, 1985), pp. 6–7, 101.

19. Ibid., pp. 44–53. For the magazines, see below, pp. 110–14.

20. Feather, *Provincial Book Trade*, pp. 55–9.

21. Ibid., pp. 4–5.

Chapter 7

1. For Locke's views, see Raymond Astbury, 'The renewal of the Licensing Act in 1693 and its lapse in 1695', *Libr.*, 5th ser., 33 (1978), pp. 381–21.

2. See Peter Fraser. *The Intelligence of the Secretaries of State and their Monopoly of Licensed News 1660–1698* (Cambridge University Press, Cambridge, 1956), pp. 35–6.

3. For these Bills, see John Feather. 'The book trade in politics: the making of the Copyright Act of 1710', *PH*, 8 (1980), pp. 20–8.

4. See Harold Herd. *The March of Journalism. The Story of the British Press from 1622 to the Present Day* (Allen and Unwin, London, 1952), pp. 39–45.

5. See J.A. Downie. *Robert Harley and the Press* (Cambridge University Press, Cambridge, 1979), *passim*; and Laurence Hanson. *Government and the Press 1695–1763* (Clarendon Press, Oxford, 1936), pp. 14–90.

6. John Feather, 'The English book trade and the law 1695–1799', *PH*, 12 (1982), pp. 53–5.

7. For a general history of the stamp duties, see Edward Hughes.

'The English Stamp Duties, 1664–1764', *EHR*, 56 (1941), pp. 234–64.

8. See Downie, *Robert Harley*, pp. 149–61; and Alan Downie. 'The growth of government tolerance of the press to 1790', in Robin Myers and Michael Harris (eds). *Development of the English Book Trade* (Oxford Polytechnic Press, Oxford, 1981), pp. 52–6.

9. James R. Sutherland. 'The circulation of newspapers and literary periodicals, 1700–1730', *Libr.*, 4th ser., 15 (1934–5), pp. 110–24.

10. Joel H. Weiner. *The War of the Unstamped. The Movement to Repeal the British Newspaper Tax, 1830–1836* (Cornell University Press, Ithaca, N.Y., 1969), pp. 2–9.

11. See below, pp. 116–17.

12. David Foxon. *Libertine Literature in England 1660–1745* (The Book Collector, London, 1964), pp. 7–13.

13. Ibid., pp. 14–15.

14. Ibid., pp. 15–18.

15. Donald Thomas. *A Long Time Burning* (Routledge and Kegan Paul, London, 1969), pp. 113–28. For the nineteenth century, see below, pp. 156–7.

16. For the law of blasphemy, see Thomas, *A Long Time Burning*, pp. 63–73; and Feather, 'The English book trade and the law', pp. 56, 60–1.

17. See Thomas, *A Long Time Burning*, pp. 34–62; and John Feather. 'From censorship to copyright: aspects of the government's role in the English book trade 1695–1775', in Kenneth E. Carpenter (ed.). *Books and Society in History* (Bowker, New York, 1983), pp. 173–81.

18. For examples, see Downie, *Robert Harley*, pp. 80–100; and Feather, 'From censorship to copyright', pp. 178–9.

19. See Hanson, *Government and the Press*, pp. 36–83.

20. Feather, 'The English book trade and the law', p. 58.

21. Thomas, *A Long Time Burning*, pp. 129–52.

22. Feather, 'The English book trade and the law', pp. 58–9.

Chapter 8

1. See J.H. Plumb. *The Commercialisation of Leisure* (University of Reading, Reading, 1973); and Peter Borsay. 'The English urban renaissance: the development of provincial urban culture *c*.1680–*c*.1760', *Soc. Hist.*, no. 5 (1977), pp. 581–603.

2. Benjamin Franklin. *Autobiography and Other Writings*. Ed. Russel B. Nye (Houghton Mifflin, Boston, Mass., 1958), p. 41.

3. William M. Sale. *Samuel Richardson: Master Printer* (Cornell University Press, Ithaca, N.Y., 1950), p. 21.

4. A famous example of a schoolbook printed on this scale is Dyche's *Guide to the English Tongue*, for which see D.F. McKenzie and J.C. Ross (eds). *A Ledger of Charles Ackers* (Oxford Bibliographical Society, new ser., 15, Oxford, 1968), pp. 249–52. For almanacs, see above, p. 23. For chapbooks, see Victor Neuburg. 'The Diceys and the chapbook trade', *Libr.*, 5th ser., 24 (1969), pp. 219–31.

5. See Thomas Laqueur. 'The cultural origins of popular literacy in

England 1500–1850', *ORE*, 2 (1976), pp. 255–75.

6. See Michael Sanderson. 'Literacy and social mobility in the industrial revolution in England', *PP*, 56 (1972), pp. 75–104. Sanderson's view was challenged by Laqueur in *PP*, 64 (1974), pp. 96–107, and defended by him in ibid., pp. 108–12.

7. This is the essence of Laqueur's argument in 'The cultural origins of popular literacy'.

8. See R.S. Schofield. 'Dimensions of illiteracy, 1750–1850', *EEH*, 10 (1972–3), pp. 437–54.

9. See R.S. Schofield. 'The measurement of literacy in pre-industrial England' in Jack Goody (ed.). *Literacy in Traditional Societies* (Cambridge University Press, Cambridge, 1968), pp. 311–25.

10. See John Feather. 'British publishing in the eighteenth century: a preliminary subject analysis', *Libr.*, 6th ser., 8 (1986), pp. 32–46.

11. See above, pp. 85–6.

12. See above, p. 57.

13. See Walter Allen. *The English Novel* (Phoenix House, London, 1954), pp. 19–39.

14. The flavour of them can be judged from the reviews in such journals as *The Critical Review* and *The Monthly Review* which devoted a considerable amount of space to them.

15. See above, pp. 60–1, 68–71.

16. This and the following paragraphs are based on John Feather, *The Provincial Book Trade in Eighteenth-Century England* (Cambridge University Press, Cambridge, 1985), *passim*. For the provincial market, see R.M. Wiles. 'The relish for reading in provincial England two centuries ago', in Paul J. Korshin (ed.). *The Widening Circle* (University of Pennsylvania Press, Philadelphia, Pa., 1976), pp. 86–116. For Wales, see Eiluned Rees. 'Developments in the book trade in eighteenth-century Wales', *Libr.*, 5th ser., 24 (1969), pp. 33–43.

17. For the early provincial newspapers, see G.A. Cranfield. *The Development of the Provincial Newspaper 1700–1760* (Oxford University Press, Oxford, 1962); and R.M. Wiles. *Freshest Advices. Early Provincial Newspapers in England* (Ohio State University Press, Columbus, Ohio, 1965).

18. For the early history of the circulating libraries, see Paul Kaufman. 'The community library: a chapter in English social history', *TAAS*, 57:2 (1967).

19. See above, pp. 60–1.

20. See below, pp. 110–12.

21. See Graham Pollard. 'Bibliographical aids to research. IV. General lists of books printed in England', *BIHR*, 12 (1934–5), pp. 168–9.

22. John Dawson Carl Buck. 'The motives of puffing: John Newbery's advertisements 1742–1767', *SB*, 30 (1977), pp. 196–210.

23. Michael Harris. 'The structure, ownership and control of the press, 1620–1780', in George Boyce, James Curran and Pauline Wingate (eds). *Newspaper History from the Seventeenth Century to the Present Day* (Constable, London, 1978), pp. 89–92.

24. See Derek Roper. *Reviewing Before the 'Edinburgh'* (Methuen, London, 1978), pp. 20–2.

25. See G.F. Papali. *Jacob Tonson, Publisher* (Tonson Publishing,

Auckland, 1968), for a list of the Tonsons' publications. For more up-to-date accounts of the family and the business (Papali's was written in 1933), see Kathleen M. Lynch, *Jacob Tonson, Kit-Kat Publisher* (University of Tennessee Press, Knoxville, Tenn., 1971), and Harry M. Geduld. *Prince of Publishers* (Indiana University Press, Bloomington, Ind., 1969).

26. For a brief history of the firm, see Philip Wallis. *At the Sign of the Ship* (Longman, London, 1974).

27. See Ralph Straus. *Robert Dodsley* (London, 1910).

28. Robert Ogilvie. 'Latin for yesterday', in Asa Briggs (ed.). *Essays in the History of Publishing* (Longman, London, 1974), pp. 219–44.

29. For a general account, see J.W. Saunders. *The Profession of English Letters* (Routledge and Kegan Paul, London, 1964), pp. 93–145.

30. See A.S. Collins. *Authorship in the Days of Johnson* (Routledge, London, 1927), pp. 189–93; and J.D. Fleeman, 'The revenue of a writer: Samuel Johnson's literary earnings', in R.W. Hunt, I.G. Philip and R.J. Roberts (eds). *Studies in the Book Trade* (Oxford Bibliographical Society, new ser., 18, Oxford, 1975), pp. 211–30.

31. For Pope's use of the 1710 Act, see James R. Sutherland. 'The Dunciad of 1729', *MLR*, 32 (1936), pp. 347–53; and John Feather. 'The publishers and the pirates: British copyright law in theory and practice 1710–1775', *PH*, 22 (1987), pp. 14–16.

32. See Straus, *Robert Dodsley*, pp. 36–57, 67–88.

33. See J. McLaverty. *Pope's Printer, John Wright* (Oxford Bibliographical Society, occ. pub., 11, Oxford, 1976); and the same author's 'Lawton Gilliver: Pope's bookseller', *SB*, 32 (1979), pp. 101–24.

34. For Markham, see F.N.L. Poynter. *A Bibliography of Gervase Markham 1568?–1637* (Oxford Bibliographical Society, new ser., 11, Oxford, 1962).

35. For a sensible account of authorship in the early eighteenth century, see Pat Rogers. *Grub Street. Studies in a Sub-culture* (Methuen, London, 1972).

36. For some examples, see G.E. Bentley, Jr. 'Copyright documents in the George Robinson archive: William Godwin and others 1713–1820', *SB*, 35 (1982), pp. 67–110. For a detailed study of a mid-eighteenth-century publisher and a small group of authors, see John Feather, 'John Nourse and his authors', *SB*, 34 (1981), pp. 205–26.

37. See above, pp. 79.

38. See Giles Barber. 'Books from the old world and for the new: the British international trade in books in the eighteenth century', *SVEC*, 151 (1976), pp. 185–224.

39. See Bernhard Fabian. 'English books and their eighteenth-century German readers', in Paul J. Korshin (ed.). *The Widening Circle*, (University of Pennsylvania Press, Philadelphia, Pa., 1976), pp. 117–96; and the same author's 'The beginnings of English-language publishing in Germany in the eighteenth century', in Kenneth E. Carpenter (ed.). *Books and Society in History* (Bowker, New York, 1983), pp. 115–44.

40. See John Tebbel. *A History of Book Publishing in the United States*. 3 vols. (Bowker, New York, 1972–8), vol. 1, pp. 134–7.

Chapter 9

1. See above, pp. 96–7 for novels, and pp. 45–6 for newspapers; and below, pp. 118–19 for children's books.

2. Raymond Birn. 'Le *Journal des savants* sous l'Ancien Régime', *Journal des Savants* (1965), pp. 15–35.

3. A.A. Manten. 'Development of European scientific journal publishing before 1850', in A.J. Meadows (ed.). *Development of Science Publishing in Europe* (Elsevier, Amsterdam, 1980), p. 7; and R.K. Bluhm, 'Henry Oldenburg, F.R.S. (*c*.1615–1677)', in Sir Harold Hartley. *The Royal Society. Its Origins and Founders* (Royal Society, London, 1960), pp. 189–93.

4. Walter Graham. *English Literary Periodicals* (Nelson, London, 1930), pp. 28–9.

5. See Stephen Parks. *John Dunton and the English Book Trade* (Garland Publishing, New York, 1976), pp. 74–108.

6. Graham, *English Literary Periodicals*, p. 46.

7. G.A. Cranfield. *The Press and Society from Caxton to Northcliffe* (Longman, London, 1978), p. 217.

8. Parks, *John Dunton*, pp. 175–76, 209–10.

9. See Dorothy Foster. 'The earliest precursor of our present-day monthly miscellanies', *PMLA*, 32 (1917), pp. 22–58.

10. See J.A. Downie, *Robert Harley and the Press* (Cambridge University Press, Cambridge, 1979), pp. 64–70, for the origins and purpose of the *Review*.

11. Graham, *English Literary Periodicals*, pp. 65–77; and Louis T. Milic. 'Tone in Steele's *Tatler*', in Donovan H. Bond and W. Reynolds McLeod (eds). *Newsletters to Newspapers: Eighteenth-century Journalism* (School of Journalism, West Virginia University, Morgantown, W.V., 1977), pp. 33–46.

12. Donald F. Bond (ed.). *The Spectator*. 5 vols. (Clarendon Press, Oxford, 1965), vol. 1, pp. xxvi–xxvii. For the Stamp Act, see above, pp. 86–8.

13. John Calhoun Stephens (ed.). *The Guardian* (University of Kentucky Press, Lexington, Ky., 1982), pp. 14–15.

14. W. Jackson Bate and Albrecht R. Strauss (eds). *The Rambler* (Yale University Press, *The Yale Edition of the Works of Samuel Johnson*, vol. 3, New Haven, Conn., 1969), pp. xxi–xxii.

15. See James R. Sutherland, 'The circulation of newspapers', p. 111. For *The Daily Courant*, see above, p. 85.

16. For the trade publishers, see above, p. 62. For Abigail Baldwin, see Michael Treadwell, 'London trade publishers', 1675–1750', *Libr.*, 6th ser., 4 (1982), pp. 109–10; and, somewhat more fancifully, Leona Rostenberg. 'Richard and Anne [*sic; recte* Abigail] Baldwin: Whig patriot publishers', *PBSA*, 47 (1953), pp. 1–42.

17. Bond, *The Spectator*. vol. 1, p. xx.

18. Bond, *The Spectator*, vol. 1, p. xxiii.

19. Stephens, *The Guardian*, pp. 14–15.

20. See Michael Harris. 'Periodicals and the book trade', in Robin

Myers and Michael Harris (eds). *Development of the English Book Trade, 1700–1899* (Oxford Polytechnic Press, Oxford, 1981), pp. 66–94.

21. See above, pp. 97–9.

22. For Cave's background, see C. Lennart Carlson. *The First Magazine. A History of 'The Gentleman's Magazine'* (Brown University Press, Providence, RI, 1938), pp. 5–12.

23. Ibid., pp. 83–109. Parliamentary reporting was not formally recognised until 1771, for which see A. Aspinall. 'The reporting and publishing of the House of Commons' debates 1771–1834', in Richard Pares and A.J.P. Taylor (eds). *Essays Presented to Sir Lewis Namier* (Macmillan, London, 1956), pp. 227–57.

24. Carlson, *The First Magazine*, p. 95.

25. See Donald Greene. 'Samuel Johnson, journalist', in Donovan H. Bond and W. Reynolds McLeod (eds). *Newsletters to Newspapers: Eighteenth-century Journalism* (School of Journalism, West Virginia University, Morgantown, W.V., 1977), pp. 87–101.

26. See Michael Harris. 'Journalism as a profession or trade in the eighteenth century', in Robin Myers and Michael Harris (eds). *Author/Publisher Relations During the Eighteenth and Nineteenth Centuries* (Oxford Polytechnic Press, Oxford, 1983) pp. 37–62.

27. See above, p. 99, for the book lists.

28. For this, see William F. Belcher. 'The sale and distribution of *The British Apollo*', in Richmond P. Bond (ed.). *Studies in the Early English Periodical* (University of North Carolina Press, Chapel Hill, N.C., 1957), pp. 73–101.

29. Because of this, very few copies survive in the blue-paper wrappers, although there are some examples extant.

30. See Wilbur L. Cross. *The History of Henry Fielding*. 3 vols. (Russell and Russell, New York, 1963), vol. 1, p. 250; vol. 2, pp. 18–20, 64, 66, 77–9, 364–5; and Gerard E. Jones (ed.). *The Covent-Garden Journal* (Yale University Press, New Haven, Conn., 1915), pp. 30–40.

31. Lewis M. Knapp. *Tobias Smollett. Doctor of Men and Manners* (Princeton University Press, Princeton, N.J., 1949), pp. 178–81. See also above, pp. 100–1.

32. Carlson, *The First Magazine*, p. 242; and James M. Kuist. '*The Gentleman's Magazine* in the Folger Library: the history and significance of the Nichols family collection', *SB*, (1976), pp. 307–22.

33. Alison Adburgham. *Women in Print* (Allen and Unwin, London, 1972), pp. 273–81. For a study of one women's magazine of the mid-eighteenth century, see Jean E. Hunter, '*The Lady's Magazine* and the study of Englishwomen in the eighteenth century', in Donovan H. Bond and W. Reynolds McLeod (eds). *Newsletters to Newspapers: Eighteenth-century Journalism* (School of Journalism, West Virginia University, Morgantown, W.V., 1977), pp. 103–17.

34. John J. McCusker. 'The business press in England before 1775', *Libr.*, 6th ser., 8 (1986), pp. 205–31.

35. G.R. Seaman. 'Eighteenth-century English periodicals and music', *BJECS*, 7 (1984), pp. 69–76.

36. 62 per cent of all European scientific journals in the eighteenth century were published in Germany, and just 7 per cent in England. See

David A. Kronick. *A History of Scientific & Technical Periodicals. The Origin and Development of the Scientific and Technical Press 1665–1790* (Scarecrow, Metuchen, N.J., 1976), p. 89. For the later developments, see ibid., pp. 118–21. See also David A. Kronick. 'Scientific journal publication in the eighteenth century', *PBSA*, 59 (1965), pp. 28–44.

37. On this subject see Robert D. Mayo. *The English Novel in the Magazines 1740–1815* (Northwestern University Press, Evanston, Ill., 1962).

38. John R. Millburn. '*Martin's Magazine: The General Magazine of Arts and Sciences*, 1755–65', *Libr.*, 5th ser., 28 (1973), pp. 221–39.

39. R.M. Wiles. *Serial Publication in England Before 1750* (Cambridge University Press, Cambridge, 1957), pp. 75–80.

40. Ibid., pp. 106–9, 117–18.

41. John Feather. *The Provincial Book Trade in Eighteenth-Century England* (Cambridge University Press, Cambridge, 1985), pp. 49–50.

Chapter 10

1. See above, p. 55; and Cyprian Blagden. 'Thomas Carnan and the almanack monopoly', *SB*, 14 (1961), pp. 23–43.

2. See Ellic Howe. 'The Stationers' Company almanacks: a late eighteenth-century printing and publishing operation', in Giles Barber and Bernhard Fabian (eds). *Buch und Buchhandel in Europa im achtzehnten Jahrhundert* (Hauswedell, Hamburg, 1981), pp. 195–209; and Bernard Capp. *Astrology and the Popular Press. English Almanacs 1500–1800* (Faber and Faber, London, 1979), pp. 263–4.

3. Stanley Morison. *John Bell, 1745–1831* (First Editions Club, London, 1930), pp. 5–6.

4. See W. Jackson Bate. *Samuel Johnson* (Chatto and Windus, London, 1978), pp. 525–7, 545–6.

5. See L.H. Butterfield. 'The American interests of the firm of E. and C. Dilly, with their letters to Benjamin Rush, 1770–1795', *PBSA*, 45 (1951), pp. 283–332; and Thomas R. Adams. 'The British pamphlet press and the American controversy, 1764–1783', *PAAS* 89 (1979), pp. 47–9.

6. See above, pp. 110–12.

7. For a general account of Newbery, see Charles Welsh. *A Bookseller of the Last Century* (Griffith, Farran, London, 1885).

8. Bruce Dickins. 'Doctor James's Fever Powder', *Life and Letters*, 2 (1929), pp. 36–47.

9. See John Alden. 'Pills and publishing: some notes on the English book trade', *Libr.*, 5th ser., 7 (1952), pp. 21–37.

10. See Leslie H. Matthews. *History of Pharmacy in Britain* (Livingstone, Edinburgh, 1962), pp. 285–8.

11. John Feather. *The Provincial Book Trade in Eighteenth-Century England* (Cambridge University Press, Cambridge, 1985), pp. 83–4.

12. See above, John Dawson Carl Buck, 'The motives of puffing: John Newbery's advertisements, 1742–1767', *SB*, 30 (1977), pp. 196–210.

13. On this, see Michael Sadleir. *The Evolution of Publishers' Binding*

Styles (Constable, London, 1930).

14. See F.J. Harvey Darton. *Children's Books in England*. 3rd edn, rev. by Brian Alderson. (Cambridge University Press, Cambridge, 1982), pp. 124–5; and Jill Grey. 'The Lilliputian Magazine — a pioneering periodical?', *J. Libr.*, 2 (1970), pp. 107–15.

15. For the most complete list of Newbery's publications, see S. Roscoe. *John Newbery and his Successors 1740–1814. A Bibliography* (Five Owls Press, Wormley, 1973). For *Goody Two-Shoes*, see R.J. Roberts. 'The 1765 edition of Goody Two-Shoes', *BMQ*, 29 (1965), pp. 67–70.

16. See M.J.P. Weedon. 'Richard Johnson and the successors to John Newbery', *Libr.*, 5th ser., 4 (1949), pp. 25–63.

17. See above, pp. 72–3.

18. Septimus Rivington. *The Publishing Family of Rivington* (Rivingtons, London, 1919), pp. 5–57.

19. For the very complex history of this large family, see Rivington, *Publishing Family, passim*. See also Henry Curwen. *A History of the Booksellers. The Old and New* (Chatto and Windus, London, 1873), pp. 296–306.

20. See above, p. 102.

21. Philip Wallis. *At the Sign of the Ship* (Longman, London, 1974), pp. 7–14, 41; and Harold Cox and John E. Chandler. *The House of Longman* (Longman, London, 1925), pp. 15–16.

22. Curwen, *History*, pp. 161–2.

23. Samuel Smiles. *A Publisher and his Friends*. 2 vols (John Murray, London, 1891), vol. 1, pp. 4–5.

24. Ibid., vol. 1, pp. 9–11, 14.

25. Ibid., pp. 29–55; and Curwen, *History*, pp. 159–80. For the changing conditions of authorship, see A.S. Collins. *The Profession of Letters. A Study of the Relation of Author to Patron, Publisher and Public, 1780–1832* (Routledge, London, 1928), pp. 105–45.

26. John Feather. 'The merchants of culture: bookselling in early industrial England', *SVEC*, 217 (1983), pp. 11–21.

27. O M Brack, Jr. 'William Strahan: Scottish printer and publisher', *Ariz. Q.*, 31 (1975), pp. 179–91.

28. Curwen, *History*, p. 110; Smiles, *A Publisher*, vol. 1, p. 18.

29. J.D. Newth. *Adam and Charles Black 1807–1957* (A. & C. Black, London, 1957).

30. Agnes A.C. Blackie. *Blackie & Son 1809–1959* (Blackie, Glasgow, 1959).

31. David Keir. *The House of Collins* (Collins, London, 1952).

32. A good general account of Robinson is a desideratum; see *DNB*, and Curwen, *History*, pp. 69–70. For Robinson as a publisher, see G.E. Bentley, Jr. 'Copyright documents in the George Robinson archives: William Godwin and others 1713–1820', *SB*, 35 (1982), pp. 67–110.

33. See Graham Pollard. 'The English market for printed books', *PH*, 4 (1978), pp. 34–7; and below, pp. 136–7.

34. See George Rudé. *Hanoverian London 1714–1808* (Secker and Warburg, London, 1981), pp. 8–10.

35. Ralph Straus, *Robert Dodsley* (London, 1910), pp. 38–9.

36. Ian Maxted. *The London Book Trades, 1775–1800: a Topographical*

Guide (The Author, Exeter, 1980), pp. 14–15.

37. James Laver. *Hatchards of Piccadilly 1797–1947* (Hatchards, London, 1947), pp. 6–14.

38. For Lackington, see Richard G. Landon. '"Small profits do great things": James Lackington and eighteenth-century bookselling', *SEEC*, 5 (1976), pp. 378–99.

Part Three: The First of the Mass Media

Chapter 11

1. See above, pp. 114–15.

2. Lucien Febvre and Henri-Jean Martin. *The Coming of the Book. The Impact of Printing 1450–1800*. Tr. by David Gerard (NLB, London, 1976), pp. 29–44.

3. Robert Darnton. *The Business of Enlightenment. A Publishing History of the 'Encyclopédie' 1775–1800* (Belknap Press, Cambridge, Mass., 1979), pp. 185–96.

4. Dard Hunter. *Papermaking. The History and Technique of an Ancient Craft*. 2nd edn (Knopf, New York, 1967), pp. 309–40.

5. Thomas Balston. *James Whatman, Father and Son* (Methuen, London, 1957), pp. 21–4.

6. Hunter, *Papermaking*, pp. 341–73.

7. D.C. Coleman. *The British Paper Industry 1495–1860* (Oxford University Press, Oxford, 1958), pp. 227–58.

8. See R.C. Alston. 'The eighteenth-century non-book. Observations on printed ephemera', in Giles Barber and Bernhard Fabian (eds). *Buch und Buchhandel in Europa im achtzehnten Jahrhundert* (Hauswedell, Hamburg, 1981), pp. 343–60.

9. John Feather. 'John Walter and the Logographic Press', *PH*, 1 (1977), pp. 92–134.

10. James Moran. *The Composition of Reading Matter* (Wace, London, 1965), pp. 52–8, 62–5.

11. For early stereotyping, see John Carter. 'William Ged and the invention of stereotype', *BC*, 7 (1958), pp. 267–9; and 'William Ged and the invention of stereotype: a postscript', *Libr.*, 5th ser., 16 (1961), pp. 143–5. For the rediscovery and commercial exploitation of the process, see Michael L. Turner. 'Andrew Wilson: Lord Stanhope's stereotype printer', *JPHS*, 9 (1975), pp. 22–65.

12. See T.A. Skingsley. 'Technical training and education in the English printing industry. A study of late-nineteenth-century attitudes', *JPHS*, 13 (1978/9), pp. 1–25; and ibid., 14 (1979/80), pp. 1–58.

13. John Child. *Industrial Relations in the British Printing Industry* (Allen and Unwin, London, 1967), pp. 47–104; and Ellic Howe and Harold E. Waite. *The London Society of Compositors. A Centenary History* (Cassell, London, 1948), pp. 84–115.

14. Ellic Howe. *The London Compositor* (The Bibliographical Society, London, 1947), pp. 69–83.

15. Horace Hart. *Charles Earl Stanhope and the Oxford University Press.* Ed. James Mosley (Printing Historical Society, London, 1966), pp. 345–405.

16. James Moran. *Printing Presses* (University of California Press, Berkeley and Los Angeles, Calif., 1978), pp. 91–100.

17. Ibid., pp. 101–11.

18. Ibid., pp. 173–83; and Frank E. Comparato. '"Old Thunderer's" American lightning. Machines and machinations in furnishing the first Hoe rotaries to *The Times*, 1856–60', *JPHS*, 13 (1978/9), pp. 27–63.

19. Michael Twyman. *Lithography 1800–1850* (Oxford University Press, London, 1970), pp. 11–12, 26–40.

20. Basil Hunnisett. *Steel-engraved Book Illustration in England* (Godine, Boston, Mass., 1980), pp. 18–31; generally, see Elizabeth M. Harris. 'Experimental graphic processes in England 1800–1859', *JPHS*, 4 (1968), pp. 33–86; ibid., 5 (1969), pp. 41–80; and ibid., 6 (1970), pp. 53–89.

21. For colour processes, see Joan M. Friedman. *Color Printing in England 1486–1870* (Yale Center for British Art, New Haven, Conn., 1978).

22. Geoffrey Wakeman. *Victorian Book Illustration. The Technical Revolution* (David and Charles, Newton Abbott, 1973), pp. 119–45.

23. Douglas Ball. *Victorian Publishers' Bindings* (The Library Association, London, 1985), pp. 17–23.

24. See above, pp. 118–19.

25. John Feather. 'The merchants of culture: Bookselling in early industrial England', *SVEC*, 217 (1983), pp. 12–14.

26. John Feather, *The Provincial Book Trade in Eighteenth-century England* (Cambridge University Press, Cambridge, 1985), pp. 44–68.

27. For railway freight arrangements and charges, see Michael Robbins. *The Railway Age* (Routledge and Kegan Paul, London, 1962), pp. 105–7; for a general account, see Jack Simmons. *The Railway in Town and Country 1830–1914* (David and Charles, Newton Abbot, 1986).

28. See R.D. Richards. *The Early History of Banking in England*. Repr. (Frank Cass, New York, 1965), pp. 189–201.

29. See below, pp. 143–4.

30. See Charles Wilson. *First with the News. The History of W.H. Smith 1792–1972* (Jonathan Cape, London, 1985), pp. 88–154; and Elizabeth James. 'An insight into the management of railway bookstalls in the eighteen fifties', *PH*, 10 (1981), pp. 65–9.

31. Wilson, *First with the News*, pp. 218–24.

32. See above, p. 124 for Lackington.

33. See above, pp. 122–3.

34. Curwen, *History*, pp. 412–20; Ian Norrie. *Mumby's Publishing and Bookselling in the Twentieth Century*. 6th edn (Bell and Hyman, London, 1982), pp. 71–2, 87.

Chapter 12

1. Charles Morgan. *The House of Macmillan (1843–1943)* (Macmillan, London, 1943), pp. 27–49.

2. Thomas Hughes. *Memoir of Daniel Macmillan* (Macmillan, London, 1882), pp. 296–302.

3. Morgan, *House of Macmillan*, pp. 101–3; see also Simon Nowell-Smith (ed.). *Letters to Macmillan* (Macmillan, London, 1967). For publishers' readers, see below, pp. 176–7.

4. Politics, of course, became something of a tradition in the Macmillan family.

5. Brian Harrison. *Drink and the Victorians. The Temperance Question in England 1815–1872* (Faber and Faber, London, 1971), p. 151. For Collins, see also David Keir. *The House of Collins* (Collins, London, 1952), pp. 258–9.

6. Simon Nowell-Smith. *The House of Cassell 1848–1958* (Cassell, London, 1958), pp. 15–16.

7. For publishing for the working-class market, see below, pp. 156–7 and 160–4.

8. Nowell-Smith, *House of Cassell*, pp. 38, 108.

9. Ibid., pp. 51–66.

10. See Louis James. *Fiction for the Working Man 1830–50* (Penguin University Books, Harmondsworth, 1974), pp. 32–50; and below, pp. 156–7.

11. For Cooke, see *DNB*.

12. See A. Warren. *The Charles Whittinghams* (Grolier Club, New York, 1896); and the entries in *DNB*.

13. For John (II) Murray, see George Paston. *At John Murray's. Records of a Literary Circle 1843–1892* (Murray, London, 1932), pp. 6–38.

14. Scott Bennett. 'John Murray's Family Library and the cheapening of books in early nineteenth century Britain', *SB*, 29 (1976), pp. 138–66.

15. For Bohn, see *DNB*.

16. See above, p. 124 and p. 137.

17. See F.A. Mumby. *The House of Routledge 1834–1934* (Routledge, London, 1934), pp. 20–8. The account in this official history is, inevitably, somewhat sanitised; the *DNB* article on Routledge is rather less reserved.

18. See James J. Barnes. *Authors, Publishers and Politicians* (Routledge and Kegan Paul, London, 1974), pp. 156–64.

19. See Elizabeth James. 'The publication of collected editions of Bulwer Lytton's novels'. *PH*, 3 (1978), pp. 46–60.

20. See W.H.G. Armytage. *Four Hundred Years of English Education*. 2nd edn (Cambridge University Press, Cambridge, 1970), p. 145.

21. See J.W. Adamson. *English Education 1789–1902* (Cambridge University Press, Cambridge, 1930), pp. 215–16.

22. For this episode, see J.M. Goldstrom. 'The correspondence between Lord John Russell and the publishing trade'. *PH*, 20 (1986), pp. 5–59.

23. See below, pp. 165–6.

24. For an overview, see J.A. Sutherland. 'The institutionalisation of the British book trade to the 1890s', in Robin Myers and Michael Harris (eds). *Development of the English Book Trade, 1700–1899* (Oxford Polytechnic Press, Oxford, 1981), pp. 95–105.

25. For this crisis, see, generally, J.H. Clapham. *An Economic History of Modern Britain*. 3 vols. (Cambridge University Press, Cambridge, 1926–38), vol. 1 (repr. 1964), pp. 272–3; and, specifically, J.A. Sutherland. 'Henry Colburn, publisher', *PH*, 19 (1986), pp. 69–70.

26. James J. Barnes. *Free Trade in Books. A Study of the London Book Trade since 1800* (Clarendon Press, Oxford, 1964), pp. 7–18.

27. See below, p. 164.

28. For Carlyle's attitude to the trade, see Heather Henderson. 'Carlyle and the book clubs: a new approach to publishing?', *PH*, 6 (1979), pp. 47–58.

29. Barnes, *Free Trade*, pp. 19–29.

30. Morgan, *House of Macmillan*, pp. 139–40.

31. Frederick Macmillan. *The Net Book Agreement 1899 and the Book War 1906–1908* (The Author, Glasgow, 1924), pp. 5–17.

32. See above, p. 137.

33. Barnes, *Free Trade*, p. 144.

34. W.G. Corp. *Fifty Years. A Brief Account of the Associated Booksellers of Great Britain and Ireland 1895–1945* (Blackwell, Oxford, [1945]), pp. 5–9.

35. R.J.L. Kingsford. *The Publishers' Association 1896–1946* (Cambridge University Press, Cambridge, 1970), pp. 8–9, 13–17.

36. See Victor Bonham-Carter. *Authors by Profession*. 2 vols (Society of Authors/Bodley Head, London, 1978–84), vol. 1, pp. 178–80. See also below, p. 175.

37. See below, pp. 175–6.

38. Peter J. Curwen. *The U.K. Publishing Industry* (Pergamon, Oxford, 1981), pp. 41–52.

39. Barnes, *Free Trade*, pp. 145–46; and Macmillan, *Net Book Agreement*, pp. 29–30.

Chapter 13

1. See above, pp. 96–7.

2. For a general account, see Peter Garside. 'Rob's last raid: Scott and the publication of the Waverley Novels', in Robin Myers and Michael Harris (eds). *Author/Publisher Relations During the Eighteenth and Nineteenth Centuries* (Oxford Polytechnic Press, Oxford, 1983), pp. 88–118.

3. For Colburn, see J.A. Sutherland. 'Henry Colburn, publisher', *PH*, 19 (1986), pp. 59–84; and for Bentley, see R.A. Gettman. *A Victorian Publisher* (Cambridge University Press, Cambridge, 1960).

4. See J.A. Sutherland. *Victorian Novelists and their Publishers* (Athlone Press, London, 1976), p. 44.

5. See Douglas C. Ewing. 'The three-volume novel', *PBSA*, 61 (1967), pp. 201–7; and Guinevere L. Greist. *Mudie's Circulating Library and the Victorian Novel* (David and Charles, Newton Abbot, 1970), pp. 40–5; Charles E. Lauterbach and Edward S. Lauterbach. 'The nineteenth century three-volume novel', *PBSA*, 51 (1957), pp. 263–302; and Michael Sadleir. 'Aspects of the Victorian novel', *PH*, 5 (1979), pp. 10–11.

6. See above, pp. 114–15.

7. See above, pp. 113–14.

8. Sutherland, *Victorian Novelists*, p. 21.

9. Robert L. Patten. *Charles Dickens and his Publishers* (Clarendon Press, Oxford, 1978), pp. 60–8.

10. Sutherland, *Victorian Novelists*, pp. 191–203; and J.A. Sutherland. 'Lytton, John Blackwood and the serialisation of *Middlemarch*', *Bibl.*, 7 (1975), pp. 98–104.

11. See below, p. 174.

12. Winifred Gérin. *Elizabeth Gaskell* (Clarendon Press, Oxford, 1976), pp. 118–26.

13. Sutherland, *Victorian Novelists*, p. 43.

14. Ibid., p. 105.

15. Ibid., pp. 37–8.

16. See Hilda M. Hamlyn. 'Eighteenth-century circulating libraries', *Libr.*, 5th ser., 1 (1947), pp. 197–222. For Gothick novels written for the libraries, see Dorothy Blakey. *The Minerva Press, 1790–1820* (The Bibliographical Society, London, 1939).

17. Greist, *Mudie's*, pp. 15–27.

18. Ibid., pp. 35–57.

19. Charles Wilson. *First with the News. The History of W.H. Smith 1792–1972* (Jonathan Cape, London, 1985), pp. 357–63.

20. Griest, *Mudie's*, pp. 171–5.

21. Wilson, *First with the News*, p. 363.

22. Victor Bonham-Carter. *Authors By Profession.* 2 vols. (Society of Authors/Bodley Head, London, 1978–84), vol. 1, p. 177.

23. See above, pp. 145–7.

24. Griest, *Mudie's*, pp. 194–7.

25. Ibid., p. 208.

26. See Annabel Jones. 'Disraeli's *Endymion*', in Asa Briggs (ed.). *Essays in the History of Publishing* (Longman, London, 1974), pp. 141–86.

27. See above, pp. 143–4.

28. Gettman, *A Victorian Publisher*, pp. 45–54.

29. Sutherland, *Victorian Novelists*, pp. 30–5.

30. Patten, *Charles Dickens*, pp. 378–80.

31. Sutherland, *Victorian Novelists*, p. 36.

32. Louis James. *Fiction for the Working Man 1830–50* (Penguin University Books, Harmondsworth, 1974), pp. 51–82. This whole section is heavily indebted to James's work.

33. Ibid., pp. 212–15.

34. Lloyd became respectable enough to be included in *DNB*.

35. See Richard D. Altick. *The English Common Reader. A Social History of the Mass Reading Public* (University of Chicago Press, Chicago, Ill., 1963), pp. 289–93.

36. There is a good account by Ronald Pearsall. *The Worm in the Bud. The World of Victorian Sexuality* (Weidenfeld and Nicolson, London, 1969), pp. 380–92.

37. Ibid., pp. 387–9.

38. Donald Thomas. *A Long Time Burning* (Routledge and Kegan Paul, London, 1969), pp. 261–4.

39. Ibid., p. 267.

40. Vera Brittain. *Radclyffe Hall. A Case of Obscenity* (Femina Books, London, 1968), pp. 84–147.

41. Edgar Johnson. *Sir Walter Scott. The Great Unknown.* 2 vols (Hamish Hamilton, London, 1970), pp. 225, 279.

42. See W.J.B. Owen. 'Costs, sales and profits of Longman's editions of Wordsworth', *Libr.*, 5th ser., 12 (1957), pp. 93–107. For the case of a comparatively minor poet, see Franklin P. Batdorf. 'The Murray reprints of George Crabbe: a publisher's record', *SB*, 4 (1951), pp. 192–9.

43. Tim Chilcott. *A Publisher and his Circle. The Life and Work of John Taylor, Keats's Publisher* (Routledge and Kegan Paul, London, 1972), p. 46.

44. Leslie A. Marchand. *Byron. A Biography.* 3 vols (Knopf, New York, 1957), pp. 325–6, 677, 804.

45. Robert Bernard Martin. *Tennyson. The Unquiet Heart* (Faber and Faber, London / Oxford University Press, Oxford, 1983), p. 160.

46. Ibid., p. 266.

47. Ibid., p. 549.

48. See Sabine Haass. 'Victorian poetry anthologies: their role and success in the nineteenth-century book market', *PH*, 17 (1985), pp. 51–64.

49. This point emerges from the figures given in John A.H. Dempster. 'Thomas Nelson and sons in the late nineteenth century: a study in motivation. Part 1', *PH*, 13 (1983), pp. 54, 58–60.

Chapter 14

1. Joseph Ellis Baker. *The Novel and the Oxford Movement* (Princeton University Press, Princeton, N.J., 1932), pp. 9–22.

2. B.E. Maidment. 'Victorian publishing and social criticism: the case of Edward Jenkins', *PH*, 11 (1982), pp. 41–71.

3. See above, p. 141.

4. R.D. Anderson. *Education and Opportunity in Victorian Scotland* (Clarendon Press, Oxford, 1983), pp. 1–6.

5. Marjorie Cruickshank. *Church and State in English Education* (Macmillan, London, 1944), p. 1; and David Cressy. *Education in Tudor and Stuart England* (Edward Arnold, London, 1975), p. 31.

6. Thomas Kelly. *Early Public Libraries* (The Library Association, London, 1966), pp. 104–14.

7. W.H.G. Armytage. *Four Hundred Years of English Education.* 2nd edn (Cambridge University Press, Cambridge, 1970), pp. 74–6.

8. Richard D. Altick. *The English Common Reader. A Social History of the Mass Reading Public* (University of Chicago Press, Chicago, Ill., 1963), pp. 34–41.

9. Ibid., p. 67.

10. G.H. Spinney. '*Cheap Repository Tracts*: Hazard and Marshall edition', *Libr.*, 4th ser., 20 (1939), pp. 295–340.

11. Altick, *English Common Reader*, pp. 102–3. For Collins's satirical view of the lady tract distributors, see his portrayal of Miss Clack in *The Moonstone*.

12. Maurice J. Quinlan. *Victorian Prelude. A History of English Manners, 1700–1830* (Columbia University Press, New York, 1941), p. 124.

13. H.F. Mathews. *Methodism and the Education of the People, 1791–1851* (Epworth Press, London, 1949), pp. 167–81. Generally, see F. Cumbers. *The Book Room. The Story of the Methodist Publishing House and the Epworth Press* (Epworth Press, London, 1956).

14. Altick, *English Common Reader*, pp. 269–77; and R.K. Webb. *The British Working Class Reader 1790–1848* (Allen and Unwin, London, 1955), pp. 60–73.

15. The best account of Knight is in his autobiography: Charles Knight. *Passages of a Working Life*. 3 vols (Bradbury and Evans, London, 1864–5).

16. Victor Neuburg. *Popular Literature* (Penguin, Harmondsworth, 1977), pp. 137–9.

17. Joel H. Weiner. *The War of the Unstamped. The Movement to Repeal the British Newspaper Tax, 1830–1836* (Cornell University Press, Ithaca, N.Y., 1969), p. 13.

18. See above, p. 146.

19. Weiner, *The War of the Unstamped*, recounts in detail the history of the agitation against the 'taxes on knowledge' in the 1830s.

20. Alan J. Lee. *The Origins of the Popular Press in England 1855–1914* (Croom Helm, London, 1976), pp. 42–9.

21. Ibid., p. 279.

22. Ibid., p. 277.

23. See Diana Dixon. 'Children and the press, 1866–1914', in Michael Harris and Alan Lee (eds). *The Press in English Society from the Seventeenth to Nineteenth Centuries* (Associated University Presses, Cranbury, N.J., 1986), pp. 133–48.

24. See Tony Mason. 'Sporting news, 1860–1914' in Michael Harris and Alan Lee (eds). *The Press in English Society from the Seventeenth to Nineteenth Centuries* (Associated University Presses, Cranbury, N.J., 1986), pp. 168–86.

25. Charles Morgan. *The House of Macmillan (1843–1943)* (Macmillan, London, 1943), p. 59.

26. See above, p. 144.

27. See Roy Yglesias. 'Education and publishing in transition', in Asa Briggs (ed.). *Essays in the History of Publishing* (Longman, London, 1974), pp. 359–77.

28. Morgan, *House of Macmillan*, pp. 189–90, although Morgan is rather cursory in his treatment of this important aspect of the firm's activities.

29. Peter Sutcliffe. *The Oxford University Press. An Informal History* (Clarendon Press, Oxford, 1978), pp. 19–24.

30. M.H. Black. *Cambridge University Press 1584–1984* (Cambridge University Press, Cambridge, 1984), pp. 158–60.

31. John A.H. Dempster. 'Thomas Nelson and Sons in the late

nineteenth century: a study in motivation. Part 1', *PH*, 13 (1983), pp. 65–7.

32. Ian Norrie. *Mumby's Publishing and Bookselling in the Twentieth Century*. 6th edn (Bell and Hyman, London, 1982), p. 55.

33. Morgan, *House of Macmillan*, p. 84.

34. H. Kay Jones. *Butterworths. History of a Publishing House* (Butterworths, London, 1980), pp. 9–30.

35. Morgan, *House of Macmillan*, pp. 84–7.

36. See Noel Annan. *Leslie Stephen. The Godless Victorian* (Weidenfeld and Nicolson, London, 1984), pp. 82–7.

37. See K.M. Elisabeth Murray. *Caught in the Web of Words. James A.H. Murray and the Oxford English Dictionary* (Yale University Press, New Haven, Conn., 1977), pp. 133–47.

Chapter 15

1. For example, he was paid £1,000 for *Marmion* before a line was written; see Edgar Johnson. *Sir Walter Scott. The Great Unknown.* 2 vols. (Hamish Hamilton, London, 1970), p. 261.

2. See above, pp. 102–3.

3. For examples of eighteenth-century agreements, see John Feather. 'John Nourse and his authors', *SB*, 34 (1981), pp. 205–26, and G.E. Bentley, Jr. 'Copyright documents in the George Robinson archive: William Godwin and others 1713–1820', *SB*, 35 (1982), pp. 67–110.

4. A.S. Collins. *The Profession of Letters. A Study of the Relation of Author to Patron, Publisher and Public, 1780–1832* (Routledge, London, 1928), p. 156.

5. Peter Garside. 'Rob's last raid: Scott and the publication of the Waverley Novels', in Robin Myers and Michael Harris (eds). *Author/ Publisher Relations During the Eighteenth and Nineteenth Centuries* (Oxford Polytechnic Press, Oxford, 1983), p. 90.

6. Robert L. Patten. *Charles Dickens and his Publishers* (Clarendon Press, Oxford, 1976), p. 237.

7. Winifred Gérin. *Elizabeth Gaskell* (Clarendon Press, Oxford, 1976), pp. 260–1.

8. See above, pp. 82–3.

9. Victor Bonham-Carter. *Authors by Profession*. 2 vols. (Society of Authors/Bodley Head, London, 1978–84), vol. 1, p. 43.

10. Ian Parsons. 'Copyright and society', in Asa Briggs (ed.). *Essays in the History of Publishing* (Longman, London, 1974), p. 44.

11. Ibid., pp. 43–4.

12. Tim Chilcott, *A Publisher and his Circle. The Life and Work of John Taylor, Keats's Publisher* (Routledge and Kegan Paul, London, 1972), p. 137.

13. Patten, *Charles Dickens and his Publishers*, pp. 70–1.

14. James J. Barnes. *Authors, Publishers and Politicians* (Routledge and Kegan Paul, London, 1974), pp. 120–6.

15. See Giles Barber. 'Galignani and the publication of English books in France, 1800–1852', *Libr.*, 5th ser., 16 (1961), pp. 267–84.

16. Barnes, *Authors, Publishers and Politicians*, pp. 94–105.

17. Simon Nowell-Smith. *International Copyright Law and the Publisher in the Reign of Queen Victoria* (Clarendon Press, Oxford, 1968), pp. 22–3, 41.

18. Ibid., pp. 23–5; Barnes, *Authors, Publishers and Politicians*, pp. 116–37.

19. Ibid., pp. 119–20.

20. See Karl H. Pressler. 'The Tauchnitz Edition: beginning and end of a famous series', *PH*, 6 (1980), pp. 63–78; and Nowell-Smith, *International Copyright Law*, pp. 42–63.

21. I am told that in the 1920s and 1930s British Customs officers would ask returning British travellers who had Tauchnitz editions with them how much of the book they had read, and then tear out all the pages up to that point so that the book could not be resold in the United Kingdom.

22. Barnes, *Authors, Publishers and Politicians*, pp. 216–62.

23. Nowell-Smith, *International Copyright Law*, pp. 68–70.

24. See Stephen M. Stewart. *International Copyright and Neighbouring Rights* (Butterworth, London, 1983), pp. 88–92.

25. Patten, *Charles Dickens and his Publishers*, pp. 63, 381.

26. R.A. Gettman. *A Victorian Publisher* (Cambridge University Press, Cambridge, 1960), pp. 114–15.

27. J.A. Sutherland. *Victorian Novelists and their Publishers* (Athlone Press, London, 1976), p. 136.

28. Asa Briggs. 'Introduction: at the Sign of the Ship', in Asa Briggs (ed.). *Essays in the History of Publishing* (Longman, London, 1974), pp. 15–16.

29. Bonham-Carter, *Authors by Profession*, vol. 1 p. 57.

30. Guinevere L. Griest. *Mudie's Circulating Library and the Victorian Novel* (David and Charles, Newton Abbot, 1970), p. 21.

31. See above, pp. 57–8.

32. Bonham-Carter, *Authors by Profession*, vol. 1, pp. 119–65.

33. Ralph Straus, *Robert Dodsley* (London, 1910), pp. 260–4.

34. For a general study, see Linda Marie Fritschner. 'Publishers' readers, publishers, and their authors'. *PH*, 7 (1980), pp. 45–100.

35. Gettman, *A Victorian Publisher*, pp. 194–230.

36. Simon Nowell-Smith (ed.). *Letters to Macmillan* (Macmillan, London, 1967), p. 161.

37. Gettman, *A Victorian Publisher*, pp. 204–5.

38. Charles Morgan. *The House of Macmillan (1843–1943)* (Macmillan, London, 1943), pp. 87–100; Nowell-Smith, *Letters to Macmillan*, pp. 129–30.

39. See James Hepburn, *The Author's Empty Purse and the Rise of the Literary Agent* (Oxford University Press, London, 1968), pp. 45–66.

40. Frederic Whyte. *William Heinemann* (Jonathan Cape, London, 1928), pp. 122–3.

41. Nowell-Smith, *Letters to Macmillan*, p. 277.

42. See Bonham-Carter, *Authors by Profession*, vol. 1, pp. 180–2.

Part Four: The Trade in the Twentieth Century

Chapter 16

1. G.A. Cranfield. *The Press and Society from Caxton to Northcliffe* (Longman, London, 1978), pp. 204–21.

2. For the decline of *The Times* at the end of the nineteenth century, see Oliver Woods and James Bishop. *The Story of 'The Times'* (Michael Joseph, London, 1983), pp. 183–8.

3. *The History of 'The Times'. The Twentieth Century Test 1884–1912* (*The Times*, London, 1947), pp. 443–4.

4. For these American developments, see John Tebbel. *A History of Book Publishing in the United States*. 3 vols. (Bowker, New York, 1972–8), vol. 2, pp. 109–12, 150–70.

5. Most of what has been written about the 'Book War', as it came to be known, is by the participants or others in the trade. An exception and the most objective account is that by Russi Jal Taraporevala. *Competition and its Control in the British Book Trade 1850–1939* (D.B. Taraporevala, Bombay, 1969), pp. 74–80.

6. *The History of 'The Times'*, pp. 448–9.

7. R.J.L. Kingsford. *The Publishers' Association 1896–1946* (Cambridge University Press, Cambridge, 1970), p. 24.

8. Edward Bell's account forms the substance of the relevant section of Sir Frederick Macmillan. *The Net Book Agreement 1899 and the Book War 1906–1908* (The Author, Glasgow, 1924).

9. Macmillan, *The Net Book Agreement*, pp. 39–45.

10. Ibid., p. 49.

11. Kingsford, *The Publishers' Association*, pp. 33–34.

12. *History of 'The Times'*, pp. 509–72; and Paul Ferris. *The House of Northcliffe* (Weidenfeld and Nicolson, London, 1971), pp. 145–8.

13. Kingsford, *The Publishers' Association*, pp. 34–5.

14. Taraporevala, *Competition and its Control*, p. 56.

15. Ibid., pp. 57, 59–60.

16. The phrase is normally used at the head of the publisher's invoice to the bookseller, or printed in his catalogue, and therefore forms part of the contract between them.

17. For a general account, see Taraporevala, *Competition and its Control*, pp. 149–69.

18. W.A. Munford. *Penny Rate. Aspects of British Public Library History 1850–1950* (The Library Association, London, 1951), pp. 23–30, 113–21.

19. Sir Stanley Unwin. *The Truth About a Publisher* (Allen and Unwin, London, 1960), p. 165.

20. Geoffrey Faber. *A Publisher Speaking* (Faber and Faber, London, 1935), p. 80.

21. Peter Mann. *From Author to Reader. A Social Study of Books* (Routledge and Kegan Paul, London, 1982), p. 98.

22. Tebbel, *History*, vol. 3, pp. 6, 182.

23. Ibid., pp. 287–95.

24. For these early clubs, see Paul Kaufman. 'English book clubs and

their role in social history', *Libri*, 14 (1964–5), pp. 1–31.

25. Kingsford, *The Publishers' Association*, p. 134.

26. George G. Harrap. *Some Memories 1901–1935* (Harrap, London, 1935), pp. 124–5.

27. Taraporevala, *Competition and its Control*, p. 179.

28. Sheila Hodges. *Gollancz. The Story of a Publishing House 1928–1978* (Gollancz, London, 1978), pp. 117–43. See also below, pp. 200–1.

29. Kingsford, *The Publishers' Association*, p. 137.

30. Michael S. Howard. *Jonathan Cape, Publisher* (Jonathan Cape, London, 1971), p. 165.

31. Printed in Taraporevala, *Competition and its Control*, pp. 237–41.

32. Printed in G.R. Davies (ed.). *Trade Reference Book*. 4th edn (Booksellers' Association, London, 1979), pp. 89–97.

33. Charles Wilson. *First With the News. The History of W.H. Smith 1792–1972* (Jonathan Cape, London, 1985), pp. 422–5.

34. See below, pp. 214–18.

35. Printed in Davies, *Trade Reference Book*, p. 5.

36. There is a complete transcript of the proceedings, on which this brief summary is based, in R.E. Barker and G.R. Davies (eds). *Books Are Different. An Account of the Defence of the Net Book Agreement* (Macmillan, London, 1966).

37. Ibid., pp. 3–38.

38. Ibid., p. 35.

39. Ibid., p. 4.

40. See above, n. 32.

41. Peter J. Curwen. *The U.K. Publishing Industry* (Pergamon, Oxford, 1981), pp. 84–5.

42. Kingsford, *The Publishers' Association*, p. 95.

43. Ian Norrie. *Mumby's Publishing and Bookselling in the Twentieth Century*. 6th edn (Bell and Hyman, London, 1982), p. 177.

44. See Davies, *Trade Reference Book*, pp. 54–5.

Chapter 17

1. See above, pp. 190–1.

2. F.A. Mumby and Frances H.S. Stallybrass. *From Swan Sonnenschein to George Allen and Unwin Ltd.* (Allen and Unwin, London, 1935), p. 79.

3. H.H. Bemrose. *The House of Bemrose 1826–1926* (Bemrose, Derby, 1926), pp. 101–3.

4. Arthur Waugh. *A Hundred Years of Publishing. Being the Story of Chapman & Hall Ltd.* (Chapman and Hall, London, 1930), pp. 203–6.

5. For production figures, see Ian Norrie. *Mumby's Publishing and Bookselling in the Twentieth Century*. 6th edn (Bell and Hyman, London, 1982), p. 220.

6. Edward Liveing. *Adventure in Publishing. The House of Ward Lock 1854–1954* (Ward Lock, London, 1954), pp. 77–80, 93.

7. Ibid., pp. 91–2.

8. Ibid., p. 69.

9. H.R. Dent (ed.). *The House of Dent 1888–1938* (Dent, London,

1938), p. 123.

10. Norrie, *Mumby's Publishing and Bookselling*, p. 56.

11. Dent, *House of Dent*, pp. 127–31, 139.

12. Peter Sutcliffe. *The Oxford University Press. An Informal History* (Clarendon Press, Oxford, 1978), pp. 140–4. For Richards's failure, see Grant Richards. *Author Hunting* (Hamish Hamilton, London, 1934), pp. 101–5.

13. Waugh, *A Hundred Years*, pp. 197–201.

14. J.D. Newth. *Adam and Charles Black 1807–1957* (A. & C. Black, London, 1957), pp. 56–61, 64–9; and Harvey Einbinder. *The Myth of the 'Britannica'* (MacGibbon and Kee, London, 1964), pp. 43–5.

15. Waugh, *A Hundred Years*, pp. 208–16.

16. Newth, *Adam and Charles Black*, pp. 70–81.

17. R.J.L. Kingsford. *The Publishers' Association 1896–1946* (Cambridge University Press, Cambridge, 1970), pp. 52–7.

18. Newth, *Adam and Charles Black*, p. 91.

19. Hector Bolitho (ed.). *A Batsford Century. The Record of a Hundred Years of Publishing and Bookselling 1843–1943* (Batsford, London, 1943), p. 52.

20. Philip Unwin. *The Publishing Unwins* (Heinemann, London, 1972), p. 66.

21. John Attenborough. *A Living Memory. Hodder and Stoughton Publishers, 1868–1975* (Hodder and Stoughton, London, 1975), pp. 81–2.

22. See above, p. 191.

23. Patricia Perelli. 'Statistical survey of the British film industry', in James Curran and Vincent Porter (eds). *British Cinema History* (Weidenfeld and Nicolson, London, 1983), pp. 372, 375.

24. See below, p. 222.

25. Asa Briggs. *The History of Broadcasting in the United Kingdom*. Vols. 1– (Oxford University Press, London, 1965–   ), vol. 2, p. 253.

26. Victor Bonham-Carter. *Authors by Profession*. 2 vols. (Society of Authors/Bodley Head, London, 1978–84), vol. 2, pp. 205–12.

27. Kingsford, *The Publishers' Association*, pp. 124–5.

28. Bonham-Carter, *Authors by Profession*, vol. 2, pp. 258–9.

29. Ibid., vol. 2, p. 256.

30. For a full account of 'rights ' from the publisher's point of view see Sir Stanley Unwin. *The Truth About Publishing*. 8th edn, rev. by Philip Unwin. (Allen and Unwin, London, 1976), pp. 171–95.

31. Philip Unwin. *The Printing Unwins. A Short History of Unwin Brothers, The Gresham Press, 1826–1926* (Allen and Unwin, London, 1976).

32. Unwin, *The Publishing Unwins*, pp. 40–4.

33. Ibid., pp. 57–61.

34. Mumby and Stallybrass, *From Swan Sonnenschein*, pp. 55–63, 75.

35. Ibid., pp. 25–7.

36. Ibid., pp. 83–4; Unwin, *The Publishing Unwins*, pp. 62–4.

37. Ibid., p. 70.

38. Ibid., p. 90.

39. Ruth Dudley Edwards. *Victor Gollancz. A Biography* (Gollancz, London, 1987), pp. 142–59; and Sheila Hodges. *Gollancz. The Story of a Publishing House 1928–1978* (Gollancz, London, 1978), pp. 16–17.

40. Norrie, *Mumby's Publishing and Bookselling*, p. 220.

41. Attenborough, *A Living Memory*, p. 122.

42. The history of the Left Book Club is still a controversial issue. The 'official' version, is John Lewis. *The Left Book Club. An Historical Record* (Gollancz, London, 1970), but that certainly plays down the extent of communist influence. The version in Hodges, *Gollancz*, pp. 117–43, is written by a woman who was left to mind the shop while Gollancz himself pursued the Club and other interests both before and after World War II. The account in Edwards, *Victor Gollancz*, pp. 194–329, has the merit of immense factual detail, and a more objective approach to some of the political issues which are raised by the history of the Club.

43. See above, p. 141.

44. Hodges, *Gollancz*, p. 39.

45. Ibid., pp. 39–42.

46. Nicolas Barker. *Stanley Morison* (Macmillan, London, 1972), p. 238.

47. Hodges, *Gollancz*, pp. 50–1.

48. Michael S. Howard. *Jonathan Cape, Publisher* (Jonathan Cape, London, 1971), p. 42.

49. Norrie, *Mumby's Publishing and Bookselling*, p. 59; and for Warburg himself, see Frederic Warburg. *An Occupation for Gentlemen* (Hutchinson, London, 1959); and George Malcolm Thomson. *Martin Secker & Warburg. The First Fifty Years* (Secker and Warburg, London, 1986).

50. Norrie, *Mumby's Publishing and Bookselling*, pp. 63–4.

51. Richard Joseph. *Michael Joseph. Master of Words*. (Ashford Press, Southampton, 1986), pp. 103–26.

52. Edwards, *Victor Gollancz*, p. 196–7.

53. Joseph, *Michael Joseph*, p. 134.

54. Ibid., pp. 142–4.

55. Waugh, *A Hundred Years*, pp. 252, 273–4.

56. Norrie, *Mumby's Publishing and Bookselling*, p. 54.

57. Dent, *House of Dent*, p. 143.

58. Simon Nowell-Smith. *The House of Cassell 1848–1958* (Cassell, London, 1958), pp. 211–12. For the Berrys, see Viscount Camrose. *British Newspapers and Their Controllers* (Cassell, London, 1947), pp. 26–36, 65–72.

59. See above, pp. 173–4.

60. Charles Morgan. *The House of Macmillan (1843–1943)* (Macmillan, London, 1943), pp. 82–3, 163–5.

61. Peter Sutcliffe. *The Oxford University Press. An Informal History* (Clarendon Press, Oxford, 1978), pp. 89–91.

62. Liveing, *Adventure in Publishing*, p. 55.

63. Newth, *Adam & Charles Black*, pp. 61–2.

64. Morgan, *House of Macmillan*, pp. 165–6.

65. Roy Yglesias. 'Education and publishing in transition', in Asa Briggs (ed.). *Essays in the History of Publishing* (Longman, London, 1974), p. 375.

66. Morgan, *House of Macmillan*, pp. 185–9.

67. Sutcliffe, *Oxford University Press*, pp. 200–2.

Chapter 18

1. David Foxon, 'Stitched books', *BC*, 24 (1975), pp. 111–24.

2. See above, pp. 172–3.

3. Hans Schmoller. 'The paperback revolution', in Asa Briggs (ed.). *Essays in the History of Publishing* (Longman, London, 1974), pp. 296–7; and John Tebbel. *A History of Book Publishing in the United States*. 3 vols. (Bowker, New York, 1972–8), vol. 3, pp. 201–14.

4. See above, pp. 117–18.

5. See above, p. 136.

6. See above, pp. 194–5.

7. See John Ryder. *The Bodley Head 1857–1957* (Bodley Head, London, 1970) for a history of the firm.

8. J.E. Morpurgo. *Allen Lane. King Penguin* (Hutchinson, London, 1979), p. 17.

9. Ibid., pp. 75–8; and Donald Thomas. *A Long Time Burning* (Routledge and Kegan Paul, London, 1969), p. 303. For the earlier history of *Ulysses*, see Noel Riley Fitch. *Sylvia Beach and the Lost Generation* (Souvenir Press, London, 1984), pp. 115–40.

10. See, for example, Sir Allen Lane. 'Paper-bound books', in John Hampden (ed.). *The Book World Today* (Allen and Unwin, London, 1957), p. 101.

11. Schmoller, 'The paperback revolution', pp. 293–4.

12. Ibid., p. 299.

13. Michael S. Howard. *Jonathan Cape, Publisher* (Jonathan Cape, London, 1971), pp. 164–5.

14. Sir Stanley Unwin. *The Truth About Publishing*. 8th edn, rev. by Philip Unwin (Allen and Unwin, London, 1976), p. 241.

15. Ruth Dudley Edwards. *Victor Gollancz. A Biography* (Gollancz, London, 1987), p. 365.

16. Sheila Hodges. *Gollancz. The Story of a Publishing House 1928–1978* (Gollancz, London, 1978), pp. 50–4.

17. Schmoller, 'The paperback revolution', pp. 298–300.

18. Ibid., p. 299.

19. Morpurgo, *Allen Lane*, pp. 92–4.

20. See Piet Schreuders. *The Book of Paperbacks. A Visual History of the Paperback*. Tr. by Josh Pachter (Virgin, London, 1981), pp. 31–6. For an American view of the importance of pictorial covers, see Lewis A. Coser, Charles Kadushin and Walter W. Powell. *Books. The Culture and Commerce of Publishing* (Basic Books, New York, 1982), pp. 218–20.

21. Ian Norrie. *Mumby's Publishing and Bookselling in the Twentieth Century*. 6th edn (Bell and Hyman, London, 1982), p. 160.

22. Morpurgo, *Allen Lane*, pp. 343–4.

23. Tebbel, *History*, vol. 3, pp. 508–10.

24. Morpurgo, *Allen Lane*, p. 183.

25. Norrie, *Mumby's Publishing and Bookselling*, p. 90.

26. John Attenborough. *A Living Memory. Hodder and Stoughton Publishers, 1868–1975* (Hodder and Stoughton, London, 1975), pp. 150–1.

27. Anthony Blond. *The Publishing Game* (Jonathan Cape, London, 1971), pp. 84–5.

28. Ibid., p. 87.

29. Morpurgo, *Allen Lane*, p. 362.

30. Peter Sutcliffe. *The Oxford University Press. An Informal History* (Clarendon Press, Oxford, 1978), pp. 273–4.

31. Publishers' Association. *Quarterly Statistical Bulletin. June 1986* (Publishers' Association, London, 1986), p. 40.

32. See below, p. 218.

33. Price Commission. *Prices, Costs and Margins in the Publishing, Printing and Binding, and Distribution of Books* (HMSO [HC 527 (1978)], London, 1979), p. 36.

34. Peter H. Mann. *Book Publishing, Book Selling and Book Reading* (Book Marketing Council, London, 1979), p. 17.

Chapter 19

1. Sir Stanley Unwin. *The Truth About a Publisher* (Allen and Unwin, London, 1960), pp. 260–1, 272.

2. Michael S. Howard. *Jonathan Cape, Publisher* (Jonathan Cape, London, 1971), pp. 190–1.

3. Ian Norrie. *Mumby's Publishing and Bookselling in the Twentieth Century*. 6th edn (Bell and Hyman, London, 1982), p. 220.

4. Peter Sutcliffe. *The Oxford University Press. An Informal History* (Clarendon Press, Oxford, 1978), p. 256.

5. Norrie, *Mumby's Publishing and Bookselling*, p. 221.

6. For the wartime problems encountered by a major papermaker, see Joan Evans. *The Endless Web. John Dickinson & Co. 1804–1954* (Jonathan Cape, London, 1955), pp. 213–21.

7. R.J.L. Kingsford. *The Publishers' Association 1896–1946* (Cambridge University Press, Cambridge, 1970), pp. 162–3.

8. Hugh Barty-King. *Her Majesty's Stationery Office. The Story of the First 200 Years 1786–1986* (HMSO, London, 1986), pp. 76–7.

9. J.E. Morpurgo. *Allen Lane. King Penguin* (Hutchinson, London, 1979), pp. 156–7.

10. Kingsford, *The Publishers' Association*, pp. 165–6, 168–70.

11. Ibid., p. 171.

12. Unwin, *Truth About a Publisher*, pp. 267–8.

13. See below, p. 217.

14. Unwin, *Truth About a Publisher*, pp. 278–9.

15. Philip Unwin. *The Publishing Unwins* (Heinemann, London, 1972), p. 121.

16. Edward Liveing. *Adventure in Publishing. The House of Ward Lock 1854–1954* (Ward Lock, London, 1954), pp. 98–9.

17. Norrie, *Mumby's Publishing and Bookselling*, p. 88.

18. Hector Bolitho. *A Batsford Century. The Record of a Hundred Years of Publishing and Bookselling 1843–1943* (Batsford, London, 1943), pp. 90–3.

19. Charles Morgan. *The House of Macmillan (1843–1943)* (Macmillan, London, 1943), pp. 236–8.

20. Philip Unwin. *The Stationers' Company 1918–1977. A Livery Company in the Modern World* (Benn, London, 1978), pp. 43–5.

21. Norrie, *Mumby's Publishing and Bookselling*, pp. 91–92.

22. Richard Joseph. *Michael Joseph. Master of Words* (Ashford Press, Southampton, 1986), p. 157.

23. Unwin, *The Publishing Unwins*, p. 138.

24. Ibid., p. 139.

25. Kingsford, *The Publishers' Association*, pp. 167–8.

26. Norrie, *Mumby's Publishing and Bookselling*, p. 220.

27. See above, pp. 209–10.

28. Asa Briggs. *The History of Broadcasting in the United Kingdom.* Vols. 1– (Oxford University Press, London, 1965–), vol. 4, pp. 198, 252–3.

29. Norrie, *Mumby's Publishing and Bookselling*, pp. 96–7.

30. See Arthur Coleridge. 'Wholesale bookselling', in John Hampden (ed.). *The Book World Today* (Allen and Unwin, London, 1957), pp. 151–6.

31. For the trade's own views, see Book Trade Working Party. *Report and Recommendations* (Book Trade Working Party, London, 1972), pp. 14–15. For some of the arrangements which have been developed, see Publishers' Association. *Book Distribution. A Handbook for Booksellers and Publishers.* 2nd edn (Publishers' Association, London, 1972).

32. Peter J. Curwen. *The UK Publishing Industry* (Pergamon, Oxford, 1981), pp. 73–5.

33. See Kirsten Schlesinger. 'Suppliers' delivery times: can booksellers ever hope for better distribution?', *Bookseller*, no. 4168 (9 Nov. 1982), pp. 1932–42.

34. Leisure Consultants. *Annual Leisure Review, 1982* (Leisure Consultants, Sudbury, 1982), p. 41.

35. Ibid., p. 13.

36. Peter H. Mann. *Book Publishing, Book Selling and Book Reading* (Book Marketing Council, London, 1979), pp. 5–6, 21–2, 24.

37. Curwen, *The UK Publishing Industry*, pp. 79–81.

38. Norrie, *Mumby's Publishing and Bookselling*, p. 220.

39. Publishers' Association. *Quarterly Statistical Bulletin. June 1986* (Publishers' Association, London, 1986), p. 49.

40. See above, pp. 202–4.

41. Sutcliffe, *Oxford University Press*, p. 268.

42. See S.I.A. Kotei. *The Book Today in Africa* (Unesco, Paris, 1981), pp. 87–100.

43. John Attenborough. *A Living Memory. Hodder and Stoughton Publishers, 1868–1975* (Hodder and Stoughton, London, 1975), pp. 173–6.

44. See Sir Stanley Unwin. *The Truth About Publishing.* 8th edn., rev. by Philip Unwin (Allen and Unwin, London, 1976), pp. 140–1.

45. Curwen, *The UK Publishing Industry*, pp. 75–6.

46. Publishers' Association, *Quarterly statistical bulletin, June 1986*, p. 35.

47. Norrie, *Mumby's Publishing and Bookselling*, p. 223.

48. See above, p. 191.

49. See the statistics in Clive Bradley. 'Publishing: a vital national and international asset', *JRSA*, 130 (1981–2), pp. 376–93.

50. See, for a detailed example, Educational Publishers' Council. *Schoolbook Spending Series 2. The West Midlands* (Publishers' Association,

London, 1982), which shows a decline of 13 per cent in the primary sector and 16 per cent in the secondary sector between 1978/9 and 1982/3. For a national overview, see British Educational Equipment Association. *Expenditure on Teaching Materials, Schoolbooks, Equipment and Stationery 1978/79–1982/83* (Publishers' Association, London, 1984).

51. National Book Committee. *Public Library Spending in England and Wales* (National Book League, London, 1983). For a very detailed analysis, see LIBTRAD. *Library Book Funds 1980/81* (Grasshopper Press, Fenstanton, 1982), and subsequent annual reviews.

52. Norrie, *Mumby's Publishing and Bookselling*, pp. 169–70.

53. Charles Wilson. *First With the News. The History of W.H. Smith 1792–1972* (Jonathan Cape, London, 1985), pp. 422–5.

54. See F.T. Bell. 'The library supplier', in Raymond Astbury (ed.). *Libraries and the Book Trade* (Bingley, London, 1968), pp. 149–62.

55. Book Trade Working Party, *Report and Recommendations*, pp. 20–3.

56. Booksellers' Association Charter Group. *Economic Survey 1978–79* (Booksellers' Association, London, 1980), p. 2.

57. See above, pp. 202–3.

58. This paragraph is heavily indebted to Lamata Mitchell. 'Mergers and Takeovers in the British Publishing Industry 1970–1986' (Loughborough University MA thesis, 1986), pp. 4–16.

59. Lewis A. Coser, Charles Kadushin and Walter W. Powell. *Books. The Culture and Commerce of Publishing* (Basic Books, New York, 1982), pp. 135–47.

60. See above, pp. 156–7.

61. For an example, see J.A. Sutherland. *Fiction and the Fiction Industry* (Athlone Press, London, 1978), pp. 63–83.

Bibliography

Adams, Thomas R. 'The British pamphlet press and the American controversy, 1764–1783'. *PAAS*, 89 (1979), pp. 33–88.

Adamson, J.W. *English Education 1789–1902* (Cambridge University Press, Cambridge, 1930).

Adburgham, Alison. *Women in Print* (Allen and Unwin, London, 1972).

Alden, John. 'Pills and publishing: some notes on the English book trade', *Libr.*, 5th ser., 7 (1952), pp. 21–37.

Allen, Walter. *The English Novel* (Phoenix House, London, 1954).

Allison, A.F. and Rogers, D.M. *A Catalogue of Catholic Books in English Printed Abroad or Secretly in England 1558–1640* (Catholic Record Society, Biographical Studies 3:3,4, Bognor Regis, 1956).

Alston, R.C. 'The eighteenth-century non-book. Observations on printed ephemera', in Giles Barber and Bernhard Fabian (eds). *Buch und Buchhandel in Europa im achtzehnten Jahrhundert* (Hauswedell, Hamburg, 1981), pp. 343–60.

Altick, Richard D. *The English Common Reader. A Social History of the Mass Reading Public* (University of Chicago Press, Chicago, Ill., 1963).

Anders, H. 'The Elizabethan *ABC* with The Catechism', *Libr.*, 4th ser., 16 (1935–6), pp. 32–48.

Anderson, R.D. *Education and Opportunity in Victorian Scotland* (Clarendon Press, Oxford, 1983).

Annan, Noel. *Leslie Stephen. The Godless Victorian* (Weidenfeld and Nicolson, London, 1984).

Arber, Edward. *Transcript of the Registers of the Company of Stationers of London (1554–1640)*. 5 vols. (The Editor, Birmingham, 1875–94).

Armstrong, Elizabeth. 'English purchases of printed books from the continent 1465 to 1526', *EHR*, 94 (1979), pp. 268–90.

Armytage, W.H.G. *Four Hundred Years of English Education*. 2nd edn (Cambridge University Press, Cambridge, 1970).

Aspinall, A. 'The reporting and publishing of the House of Commons' debates 1771–1834', in Richard Pares and A.J.P. Taylor (eds). *Essays Presented to Sir Lewis Namier* (Macmillan, London, 1956), pp. 227–57.

Astbury, Raymond. 'The renewal of the Licensing Act in 1693 and its lapse in 1695', *Libr.*, 5th ser., 33 (1978), pp. 291–322.

Attenborough, John. *A Living Memory. Hodder and Stoughton Publishers, 1868–1975* (Hodder and Stoughton, London, 1975).

Avis, Frederick C, 'Book smuggling into England during the sixteenth century', *GJ*, 1972, pp. 180–7.

—— 'An enquiry into English privilege printing, 1582', *GJ*, 1975, pp. 150–5.

Baker, Joseph Ellis. *The Novel and the Oxford Movement* (Princeton University Press, Princeton, N.J., 1932).

Bald, R.C. 'Early copyright litigation and its bibliographical interest', *PBSA*, 36 (1942), pp. 81–96.

Ball, Douglas. *Victorian Publishers' Bindings* (The Library Association,

London, 1985).

Balston, Thomas. *James Whatman, Father and Son* (Methuen, London, 1957).

Barber, Giles. 'Books from the old world and for the new: the British international trade in books in the eighteenth century', *SVEC*, 151 (1976), pp. 185–224.

—— 'Galignani and the publication of English books in France, 1800–1852', *Libr.*, 5th ser., 16 (1961), pp. 267–84.

Barker, Nicolas. 'The St Albans press: the first punch-cutter in England and the first native typefounder?', *TCBS*, 7 (1979), pp. 257–78.

—— *Stanley Morison* (Macmillan, London, 1972).

Barker, R.E. and Davies, G.R. (eds). *Books Are Different. An Account of the Defence of the Net Book Agreement* (Macmillan, London, 1966).

Barnes, James J. *Authors, Publishers and Politicians* (Routledge and Kegan Paul, London, 1974).

—— *Free Trade in Books. A Study of the London Book Trade Since 1800* (Clarendon Press, Oxford, 1964).

Barty-King, Hugh. *Her Majesty's Stationery Office. The Story of the First 200 Years 1786–1986* (HMSO, London, 1986).

Batdorf, Franklin P. 'The Murray reprints of George Crabbe: a publisher's record', *SB*, 4 (1951), pp. 192–9.

Bate, W. Jackson. *Samuel Johnson* (Chatto and Windus, London, 1978).

—— and Strauss, Albrecht B. (eds). *The Rambler* (Yale University Press, *The Yale Edition of the Works of Samuel Johnson*, vol. 3, New Haven, Conn., 1969).

Belanger, Terry. 'Booksellers' trade sales, 1718–1768', *Libr.*, 5th ser., 30 (1975), pp. 281–302.

Belcher, William F. 'The sale and distribution of *The British Apollo*', in Richmond P. Bond (ed.). *Studies in the Early English Periodical* (University of North Carolina Press, Chapel Hill, N.C., 1957), pp. 73–101.

Bell, F.T. 'The library supplier', in Raymond Astbury (ed.). *Libraries and the Book Trade* (Bingley, London, 1968), pp. 149–62.

Bell, H.E. 'The price of books in mediéval England', *Libr.*, 4th ser., 17 (1936–7), pp. 311–32.

Bemrose, H.H. *The House of Bemrose 1826–1926* (Bemrose, Derby, 1926).

Bennett, H.S. *English Books & Readers 1475 to 1557*. 2nd edn (Cambridge University Press, Cambridge, 1969).

—— *English Books & Readers 1558 to 1603* (Cambridge University Press, Cambridge, 1965).

—— *English Books & Readers 1603 to 1640* (Cambridge University Press, Cambridge, 1970).

—— 'The production and dissemination of vernacular manuscripts in the fifteenth century', *Libr.*, 5th ser., 1 (1946–7), pp. 167–78.

Bennett, Scott. 'John Murray's Family Library and the cheapening of books in early nineteenth century Britain', *SB*, 29 (1976), pp. 138–66.

Bentley, G.E., Jr. 'Copyright documents in the George Robinson archive: William Godwin and others 1713–1820', *SB*, 35 (1982), pp. 67–110.

Bentley, Gerald Eades. *The Profession of Dramatist in Shakespeare's Time*

1590–1642 (Princeton University Press, Princeton, N.J., 1971).

Birn, Raymond. 'Le *Journal des savants* sous l'Ancien Régime', *Journal des Savants* (1965), pp. 15–35.

Black, M.H. *Cambridge University Press 1584–1984* (Cambridge University Press, Cambridge, 1984).

Blackie, Agnes A.C. *Blackie & Son 1809–1959* (Blackie, Glasgow, 1959).

Blagden, Cyprian. 'Booksellers' trade sales 1718–1768', *Libr.*, 5th ser., 5 (1950–1), pp. 243–57.

—— 'The "Company" of Printers', *SB*, 13 (1960), pp. 1–15.

—— 'The distribution of almanacs in the second half of the seventeenth century', *SB*, 11 (1958), pp. 107–16.

—— 'The English Stock of the Stationers' Company. An account of its origins', *Libr.*, 5th ser., 10 (1955), pp. 163–85.

—— 'The English Stock of the Stationers' Company in the time of the Stuarts', *Libr.*, 5th ser., 12 (1957), pp. 167–86.

—— 'Notes on the ballad market in the second half of the seventeenth century', *SB*, 6 (1954), pp. 161–80.

—— *The Stationers' Company. A History, 1403–1959* (Allen and Unwin, London, 1960).

—— 'The Stationers' Company in the Civil War period', *Libr.*, 5th ser., 13 (1958), pp. 1–17.

—— 'Thomas Carnan and the almanack monopoly', *SB.*, 14 (1961), pp. 23–43.

Blake, N.F. 'Wynkyn de Worde: the early years', *GJ*, 1971, pp. 62–9.

—— 'Wynkyn de Worde: the later years', *GJ*, 1972, pp. 128–38.

Blakey, Dorothy. *The Minerva Press, 1790–1820* (The Bibliographical Society, London, 1939).

Blayney, Peter W.M. 'The prevalance of shared printing in the early seventeenth century', *PBSA*, 67 (1973), pp. 437–42.

Blond, Anthony. *The Publishing Game* (Jonathan Cape, London, 1971).

Bluhm, R.K. 'Henry Oldenburg, F.R.S. (*c*.1615–1677)', in Sir Harold Hartley. *The Royal Society. Its Origins and Founders* (Royal Society, London, 1960), pp. 183–97.

Bolitho, Hector (ed.). *A Batsford Century. The Record of a Hundred Years of Publishing and Bookselling 1843–1943* (Batsford, London, 1943).

Bond, Donald F. (ed.). *The Spectator.* 5 vols. (Clarendon Press, Oxford, 1965).

Bonham-Carter, Victor. *Authors by Profession.* 2 vols. (Society of Authors / Bodley Head, London, 1978–84).

Book Trade Working Party. *Report and Recommendations* (Book Trade Working Party, London, 1972).

Booksellers' Association Charter Group. *Economic Survey 1978–79* (Booksellers' Association, London, 1980).

Borsay, Peter. 'The English urban renaissance: the development of provincial urban culture *c*.1680–*c*.1760', *Soc. Hist.*, no. 5 (1977), pp. 581–603.

Bosanquet, E.F. *English Printed Almanacks and Prognostications. A Bibliographical History to the Year 1600* (The Bibliographical Society, London, 1917).

Bourgain, Pascale. 'L'édition des manuscrits', in Henri-Jean Martin and

Roger Chartier (eds). *Histoire de l'édition française*. 3 vols. (Promodis, Paris, 1982–85), vol. 1, pp. 48–75.

Bowen, James. *A History of Western Education. Vol. 3. The Modern West* (Methuen, London, 1981).

Brack, O M Jr. 'William Strahan: Scottish printer and publisher', *Ariz. Q.*, 31 (1975), pp. 179–91.

Bradley, Clive. 'Publishing: a vital national and international asset', *JRSA*, 130 (1981–2), pp. 376–93.

Briggs, Asa. 'Introduction: at the Sign of the Ship', in Asa Briggs (ed.). *Essays in the History of Publishing* (Longman, London, 1974), pp. 1–28.

—— *The History of Broadcasting in the United Kingdom*. Vols. 1– (Oxford University Press, London, 1965–).

British Educational Equipment Association. *Expenditure on Teaching Materials, Schoolbooks, Equipment and Stationery 1978/79–1982–83* (Publishers' Association, London, 1984).

Brittain, Vera. *Radclyffe Hall. A Case of Obscenity* (Femina Books, London, 1968).

Buck, John Dawson Carl. 'The motives of puffing: John Newbery's advertisements 1742–1767', *SB*, 30 (1977), pp. 196–210.

Bühler, Curt F. *William Caxton and his Critics* (Syracuse University Press, Syracuse, N.Y., 1960).

Butterfield, L.H. 'The American interests of the firm of E. and C. Dilly, with their letters to Benjamin Rush, 1770–1795', *PBSA*, 45 (1951), pp. 283–332.

Camrose, Viscount. *British Newspapers and Their Controllers* (Cassell, London, 1947).

Capp, Bernard. *Astrology and the Popular Press. English Almanacs 1500–1800* (Faber and Faber, London, 1979).

Carlson, C. Lennart. *The First Magazine. A History of 'The Gentleman's Magazine'* (Brown University Press, Providence, R.I., 1938), pp. 5–12.

Carter, Harry. *A History of the Oxford University Press. Vol. 1. To the Year 1780* (Clarendon Press, Oxford, 1975).

Carter, John, 'William Ged and the invention of stereotype', *BC*, 7 (1958), pp. 267–9.

—— 'William Ged and the invention of stereotype: a postscript', *Libr.*, 5th ser., 16 (1961), pp. 143–5.

Chilcott, Tim. *A Publisher and his Circle. The Life and Work of John Taylor, Keats's Publisher* (Routledge and Kegan Paul, London, 1972).

Child, John. *Industrial Relations in the British Printing Industry* (Allen and Unwin, London, 1967).

Clair, Colin. *A History of Printing in Britain* (Cassell, London, 1965).

Clapham, J.H. *An Economic History of Modern Britain*. 3 vols. (Cambridge University Press, Cambridge, 1926–38).

Clyde, W.M. 'Parliament and the press, 1643–7', *Libr.*, 4th ser., 13 (1932–3), pp. 399–424.

—— 'Parliament and the press, II', *Libr.*, 4th ser., 14 (1933–4), pp. 39–58.

Coleman, D.C. *The British Paper Industry 1495–1860* (Oxford University Press, Oxford, 1958).

Coleridge, Arthur. 'Wholesale bookselling', in John Hampden (ed.). *The Book World Today* (Allen and Unwin, London, 1957), pp. 151–6.

Collins, A.S. *Authorship in the Days of Johnson* (Routledge, London, 1927).

—— *The Profession of Letters. A Study of the Relation of Author to Patron, Publisher and Public, 1780–1832* (Routledge, London, 1928).

Comparato, Frank E. '"Old Thunderer's" American lightning. Machines and machinations in furnishing the first Hoe rotaries to *The Times*, 1856–60', *JPHS*, 13 (1978/9), pp. 27–63.

Corp, W.G. *Fifty Years. A Brief Account of the Associated Booksellers of Great Britain and Ireland 1895–1945* (Blackwells, Oxford, [1945]).

Corsten, Severin. 'Caxton in Cologne', *JPHS*, 11 (1976/7), pp. 1–18.

Coser, Lewis A. Charles Kadushin and Walter W. Powell. *Books. The Culture and Commerce of Publishing* (Basic Books, New York, 1982).

Cox, Harold and Chandler, John E. *The House of Longman* (Longman, London, 1925).

Crane, R.S. and Kaye, F.B. *A Census of British Newspapers and Periodicals 1620–1800* (University of North Carolina Press, Chapel Hill, N.C., 1927).

Cranfield, G.A. *The Development of the Provincial Newspaper 1700–1760* (Oxford University Press, Oxford, 1962).

—— *The Press and Society from Caxton to Northcliffe* (Longman, London, 1978).

Cressy, David. *Education in Tudor and Stuart England* (Edward Arnold, London, 1975).

—— *Literacy and the Social Order. Reading and Writing in Tudor and Stuart England* (Cambridge University Press, Cambridge, 1980).

Crist, Timothy. 'Government control of the press after the expiration of the Printing Act in 1679', *PH*, 5 (1979), pp. 49–77.

Cross, Wilbur L. *The History of Henry Fielding*. 3 vols. (Russell and Russell, New York, 1963).

Cruickshank, Marjorie. *Church and State in English Education* (Macmillan, London, 1944).

Cumbers, F. *The Book Room. The Story of The Methodist Publishing House and The Epworth Press* (Epworth Press, London, 1956).

Curwen, Henry. *A History of the Booksellers. The Old and New* (Chatto and Windus, London, 1873).

Curwen, Peter J. *The UK Publishing Industry* (Pergamon Oxford, 1981).

Darnton, Robert. *The Business of Enlightenment. A Publishing History of the 'Encyclopédie' 1775–1800* (Belknap Press, Cambridge, Mass., 1979).

Darton, F.J. Harvey. *Children's Books in England*. 3rd edn, rev. by Brian Alderson. (Cambridge University Press, Cambridge, 1982).

Davies, G.R. (ed.). *Trade Reference Book*. 4th edn (Booksellers' Association, London, 1979).

Davis, Lennart J. *Factual Fictions. The Origins of the English Novel* (Columbia University Press, New York, 1983).

de Hamel, Christopher. *Glossed Books of the Bible and the Origins of the Paris Book Trade* (Brewer, Cambridge, 1984).

Dempster, John A.H. 'Thomas Nelson and Sons in the late nineteenth century: a study in motivation. Part 1', *PH*, 13 (1983), pp. 41–87.

Dent, H.R. (ed.). *The House of Dent 1888–1938* (Dent, London, 1938).

Dickins, Bruce. 'Doctor James's Fever Powder', *Life and Letters*, 2 (1929), pp. 36–47.

Diehl, Edith. *Bookbinding. Its Background and Techniques*. 2 vols. Repr. (Hacker, New York, 1979).

Dixon, Diana. 'Children and the press, 1860–1914', in Michael Harris and Alan Lee (eds). *The Press in English Society from the Seventeenth to Nineteenth Centuries* (Associated University Presses, Cranbury, N.J., 1986), pp. 133–48.

Downie, J.A. 'The growth of government tolerance of the press to 1790', in Robin Myers and Michael Harris (eds). *Development of the English Book Trade* (Oxford Polytechnic Press, Oxford, 1981), pp. 36–65.

—— *Robert Harley and the Press* (Cambridge University Press, Cambridge, 1979).

Doyle, A.I. and Parkes, M.B. 'The production of copies of the *Canterbury Tales* and the *Confessio amantis* in the early fifteenth century', in M.B. Parkes and Andrew G. Watson (eds). *Medieval Scribes, Manuscripts & Libraries. Essays Presented to N.R. Ker* (Scolar Press, London, 1979), pp. 163–210.

Duff, E. Gordon. *A Century of the English Book Trade* (The Bibliographical Society, London, 1905).

Eade, Simon H. 'English Legal Printing, 1476–1550' (Loughborough University MLS thesis, 1982).

Educational Publishers' Council. *Schoolbook Spending Series 2. The West Midlands* (Publishers' Asssociation, London, 1982).

Edwards, A.S.G. 'Lydgate manuscripts: some directions for future research', in Derek Pearsall (ed.). *Manuscripts and Readers in Fifteenth-century England* (Brewer, Cambridge, 1983), pp. 15–26.

Edwards, Ruth Dudley. *Victor Gollancz. A Biography* (Gollancz, London, 1987).

Einbinder, Harvey. *The Myth of the 'Britannica'* (MacGibbon and Kee, London, 1964).

Eisenstein, Elizabeth L. *The Printing Press as an Agent of Change*. 2 vols. (Cambridge University Press, Cambridge, 1979).

Ellis, Aytoun. *The Penny Universities. A History of the Coffee-houses* (Secker and Warburg, London, 1956).

Evans, Joan. *The Endless Web. John Dickinson & Co. 1804–1954* (Jonathan Cape, London, 1955).

Ewing, Douglas C. 'The three-volume novel', *PBSA*, 61 (1967), pp. 201–7.

Faber, Geoffrey. *A Publisher Speaking* (Faber and Faber, London, 1935).

Fabian, Bernhard. 'The beginnings of English-language publishing in Germany in the eighteenth century', in Kenneth E. Carpenter (ed.). *Books and Society in History* (Bowker, New York, 1983), pp. 115–44.

—— 'English books and their eighteenth-century German readers', in Paul J. Korshin (ed.). *The Widening Circle* (University of Pennsylvania Press, Philadelphia, Pa., 1976), pp. 117–96.

Feather, John. 'The book trade in politics: the making of the Copyright Act of 1710', *PH*, 8 (1980), pp. 19–44.

—— 'British publishing in the eighteenth century: a preliminary subject analysis', *Libr.*, 6th ser., 8 (1986), pp. 32–46.

—— *English Book Prospectuses. An Illustrated History* (Bird and Bull Press, Newton, Pa., 1984).

—— 'The English book trade and the law 1695–1799', *PH*, 12 (1982), pp. 51–75.

—— 'From censorship to copyright: aspects of the government's role in the English book trade 1695–1775', in Kenneth E. Carpenter (ed.). *Books and Society in History* (Bowker, New York, 1983), pp. 173–81.

—— 'John Nourse and his authors', *SB*, 34 (1981), pp. 205–26.

—— 'John Walter and the Logographic Press', *PH*, 1 (1977), pp. 92–134.

—— 'The merchants of culture: bookselling in early industrial England', *SVEC*, 217 (1983), pp. 11–21.

—— *The Provincial Book Trade in Eighteenth-century England* (Cambridge University Press, Cambridge, 1985).

—— 'The publishers and the pirates: British copyright law in theory and practice 1710–1775', *PH*, 22 (1987), pp. 5–32.

Febvre, Lucien and Martin, Henri-Jean. *The Coming of the Book. The Impact of Printing 1450–1800.* Tr. by David Gerard (NLB, London, 1976).

Ferris, Paul. *The House of Northcliffe* (Weidenfeld and Nicolson, London, 1971).

Fitch, Noel Riley. *Sylvia Beach and the Lost Generation* (Souvenir Press, London, 1984).

Fleeman, J.D. 'The revenue of a writer: Samuel Johnson's literary earnings', in R.W. Hunt, I.G. Philip and R.J. Roberts (eds). *Studies in the Book Trade* (Oxford Bibliographical Society, Oxford, new ser., 18. 1975), pp. 211–30.

Fortescue, G.K. *Catalogue of the Pamphlets, Books, Newspapers and Manuscripts . . . Collected by G. Thomason 1640–1661.* 2 vols. (British Museum, London, 1908).

Foster, Dorothy. 'The earliest precursor of our present-day monthly miscellanies', *PMLA*, 32 (1917), pp. 22–58.

Foxon, David. *Libertine Literature in England 1660–1745* (The Book Collector, London, 1964).

—— 'Stitched books', *BC*, 24 (1975), pp. 111–24.

Frank, Joseph. *The Beginnings of the English Newspaper 1620–1660* (Harvard University Press, Cambridge, Mass., 1961).

Franklin, Benjamin. *Autobiography and Other Writings.* Ed. Russel B. Nye (Houghton Mifflin, Boston, Mass., 1958).

Fraser, Peter. *The Intelligence of the Secretaries of State and their Monopoly of Licensed News 1660–1698* (Cambridge University Press, Cambridge, 1956).

Friedman, Joan M. *Color Printing in England 1486–1870* (Yale Center for British Art, New Haven, Conn., 1978).

Fritschner, Linda Marie. 'Publishers' readers, publishers and their authors', *PH*, 7 (1980), pp. 45–100.

Gamzue, B.B. 'Elizabeth and literary patronage', *PMLA*, 49 (1943), pp. 1041–9.

Garside, Peter, 'Rob's last raid: Scott and the publication of the Waverley novels', in Robin Myers and Michael Harris (eds). *Author/*

Publisher Relations during the Eighteenth and Nineteenth Centuries (Oxford Polytechnic Press, Oxford, 1983), pp. 88–118.

Geduld, Harry M. *Prince of Publishers* (Indiana University Press, Bloomington, Ind., 1969).

Gérin, Winifred. *Elizabeth Gaskell* (Clarendon Press, Oxford, 1976).

Gerulaitas, Leonardas Vyantas. *Printing and Publishing in Fifteenth-century Venice* (Mansell, London, 1976).

Gettman, R.A. *A Victorian Publisher* (Cambridge University Press, Cambridge, 1960).

Gibson, Strickland. 'A bibliography of Francis Kirkman', *OBSP*, new ser., 1 (1947).

Goldschmidt, E. Ph. *Medieval Texts and their First Appearance in Print* (The Bibliographical Society, Suppl. to The Bibliographical Society's Transactions, 16, London, 1943).

Goldstrom, J.M. 'The correspondence between Lord John Russell and the publishing trade', *PH*, 20 (1986), pp. 5–59.

Graham, Walter. *English Literary Periodicals* (Nelson, London, 1930).

Greene, Donald. 'Samuel Johnson, journalist', in Donovan H. Bond and W. Reynolds McLeod (eds). *Newsletters to Newspapers: Eighteenth-century Journalism* (School of Journalism, West Virginia University, Morgantown, W.V., 1977), pp. 87–101.

Greg, W.W. *A Bibliography of the English Printed Drama to the Restoration.* 4 vols. (The Bibliographical Society, London, 1939–59).

—— *Some Aspects and Problems of London Publishing between 1550 and 1650* (Clarendon Press, Oxford, 1956).

—— and Boswell, E. (eds). *Records of the Court of the Stationers' Company 1576 to 1602 from Register B* (The Bibliographical Society, London, 1930).

Gregg, Pauline. *Free-born John. A Biography of John Lilburne* (Harrap, London, 1961).

Greist, Guinevere L. *Mudie's Circulating Library and the Victorian Novel* (David and Charles, Newton Abbot, 1970).

Grey, Jill. 'The Lilliputian Magazine — a pioneering periodical?', *J. Libr.*, 2 (1970), pp. 107–15.

Haass, Sabine. 'Victorian poetry anthologies: their role and success in the nineteenth-century book market', *PH*, 17 (1985), pp. 51–64.

Hamlyn, H.M. 'Eighteenth-century circulating libraries', *Libr.*, 5th ser., 1 (1947), pp. 197–222.

Handover, P.M. *A History of 'The London Gazette' 1665–1965* (HMSO, London, 1965).

Hanson, Laurence. *Government and the Press 1695–1763* (Clarendon Press, Oxford, 1936).

Harrap, George G. *Some Memories 1901–1935* (Harrap, London, 1935).

Harris, Elizabeth M. 'Experimental graphic processes in England 1800–1859', *JPHS*, 4 (1968), pp. 33–86; ibid., 5 (1969), pp. 41–80; and ibid., 6 (1970), pp. 53–89.

Harris, Michael. 'Journalism as a profession or trade in the eighteenth century', in Robin Myers and Michael Harris (eds.). *Author/Publisher Relations During the Eighteenth and Nineteenth Centuries* (Oxford Polytechnic Press, Oxford, 1983), pp. 37–62.

—— 'Periodicals and the book trade', in Robin Myers and Michael Harris (eds). *Development of the English Book Trade, 1700–1899* (Oxford Polytechnic Press, Oxford, 1981), pp. 66–94.

—— 'The structure, ownership and control of the press, 1620–1780', in George Boyce, James Curran and Pauline Wingate (eds). *Newspaper History from the Seventeenth Century to the Present Day* (Constable, London, 1978), pp. 82–97.

Harrison, Brian. *Drink and the Victorians. The Temperance Question in England 1815–1872* (Faber and Faber, London, 1971).

Hart, Horace. *Charles Earl Stanhope and the Oxford University Press*. Ed. James Mosley (Printing Historical Society, London, 1966).

Heawood, Edward. 'Sources of early English paper supply', *Libr.*, 4th ser., 10 (1929–30), pp. 282–307, 427–54.

Heckethorn, Charles W. *The Printers of Basle in the XV and XVI Centuries* (Fisher Unwin, London, 1897).

Hellinga, Lotte and Wytze. 'Caxton in the Low Countries', *JPHS*, 11 (1976/7), pp. 19–32.

Henderson, Heather. 'Carlyle and the book clubs: a new approach to publishing?', *PH*, 6 (1979), pp. 37–62.

Hepburn, James. *The Author's Empty Purse and the Rise of the Literary Agent* (Oxford University Press, London, 1968).

Herd, Harold. *The March of Journalism. The Story of the British Press from 1622 to the Present Day* (Allen and Unwin, London, 1952).

The History of 'The Times'. The Twentieth Century Test 1884–1912 (*The Times*, London, 1947).

Hodges, Sheila. *Gollancz. The Story of a Publishing House 1928–1978* (Gollancz, London, 1978).

Hodgson, Norma and Blagden, Cyprian. *The Notebook of Thomas Bennet and Henry Clements (1686–1719)* (Oxford Bibliographical Society, new ser., 6, Oxford, 1956).

Hoppe, Harry R. 'John Wolfe, printer and publisher, 1579–1601', *Libr.*, 4th ser., 14 (1933–4), pp. 241–88.

Howard, Michael S. *Jonathan Cape, Publisher* (Jonathan Cape, London, 1971).

Howe, Ellic. *The London Compositor* (The Bibliographical Society, London, 1947).

—— 'The Stationers' Company almanacks: a late eighteenth-century printing and publishing operation', in Giles Barber and Bernhard Fabian (eds). *Buch und Buchhandel in Europa im achtzehnten Jahrhundert* (Hauswedell, Hamburg, 1981), pp. 195–209.

—— and Waite, Harold E. *The London Society of Compositors. A Centenary History* (Cassell, London, 1948).

Hughes, Edward. 'The English Stamp Duties, 1664–1764, *EHR*, 56 (1941), pp. 234–64.

Hughes, Thomas. *Memoir of Daniel Macmillan* (Macmillan, London, 1882).

Humphreys, K.W. 'Distribution of books in the English West Midlands in the later middle ages', *Libri*, 17 (1967), pp. 1–12.

Hunnisett, Basil. *Steel-engraved Book Illustration in England* (Godine, Boston, Mass., 1980).

Hunter, Dard. *Papermaking. The History and Technique of an Ancient Craft.* 2nd edn (Knopf, New York, 1967).

Hunter, Jean E. *'The Lady's Magazine* and the study of Englishwomen in the eighteenth century', in Donovan H. Bond and W. Reynolds McLeod (eds). *Newsletters to Newspapers: Eighteenth-century Journalism* (School of Journalism, West Virginia University, Morgantown, W.V., 1977), pp. 103–17.

Isaac, P.C.G. (ed.). *Third Seminar on the British Book Trade. Report* (British Book Trade Index [Newcastle-upon-Tyne], 1985).

James, Elizabeth. 'An insight into the management of railway bookstalls in the eighteen fifties', *PH*, 10 (1981), pp. 65–9.

—— 'The publication of collected editions of Bulwer Lytton's novels', *PH*, 3 (1978), pp. 46–60.

James, Louis. *Fiction for the Working Man 1830–50* (Penguin University Books, Harmondsworth, 1974).

Johnson, A.F. 'The King's Printers, 1660–1742', *Libr.*, 5th ser., 3 (1949), pp. 33–8.

Johnson, Edgar. *Sir Walter Scott. The Great Unknown.* 2 vols. (Hamish Hamilton, London, 1970).

Johnson, Gerald D. 'John Trundle and the book-trade 1603–1626', *SB*, 39 (1986), pp. 177–99.

—— 'Nicholas Ling, publisher, 1580–1607', *SB*, 38 (1985), pp. 203–14.

Jones, Annabel. 'Disraeli's *Endymion*', in Asa Briggs (ed.). *Essays in the History of Publishing* (Longman, London, 1974), pp. 141–86.

Jones, Gerard E. (ed.). *The Covent-Garden Journal* (Yale University Press, New Haven, Conn., 1915).

Jones, H. Kay. *Butterworths. History of a Publishing House* (Butterworths, London, 1980).

Joseph, Richard. *Michael Joseph. Master of Words* (Ashford Press, Southampton, 1986).

Jusserand, J.J. *The English Novel in the Time of Shakespeare.* Tr. Elizabeth Lee. (Fisher Unwin, London, 1890).

Kaufman, Paul. 'The community library: a chapter in English social history', *TAAS*, 57:2 (1967).

—— 'English Book Clubs and Their Role in Social History', *Libri.*, 14 (1964–5), pp. 1–31.

Keir, David. *The House of Collins* (Collins, London, 1952).

Kelly, Thomas. *Early Public Libraries* (The Library Association, London, 1966).

Kenyon, Sir Frederic. *Books and Readers in Ancient Greece and Rome* (Clarendon Press, Oxford, 1932).

Ker, N.R. *Medieval Libraries of Great Britain.* 2nd edn (Royal Historical Society, London, 1964).

—— 'Oxford college libraries before 1500', in J. Ijsewijn and J. Paquet (eds). *The Universities in the Later Middle Ages* (Louvain University Press, Louvain, 1978), pp. 293–311.

Kerling, Nellie J.M. 'Caxton and the trade in printed books', *BC*, 4 (1955), pp. 190–9.

King, John N. *English Reformation Literature. The Tudor Origins of the Protestant Tradition* (Princeton University Press, Princeton, N.J., 1982).

Kingsford, R.J.L. *The Publishers' Association 1896–1946* (Cambridge University Press, Cambridge, 1970).

Kirschbaum, Leo. 'The copyright of Elizabethan plays', *Libr.*, 5th ser., 14 (1959), pp. 231–50.

Knapp, Lewis M. *Tobias Smollett. Doctor of Men and Manners* (Princeton University Press, Princeton, N.J., 1949).

Knight, Charles. *Passages of a Working Life*. 3 vols. (Bradbury and Evans, London, 1864–5).

Knowles, David. *The Religious Orders in England*. 3 vols. (Cambridge University Press, Cambridge, 1948–59).

—— and Hadock, R. Neville. *Medieval Religious Houses in England and Wales* (Longman, London, 1971).

Kotei, S.I.A. *The Book Today in Africa* (Unesco, Paris, 1981).

Kronick, David A. *A History of Scientific & Technical Periodicals. The Origin and Development of the Scientific and Technical Press 1665–1790* (Scarecrow, Metuchen, N.J., 1976).

—— 'Scientific journal publication in the eighteenth century', *PBSA*, 59 (1965), pp. 28–44.

Kuist, James M. '*The Gentleman's Magazine* in the Folger Library: the history and significance of the Nichols family collection', *SB*, (1976), pp. 307–22.

Lacqueur, Thomas. 'The cultural origins of popular literacy in England 1500–1850', *ORE*, 2 (1976), pp. 255–75.

Landon, Richard G. '"Small profits do great things": James Lackington and eighteenth-century bookselling', *SEEC*, 5 (1976), pp. 378–99.

Lane, Sir Allen. 'Paper-bound books', in John Hampden (ed.). *The Book World Today* (Allen and Unwin, London, 1957).

Lathrop, Henry B. *Translations from the Classics into English from Caxton to Chapman 1477–1610* (University of Wisconsin Press, Madison, Wis., 1932).

Lauterbach, Charles E. and Lauterbach, Edward S. 'The nineteenth century three-volume novel', *PBSA*, 51 (1957), pp. 263–302.

Laver, James. *Hatchards of Piccadilly 1797–1947* (Hatchards, London, 1947).

Lawlor, John. *Book Auctions in England in the Seventeenth Century* (Elliot Stock, London, 1898).

Lee, Alan J. *The Origins of the Popular Press in England 1855–1914* (Croom Helm, London, 1976).

Leisure Consultants. *Annual Leisure Review, 1982* (Leisure Consultants, Sudbury, 1982).

Lewis, John. *The Left Book Club. A Historical Record* (Gollancz, London, 1970).

LIBTRAD. *Library Book Funds 1980/81* (Grasshopper Press, Fenstanton, 1982).

Lievsay, John L. *The Englishman's Italian Books 1550–1700* (University of Pennsylvania Press, Philadelphia, Pa., 1969).

Lipson, E. *The Economic History of England*. 3 vols. 5th edn (A. & C. Black, London, 1929–48).

Liveing, Edward. *Adventure in Publishing. The House of Ward Lock 1854–1954* (Ward Lock, London, 1954).

Lucas, Peter J. 'The growth and development of English literary patronage in the later Middle Ages and the early Renaissance', *Libr.*, 6th ser., 4 (1982), pp. 218–48.

Lynch, Kathleen M. *Jacob Tonson, Kit-Kat Publisher* (University of Tennessee Press, Knoxville, Tenn., 1971).

McCusker, John J. 'The business press in England before 1775', *Libr.*, 6th ser., 8 (1986), pp. 205–31.

Macdonald, Hugh. *John Dryden. A bibliography of the Early Editions* (Clarendon Press, Oxford, 1939).

McKenzie, D.F. *The Cambridge University Press 1696–1712.* 2 vols. (Cambridge University Press, Cambridge, 1966).

—— *The London Book Trade in the Later Seventeenth Century* (Privately printed, Cambridge, 1976).

—— (ed.). *Stationers' Company Apprentices 1701–1800* (Oxford Bibliographical Society, new ser., 19, Oxford, 1978).

—— and Ross, J.C. (eds). *A Ledger of Charles Ackers* (Oxford Bibliographical Society, new ser., 15, Oxford, 1968).

McKerrow, R.B. *A Dictionary of the Printers and Booksellers in England, Scotland and Ireland, and of Foreign Printers of English Books, 1557–1640* (The Bibliographical Society, London, 1910).

McLaverty, J. 'Lawton Gilliver: Pope's bookseller', *SB*, 32 (1979), pp. 101–24.

—— *Pope's Printer, John Wright* (Oxford Bibliographical Society, occ. pub. 11, Oxford, 1976).

Macmillan, Sir Frederick. *The Net Book Agreement 1899 and The Book War 1906–1908* (The Author, Glasgow, 1924).

Maidment, B.E. 'Victorian publishing and social criticism: the case of Edward Jenkins', *PH*, 11 (1982), pp. 41–71.

Mann, Peter H. *Book Publishing, Book Selling and Book Reading* (Book Marketing Council, London, 1979).

—— *From Author to Reader. A Social Study of Books* (Routledge and Kegan Paul, London, 1982).

Manten, A.A. 'Development of European scientific journal publishing before 1850', in A.J. Meadows (ed.). *Development of Science Publishing in Europe* (Elsevier, Amsterdam, 1980), pp. 1–22.

Marchand, Leslie A. *Byron. A Biography.* 3 vols. (Knopf, New York, 1957).

Martin, J.W. 'The Marian regime's failure to understand the importance of printing', *HLQ*, 44 (1980–1), pp. 231–47.

Martin, Robert Bernard. *Tennyson. The Unquiet Heart* (Faber and Faber, London / Oxford University Press, Oxford, 1983).

Mason, Tony. 'Sporting news, 1860–1914', in Michael Harris and Alan Lee (eds). *The Press in English Society from the Seventeenth to Nineteenth Centuries* (Associated University Presses, Cranbury, N.J., 1986), pp. 168–86.

Mathews, H.F. *Methodism and the Education of the People, 1791–1851* (Epworth Press, London, 1949).

Matthews, Leslie H. *History of Pharmacy in Britain* (Livingstone, Edinburgh, 1962).

Maxted, Ian. *The London Book Trades, 1775–1800: a Topographical Guide*

(The Author, Exeter, 1980).

Mayo, Robert D. *The English Novel in the Magazines 1740–1815* (Northwestern University Press, Evanston, Ill., 1962).

Milic, Louis T. 'Tone in Steele's *Tatler*', in Donovan H. Bond and W. Reynolds McLeod (eds). *Newsletters to Newspapers: Eighteenth-century Journalism* (School of Journalism, West Virginia University, Morgantown, W.V., 1977), pp. 33–46.

Millburn, John R. '*Martin's Magazine: The General Magazine of Arts and Sciences*, 1755–65', *Libr.*, 5th ser., 28 (1973), pp. 221–39.

Miller, C. William. 'Henry Herringman, Restoration bookseller-publisher', *PBSA*, 42 (1948), pp. 292–306.

Miller, Edwin H. *The Professional Writer in Elizabethan England* (Harvard University Press, Cambridge, Mass., 1959).

Mitchell, Lamata. 'Mergers and Takeovers in the British Publishing Industry' (Loughborough University MA thesis, 1986).

Moran, James. *The Composition of Reading Matter* (Wace, London, 1965).

—— *Printing Presses* (University of California Press, Berkeley and Los Angeles, Calif., 1978).

Moran, Jo Ann Hoeppner. *The Growth of English Schooling 1340–1548* (Princeton University Press, Princeton, N.J., 1985).

Morgan, Charles. *The House of Macmillan (1843–1943)* (Macmillan, London, 1943).

Morison, Stanley. *John Bell, 1745–1831* (First Editions Club, London, 1930).

Morpurgo, J.E. *Allen Lane. King Penguin* (Hutchinson, London, 1979).

Moseley, C.W.R.D. 'The availability of *Mandeville's Travels* in England, 1356–1750', *Libr.*, 5th ser., 30 (1975), pp. 125–33.

Mumby, F.A. *The House of Routledge 1834–1934* (Routledge, London, 1934).

—— and Frances H.S. Stallybrass. *From Swan Sonnenschein to George Allen and Unwin Ltd.* (Allen and Unwin, London, 1935).

Munford, W.A. *Penny Rate. Aspects of British Public Library History 1850–1950* (The Library Association, London, 1951).

Murray, K.M. Elisabeth. *Caught in the Web of Words. James A.H. Murray and the Oxford English Dictionary* (Yale University Press, New Haven, Conn., 1977).

National Book Committee. *Public Library Spending in England and Wales* (National Book League, London, 1983).

Neuburg, Victor. 'The Diceys and the chapbook trade', *Libr.*, 5th ser., 24 (1969), pp. 219–31.

—— *Popular Literature* (Penguin, Harmondsworth, 1977).

Newth, J.D. *Adam and Charles Black 1807–1957* (A. & C. Black, London, 1957).

Nixon, Howard, M. 'Caxton, his contemporaries and successors in the book trade from Westminster documents', *Libr.*, 5th ser., 31 (1976), pp. 305–26.

—— 'William Caxton and bookbinding', *JPHS*, 11 (1975/6), pp. 92–113.

Norrie, Ian. *Mumby's Publishing and Bookselling in the Twentieth Century*. 6th edn (Bell and Hyman, London, 1982).

Nowell-Smith, Simon. *The House of Cassell 1848–1958* (Cassell, London,

1958).

—— *International Copyright Law and the Publisher in the Reign of Queen Victoria* (Clarendon Press, Oxford, 1968).

—— (ed.) *Letters to Macmillan* (Macmillan, London, 1967).

Oastler,C.L. *John Day, the Elizabethan Printer* (Oxford Bibliographical Society, occ. publ. 10, Oxford, 1975).

Oates, J.C.T. 'The Trewe encountre: a pamphlet on Flodden Field', *TCBS*, 1 (1950), pp. 126–9.

Ogilvie, Robert. 'Latin for yesterday', in Asa Briggs (ed.). *Essays in the History of Publishing* (Longman, London, 1974), pp. 219–44.

Orme, Nicholas. *English Schools in the Middle Ages* (Methuen, London, 1973).

Owen,W.J.B. 'Costs, sales and profits of Longman's editions of Wordsworth', *Libr.*, 5th ser., 12 (1957), pp. 93–107.

Painter, George D. *William Caxton* (Chatto and Windus, London, 1976).

Pantzer, Katherine F. 'Printing the English statutes, 1484–1640: some historical implications', in Kenneth E. Carpenter (ed.). *Books and Society in History* (Bowker, New York, 1983), pp. 69–114.

Papali, G.F. *Jacob Tonson, Publisher* (Tonson Publishing, Auckland, 1968).

Parks, Stephen. *John Dunton and the English Book Trade* (Garland Publishing, New York, 1976).

Parsons, Ian. 'Copyright and society', in Asa Briggs (ed.). *Essays in the History of Publishing* (Longman, London, 1974), pp. 29–60.

Paston, George. *At John Murray's. Records of a Literary Circle 1843–1892* (Murray, London, 1932).

Patten, Robert L. *Charles Dickens and his Publishers* (Clarendon Press, Oxford, 1976).

Pearsall, Ronald. *The Worm in the Bud. The World of Victorian Sexuality* (Weidenfeld and Nicolson, London, 1969).

Perelli, Patricia. 'Statistical survey of the British film industry', in James Curran and Vincent Porter (eds). *British Cinema History* (Weidenfeld and Nicolson, London, 1983), pp. 372–82.

Plant, Marjorie. *The English Book Trade.* 2nd edn (Allen and Unwin, London, 1965).

Plomer, Henry R. *A Dictionary of the Booksellers and Printers who Were at Work in England, Scotland and Ireland from 1641 to 1667* (The Bibliographical Society, London, 1908).

Plumb, J.H. *The Commercialisation of Leisure* (University of Reading, Reading, 1973).

Pollard, Alfred W. 'The new Caxton indulgence', *Libr.*, 4th ser., 11 (1928–9), pp. 86–9.

—— *Shakespeare's Fight with the Pirates.* 2nd edn (Cambridge University Press, Cambridge, 1920).

Pollard, Graham. 'Bibliographical aids to research. IV. General lists of books printed in England', *BIHR*, 12 (1934–5), pp. 165–74.

—— 'Changes in the style of bookbindings, 1550–1830', *Libr.*, 5th ser., 11 (1956), pp. 71–94.

—— 'The Company of Stationers before 1557', *Libr.*, 4th ser., 18 (1937–8), pp. 1–38.

—— 'The early constitution of the Stationers' Company', *Libr.*, 4th ser., 18 (1937–8), pp. 235–60.

—— 'The English market for printed books', *PH*, 4 (1978), pp. 7–48.

—— 'The names of some English fifteenth-century binders', *Libr.*, 5th ser., 25 (1970), pp. 193–218.

—— 'The *pecia* system in the medieval universities', in M.B. Parkes and Andrew G. Watson (eds). *Medieval Scribes, Manuscripts & Libraries. Essays Presented to N.R. Ker* (Scolar Press, London, 1979), pp. 145–61.

Poynter, F.N.L. *A Bibliography of Gervase Markham 1568?–1637* (Oxford Bibliographical Society, new ser., 11, Oxford, 1962).

Pressler, Karl H. 'The Tauchnitz Edition: beginning and end of a famous series', *PH*, 6 (1980), pp. 63–78.

Price Commission. *Prices, Costs and Margins in the Publishing, Printing and Binding, and Distribution of Books* (HMSO [HC 527 (1978)], London, 1979).

Proctor, Robert. 'The French Royal Greek types and the Eton *Chrysostom*', in A.W. Pollard (ed.). *Bibliographical Essays by Robert Proctor*. Repr. (Franklin, New York, 1969), pp. 89–119.

Publishers' Association. *Book Distribution. A Handbook for Booksellers and Publishers.* 2nd edn (Publishers' Association, London, 1972).

—— *Quarterly Statistical Bulletin. June 1986* (Publishers' Association, London, 1986).

Quinlan, Maurice J. *Victorian Prelude. A History of English Manners, 1700–1830* (Columbia University Press, New York, 1941).

Reed, Arthur W. 'The regulation of the book trade before the proclamation of 1538', *TBS*, 15 (1919), pp. 157–84.

Rees, Eiluned. 'Developments in the book trade in eighteenth-century Wales', *Libr.*, 5th ser., 24 (1969), pp. 33–43.

Richards, Grant. *Author Hunting* (Hamish Hamilton, London, 1934).

Richards, R.D. *The Early History of Banking in England*. Repr. (Frank Cass, New York, 1965).

Rivington, Septimus. *The Publishing Family of Rivington* (Rivingtons, London, 1919).

Robbins, Michael. *The Railway Age* (Routledge and Kegan Paul, London, 1962).

Roberts, Colin H. and Skeat, T.C. *The Birth of the Codex* (British Academy, London, 1983).

Roberts, R.J. 'The 1765 edition of Goody Two-Shoes', *BMQ*, 29 (1965), pp. 67–70.

Roberts, S.C. *The Evolution of Cambridge Publishing* (Cambridge University Press, Cambridge, 1956).

Rogers, Pat. *Grub Street. Studies in a Sub-culture* (Methuen, London, 1972).

Roper, Derek. *Reviewing Before the 'Edinburgh'* (Methuen, London, 1978).

Roscoe, S. *John Newbery and his Successors 1740–1814. A Bibliography* (Five Owls Press, Wormley, 1973).

Rosenberg, Eleanor. *Leicester. Patron of Letters* (Columbia University Press, New York, 1955).

Rostenberg, Leona. 'Richard and Anne Baldwin: Whig patriot publishers', *PBSA*, 47 (1953), pp. 1–42.

Rude, David, W. and Berry, Lloyd E. 'Tanner manuscript no. 33: new light on the Stationers' Company in the early seventeenth century', *PBSA*, 66 (1972), pp. 105–34.

Rudé, George. *Hanoverian London 1714–1808*. (Secker and Warburg, London, 1981).

Ryder, John. *The Bodley Head 1857–1957* (Bodley Head, London, 1970).

Sadleir, Michael. 'Aspects of the Victorian novel', *PH*, 5 (1979), pp. 7–47.

—— *The Evolution of Publishers' Binding Styles* (Constable, London, 1930).

Sale, William M. *Samuel Richardson: Master Printer* (Cornell University Press, Ithaca, N.Y., 1950).

Sanderson, Michael. 'Literacy and social mobility in the industrial revolution in England', *PP*, 56 (1972), pp. 75–104.

Saunders, J.W. *The Profession of English Letters* (Routledge and Kegan Paul, London, 1964).

Savage, Ernest A. *Old English Libraries* (Methuen, London, 1911).

Schlesinger, Kirsten. 'Suppliers' delivery times: can booksellers ever hope for better distribution?', *Bookseller*, no. 4168 (9 Nov. 1982), pp. 1932–42.

Schmoller, Hans. 'The paperback revolution', in Asa Briggs (ed.). *Essays in the History of Publishing* (Longman, London, 1974), pp. 283–318.

Schofield, R.S. 'Dimensions of illiteracy, 1750–1850', *EEH*, 10 (1972–3), pp. 437–54.

—— 'The measurement of literacy in pre-industrial England', in Jack Goody (ed.). *Literacy in Traditional Societies* (Cambridge University Press, Cambridge, 1968), pp. 311–25.

Schreuders, Piet. *The Book of Paperbacks. A Visual History of the Paperback*. Tr. by Josh Pachter (Virgin, London, 1981).

Scott, Mary A. *Elizabethan Translations from the Italian*. Repr. (Franklin, New York, 1969).

Seaman, G.R. 'Eighteenth-century English periodicals and music', *BJECS*, 7 (1984), pp. 69–76.

Sessions, William K. *The King's Printer at Newcastle-upon-Tyne in 1639, at Bristol in 1643–1645 and at Exeter in 1645–1646* (Ebor Press, York, 1982).

—— *A Printer's Dozen. The First British Printing Centres to 1557 outside Westminster and London* (Ebor Press, York, 1983).

—— *A World of Mischiefe. The King's Printer in York in 1642 and in Shrewbury in 1642–1643* (Ebor Press, York, 1981).

—— and Sessions, E. Margaret. *Printing in York* (William Sessions Ltd., York, 1976).

Shaylor, Joseph. *The Fascination of Books* (Simpkin, Marshall, London, 1912).

Shearyn, Phoebe. *The Literary Profession in the Elizabethan Age*. 2nd edn., rev. J.W. Saunders (Manchester University Press, Manchester, 1967).

Siebert, Frederick Seaton. *Freedom of the Press in England 1476–1776* (University of Illinois Press, Urbana, Ill., 1965).

Simmons, Jack. *The Railway in Town and Country 1830–1914* (David and Charles, Newton Abbot, 1986).

Simon, Joan. *Education and Society in Tudor England* (Cambridge University Press, Cambridge, 1967).

Sisson, C.J. 'The laws of Elizabethan copyright: the Stationers' view', *Libr.* 5th ser., 15 (1960) pp. 8–21.

Skingsley, T.A. 'Technical training and education in the English printing industry. A study of late-nineteenth-century attitudes', *JPHS*, 13 (1978/9), pp. 1–25; and ibid., 14 (1979/80), pp. 1–58.

Slavin, Arthur J. 'The Gutenberg galaxy and the Tudor revolution', in Gerald P. Tyson and Sylvia S. Wagonheim (eds). *Print and Culture in the Renaissance. Essays on the Advent of Printing in Europe* (University of Delaware Press, Newark, N.J., 1986), pp. 90–109.

—— 'The Tudor revolution and the devil's art: Bishop Bonner's printed forms', in D.J. Guth and J.W. McKenna (eds). *Tudor Rule and Revolution* (Cambridge University Press, Cambridge, 1982), pp. 3–23.

Smiles, Samuel. *A Publisher and his Friends*. 2 vols. (John Murray, London, 1891).

Southern, A.C. *Elizabethan Recusant Prose 1559–1582* (Sands, London, 1950).

Spencer, Lois. 'The politics of George Thomason', *Libr.*, 5th ser., 14 (1959), pp. 11–27.

—— 'The professional and literary connexions of George Thomason', *Libr.*, 5th ser., 13 (1958), pp. 102–18.

Spinney, G.H. '*Cheap Repository Tracts*: Hazard and Marshall edition', *Libr.*, 4th Ser., 20 (1939), pp. 295–340.

Spufford, Margaret. *Small Books and Pleasant Histories* (Cambridge. University Press, Cambridge, 1985).

Stephens, John Calhoun (ed.). *The Guardian* (University of Kentucky Press, Lexington, Ky., (1982).

Stewart, Stephen M. *International Copyright Law and Neighbouring Rights* (Butterworth, London, 1983).

Straus, Ralph. *Robert Dodsley* (London, 1910).

Sutcliffe, Peter. *The Oxford University Press. An Informal History* (Clarendon Press, Oxford, 1978).

Sutherland, J.A. *Fiction and the Fiction Industry* (Athlone Press, 1978).

—— 'Henry Colburn, publisher', *PH*, 19 (1986), pp. 59–84.

—— 'The institutionalisation of the British book trade to the 1890s', in Robin Myers and Michael Harris (eds). *Development of the English Book Trade, 1700–1899* (Oxford Polytechnic Press, Oxford, 1981), pp. 95–105.

—— 'Lytton, John Blackwood and the serialisation of *Middlemarch*', *Bibl.*, 7 (1975), pp. 98–104.

—— *Victorian Novelists and their Publishers* (Athlone Press, London, 1976).

Sutherland, James R. 'The circulation of newspapers and literary periodicals, 1700–1730', *Libr.*, 4th ser., 15 (1934–5), pp. 110–24.

—— 'The Dunciad of 1729', *MLR*, 32 (1936), pp. 347–53.

Taraporevala, Russi Jal. *Competition and its Control in the British Book Trade 1850–1939* (D.B. Taraporevala, Bombay, 1969).

Tebbel, John. *A History of Book Publishing in the United States*. 3 vols. (Bowker, New York, 1972–8).

Thomas, Donald. *A Long Time Burning* (Routledge and Kegan Paul, London, 1969).

Thomas, Keith. *Religion and the Decline of Magic* (Penguin, Harmondsworth, 1978).

Thomas, P.W. *Sir John Berkenhead 1617–1679. A Royalist Career in Politics and Polemics* (Clarendon Press, Oxford, 1969).

Thomson, George Malcolm. *Martin Secker & Warburg. The First Fifty Years* (Secker and Warburg, London, 1986).

Thrupp, Sylvia L. *The Merchant Class of Medieval London 1300–1500* (University of Michigan Press, Ann Arbor, Mich., 1968).

Treadwell, Michael. 'London trade publishers 1675–1750', *Libr.*, 6th ser., 4 (1982), pp. 99–134.

Treptow, Otto. *John Siberch. Johann Lair von Siegburg.* Tr. by Trevor Jones, abridged and ed. John Morris and Trevor Jones. (Cambridge Bibliographical Society, monograph 6, Cambridge, 1970).

Turner, Michael L. 'Andrew Wilson: Lord Stanhope's stereotype printer', *JPHS*, 9 (1975), pp. 22–65.

Turville-Petre, Thorlac. 'Some medieval English manuscripts in the north-east Midlands', in Derek Pearsall (ed.). *Manuscripts and Readers in Fifteenth-century England* (Brewer, Cambridge, 1983), pp. 125–41.

Twyman, Michael. *Lithography 1800–1850* (Oxford University Press, London, 1970).

Unwin, George. *Gilds and Companies of the City of London* (Methuen, London, 1908).

Unwin, Philip. *The Printing Unwins, A Short History of Unwin Brothers. The Gresham Press, 1826–1926* (Allen and Unwin, London, 1976).

—— *The Publishing Unwins* (Heinemann, London, 1972).

—— *The Stationers' Company 1918–1977. A Livery Company in the Modern World* (Benn, London, 1978).

Unwin, Sir Stanley. *The Truth About a Publisher* (Allen and Unwin, London, 1960).

—— *The Truth About Publishing.* 8th edn, rev. by Philip Unwin (Allen and Unwin, London, 1976).

Wakeman, Geoffrey. *Victorian Book Illustration. The Technical Revolution* (David and Charles, Newton Abbot, 1973).

Walker, J. 'The censorship of the press during the reign of Charles II', *Hist.*, 25 (1950), pp. 219–38.

Wallis, Philip. *At the Sign of the Ship* (Longman, London, 1974).

Warburg, Frederic. *An Occupation for Gentlemen* (Hutchinson, London, 1959).

Warren, A. *The Charles Whittinghams* (Grolier Club, New York, 1896).

Watson, S.F. 'Some materials for a history of printing and publishing in Ipswich', *PSIANH*, 24 (1946/7), pp. 182–227.

Waugh, Arthur. *A Hundred Years of Publishing. Being the Story of Chapman & Hall Ltd.* (Chapman and Hall, London, 1930).

Webb, R.K. *The British Working Class Reader 1790–1848* (Allen and Unwin, London, 1955).

Weedon, M.J.P. 'Richard Johnson and the successors to John Newbery', *Libr.*, 5th ser., 4 (1949), pp. 25–63.

Weiner, Joel H. *The War of the Unstamped. The Movement to Repeal the British Newspaper Tax, 1830–1836* (Cornell University Press, Ithaca, N.Y., 1969).

Welsh, Charles. *A Bookseller of the Last Century* (Griffith, Farran, London,

1885).

Whyte, Frederic. *William Heinemann* (Jonathan Cape, London, 1928).

Wiles, R.M. *Freshest Advices. Early Provincial Newspapers in England* (Ohio State University Press, Columbus, Ohio, 1965).

—— 'The relish for reading in provincial England two centuries ago', in Paul J. Korshin (ed.). *The Widening Circle* (University of Pennsylvania Press, Philadelphia, Pa., 1976), pp. 86–116.

—— *Serial Publication in England Before 1750* (Cambridge University Press, Cambridge, 1957), pp. 75–80.

Williams, Franklin B., Jr. *Dedications and Verses through 1640* (The Bibliographical Society, Suppl. to *Libr.*, 30:1, London, 1975).

—— *Index of Dedications and Commendatory Verses in English Books Before 1641* (The Bibliographical Society, London, 1962).

Wilson, Charles. *First with the News. The History of W.H. Smith 1792–1972* (Jonathan Cape, London, 1985).

Wolfe, Don M. *Milton in the Puritan Revolution* (Humanities Press, New York, 1963).

Woodfield, Denis B. *Surreptitious Printing in England 1550–1640* (Bibliographical Society of America, New York, 1973).

Woods, Oliver, and Bishop, James. *The Story of 'The Times'* (Michael Joseph, London, 1983).

Wright, Louis B. *Middle-class Culture in Elizabethan England* (University of North Carolina Press, Chapel Hill, N.C., 1935).

Yglesias, Roy. 'Education and publishing in transition', in Asa Briggs (ed.). *Essays in the History of Publishing* (Longman, London, 1974), pp. 357–88.

Zell, Michael L. 'An early press in Canterbury?', *Libr.*, 5th ser., 32 (1977), pp. 155–6.

Index